Spelling

W9-DHF-972

purposeful design
PUBLICATIONS
A Division of ACSI

Colorado Springs, CO

Development Team

First Edition

Editorial Team

Dr. Sharon Berry	*Managing Editor*
Dr. Barry Morris	*Content Manager*
Dr. Ollie Gibbs	*Project Manager*

Author Team

Sharon Bird	Linda Miller
Cathy Guy	Nancy Wetsel
Eunice Harris	Connie Williams

Project Consultants

Dr. Barbara Bode	Ruth McBride
Dr. Richard Edlin	Dr. Connie Pearson
Dr. Omer Bonenberger	Patti Rhan
Dr. Linda Goodson	Dr. Milton Uecker
Dr. Alex Lackey	Dr. Ray White

Second Edition

Editorial Team

JoAnn Keenan	*Managing Editor*
Maria L. Deckard	*Editor*
Cynthia C. Shipman	*Editor*
Lorraine Wadman	*Editor*
Dr. June Hetzel	*Senior Content Editor*
Dr. Claire Sibold	*Content Editor*

Design Team

Monica Starr Brown	*Graphic Designer, Photographer*
Susanna Garmany	*Graphic Designer*
Daron Short	*Graphic Designer, Photographer*

Project Consultants

Dr. Derek Keenan	*ACSI Vice President for Academic Affairs*
Steven Babbitt	*Director, Purposeful Design Publications*
Don Hulin	*Assistant Director, Textbook Development*

Purposeful Design

Spelling

Grade 5
Teacher Edition

ecosystem
courageous
plumage
aquamarine
vitality

Managing Editor
JoAnn Keenan

Editors
Maria L. Deckard
Cynthia C. Shipman
Lorraine Wadman

Designers
Monica Starr Brown
Susanna Garmany
Daron Short

Senior Content Editor
Dr. June Hetzel

Content Editor
Dr. Claire Sibold

Purposeful Design Publications is the publishing division of the Association of Christian Schools International (ACSI) and is committed to the ministry of Christian school education, to enable Christian educators and schools worldwide to effectively prepare students for life. As the publisher of textbooks, trade books, and other educational resources within ACSI, Purposeful Design Publications strives to produce biblically sound materials that reflect Christian scholarship and stewardship and that address the identified needs of Christian schools around the world.

References to books, computer software, and other ancillary resources in this series are not endorsements by ACSI. These materials were selected to provide teachers with additional resources appropriate to the concepts being taught and to promote student understanding and enjoyment.

Unless otherwise identified, all Scripture quotations are taken from the Holy Bible, New King James Version (NKJV), © 1982 by Thomas Nelson, Inc. Used by permission. All rights reserved.

Illustrations on Student Edition pages 6, 32, and 66 by Aline Heiser, North Ridgeville, OH.
Image of Franklin-Folger chart of the Gulf Stream on Student Edition page 58 courtesy of the Geography and Map Division, Library of Congress.
Photographs on Student Edition pages 122, 126, 132, 134, 135, 136, 137, 138, 139, 140, 141, and 142 courtesy of NASA.
Photographs on Blackline Masters SP5-34A, SP5-34C, SP5-35A, and SP5-36B–C courtesy of NASA.

Printed in the United States of America
18 17 16 15 14 13 12 11 10 09   1 2 3 4 5 6 7

Spelling, grade five
Purposeful Design Spelling series
Second edition
ISBN 978-1-58331-245-2   Teacher edition   Catalog #7416

Purposeful Design Publications
A Division of ACSI
PO Box 65130 • Colorado Springs, CO 80962-5130
Customer Service: 800-367-0798 • www.acsi.org

Table of Contents

Lesson		**Page**

Lesson		Page

Teacher Resources

© Spelling Grade 5

Blackline Master List

Transparency List

Poster List

Foreword

The fourfold educational mission of Christian schools is to prepare young people as disciples of Christ who are spiritually-formed thinkers. Education implies the development of the mind by the acquisition of knowledge and the ability to think and understand. Schools also equip students with a set of skills that are essential for life and vocation. In addition, the training process seeks to ground pupils with a worldview that is biblical and that shapes their lives into a God-pleasing spiritual pattern. In order to fulfill this Kingdom mandate, schools need to do their educational work carefully and responsibly. Purposeful Design Publications exists to assist educators in the fulfillment of that mission.

Over the past decades there continues to be a plethora of approaches to many aspects of the language arts. The research literature is somewhat conflicted about what is most effective in preparing students to be good readers, but it is quite clear about developing strong spellers. We have been through an era where spelling did not need to be taught explicitly but as an outgrowth of reading (Smith 1971). Several things from the research about spelling instruction are quite clear:

- Effective spelling instruction strengthens reading
- There are multiple benefits to explicit spelling instruction
- Strategies must be matched according to the age and level of spelling ability
- Well-developed and current spelling resources incorporate comprehensive tested strategies that match a variety of learners

(Gentry 2004)

The revised Purposeful Design Spelling series approaches spelling as a critical literacy skill that strengthens reading and writing ability. Spelling strategies such as word sorting by phonetic pattern, developing vocabulary through word study, and using the writing process to compose original stories pervade the books. Each of these strategies has a direct correlation to more effective and efficient reading and writing. Just as manipulatives are critical to mathematics understanding, spelling activities are crucial to the long-term acquisition by students of a significant bank of words they can spell correctly.

Each grade level and each lesson in the series has been thoroughly revised with updated strategies and research-based activities. Every page has been redesigned for readability, instructional flow and sequence, and attractive pictures and illustrations that draw students into and through each lesson.

Purposeful Design Publications, the publishing division of the Association of Christian Schools International, is indebted to a fine team of consultants, editors, and contributors who have invested themselves in this revision project. It was clear from the outset that some of the core concepts of the original spelling series were sound, but this team, backed by extensive research findings, has thoroughly revised these books into an outstanding series.

Your students will be well served by utilizing Purposeful Design Spelling in your classroom. We are certain that it will assist you to produce students who know how to spell, enjoy the activities of learning to spell, and embed in their minds a growing bank of words that support and strengthen vocabulary acquisition and reading skills.

Derek J. Keenan, Ed.D.
Vice President, Academic Affairs

Gentry, J. Richard. 2004 *The Science of Spelling*. Portsmouth, New Hampshire: Heinemann.

Smith, F. 1971 *Understanding Reading: A Psycholinguistic Analysis of Reading and Learning to Read*. New York: Holt, Rinehart and Winston.

"You are worthy, O Lord,
To receive glory and honor and power;
For You created all things,
And by Your will they exist and were created."
Revelation 4:11

Preface

The Purposeful Design Publications Team carefully crafted this revised spelling series with you and your Christian School students in mind. The philosophical underpinnings of this grades 1–6 series are as follows:

The ultimate aim of Christian education is to bring students to a saving knowledge of Jesus Christ, to know His Word, and to live Christianly in right relationship with God and others. Therefore, literacy contributes to a child's spiritual maturity as he or she develops as a reader and a writer, processing the truths of Scripture. Mastery of conventional spelling and word study become critical subsets of the writing branch of literacy, sharpening the student's literacy tools and his/her ability to accurately convey love and truth to others through the written word.

Conventional spelling contributes to the accuracy with which a writer can convey his message. Therefore, this series provides delightfully interesting and varied word study activities for both phonetically-consistent pattern words as well as high-frequency words. Study of phonetically-consistent pattern words supports students' acquisition of spelling generalizations, and study of high-frequency words promotes writing fluency with high-utility words. Writing assignments provide opportunities for learners to apply spelling in context, accurately conveying messages to readers through the encoding process.

Children are unique image bearers of God. Therefore, the learning process must take into account child development, academic strengths and weaknesses, learning styles, learning modalities, and learning rates. The Purposeful Design editorial team has ensured that you have straightforward methods to differentiate the learning process for high achievers, average performers, and struggling learners. Each lesson provides opportunities for high achievers to study challenge words and for struggling learners to receive additional spelling support. Additionally, a website has been developed to provide a plethora of resources to assist you in strategically planning for all learners.

Parents and teachers jointly share the responsibility of the child's education. Therefore, this series provides spelling study activities for both school and home, conceptualizing the training of the child as a partnership between parents and teachers.

Learning should satisfy the God-given curiosity of a child and inspire increased desire for learning. Therefore, the creative design team of Purposeful Design Publications has provided inviting images of God's creation and attractive layouts of student workbook pages and blackline masters. Additionally, the editorial team has carefully crafted lessons to include games, puzzles, stories, poems, and other inspiring, fun activities.

The Purposeful Design Publications Team desires that this series ministers to the educational needs of your students and that spelling becomes a favorite part of their day and your day as students study spelling "their way"—actively and joyfully! May the Lord bless you as you continue to press on in the name of the Lord Jesus Christ, training the next generation of Kingdom writers.

June Hetzel, Ph.D.
Professor of Education
Biola University

Acknowledgments

The Peer Review process is an important step in the development of this textbook series. ACSI and the Purposeful Design staff greatly appreciate the feedback we receive from the schools and teachers who participate. We highly value the efforts and input of these faculty members; their recommendations and suggestions are extremely helpful. The institutions listed below have assisted us in this way.

American Christian Academy, Tuscaloosa, AL

Asheville Christian Academy, Swannanoa, NC

Calvary Christian Academy, Philadelphia, PA

Cedar Park Christian School, Bothell, WA

Cincinnati Hills Christian Academy, Cincinnati, OH

Colorado Springs Christian Schools, Colorado Springs, CO

Cypress Christian School, Houston, TX

Evangelical Christian Academy, Colorado Springs, CO

Faith Christian Academy, Arvada, CO

Faith Christian School, Rocky Mount, NC

Forest Lake Christian School, Auburn, CA

Fresno Christian Schools, Fresno, CA

Grace Community School, Tyler, TX

Greenbrier Christian Academy, Chesapeake, VA

Harvest Christian Academy, Elgin, IL

Heritage Christian School, Brookfield, WI

Jupiter Christian School, Jupiter, FL

Kodiak Christian School, Kodiak, AK

Light and Life Christian School, Escondido, CA

Mount Hope School, Burlington, MA

North Cobb Christian School, Kennesaw, GA

North County Christian School, Florissant, MO

North Heights Christian Academy, Roseville, MN

Northwest Christian School, Phoenix, AZ

Oak Park Christian Academy, Oak Park, IL

Oakland Christian School, Auburn Hills, MI

Peoria Christian School, Peoria, IL

Pine Castle Christian Academy, Orlando, FL

Rocky Bayou Christian School, Niceville, FL

Salisbury Christian School, Salisbury, MD

Santiam Christian School, Corvallis, OR

Schenectady Christian School, Schenectady, NY

Smithtown Christian School, Smithtown, NY

Southwest Christian School, Fort Worth, TX

The Pilgrim Academy, Egg Harbor City, NJ

Traders Point Christian Academy, Indianapolis, IN

Tri-City Christian Schools, Vista, CA

Trinity Christian Academy, Jackson, TN

Trinity Christian School, Addison, TX

Wesleyan School, Norcross, GA

West Bay Christian Academy, North Kingston, RI

West-Mont Christian Academy, Pottstown, PA

Spelling Series Task Force

June Hetzel, Ph.D.
Biola University

Pam Levicki
St. Stephen's Episcopal Day School

Anne Lichlyter
Evangelical Christian Academy

Victoria Lierheimer
Evergreen Academy

Keith McAdams
Cornerstone University

Rebecca Pennington
Covenant College

Julia Taves
Colorado Springs Christian School

Carolyn Ware
North Cobb Christian School

Amy Young
Rocky Mountain Christian Academy

Using the Teacher and Student Editions

Welcome to Purposeful Design Grade Five Spelling!

We believe that you will enjoy the new format, including beautiful, full-color photographs; well-researched word lists that include pattern words, content area words, and vocabulary words with Greek and Latin roots; and teacher-friendly lesson instructions. This instructional program, comprised of a Teacher Edition, Student Edition, Blackline Masters CD, Color Transparencies, and Posters, are all designed to assist you in engaging and challenging your students to become excellent spellers.

Visit www.acsi.org/~spellingresources for a listing of a wide variety of resources specifically selected to provide you with classroom tools in support of spelling and language arts instruction. Resources listed, although not endorsed by Purposeful Design Publications, are recommended by local educators for supporting grade five spelling.

Grade five of the revised spelling series consists of 36 lessons, primarily using whole-group activities; however, guidance for supporting students who struggle as well as students who are advanced is also included. Each weekly word list lesson is designed for five days, 30–40 minutes of instruction per day. After each five-week set of word list lessons, a review lesson is provided.

Teacher Edition

Each Teacher Edition lesson includes an instructional "Objective," lesson "Introduction," and "Directed Instruction" in a step-by-step format. All the materials needed to teach each lesson are listed in the Lesson Materials. Instructional objectives and lesson content meet criteria set by state and national language arts standards.

The five-day instructional format of the word list lessons begins with the "Pretest" on Day 1 and concludes with the "Posttest" on Day 5. Day 2 is reserved for "Word Analysis and Vocabulary" instruction, Day 3 for "Word Study Strategies," and Day 4 for "Writing." Lesson activities strengthen the students' skills in decoding, encoding, vocabulary, word building, proofreading, and creative word application in daily writing.

The "Pretest" is written on the students' own paper. It is self-corrected for immediate feedback without formal grades recorded. Each "Pretest" assesses current skill levels of individual students, as well as the skills of the entire class, in the context of the list words provided. If your students miss several words on the "Pretest," more practice will be needed throughout the week. It is important to teach your students to check the accuracy of their own "Pretest" so that they strengthen proofreading skills and understand their own error patterns. An extremely helpful tool for spelling practice is "A Spelling Study Strategy" found on a poster (P-1), color transparency (T-1), and blackline master (BLM SP5-01A). "A Spelling Study Strategy" is also found on the inside cover of the Student Edition. Demonstrate the use of "A Spelling Study Strategy" before beginning Lesson 1.

On weekly "Posttests," students write their spelling words and five dictated sentences on lined paper. Your students may write the dictation sentences as a paragraph. Dictation is an excellent way to integrate auditory and visual memory skills, as well as writing skills and conventions, such as capitalization and punctuation, in context. Dictation also provides a model of a complete sentence or paragraph. Many dictation sentences include words on previous spelling lists for review. We suggest that you read each sentence slowly, have the students repeat the sentence, and then read it once again before the students begin to write the sentence. Score the dictation sentences as a part of the overall grade on the "Posttest"; however, the scoring procedure is up to you.

Every sixth lesson is a review lesson and the "Assessment" for each review lesson is given on Day 5. The "Assessment" is cumulative, covering words from the five previous lessons. Each "Assessment" is helpful in preparation for achievement testing since it is in standardized test format; words are presented in the context of a sentence that contains three underlined words, one of which may be misspelled, and a fourth choice of *All correct*. Students use a Student Answer Form to indicate the misspelled word or choose *All correct* if there are no misspellings. To extend each "Assessment," you may choose to have the students rewrite each misspelled word correctly.

The "Student Spelling Support" appears as a sidebar. The "Student Spelling Support" is a selection of optional activities that extends the spelling lessons, provides additional ideas for different learning styles, and incorporates spelling with other curriculum areas. The "Student Spelling Support" also gives ideas for discussion of the Scripture verses on the Student Edition pages, lists additional Scripture references, and promotes biblical integration. There are suggested writing challenge activities. You will not be able to use every suggestion listed for each lesson; however, a rich selection of spelling support strategies enables you to pick and choose as you carefully craft activities tailored to student needs. All materials needed for the "Student Spelling Support" are listed in "Student Spelling Support Materials."

One of the "Student Spelling Support" suggestions calls for starting and adding words to a classroom "Word Wall." Develop student-generated "Word Walls," using each week's spelling words. Write the words, categorize the Pattern, Content, and Vocabulary Words, and attach to the wall. The example given in Lesson one and the example shown below contain only a few of the list words, but teachers should add all of the words to their Word Wall. Allow students to spontaneously add new words to the list during the week. Categorizing words by patterns helps students internalize generalizations.

Word Wall

Short Vowel Sounds		Mountains	
chilly	value	granite	erosion
humble	shelving	summit	igneous

Vocabulary Words				
frag	+	ile	=	fragile
frag	+	ment	=	fragment
de	+	posit	=	deposit
ex	+	pos(e)	=	expose

Blackline Masters and Other Resources

Each lesson includes one or more blackline masters on CD. The CD is found on the inside back cover of the Teacher Edition. You will find the title and other useful information in the upper right-hand corner. The title is in the uppermost box. The second box contains the abbreviation, BLM SP5, followed by the lesson number and a letter. For example, BLM SP5-06C indicates that this blackline master is found in grade five (SP5), lesson six (06), and is the third (C) blackline master in that lesson. Additionally, each blackline master has a circled letter code that indicates the primary use for the blackline. **A** stands for Assessment, **H** for Homework, **P** for Practice, and **T** for Teacher Tools.

- The blackline masters labeled **A for Assessment** are needed for the Review Assessment. Day 5 of each review lesson indicates the blackline masters needed.   **(A)**

- The blackline masters labeled **H for Homework** provide practice with the skills taught in class. Answers are provided on the blackline master CD. Homework suggestions are given for three nights per week to accommodate evening worship schedules. Some of the activities call for students to choose a correctly spelled word from a group of misspelled words. This can be extremely challenging for students with visual processing disorders. You may choose to reduce the number of exercises, or choose to assign a different activity to these students.   **(H)**

- The blackline masters labeled **P for Practice** mirror the concepts and skills taught in the Student Edition.   **(P)**

- The blackline masters labeled **T for Teacher Tools** are the answer keys for the proofreading lesson transparencies and review "Assessments."   **(T)**

Note to Macintosh Users: Double-click the disc icon on the desktop, go to the folder named "PDF," open the file containing the blackline masters, and access the list.

Color transparencies are coded with *T* plus a number and posters are coded with *P* plus a number for identification. Transparencies and Posters are used in different lessons, and instructions for their use are included in the Teacher Edition.

Student Edition

The theme of grade five is Created Wonders. Students will be introduced to the natural wonders of God's creation in the heavens and on the earth. The weekly theme provides an opportunity for students to learn to spell words from a variety of thematic content areas related to God's purposeful design.

The handwriting styles presented as penmanship models in the lessons include both standard manuscript and cursive forms commonly used in Christian schools. Word lists are presented in a manuscript form on odd-numbered pages; word lists are presented in a standard cursive form on even-numbered pages. Either handwriting form can be viewed by flipping the page or looking at the adjacent page. Please note that most visual memory and recall of spelling words is in manuscript. Students struggling with spelling should study their words exclusively in manuscript. It would be helpful to copy and paste manuscript lists over cursive lists for students with visual perceptual disorders.

Each word list lesson is organized around phonetic generalizations, content themes, and morphemic patterns. We use the term generalizations as opposed to rules because we realize that most, but not all, words follow these principles. An understanding of these generalizations will give your students knowledge of the spelling patterns required to spell phonetically-consistent Pattern Words and morphemically-consistent Vocabulary Words. Vocabulary Words all contain roots or affixes originating from Greek or Latin. Etymology, or the study of word orgins, is important in helping students develop strong spelling and vocabulary skills. Word lists also incorporate content area words. Content Words do not always follow a phonetic pattern, but they provide additional vocabulary to enhance students' ability to write proficiently within a subject area. Lists also include space on the student pages for the assignment of Challenge Words. You may choose Challenge Words based on the phonetic pattern targeted in the lesson, words previously misspelled, or content area words from other subjects you are studying, including social studies, science, and Bible. Students are often motivated to spell content area words by their interest in those subjects. You may also want to have your students self-select their own Challenge Words.

Some instructions on the Student Edition pages specify using only Pattern, Content, and/or Vocabulary Words. Other instructions specify using list words—a combination of all three categories.

A "Word Bank" is found in the back of the Student and Teacher Editions. In this section, students add Challenge Words that serve as a reference for their writing. Following this section is the "Spelling Dictionary," which is needed for the completion of several student pages. The syllabication, pronunciation, part(s) of speech, definition(s), and a sample sentence(s) are provided for each fifth grade spelling word.

Elements of the Student Edition include the following:

- Pages are perforated and each lesson may be removed without losing a page from the next lesson.
- A name line is provided on each odd-numbered page.
- Colored boxes at the top of the page highlight the skill(s) practiced on each page.
- Exercises are numbered from left to right on pages with columns. Otherwise, the numbers are read vertically.
- Terminology that may be new to students is highlighted in yellow the first time it appears.
- The first letter of each Content Word is provided as a clue for students to complete sentences on the Word Analysis page of each lesson.

Differentiated Instruction

We have included options for differentiating instruction because no textbook series is "one size fits all." These suggestions for "Differentiated Instruction" include changing the number of spelling words for learners who are either behind or ahead of their peers in spelling so as to secure an appropriate level of difficulty for each student.

There are important considerations when spelling is differentiated. The first is clear communication with parents, and the second is evaluation and grading. Parents need to be partners in the differentiation process. Parents need to know which words their child will be responsible for learning and how he or she will be evaluated. We suggest that you hold a meeting early in the school year with parents of students whose skills were below grade level expectations, or who missed more than half of the words on the first two or three spelling list lessons. Let the parents know that students acquire skills at different rates, and that phonetic spelling skills and visual memory skills should improve throughout the fifth grade year, paralleling individual developmental progress which may be ahead or behind student peers. Assign more words as each student's progress dictates. Develop a method of communicating with parents, such as a weekly e-mail, which words students need to study.

It is suggested that, if possible, the students attempt to spell every word on the "Pretest" and "Posttest," even though they will be graded only on words that they were assigned. This is not only good practice for the students, but it reduces the chance of students being questioned or ridiculed for having fewer words on their tests. All students should complete every page in the Student Edition in preparation for the weekly "Posttest." The "Assessment" for the review lessons is cumulative and has been organized so that the first twelve sentences contain the spelling words that have been assigned to students who have reduced word lists.

For students who are ahead of their peers, we suggest that Extra Challenge Words be assigned. The words suggested are taken from lists of words that are ranked by usage and grade level. You may use the words suggested, develop your own list from content area study, or invite advanced students to suggest their own Extra Challenge Words. Extra Challenge Words may be sent home via e-mail. Decide with parents whether or not to include these words in each student's overall spelling grade.

Discuss the evaluation and grading of students who have differentiated lists with your administrator and teammates to provide grade level and/or schoolwide consistency.

Finally, enjoy using Purposeful Design Spelling, Grade Five. It has been our pleasure to receive teacher input and revise this series to better meet your students' needs. Enjoy the journey.

Preparing a Lesson

Read through the lesson and make notes regarding preparation.

Read the lesson objective so that it is clear in your mind.

Note the materials needed to teach the lesson as well as where and how each item is used.

Read the Created Wonders theme presented on the sidebar.

Lesson 28 — Plurals

Student Pages
Pages 109–112

Lesson Materials
BLM SP5-28A
3" × 5" Index cards
BLM SP5-28B
T-18
BLM SP5-28C

Created Wonders
The theme of this lesson is spring. Spring falls between winter and summer, from mid March to mid June in the northern hemisphere. The vernal equinox, the day when the number of daylight and nighttime hours is almost the same, signals the beginning of spring. Springtime holidays celebrated in the United States include Easter and Mother's Day.

Day 1 Pretest

Objective
The students will accurately spell and write words that are **plural** nouns. They will spell and write content, vocabulary, and challenge words.

Introduction
Before class, select Challenge Words for numbers 24 and 25 from a cross-curricular subject, words misspelled on previous assignments, or words that interest your students. The word *affixes* is **plural** and is suggested for number 24. Administer the Pretest.

Directed Instruction
1 Say each word, use it in a sentence, and then repeat the word.
Pattern Words
  1. Three <u>businesses</u> promised to support our school fund-raising drive.
  2. The <u>aircraft</u> were taking off from the airport.
  3. <u>Countries</u> in the northern hemisphere have spring weather in April.
  4. The library contains <u>dictionaries</u> printed by different companies.
  5. Nina used sprigs of parsley as <u>garnishes</u> for her salad.
  6. The family received the <u>kindnesses</u> of others with joy.
  7. The <u>missionaries</u> planted several new churches in Asia.
  8. Rabbits may have four or more <u>offspring</u> per litter.
  9. <u>Onions</u> grow below the ground.
  10. Baseball players need sharp <u>reflexes</u> to make plays quickly.
  11. <u>Salmon</u> swim upstream to lay their eggs.
  12. Tia made several egg salad <u>sandwiches</u>.
Content Words
  13. Is Easter an <u>annual</u> celebration?
  14. Followers of <u>Christianity</u> believe that Jesus rose from the dead.
  15. Livia enjoys <u>gardening</u> in the spring.
  16. April showers provided much needed <u>precipitation</u>.
  17. Easter is the celebration of Jesus' <u>resurrection</u>.
  18. Daffodils and crocuses bloom in <u>springtime</u>.
  19. The <u>vernal</u> equinox occurs during the spring.
Vocabulary Words
  20. A <u>juvenile</u> rabbit is called a bunny.
  21. The tulips bloomed in <u>vivid</u> shades of red and pink.
  22. The spring thaw seemed to <u>rejuvenate</u> the mountain meadow.
  23. A <u>vivacious</u> little robin perched on a branch.
Challenge Words
  24.
  25.

2 Allow students to self-correct their Pretest. Write each word on the board. Point out that each Pattern Word is a plural noun. Note that most of the plural nouns in this lesson follow a predictable pattern. The irregular **plurals** are *salmon, aircraft,* and *offspring*. The irregular **plurals** have the same spelling in both the singular and plural forms. *Christianity* is always capitalized because it is a proper noun. Note the roots *juven* and *viv* in the Vocabulary Words.
3 As a class, read, spell, and read each word. Direct students to circle misspelled words with a colored pencil and rewrite them correctly.
4 Proof each student's Pretest. This becomes an individualized study

110

---

sheet that can be used at school or at home.
5 Homework suggestion: Distribute a copy of **BLM SP5-28A Lesson 28 Words and Phrases** to each student.

Day 2 Word Analysis and Vocabulary

Objective
The students will sort and write words that are **plurals** and complete sentences with content words. They will use a table to write vocabulary words, match definitions, complete sentences, and choose the best meaning for underlined words.

Introduction
Write the singular form of each Pattern Word on one side and the plural form on the other side of 3" × 5" INDEX CARDS. The irregular **plurals**, *salmon, aircraft,* and *offspring,* will be the same on both sides. Distribute the cards to twelve students. Write the following generalizations on the board:
• To make most nouns plural, add -s. (onions)
• To make nouns ending in *ch, s, sh,* or *x* plural, add -es. (sandwiches, kindnesses, businesses, garnishes, reflexes)
• To make nouns ending in a consonant *y* pattern plural, change *y* to *i* and add -es. (countries, dictionaries, missionaries)
• Some irregular plural nouns are spelled alike, whether singular or plural. (salmon, aircraft, offspring)
Instruct students to look at both sides of their cards to determine what was done to each singular noun to form the plural noun. Read each generalization aloud. Have students raise their card if they have a word that follows the generalization mentioned. Invite students to spell both the singular and plural forms. Retain the index cards for use in Student Spelling Support, number 7.

Directed Instruction
1 Choose a student to look up the Content Words *vernal* and *precipitation* in their Spelling Dictionary. Invite the student to share the pronunciation,

Differentiated Instruction
• For students who spelled all the words correctly on the Pretest, select and assign Extra Challenge Words from the following list: sonata, ambitious, representative, appendectomy, character, external.
• For students who spelled less than half correctly, assign the following Pattern, Content, and Vocabulary Words: onions, salmon, reflexes, offspring, countries, missionaries, annual, gardening, springtime, resurrection, rejuvenate, vivid. On the Posttest, evaluate these students on the twelve words assigned; however, encourage them to attempt to spell all the list words to the best of their ability. They are also responsible for writing the dictated sentences.

Take note of the suggestions given in the Differentiated Instruction section if you plan to differentiate instruction.

Look at the lesson Introduction for ways to engage the students' interest in the lesson.

Review the Directed Instruction section to become familiar with the sequence of procedures to follow.

111

xviii

Look at the Student Spelling Support section of suggested activities to extend the spelling lessons, provide additional ideas for different learning styles, and incorporate spelling with other curriculum areas, including biblical integration.

Note the blackline masters, posters, and color transparencies provided.

Prepare the classroom for the activity noted in the lesson Introduction.

Locate definitions of new terms printed in green italics.

Use the suggestions listed for assessment to monitor student progress.

Use the answers provided on the reduced student pages for correction and evaluation of student work.

Student Spelling Support Materials

BLM SP5-01A
BLMs SP5-28D–E
Card stock
BLM SP5-01G
3″ × 5″ Index cards
Ribbon
Basket

Student Spelling Support

1. Use **BLM SP5-01A A Spelling Study Strategy** in instructional groups to provide assistance with some or all of the words.
2. Duplicate **BLMs SP5-28D–E Lesson 28 Spelling Words I** and **II** on CARD STOCK for students to use as flash cards at school or at home. Another option is to use **BLM SP5-01G Flash Cards Template** or 3″ × 5″ INDEX CARDS for students to write their own flash cards to use as a study aid.
3. Invite students to write the Challenge Words, numbers 24 and 25, in the Word Bank, in the back of their textbook.
4. Read John 11:25: "Jesus said to her, 'I am the **resurrection** and the life. He who believes in Me, though he may die, he shall live.'" These precious words of Jesus give hope to all generations. Invite students to write a brief personal account in paragraph form of how the resurrection of Jesus has impacted their own life.
5. Challenge students to write a descriptive paragraph detailing their favorite springtime memory. Roll up each student's memory, tie it with a RIBBON, and place the memory in a BASKET for all to share.
6. Write this week's words, categorize the Pattern, Cont. on page 000

112

part of speech, definition, and sample sentence with the class.
2 Proceed to *page 109*. Say, spell, and say each Pattern, Content, and Vocabulary Word. Provide this week's Challenge Words and have students write them in the spaces provided.
3 Proceed to *page 110*. Select students to build each Vocabulary Word. For example, the prefix *re-* goes with the root *juven* and the suffix *-ate* to build the word *rejuvenate*. Provide assistance as students complete the page independently.
4 Homework suggestion: Distribute a copy of **BLM SP5-28B Lesson 28 Phrases and Sentences** to each student.

Day 3 Word Study Strategies

Objective
The students will write the plural form of singular words. They will write singular or plural possessive nouns to complete phrases.

Introduction
Write the following incomplete phrases on the board, leaving blanks as indicated:
• the flavor of the onion
• the flavor of ten onions
• the customer of the business
• the customer of ten businesses

the _____ flavor (onion's)
the _____ flavor (onions')
the _____ customer (business's)
the _____ customer (businesses')

Explain that a *possessive noun shows ownership*. Possessive nouns may be singular or plural. To make singular nouns and irregular plural nouns possessive, add an apostrophe and *-s*. Choose a volunteer to fill in the first blank. To make singular nouns ending in *s* and regular plural nouns possessive, add an apostrophe after the *s*. Invite a volunteer to fill in the second, third, and fourth blanks.

Directed Instruction
1 Invite students to turn to the list of Pattern Words, found on *page 111*, and state the singular form of each plural noun.
2 Proceed to *page 111*. Remind students to look closely at the singular words shown in exercises 1–12 and to apply the generalizations for forming **plurals** covered in Day 2 Introduction. Select volunteers to spell the plural for each singular noun in exercises 1–12. Students complete the page.
3 Choose a student to read John 11:25. Share how Christ's resurrection has impacted your life.

Day 4 Writing

Objective
The students will read a report about the season of spring. They will write list words that could replace the bold words in the report.

Introduction
Display **T-18 Graphic Organizer** and explain that the diagram is a graphic organizer. A *graphic organizer is a drawing that shows how words or ideas fit together*. Graphic organizers can provide a beginning for a writing assignment. Write the word *springtime* in the oval on the transparency. Brainstorm things that would fall into the categories of sights, smells, tastes, sounds, textures, and activities associated with springtime in the area where you live. Write students' ideas on the board. Invite students to assist you in filling in the boxes in the graphic organizer on the transparency, using a separate box for each category.

Directed Instruction
1 Remind students that the Spelling Dictionary provides definitions for each list word. They may use the Spelling Dictionary as an aid to

© *Spelling Grade 5*

---

defining words and determining synonyms.
2 Proceed to *page 112*. Encourage students to read the entire report before selecting each word with the same meaning as the bold words in the report. When complete, have a volunteer read the report, replacing the bold words with list words.
3 Invite students to reference the graphic organizer in the lesson Introduction as a framework for writing the suggested paragraph at the bottom of the page.
4 Homework suggestion: Distribute a copy of **BLM SP5-28C Lesson 28 Test Prep** to each student.

Day 5 Posttest

Objective
The students will correctly write dictated spelling words and sentences.

Introduction
Review by using flash cards noted in Student Spelling Support, number 2.

Directed Assessment
1 Dictate the list words by using the Pretest sentences or developing original ones. Reserve *springtime*, *countries*, *offspring*, *annual*, and *vivid* for the dictation sentences.
2 Read each sentence. Repeat as needed.
• Springtime is a season between winter and summer.
• In countries north of the equator, the days grow longer in the spring.
• Many woodland animals give birth to offspring in this season.
• Easter, an annual celebration, is always in the spring.
• Flowers with vivid colors bloom in the spring.
3 If assigned, dictate Extra Challenge Words.
4 Score the test, counting each misspelled word as an error. Correct the dictation sentences by grading only the spelling words or grading the complete sentences.

Student Spelling Support

Cont. from page 000

Content, and Vocabulary Words, and attach them to the Word Wall.
7. Kinesthetic learners will enjoy matching plural nouns with their singular forms. Spread two sets of word cards like those used in Day 2 Introduction in random order on a table, placing one set with the singular words faceup and one set with the plural words faceup. Invite a student to match each singular noun with its plural form quickly while you time the activity using a clock with a second hand. Record the length of time needed to match the cards. Invite a second student to repeat the activity in less time.
8. Challenge students to interview missionaries and then write a description of their ministry setting—both geographically and spiritually. Collect these writings in a class book entitled "Christianity at Work."

© *Spelling Grade 5*

A Spelling Study Strategy

Teacher Note: Instruct students in the use of **A Spelling Study Strategy** prior to Lesson 1.

Display P-1 A Spelling Study Strategy.

Duplicate one copy of **BLM SP5-01A A Spelling Study Strategy** for each student. Write *chilly, value, humble, pattern,* and *shelving* in the left-hand column. Model each step.

- Look at the first spelling word, say it, and listen to the sounds. Think about the sounds.
- Fold the paper.
- Picture the word in your mind, identify spelling patterns, and write the word.
- Unfold the paper.
- Use a colored pencil for checking and making corrections. If a word is misspelled, direct students to circle it, go back to the first column, and write the word in the faded column.

Student Pages

Pages 1–4

Lesson Materials

BLM SP5-01B
T-2
P-2
P-3
BLM SP5-01C
BLM SP5-01D

Created Wonders

Genesis 1:1 says, "In the beginning God created the heavens and the earth." Our loving God chose to create the universe and everything within it. Through His creation, we can see just how amazing our God is.

Lessons 1–5 utilize the theme of different aspects of land structure. Lesson 1 begins with mountains. Mountains are regions of land that are raised sharply above the surrounding landscape. Mountains are formed in three general ways—movement of plates in the earth's crust, volcanic activity, or erosion.

Day 1 Pretest

Objective

The students will accurately spell and write words with **short vowels**, content, vocabulary, and challenge words.

Introduction

The Pretest is an ungraded assessment to assist students in studying the list words—Pattern, Content, Vocabulary, and Challenge. To meet your students' needs, select Challenge Words from a cross-curricular subject, common misspellings for fifth graders, or words that interest your students. The word *industrial* has **short i** in the first syllable and is suggested for number 24. Explain that they are to attempt to write all the spelling words.

Directed Instruction

1 Use the sentences that follow or develop original ones.

2 Say each word, use it in a sentence, and then repeat the word.

Pattern Words
1. The <u>value</u> of the mountain-climbing lesson was tremendous.
2. Jesus wants all of us to be <u>humble</u> and serve one another.
3. The <u>shelving</u> on the mountainside was very steep and dangerous.
4. Cary spoke in a <u>whisper</u> so he would not disturb the quiet camp.
5. Sarah learned about <u>puppetry</u> at summer camp on Mount Whitney.
6. Joan bought some <u>magazines</u> for her long flight to the Himalayas.
7. Trina had a <u>headache</u> from the change in altitude during her hike.
8. Snow is a <u>common</u> sight on the top of tall mountain ranges.
9. Xavier read through the <u>volumes</u> of mountain-climbing information.
10. Geologists study the <u>pattern</u> of movements in the earth's crust.
11. Does the mountain <u>separate</u> the two valleys?
12. Rachel felt a <u>chilly</u> wind when she reached the mountaintop.

Content Words
13. The small stream carried <u>sediment</u> from the mountain to the lake.
14. <u>Igneous</u> rock is formed when volcanic rock hardens.
15. Many people have tried to climb to the <u>summit</u> of Mount Everest.
16. Joseph wrote a report about the <u>mountains</u> in the European Alps.
17. Through <u>erosion</u>, the surface of the earth is constantly changing.
18. The <u>snowcapped</u> top of Pikes Peak is often photographed.
19. The <u>granite</u> on Mount Rushmore was blasted and sculpted.

Vocabulary Words
20. A <u>fragment</u> of rock broke off the cliff as the wind rushed by.
21. Derrell decided not to climb onto the <u>fragile</u> mountain cliff.
22. The wind and rain will slowly <u>expose</u> the mountainside.
23. A vast mineral <u>deposit</u> was found in the mountainous area.

Challenge Words
24. _____ (Insert your choice.)
25. _____ (Insert your choice.)

3 Allow students to self-correct their Pretest. Write each word on the board. Point out the **short vowels** in the first syllable of each Pattern Word. Note the roots *frag*, *posit*, and *pos* in the Vocabulary Words.

4 As a class, read, spell, and read each word. Direct students to circle misspelled words with a colored pencil and rewrite them correctly.

5 Proof each student's Pretest. This becomes an individualized study

sheet that can be used at school or at home.

6 Homework suggestion: Distribute a copy of **BLM SP5-01B Lesson 1 Words and Phrases** to each student.

Day 2 Word Analysis and Vocabulary

Objective

The students will sort words with **short vowels** according to the first syllable sound. They will complete sentences with content words. They will use a table to write vocabulary words, match vocabulary words to their definitions, and complete a sentence.

Introduction

Proceed to page 1. Define the following categories of words: Pattern Words—words with similar spellings or sounds; Content Words—words related to a specific content area indicated by the theme of the lesson; Vocabulary Words—words with prefixes, suffixes, and Greek and Latin roots; Challenge Words—words that may be harder to spell. Provide this week's Challenge Words and have students write the words on their page.

Directed Instruction

1 Invite students to refer to the list words, found on page 1, for this activity. Chorally read each Pattern Word. Point out that the Pattern Words in this lesson all contain a short vowel sound in the first syllable. A *syllable* is <u>a word or a part of a word with one vowel sound</u>. Have students identify the short vowel sound within each word. Categorize the words on the board. (**short a—value, pattern, magazines; short e—shelving, separate, headache; short i—chilly, whisper; short o—volumes, common; short u—humble, puppetry**) Use the categorized words as a guide to complete exercises 1–12. Read the directions for exercises 13–19 and complete together.

2 Proceed to page 2. Display **T-2 Word Origins Practice** on the overhead and invite students to follow along as you build the foundation of studying word origins. The transparency is an exact replica of student

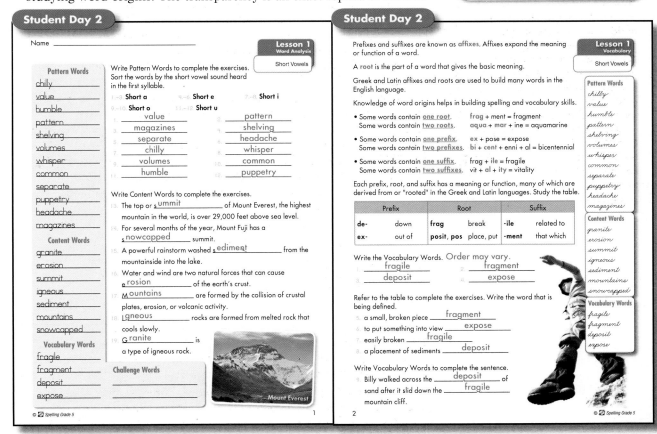

**Student Spelling
Support Materials**

T-1
BLM SP5-01A
BLMs SP5-01E–F
Card stock
BLM SP5-01G
3" × 5" Index cards
BLM Parent Letter

**Student
Spelling Support**

1. Use **T-1 A Spelling Study Strategy** and **BLM SP5-01A A Spelling Study Strategy** for students who demonstrate the need for additional practice with some or all of the words.

2. Duplicate **BLMs SP5-01E–F Lesson 1 Spelling Words I** and **II** on CARD STOCK for students to use as flash cards at school or at home. Another option is to use **BLM SP5-01G Flash Cards Template** or 3" × 5" INDEX CARDS for students to write their own flash cards to use as a study aid.

3. Invite students to write the Challenge Words, numbers 24 and 25, in the Word Bank, in the back of their textbook.

4. Read Genesis 1:1: "In the beginning God created the heavens and the earth." Discuss with students the marvelous things that God has created. God's majesty is seen throughout His creation—land, plants, oceans, living things, seasons, and the universe!

5. Challenge students to research and write interesting facts about the lesson theme—mountains. Students compile facts and draw pictures in a journal or notebook to build an informative resource. Do this with each lesson theme in the textbook as the year

Cont. on page 5

page 2. Use the transparency to instruct students on how to build each Vocabulary Word. For example, the prefix *de-* goes with the root *posit* to get the word *deposit*; the root *frag* goes with the suffix *-ile* to get the word *fragile*; the root *frag* goes with the suffix *-ment* to get the word *fragment*. Note that the prefix *ex-* goes with the root *pos* to get the word *expose* and silent *e* is not in the original root spelling. Read each sentence and complete the page as a class.

3 Display **P-2** and **P-3 Greek and Latin Roots** for students to reference roots and their meanings. Leave posters up throughout the year.

4 Homework suggestion: Distribute a copy of **BLM SP5-01C Lesson 1 Phrases and Sentences** to each student.

Day 3 Word Study Strategies
Objective
The students will write synonyms and syllabicate words between double consonants. They will use the context of a sentence to determine the meaning of underlined words.

Introduction
Invite students to follow along as you write the following words on the board: pretty, happy, caring, fast. Allow students to recite any word that comes to mind that is a synonym of each word that you are writing. A *synonym* is a word that means the same or almost the same as another word. Write the recited synonyms on the board. (**Possible synonyms: beautiful, joyful, loving, quick**)

Directed Instruction
1 Write the following words on the board: valley, narrow, surround, collide. Challenge students to identify the commonality in the words. (**All of the words contain double consonants.**) State the following syllabication generalization: Divide between double consonants. Draw a vertical line between double consonants in each word to show syllabication. (**val|ley, nar|row, sur|round, col|lide**)

2 Reinforce the meanings of *shelving, erosion,* and *sediment* by reading each definition and sentence from the Spelling Dictionary found in the back of the text.

3 Proceed to page 3. Students independently complete the page. Select a student to read Genesis 1:1 and discuss the magnificence of God's creation as mentioned in Student Spelling Support, number 4.

Day 4 Writing
Objective
The students will complete a descriptive e-mail in the context of a cloze activity using pattern, content, and vocabulary words.

Introduction
Teacher Note: The descriptive domain is the focus for the writing pages in Lessons 1–5.

Before class, write the following word choices and e-mail on the board: value, common, separate.

> Dear Consumer,
> Welcome to our new web store! On this site, our team has chosen to __1__ the __2__ items from the hard-to-find items. We hope your shopping experience will be a benefit and __3__ to you. Contact customer support if you need any assistance. Happy shopping!
> Cordially,
> The Bargain Team

Discuss the benefits of communicating by e-mail. (**Possible benefits: quick delivery, direct response, instant contact**) Chorally read the incomplete e-mail aloud.

Directed Instruction

1 Select a volunteer to complete the cloze activity by writing in the missing words. (1—separate; 2—common; 3—value) A *cloze activity consists of a sentence or passage with blanks.*

2 Proceed to page 4 and select a volunteer to read the sentences at the top of the page. Students complete the cloze activity independently. When complete, select a volunteer to read the e-mail aloud.

3 Homework suggestion: Distribute a copy of **BLM SP5-01D Lesson 1 Test Prep** to each student.

Day 5 Posttest

Objective

The students will correctly write dictated spelling words and sentences.

Introduction

Review by using flash cards noted in Student Spelling Support, number 2.

Directed Assessment

1 Dictate the list words by using the Pretest sentences or developing original ones. Reserve *magazines*, *fragile*, *summit*, *chilly*, and *granite* for the dictation sentences.

2 Read each sentence. Repeat as needed.
- Sue bought some <u>magazines</u> about hiking.
- She read about hiking in <u>fragile</u> mountain areas.
- Sue wanted to hike to the <u>summit</u> before dark.
- It was <u>chilly</u> on the top of the mountain.
- The mountain was made of <u>granite</u>.

3 If assigned, dictate Extra Challenge Words.

4 Score the test, counting each misspelled word as an error. Correct the dictation sentences by grading only the spelling words or grading the complete sentences.

Student Spelling Support
Cont. from page 4

progresses. At the end of the year, invite students to share their progressive journals.

6. Make a Word Wall using this week's spelling words. Write the words, categorize the Pattern, Content, and Vocabulary Words, and attach to the wall. Allow students to spontaneously add new words to the list during the week. Categorizing by patterns helps students internalize generalizations.

Short vowel in the first syllable
value　shelving　chilly
volumes　humble
Content: Mountains
granite　erosion
Vocabulary
fragile　deposit

7. Provide a copy of the **BLM Parent Letter** for each student to take home. This will inform parents about their child's spelling class.

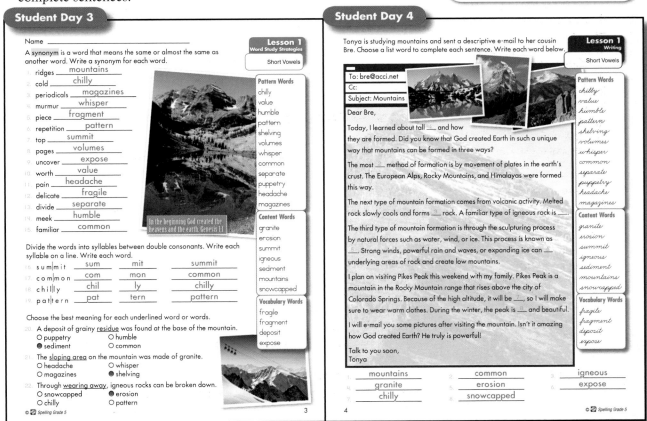

Student Pages

Pages 5–8

Lesson Materials

BLM SP5-02A
T-2
BLM SP5-02B
3" × 5" Index cards
BLM SP5-02C

Created Wonders

The theme of this lesson is volcanoes. Volcanoes are formed by the accumulation of magma, molten rock beneath the earth's surface. When pressure builds up, magma rises to the surface, resulting in an eruption. Gases, tephra, and lava may emerge during an eruption. While some volcanoes pose a threat to populated areas, the majority of volcanoes are under the oceans.

Day 1 Pretest

Objective

The students will accurately spell and write words with **long a**, content, vocabulary, and challenge words.

Introduction

The Pretest is an ungraded assessment to assist students in studying the Pattern, Content, Vocabulary, and Challenge Words. To meet your students' needs, select Challenge Words from a cross-curricular subject or words misspelled on previous assignments. The word *congratulations* has **long a** in the fourth syllable and is suggested for number 24. Explain that they are to attempt to write all the spelling words.

Directed Instruction

1 Use the sentences that follow or develop original ones.

2 Say each word, use it in a sentence, and then repeat the word.

Pattern Words

1. Mr. Santos is an <u>agent</u> for the Volcanic Study Agency.
2. Ash from Mount Saint Helens turned our car <u>beige</u>.
3. Natalie never had a <u>complaint</u> about the hike up Mount Rainier.
4. Forest fires are a <u>major</u> problem after volcanic eruptions.
5. Adam put all the <u>details</u> that he could into his report on volcanoes.
6. We <u>obeyed</u> the rangers and evacuated before Kilauea erupted.
7. The Lord preserves all those who are <u>faithful</u> to Him.
8. Could seismic activity delay the arrival of the <u>freight</u>?
9. Scientists made a geodetic <u>survey</u> when volcanic activity ceased. je ō det´ic
10. Charles <u>prepaid</u> for the tickets to the natural history museum.
11. People provided <u>neighborly</u> assistance after the volcanic explosion.
12. Jesus will <u>reign</u> for all eternity.

Content Words

13. <u>Magma</u> formed a bulge in the side of the mountain.
14. A great quantity of <u>lava</u> started to flow down the mountain.
15. Igneous materials move toward areas of lower <u>pressure</u>.
16. <u>Molten</u> rock accumulates below the earth's surface.
17. Geologists found <u>tephra</u> hundreds of miles from the explosion site.
18. Mount Shasta is a dormant <u>volcano</u>.
19. The <u>eruption</u> of Mount Vesuvius destroyed the town of Pompeii.

Vocabulary Words

20. Lines of latitude and longitude <u>intersect</u>.
21. Jessica used coordinates to find the <u>intersection</u> on the map.
22. The college will <u>induct</u> Dr. Brown as the geology department head.
23. High winds provided <u>conduction</u> for ashes across the state.

Challenge Words

24. _____ (Insert your choice.)
25. _____ (Insert your choice.)

3 Allow students to self-correct their Pretest. Write each word on the board. Point out the following **long a** spellings: *a* in an open syllable, ai, ei, eigh, ey. Remind students that each Vocabulary Word is made up of a root and an affix(es). *Duct* and *sect* are the roots in this lesson.

4 As a class, read, spell, and read each word. Direct students to circle misspelled words with a colored pencil and rewrite them correctly.

5 Proof each student's Pretest. This becomes an individualized study sheet that can be used at school or at home.

6 Homework suggestion: Distribute a copy of **BLM SP5-02A Lesson 2 Words and Phrases** to each student.

Day 2 Word Analysis and Vocabulary

Objective

The students will sort words with **long a** according to spelling. They will write content words to complete sentences. The students will use a table to write vocabulary words to match a given definition and in context. They will choose the best meaning for the underlined word.

Introduction

Invite students to turn to page 5 to use as a reference for the list words. Review the spellings for **long a** by calling out the various spellings and asking students to give examples of Pattern Words that contain each spelling. (*a* in an open syllable—agent, major; ai—details, faithful, prepaid, complaint; eigh—freight, neighborly; ei—reign, beige; ey—survey, obeyed)

Directed Instruction

1 Display **T-2 Word Origins Practice** to review the definitions of a root and affix. Remind students that many words have more than one affix. The words *conduction* and *intersection* in this lesson each have more than one affix. The prefixes are *con-* and *inter-*, and the suffix in both words is *-ion*. The root *duct* means *lead*, and the root *sect* means *cut*. Knowing the meaning or function of roots and affixes helps students in defining each word.

2 Proceed to page 5. Say, spell, and say each Pattern, Content, and Vocabulary Word. Provide this week's Challenge Words and have students write them in the spaces provided. Supply the meaning of any Content Words that are unfamiliar to students.

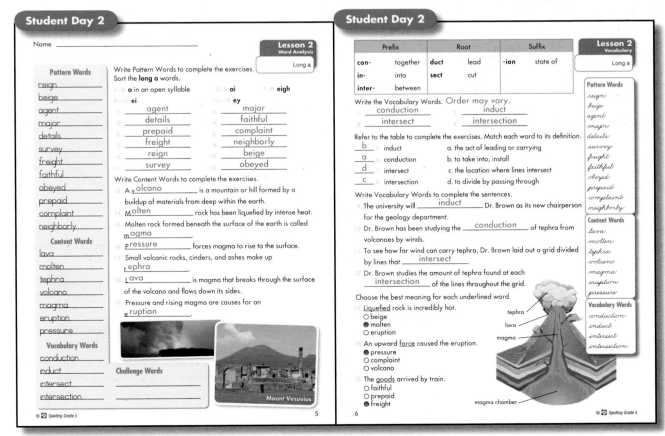

3 Proceed to page 6. Encourage students to use the table as an aid in building each Vocabulary Word. For example, the prefix *con-* goes with the root *duct* and the suffix *-ion* to make the word *conduction*. To conclude the lesson, ask students to state additional words that have the roots *duct* and *sect*. (**Possible answers: conduct, section**) Allow students to complete the page independently.

4 Homework suggestion: Distribute a copy of **BLM SP5-02B Lesson 2 Phrases and Sentences** to each student.

Day 3 Word Study Strategies

Objective

The students will use the Spelling Dictionary to correctly place words in sentence context. They will underline and write list words that are used as nouns in paragraphs.

Introduction

Direct students to turn to page 155 in the back of their textbook. Use this page to explain each component of a dictionary entry—guide words, an entry word, the pronunciation, the part of speech, the definition, and the sample sentence. Select volunteers to read each component and briefly discuss each one.

Directed Instruction

1 Challenge students to look up the word *volcano* in their Spelling Dictionary. Choose volunteers to state the guide words at the top of the page (**verbal and youthfulness**), write the pronunciation on the board (/vol ˈkā nō/), state the part of speech (**noun**), read the definition (**a mountain or hill formed by the accumulation of materials on the earth's surface**), and read the sample sentence (**Mount Shasta is a dormant volcano.**).

2 Review that the part of speech listed in the entry for *volcano* is a noun. A *noun* is <u>a person, place, thing, or idea</u>. Nouns can be singular or plural. Parts of speech vary, depending upon how a word is used in context, so a word may be used as a noun in one sentence and a different part of speech in another sentence. Most nouns in context are preceded by the articles *a*, *an*, or *the*.

3 Proceed to page 7. Allow students to independently read the directions and complete the page. Assist as needed.

Day 4 Writing

Objective

The students will read a dialogue between a teacher and students. They will locate, underline, and write the list words.

Introduction

Before class, write each of the following sentences on a 3" × 5" INDEX CARD:
- CHRIS: Hi, Lee. When did you get here?
- LEE: I just arrived. I cannot wait to get started on our science project.
- CHRIS: I do not have all the materials we need. Did you bring the microscope?
- LEE: Yes, I have the microscope! Let's get going!

Select two students to play the parts of Chris and Lee and distribute the appropriate cards. Explain that this activity is called a *dialogue*. A *dialogue* is <u>a conversation between two or more people</u>.

Directed Instruction

1 Inform students that a dialogue often involves questions and answers. When one person asks a question and another person provides an answer, a dialogue takes place. Today's lesson involves a conversation between a teacher and students while on a field trip to Mount Rainier National Park in the state of Washington.

2 Proceed to page 8. Choose a student to read the instructions for the page. Select students to play the roles of the teacher and the students and read the dialogue aloud.

3 Explain that some list words appear multiple times on the page, but each word is to be written only once. Advise students to cross off each word on the word list after they write it to avoid duplication. Allow students to complete the page.

4 Homework suggestion: Distribute a copy of **BLM SP5-02C Lesson 2 Test Prep** to each student.

Day 5 Posttest

Objective
The students will correctly write dictated spelling words and sentences.

Introduction
Review by using flash cards noted in Student Spelling Support, number 2.

Directed Assessment

1 Dictate the list words by using the Pretest sentences or developing original ones. Reserve *beige, intersect, details, volcano,* and *lava* for the dictation sentences.

2 Read each sentence. Repeat as needed.
- Jan has a beige travel notebook.
- Jan uses lines that intersect to make maps in her notebook.
- She also writes down details of her trips.
- Once, Jan wrote about a volcano that she saw on one of her trips.
- Super hot lava rushed down its sides.

3 If assigned, dictate Extra Challenge Words.

4 Score the test, counting each misspelled word as an error. Correct the dictation sentences by grading only the spelling words or grading the complete sentences.

Notes

Student Day 3

Name _____

Lesson 2
Word Study Strategies

Long a

Look up **lava** and **magma** in your Spelling Dictionary. Decide which word fits best in each sentence. Write the words.
1. Molten rock below the earth's surface is called __magma__.
2. __Lava__ erupted from Mount Saint Helens and flowed down its side.

Look up **reign** and **survey** in your Spelling Dictionary. Decide which word fits best in each sentence. Write the words.
3. The geologist made a __survey__ of the mountainside.
4. When Queen Victoria first began to __reign__, little was known about the movement of the earth's crust. Scientists have discovered many things since that time.

A **noun** is a person, place, thing, or idea. Nouns can be singular or plural. Read the paragraphs, underline the list words that are used as nouns, and write the words.

Mr. Lopez works as an <u>agent</u> for a major railroad. His job requires that he travel to different states to check on the loading and unloading of <u>freight</u>. Mr. Lopez's job is important to many people who prepaid to have their goods shipped by train.

While he was in Washington, inspecting goods at the <u>intersection</u> of two train lines, Mr. Lopez witnessed the <u>eruption</u> of Mount Saint Helens, an active <u>volcano</u>. Mr. Lopez noted the <u>details</u> of the event in his beige journal. He wrote about the speed of the <u>lava</u> as it raced down the mountain. Mr. Lopez was amazed by the quantity of <u>tephra</u> that remained in the air for some time after the explosion. Months later, Mr. Lopez reread his journal entry as a reminder of his experience near Mount Saint Helens. Order may vary.

5. __agent__ 6. __freight__ 7. __intersection__
8. __eruption__ 9. __volcano__ 10. __details__
11. __lava__ 12. __tephra__

Pattern Words
reign
beige
agent
major
survey
freight
faithful
obeyed
prepaid
complaint
neighborly

Content Words
lava
molten
tephra
volcano
magma
eruption
pressure

Vocabulary Words
conduction
induct
intersect
intersection

7

Student Day 4

Read the dialogue, between Mrs. Cole and her students, that took place at Mount Rainier National Park in Washington. Underline and write the list words. Write each word only once.

Lesson 2
Writing

Long a

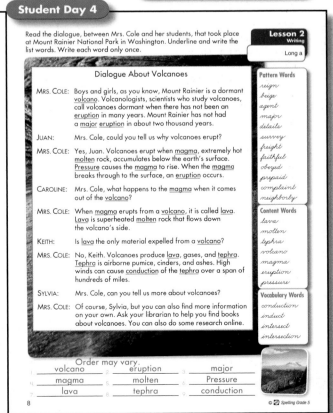

Dialogue About Volcanoes

MRS. COLE: Boys and girls, as you know, Mount Rainier is a dormant <u>volcano</u>. Volcanologists, scientists who study volcanoes, call volcanoes dormant when there has not been an <u>eruption</u> in many years. Mount Rainier has not had a <u>major</u> <u>eruption</u> in about two thousand years.

JUAN: Mrs. Cole, could you tell us why volcanoes erupt?

MRS. COLE: Yes, Juan. Volcanoes erupt when <u>magma</u>, extremely hot <u>molten</u> rock, accumulates below the earth's surface. <u>Pressure</u> causes the <u>magma</u> to rise. When the <u>magma</u> breaks through to the surface, an <u>eruption</u> occurs.

CAROLINE: Mrs. Cole, what happens to the <u>magma</u> when it comes out of the <u>volcano</u>?

MRS. COLE: When <u>magma</u> erupts from a <u>volcano</u>, it is called <u>lava</u>. <u>Lava</u> is superheated <u>molten</u> rock that flows down the <u>volcano</u>'s side.

KEITH: Is <u>lava</u> the only material expelled from a <u>volcano</u>?

MRS. COLE: No, Keith. Volcanoes produce <u>lava</u>, gases, and <u>tephra</u>. <u>Tephra</u> is airborne pumice, cinders, and ashes. High winds can cause <u>conduction</u> of the <u>tephra</u> over a span of hundreds of miles.

SYLVIA: Mrs. Cole, can you tell us more about volcanoes?

MRS. COLE: Of course, Sylvia, but you can also find more information on your own. Ask your librarian to help you find books about volcanoes. You can also do some research online.

Order may vary.
1. __volcano__ 2. __eruption__ 3. __major__
4. __magma__ 5. __molten__ 6. __Pressure__
7. __lava__ 8. __tephra__ 9. __conduction__

Pattern Words
reign
beige
agent
major
details
survey
freight
faithful
obeyed
prepaid
complaint
neighborly

Content Words
lava
molten
tephra
volcano
magma
eruption
pressure

Vocabulary Words
conduction
induct
intersect
intersection

8

© Spelling Grade 5

Student Pages

Pages 9–12

Lesson Materials

BLM SP5-03A
BLM SP5-03B
T-3
BLM SP5-03C
BLM SP5-03D

Created Wonders

The theme of this lesson is caves. Caves are hollow areas beneath the ground or in the side of a hill, cliff, or mountain. Caves also exist under water. Spelunking, exploring caves for recreation, is a hobby enjoyed by people all over the world.

Day 1 Pretest

Objective

The students will accurately spell and write words with **long e**, content, vocabulary, and challenge words.

Introduction

The Pretest is an ungraded assessment to assist students in studying the Pattern, Content, Vocabulary, and Challenge Words. To meet your students' needs, select Challenge Words from a cross-curricular subject or words misspelled on previous assignments. The word *convenience* has **long e** and is suggested for number 24. Explain that they are to attempt to write all the spelling words.

Directed Instruction

1 Use the sentences that follow or develop original ones.

2 Say each word, use it in a sentence, and then repeat the word.

Pattern Words
  1. Cara and her sisters enjoy playing <u>volleyball</u>.
  2. The bus driver drove through the <u>alley</u> to get to the main street.
  3. My <u>belief</u> in God is solid as a rock.
  4. Have you <u>received</u> Jesus as your Savior?
  5. Tucker wants to <u>achieve</u> a high score on his science project.
  6. The spelunker discussed how to explore a cave at an <u>assembly</u>.
  7. Sunglasses are a <u>shield</u> that protects our eyes from ultraviolet rays.
  8. <u>Neither</u> Ramon nor Pedro attended the field trip to the cave.
  9. Kirk took some medicine to <u>relieve</u> his headache.
  10. Anya bought souvenirs from the gift shop with her own <u>money</u>.
  11. Mrs. McIntire earns a <u>salary</u> as a tour guide.
  12. Many caves were found when people explored the <u>territory</u>.

Content Words
  13. <u>Stalactites</u> grow downward from the ceiling of caves.
  14. A cave can have more than one <u>chamber</u>.
  15. My class enjoyed touring the beautiful <u>cavern</u>.
  16. Many <u>columns</u> are formed in caves by water seeping through the roof.
  17. <u>Stalagmites</u> grow upward from the floor of caves.
  18. The stream disappeared into the <u>sinkhole</u>.
  19. Many caves are formed from <u>limestone</u>.

Vocabulary Words
  20. A <u>section</u> of the cave was off-limits to visitors.
  21. Our class was told to not make <u>contact</u> with the cave walls.
  22. The cave opening was <u>intact</u> after the earthquake.
  23. After learning about caves, we will <u>dissect</u> owl pellets.

Challenge Words
  24. _____ (Insert your choice.)
  25. _____ (Insert your choice.)

3 Allow students to self-correct their Pretest. Write each word on the board. Point out the following **long e** spellings: ei, ey, ie, y. Review that *i* usually comes before *e* except after the letter *c*. The word *neither* is an exception to this generalization. Remind students that each Vocabulary Word is made up of a root and an affix. *Sect* and *tact* are the roots in this lesson.

4 As a class, read, spell, and read each word. Direct students to circle misspelled words with a colored pencil and rewrite them correctly.

5 Proof each student's Pretest. This becomes an individualized study sheet that can be used at school or at home.

6 Homework suggestion: Distribute a copy of **BLM SP5-03A Lesson 3 Words and Phrases** to each student.

Day 2 Word Analysis and Vocabulary

Objective
The students will accurately sort **long e** words, write content words to complete sentences, and use a table to correctly write vocabulary words. They will select definitions for list words.

Introduction
Write the following **long e** spellings on the board: ei, ey, ie, y. Explain that these four spellings make the **long e** sound in the Pattern Words. Read each Pattern Word aloud and select a student to state the **long e** spelling in that particular word.

Directed Instruction

1 Explain that the Content Words relate to the theme of caves. Two words that are easily confused are *stalactites* and *stalagmites*. Write the words on the board, underlining *ct* in *stalactites* and *gm* in *stalagmites*. Teach the following helpful hints:
- Stala<u>ct</u>ites grow downward from the <u>c</u>eiling, and if you grab one, you can hold on <u>t</u>ight.
- Stala<u>gm</u>ites grow upward from the <u>g</u>round, and if you're not careful, you <u>m</u>ight run into one.

2 Have students turn to page 9 to refer to the list words. Using the Spelling Dictionary in the back of the book, read a few definitions of list words, one at a time, asking students to name the list word. Some of the following are choices: a narrow street (**alley**), a large cave (**cavern**), unbroken (**intact**).

Differentiated Instruction

Differentiating spelling instruction is an option to consider.
- For students who spelled all the words correctly on the Pretest, select and assign Extra Challenge Words from the following list: applause, Sinai, judicial, pneumonia, interrogative, programming.
- For students who spelled less than half correctly, assign the following Pattern, Content, and Vocabulary Words: shield, salary, relieve, money, received, assembly, cavern, sinkhole, chamber, limestone, section, intact. On the Posttest, evaluate these students on the twelve words assigned; however, encourage them to attempt to spell all the list words to the best of their ability. They are also responsible for writing the dictated sentences.

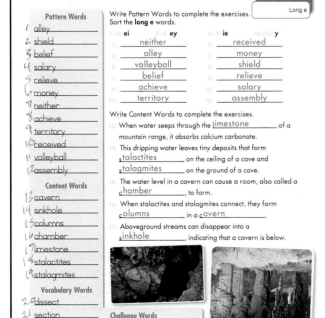

Student Day 2

Name _____

Lesson 3 Word Analysis — Long e

61 pts.

Pattern Words
1 alley
2 shield
3 belief
4 salary
5 relieve
6 money
7 neither
8 achieve
9 territory
10 received
11 volleyball
12 assembly

Content Words
13 cavern
14 sinkhole
15 columns
16 chamber
17 limestone
18 stalactites
19 stalagmites

Vocabulary Words
20 dissect
21 section
22 contact
23 intact

Write Pattern Words to complete the exercises. Sort the **long e** words.

| 1–2 ei | 3–5 ey | 6–9 ie | 10–12 y |

1. neither
2. received
3. alley
4. money
5. volleyball
6. shield
7. belief
8. relieve
9. achieve
10. salary
11. territory
12. assembly

Write Content Words to complete the exercises.

13. When water seeps through the limestone of a mountain range, it absorbs calcium carbonate.

14. This dripping water leaves tiny deposits that form stalactites on the ceiling of a cave and stalagmites on the ground of a cave.

15. The water level in a cavern can cause a room, also called a chamber, to form.

16. When stalactites and stalagmites connect, they form columns in a cavern.

17. Aboveground streams can disappear into a sinkhole, indicating that a cavern is below.

Challenge Words

cave

Student Day 2

Prefix		Root		Suffix	
dis-	apart	sect	cut	-ion	state of
con-	together	tact	touch		
in-	not				

Lesson 3 Vocabulary — Long e

Write the Vocabulary Words. Order may vary.
1. dissect
2. section
3. contact
4. intact

Refer to the table to complete the exercises. Write the word that is being defined.

5. a piece separated from a whole — section
6. not touched or broken — intact
7. a touch — contact
8. to cut apart — dissect

Write Vocabulary Words to complete the sentences.

9. A section of the cave was blocked by a broken stalactite.
10. The tour guide allowed us to make contact with the broken stalactite.
11. The large columns in the cavern have remained intact for many years.
12. Addie will dissect a bat that once lived in a cave.

Choose the best meaning for each word.

13. received
   - ○ to have disappeared
   - ○ to have spoken
   - ● to have acquired

14. alley
   - ○ a dead-end street
   - ● a narrow street
   - ○ a wide street

15. territory
   - ● an area of land
   - ○ a type of dog
   - ○ a piece of a rock

16. salary
   - ○ a vegetable
   - ● money earned
   - ○ a sport

Pattern Words
alley
shield
belief
salary
relieve
money
neither
achieve
territory
received
volleyball
assembly

Content Words
cavern
sinkhole
columns
chamber
limestone
stalactites
stalagmites

Vocabulary Words
dissect
section
contact
intact

© Spelling Grade 5 9

10 © Spelling Grade 5

3 Proceed to page 9. Say, spell, and say each Pattern, Content, and Vocabulary Word. Provide this week's Challenge Words and have students write them in the spaces provided before completing the page.

4 Proceed to page 10. Remind students to use the table to assist in building each Vocabulary Word. For example, the prefix *dis-* and the root *sect* make the word *dissect*. To conclude the lesson, ask students to state additional words that have the prefixes *dis-* and *in-*. (**Possible answers: dissection, insect**) Allow students to complete the page independently.

5 Homework suggestion: Distribute a copy of **BLM SP5-03B Lesson 3 Phrases and Sentences** to each student.

Day 3 Word Study Strategies

Objective

The students will complete analogies. They will syllabicate words between double consonants and compound words, and write the words.

Introduction

Write the following incomplete analogies on the board:
- Blouse is to shirt as cash is to _____. (**money**)
- Foot is to football as volley is to _____. (**volleyball**)

Ask students to name these types of sentences. (**analogies**) Remind students that an *analogy* is made up of two word pairs. Both pairs of words have the same kind of relationship. Read the first analogy and ask a volunteer to state how the words *blouse* and *shirt* are related. (**Possible answer: A *blouse* is the same as a *shirt*.**) Apply the same relationship to the second part of the analogy by asking students which list word, found on page 11, means the same as *cash*. (**money**) In the next analogy, assist students in understanding the relationship between *foot* and *football*. (***Foot* is the first word in the compound word *football*.**) Apply the same relationship to *volley*. (**volleyball**)

Directed Instruction

1 Write *pattern* and *summit* on the board. Remind students that words with double consonants are divided into syllables between the double consonants. Syllabicate *pattern* and *summit*. (**pat|tern, sum|mit**)

2 Write *snowcapped* and *evergreen* on the board. State the following syllabication generalization: Divide a compound word into two smaller words. Challenge students to state the two smaller words in *snowcapped* and *evergreen*. (**snow and capped; ever and green**) Select a student to show the syllabication of *snowcapped* and *evergreen*. (**snow|capped, ever|green**)

3 Proceed to page 11. Allow students to read the directions and complete the page independently. Assist as needed.

Day 4 Writing

Objective

The students will use proofreading marks to identify mistakes in a tour guide's descriptive notes. They will correctly write misspelled words.

Introduction

Display **T-3 Proofreading Descriptive Notes**, keeping the bottom portion of the transparency covered. Relate that the tour guide's notes are fiction, but the facts about a cave are nonfiction. Define *spelunker* as *one who explores a cave*. Tell students that the errors will be corrected using proofreading marks located in the Proofreading Marks box. Review each proofreading mark. Orally read the text and challenge students to locate the mistakes. Correct the mistakes on the overhead using the appropriate proofreading mark. Use **BLM SP5-03C T-3 Answer Key** as a guide. Uncover the bottom of the transparency so students can see a corrected version.

Directed Instruction

1 Proceed to page 12. Select a student to read the sentences at the top of the page. Allow students to work independently, assisting as needed to ensure each error is corrected. Encourage students to edit their papers using the proofreading marks. (**9 misspellings; 4 capital letters needed; 1 period needed; 3 deletes; 1 add something—*of*; 3 small letters needed; 2 new paragraphs**)

2 Homework suggestion: Distribute a copy of **BLM SP5-03D Lesson 3 Test Prep** to each student.

Day 5 Posttest

Objective
The students will correctly write dictated spelling words and sentences.

Introduction
Review by using flash cards noted in Student Spelling Support, number 2.

Directed Assessment

1 Dictate the list words by using the Pretest sentences or developing original ones. Reserve *cavern*, *money*, *received*, *chamber*, and *section* for the dictation sentences.

2 Read each sentence. Repeat as needed.
- My family and I visited a famous <u>cavern</u>.
- My brother Tom gave the ticket agent our <u>money</u>.
- Tom <u>received</u> the tickets after he paid.
- The first <u>chamber</u> we walked into was very large.
- The deepest <u>section</u> of the cave was chilly.

3 If assigned, dictate Extra Challenge Words.

4 Score the test, counting each misspelled word as an error. Correct the dictation sentences by grading only the spelling words or grading the complete sentences.

Notes

Do pg. 12 in class—
Use overhead in Sp. files
(No points for lesson)

Student Day 3

Name _____

An analogy is made up of two word pairs. Both pairs of words have the same kind of relationship.

Lesson 3
Word Study Strategies

Long e

Choose the best word for each analogy. Write it on the line.

1. **Ground** is to **stalagmites** as **ceiling** is to ____ stalactites
2. **Students** is to **pupils** as **pillars** is to ____ columns
3. **Beagle** is to **dog** as **umbrella** is to ____ shield
4. **Assistant** is to **helper** as **currency** is to ____ money
5. **Denied** is to **refused** as **acquired** is to ____ received
6. **Street** is to **alley** as **wage** is to ____ salary
7. **Room** is to **chamber** as **accomplish** is to ____ achieve
8. **Unable** is to **able** as **unbelief** is to ____ belief
9. **Beginning** is to **end** as **whole** is to ____ section
10. **Stroll** is to **walk** as **untouched** is to ____ intact

Divide the words into syllables between double consonants. Write each syllable on a line. Write each word.

11. d i s s e c t ____ dis ____ sect ____ dissect
12. a l l e y ____ al ____ ley ____ alley

Multisyllable words are divided more than one time. Notice how each word is divided. Write the word.

13. a s | s e m | b l y ____ assembly
14. t e r | r i | t o r | y ____ territory

Divide each compound word into two smaller words. Write each syllable on a line. Write each word.

15. l i m e | s t o n e ____ lime ____ stone ____ limestone
16. s i n k | h o l e ____ sink ____ hole ____ sinkhole

Write the list word that has two double consonants and is a compound word. Write each syllable.

17. ____ volleyball ____ vol ____ ley ____ ball

Pattern Words
alley
shield
belief
salary
relieve
money
neither
achieve
territory
received
volleyball
assembly

Content Words
cavern
sinkhole
columns
chamber
limestone
stalactites
stalagmites

Vocabulary Words
dissect
section
contact
intact

© Spelling Grade 5 — 11

Student Day 4

Chad is a new tour guide at Windy Cave. He wrote descriptive notes about what he should say to the tourists. Use the proofreading marks to identify mistakes in his notes. Correctly write the misspelled words.

Lesson 3
Writing

Long e

My Tour Guide Notes

Good Morning and welcome to Windy Cave. my name is chad and I am your tour guide today. Please listen carefully and stay together as I will be explaining interesting facts about the cavern. Before we enter, let me tell you about the cave's entrance. The original opening to the cave was a sinkhold which two boys discovered one afternoon in the late 1800s. The original entrance has not been inntact since it was widened and steps were built to allow tourists easy access into into the cave. please be careful as we descend down the ninety-six steps into the largest chammber in this cave, the Grand Ballroom.

This is a limestone cave. As water aboveground seeps into the soil, it collects acid from Lymestone. Over a period of time, the acidic water dissolves the Limestone in the ground, creating caves. The beautiful formations you see on the ceiling are known as stallactites and the ones on the ground are known as stalagmites. These beautiful structures are also formed from the acidic water that seeps through the ground. As water continues seeping through the ground, these structures keep growing. Sometimes stalactites and stalagmites meet and colums are formed. This next room is called the Hall Of Giants since giant pillars have formed from the continual flow water.

The last section of the cave on today's tour is the Bat Room. Bats are are known to live in caves. Over in the corner you can see several bats asleep and their bat droppings underneath them. Bat droppings are called guano and were once collected and sold to use in gunpowder and fertilizer. It was a pleasure being your tour guide today. I hope hope you will join us sometime for our new Lantern Tours held each saturday evening.

Proofreading Marks
○ Circle misspellings.
≡ Make a capital letter.
⊙ Add a period.
⤶ Delete.
∧ Add something.
/ Make a small letter.
¶ Make a new paragraph.

Pattern Words
alley
shield
belief
salary
relieve
money
neither
achieve
territory
received
volleyball
assembly

Content Words
cavern
sinkhole
columns
chamber
limestone
stalactites
stalagmites

Vocabulary Words
dissect
section
contact
intact

9 pts

1. cavern	4. sinkhole	7. intact
2. chamber	5. limestone	8. stalactites
3. stalagmites	6. columns	9. section

© Spelling Grade 5

12

Day 1 Pretest

Objective

The students will accurately spell and write words with **long i and long o**, content, vocabulary, and challenge words.

Introduction

The Pretest is an ungraded assessment to assist students in studying the Pattern, Content, Vocabulary, and Challenge Words. To meet your students' needs, select Challenge Words from a cross-curricular subject or words misspelled on previous assignments. The word *kimono* has the **long o** sound twice and is suggested for number 24. Explain that they are to attempt to write all the spelling words.

Directed Instruction

1 Use the sentences that follow or develop original ones.

2 Say each word, use it in a sentence, and then repeat the word.

Pattern Words
1. <u>Although</u> it was raining, Dave took a tour of the fertile valleys.
2. <u>Cocoa</u> is grown on plantations that are situated in river valleys.
3. Dr. Schmidt placed the survey results into an <u>envelope</u>.
4. As the weather turned warmer, an <u>icicle</u> fell off a tree branch.
5. The geologist's lecture on river erosion ended at <u>midnight</u>.
6. Becka <u>thoroughly</u> understood the lecture on formation of valleys.
7. What will <u>motivate</u> you to study the different effects of erosion?
8. <u>Lightning</u> was seen during the thunderstorm in the canyon.
9. The <u>ideal</u> agent in shaping and forming valleys is rivers.
10. Les bought some <u>groceries</u> before his hike through the canyon.
11. The geological team <u>decided</u> to survey the structure of the canyon.
12. We will <u>admire</u> the view of the canyon from a mountain summit.

Content Words
13. Risa learned that a <u>glacier</u> can carve the landscape.
14. The Continental Divide is a drainage <u>basin</u> in North America.
15. A <u>valley</u> can be completely surrounded by higher ground.
16. Can you name the <u>deepest</u> valleys in the world?
17. <u>Terraces</u> can be cut by the powerful forces of a rushing river.
18. One of the most famous <u>gorges</u> in the world is the Grand Canyon.
19. The Mississippi River flows through one of the <u>broadest</u> river valleys.

Vocabulary Words
20. The fifth graders will be discussing each <u>proverb</u> in the Bible.
21. Amy gave a <u>verbal</u> description of the valley's terrain.
22. Dr. Kern will <u>proceed</u> with his lecture on valleys.
23. The canyon community hopes that the river waters will soon <u>recede</u>.

Challenge Words
24. _____ (Insert your choice.)
25. _____ (Insert your choice.)

3 Allow students to self-correct their Pretest. Write each word on the board. Point out the following **long i** spellings: *i* in an open syllable, i_e, igh. Note the following **long o** spellings: *o* in an open syllable, o_e, ough. Remind students that each Vocabulary Word is made up of a root and an affix. The roots in this lesson are *ceed*, *cede*, and *verb*.

4 As a class, read, spell, and read each word. Direct students to circle misspelled words with a colored pencil and rewrite them correctly.

Lesson Materials

BLM SP5-04A
BLM SP5-04B
T-4
BLM SP5-04C

Created Wonders

The theme of this lesson is valleys. Valleys are low areas of ground that are surrounded by higher terrain. The most common type of valley is a river valley, which is formed by the eroding effects of the river. Other types of valleys can be formed by the movement of glaciers or plates in the earth's crust. Some valleys can also be found below sea level.

5 Proof each student's Pretest. This becomes an individualized study sheet that can be used at school or at home.

6 Homework suggestion: Distribute a copy of **BLM SP5-04A Lesson 4 Words and Phrases** to each student.

Day 2 Word Analysis and Vocabulary

Objective

The students will sort words with **long i and long o** and complete sentences with content words. They will use a table to write vocabulary words, match given definitions in context, and choose the best meaning for the underlined words.

Introduction

Invite students to refer to the list words, found on page 13, for this activity. Chorally read each Pattern Word. Challenge students to quickly count how many Pattern Words contain **long i** (**6**) and how many contain **long o** (**6**). Have students identify the **long i and long o** spellings. (**long i:** *i* **in an open syllable, i_e, igh; long o:** *o* **in an open syllable, o_e, ough**) Note that *cocoa* contains two **long o** spellings—*o* in an open syllable and *oa*—but the target spelling in this word is *o* in an open syllable.

Directed Instruction

1 Call out the spellings for **long i** and ask students to give examples of Pattern Words that contain each spelling. (**i in an open syllable—ideal, icicle; i_e—admire, decided; igh—lightning, midnight**) Repeat the process for words with **long o**. (**o in an open syllable—cocoa, motivate, groceries; o_e—envelope; ough—although, thoroughly**)

2 Proceed to page 13. Say, spell, and say each Pattern, Content, and Vocabulary Word. Provide this week's Challenge Words and have students write them in the spaces provided before completing the page.

3 Proceed to page 14. Remind students that each Vocabulary Word contains a root and affix. Note the two spellings for the same root sound—*ceed* and *cede*. Build each Vocabulary Word before students

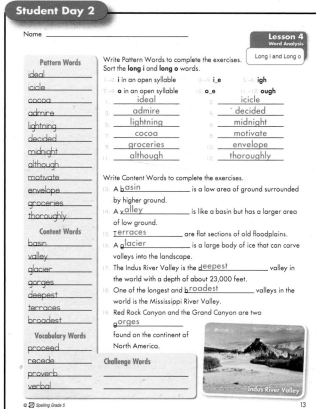

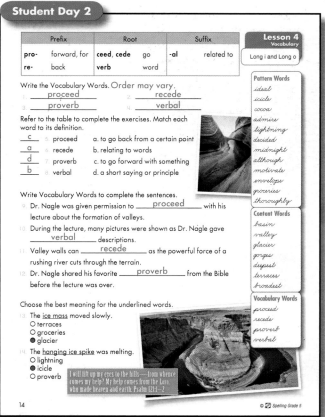

complete the page. For example, the root *verb* goes with the suffix *-al* to get the word *verbal*. Provide assistance as needed. Select a volunteer to read exercises 9–12 when complete and Psalm 121:1–2. Discuss the omnipotence of God.

4 Homework suggestion: Distribute a copy of **BLM SP5-04B Lesson 4 Phrases and Sentences** to each student.

Day 3 Word Study Strategies

Objective

The students will syllabicate words after prefixes and place an accent mark on the open syllable of list words. They will write list words to match their pronunciations and identify if the list word is a noun or verb.

Introduction

Write the following words on the board: midstream, program, recite. Challenge students to identify the commonality in the words. (**All of the words contain prefixes.**) Draw a vertical line after each prefix, in each word, to show syllabication. (**mid|stream, pro|gram, re|cite**)

Directed Instruction

1 Display **T-4 Using the Spelling Dictionary**. Read through each part of the dictionary entry to review the following information: entry word, pronunciation, part of speech, definition, sample sentence. Review that the pronunciation shows how to say the entry word. The pronunciation shows an accent mark ('), indicating the stressed syllable. A *stressed syllable* is the syllable that is pronounced with more emphasis than any other syllable in the word. Have students locate *basin* in their Spelling Dictionary, review the pronunciation of the word, and note the stressed syllable. (/'bā sən/)

2 Write the following pronunciations on the board: /ī 'dē əl/, /ȯl 'thō/. Challenge students to sound out the pronunciations and identify the words. (**ideal, although**)

3 Review the following definition of a noun: A noun is a person, place, thing, or idea. Remind students that a *verb* is an action word that can be in the present tense or past tense. Recite the following words and have students identify them as nouns or verbs: icicle (**noun**), motivate (**verb**), recede (**verb**), valley (**noun**).

4 Proceed to page 15. Students read the directions and independently complete the page. Check for accuracy as students work.

Day 4 Writing

Objective

The students will read and complete stanzas in a poem by writing list words in shape boxes.

Introduction

Write the following short poem on the board:

A lightning bolt illuminates the night,
Admire creation as it brings you delight.
A cavernous valley cuts through the land,
Thoroughly created by the Master's Hand.

Select a volunteer to read the poem aloud.

Directed Instruction

1 Invite students to refer to their list of words, found on page 16, for this activity. Challenge students to locate the list words in the poem. For each list word identified, draw a shape box around each letter—for example, l̲i̲g̲h̲t̲n̲i̲n̲g̲. (**lightning, Admire, valley, Thoroughly**)

Studying the configuration of words promotes visual memory and is an analytical tool.

2 Proceed to page 16. Students will silently read the poem and independently complete the shape boxes with list words. When complete, select volunteers to read the stanzas of the poem. The last stanza of the poem can be a discussion starter. Use the question to begin a discussion on what it means to follow God's call. This activity can be connected with Student Spelling Support, number 5.

3 Homework suggestion: Distribute a copy of **BLM SP5-04C Lesson 4 Test Prep** to each student.

Day 5 Posttest

Objective
The students will correctly write dictated spelling words and sentences.

Introduction
Review by using flash cards noted in Student Spelling Support, number 2.

Directed Assessment

1 Dictate the list words by using the Pretest sentences or developing original ones. Reserve *valley*, *glacier*, *proceed*, *decided*, and *thoroughly* for the dictation sentences.

2 Read each sentence. Repeat as needed.
- A valley is a low area of ground.
- A glacier can carve a valley's path.
- Most valleys proceed to other valleys.
- Ann decided to write a report on valleys.
- She was thoroughly looking forward to it.

3 If assigned, dictate Extra Challenge Words.

4 Score the test, counting each misspelled word as an error. Correct the dictation sentences by grading only the spelling words or grading the complete sentences.

Student Spelling Support

Cont. from page 16

of God." Encourage students to begin a Bible journal and to write down verses or prayers that keep them focused on God's will.

6. Challenge students to research the different types of valleys—river, glacial, crustal movement, and submarine. Students focus on the unique features of valley formation and how these traits influence the topography of each type of valley.

7. Write this week's words, categorize the Pattern, Content, and Vocabulary Words, and attach them to the Word Wall.

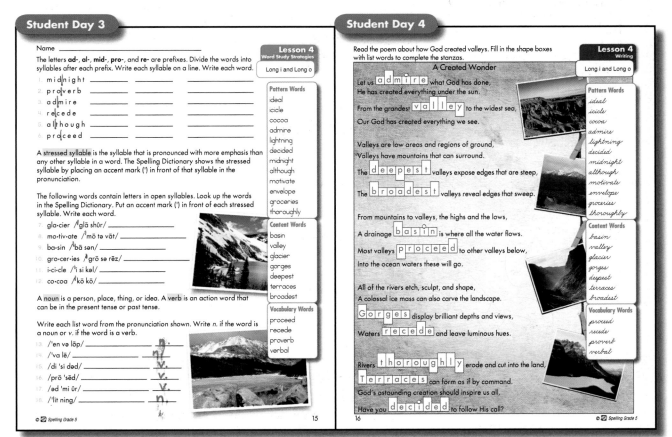

Student Pages
Pages 17–20

Lesson Materials
BLM SP5-05A
BLM SP5-05B
BLM SP5-05C

Created Wonders

The theme of this lesson is deserts. Arid and semiarid regions cover one-fourth of the world's surface. Some deserts have huge sand dunes while others have rocky hills and stony plains. Although temperatures soar above 100 degrees Fahrenheit and there is a lack of water, deserts are home to many plants, animals, and even some people.

Day 1 Pretest

Objective

The students will accurately spell and write words with **long u**, content, vocabulary, and challenge words.

Introduction

The Pretest is an ungraded assessment to assist students in studying the Pattern, Content, Vocabulary, and Challenge Words. To meet your students' needs, select Challenge Words from a cross-curricular subject or words misspelled on previous assignments. The word *fireproofing* has **long u** and is suggested for number 24. Explain that they are to attempt to write all the spelling words.

Directed Instruction

1 Use the sentences that follow or develop original ones.

2 Say each word, use it in a sentence, and then repeat the word.

Pattern Words

1. Since my shoe was too tight, I decided to <u>loosen</u> the laces.
2. The coach's pep talk will <u>unify</u> the team.
3. My brother's <u>curfew</u> is 11:00 P.M.
4. Are you <u>included</u> in the family of God?
5. Which desert plant are you <u>choosing</u> for your science project?
6. My <u>nephew</u> rode a camel at the theme park.
7. Sasha <u>bruised</u> her foot falling off her bicycle.
8. The <u>pursuit</u> to catch the thief running in the sand was difficult.
9. Jesus died on the cross to <u>rescue</u> us from the evil one.
10. Jamal <u>continued</u> working on his chores until he was finished.
11. <u>Dutiful</u> students complete their class work on time.
12. The salesclerk showed Grandma a lovely bottle of <u>perfume</u>.

Content Words

13. Camels are able to live in an <u>arid</u> climate.
14. Dry air <u>evaporates</u> moisture from the ground.
15. A desert <u>landscape</u> consists mostly of sand.
16. Tony enjoys riding his all-terrain vehicle up and down sand <u>dunes</u>.
17. Most <u>deserts</u> have a small area of water called an oasis.
18. The saguaro <u>cactus</u> can reach a height of over fifty-five feet.
19. <u>Semiarid</u> regions have an annual rainfall of ten-to-twenty inches.

Vocabulary Words

20. Plastic containers are <u>durable</u>.
21. Water is <u>vital</u> for plants and animals.
22. Sam slept the entire <u>duration</u> of the desert drive.
23. Vitamins help our body to have <u>vitality</u>.

Challenge Words

24. _____ (Insert your choice.)
25. _____ (Insert your choice.)

3 Allow students to self-correct their Pretest. Write each word on the board. Point out the following **long u** spellings: ew, oo, *u* in an open syllable, ue, u_e, ui. Note the roots *dur* and *vit* in the Vocabulary Words.

4 As a class, read, spell, and read each word. Direct students to circle misspelled words with a colored pencil and rewrite them correctly.

5 Proof each student's Pretest. This becomes an individualized study sheet that can be used at school or at home.

6 Homework suggestion: Distribute a copy of **BLM SP5-05A Lesson 5 Words and Phrases** to each student.

Day 2 Word Analysis and Vocabulary

Objective
The students will accurately sort **long u** words, write content words to complete sentences, and use a table to correctly write vocabulary words. They will select list words that match definitions.

Introduction
Write the following **long u** spellings on the board: ew, oo, *u* in an open syllable, ue, u_e, ui. Invite students to turn to page 17 for the list words. Read each Pattern Word and select volunteers to state the **long u** pattern within each word.

Directed Instruction

1 Explain that this week's Content Words relate to the theme of deserts. Two words that may be unfamiliar to students and difficult to pronounce are *arid* and *semiarid*. Explain that *arid* means *extremely dry with very little rainfall*, and *semiarid* means *very dry with little rainfall*. *Semiarid* regions are adjacent to *arid* regions. Correctly pronounce each word. Review the definitions of any other unfamiliar words.

2 Proceed to page 17. Say, spell, and say each Pattern, Content, and Vocabulary Word. Provide this week's Challenge Words and have students write them in the spaces provided. Before students complete the page, remind them that the article *an* precedes a word that begins with a vowel.

3 Proceed to page 18. Remind students to use the table to assist in building each Vocabulary Word. Explain that the prefix box is empty since each Vocabulary Word consists only of one root and one or more suffixes. The Vocabulary Word *vitality* has two suffixes, -al and -ity. Build each Vocabulary Word with the class. For example, the root *dur* goes with the suffix -able to get the word *durable*. Allow students to

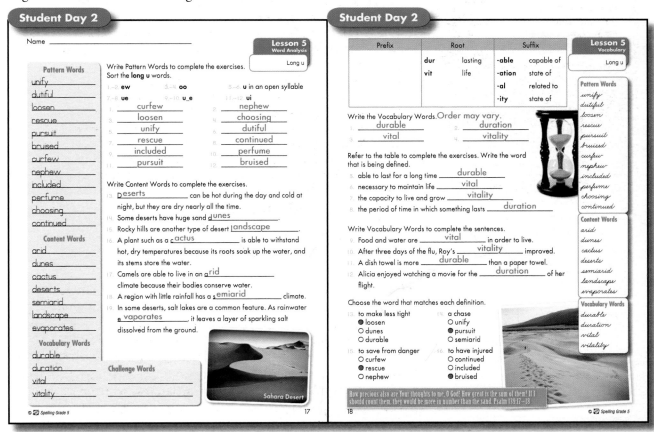

4 Homework suggestion: Distribute a copy of **BLM SP5-05B Lesson 5 Phrases and Sentences** to each student.

Day 3 Word Study Strategies

Objective

The students will syllabicate words between unlike consonants. They will write the past tense of a given verb. They will complete sentences by writing the present or past tense of a given verb.

Introduction

Write the following words on the board: humble, molten, magma, wonder, pardon. Read the words and select volunteers to syllabicate the words. (**hum|ble, mol|ten, mag|ma, won|der, par|don**) Check for accuracy and then ask what the commonality is with these words regarding the syllabication. (**Each word is divided between unlike consonants.**)

Directed Instruction

1 Ask a volunteer to state the two verbs from the group of words on the board. (**wonder, pardon**) Explain that these verbs are in the present tense. Select another volunteer to pronounce these verbs in the past tense. (**wondered, pardoned**)

2 Write the following sentences on the board:
- I _____ (wondered) what time it is right now.
  (**wonder; present tense**)
- The governor _____ (pardon) the innocent person.
  (**pardoned; past tense**)

Explain that a form of the verb is in parentheses. Using the context of the sentence, have students select the correct tense of the verb and determine if it is in the present or past tense. Complete each sentence.

3 Proceed to page 19. Tell students that for exercises 9–15, they are to look at the verb in the parentheses and determine if it should be written in the present or past tense in order to fill in each blank. All the verbs are list words.

Day 4 Writing

Objective

The students will write list words in three scenarios with problems and solutions.

Introduction

Hold a short discussion about some problems students have faced and what they did to solve or overcome the situation. Share a situation of your own. Present the following as a possible problem: A friend of yours stole some money. What would you do? Brainstorm three possible solutions to the problem. Have students vote for their favorite solution. Conclude by stating that no matter how big or small the problem may be, the Lord is always ready to guide us, help us, and comfort us. We need to place our trust in Him, step back, and allow Him to take control.

Directed Instruction

1 Explain that on today's writing page there are three scenarios with problems and solutions. Teach that when using the words *arid* and *semiarid*, the article *an* precedes *arid* and the article *a* precedes *semiarid*. Because of this, these words are not interchangeable. Students need to select words based upon whether a vowel or consonant follows the article.

2 Proceed to page 20. Allow students to complete the page. Select students to orally read each problem and solution after the page has been completed.

Student Spelling Support Materials

BLM SP5-01A
BLMs SP5-05D–E
Card stock
BLM SP5-01G
3" x 5" Index cards

Student Spelling Support

1. Use **BLM SP5-01A A Spelling Study Strategy** in instructional groups to provide assistance with some or all of the words.

2. Duplicate **BLMs SP5-05D–E Lesson 5 Spelling Words I** and **II** on CARD STOCK for students to use as flash cards at school or at home. Another option is to use **BLM SP5-01G Flash Cards Template** or 3" × 5" INDEX CARDS for students to write their own flash cards to use as a study aid.

3. Invite students to write the Challenge Words, numbers 24 and 25, in the Word Bank, in the back of their textbook.

4. Read Psalm 139:17–18: "How precious also are Your thoughts to me, O God! How great is the sum of them! If I should count them, they would be more in number than the sand." Share with the students that each one of us is precious to God. He not only loves and cares for us, he also thinks about us. God's thoughts about each one of us is more than all the grains of sand combined. To extend the discussion, invite students to journal what they imagine God might be thinking about them that day. A suggested title is "Sands of Time."

5. Challenge advanced learners to research cacti, write a brief description of each cactus, illustrate,

Cont. on page 21

3 Homework suggestion: Distribute a copy of **BLM SP5-05C Test Prep** to each student.

Day 5 Posttest

Objective
The students will correctly write dictated spelling words and sentences.

Introduction
Review by using flash cards noted in Student Spelling Support, number 2.

Directed Assessment

1 Dictate the list words by using the Pretest sentences or developing original ones. Reserve *deserts*, *arid*, *vital*, *continued*, and *dutiful* for the dictation sentences.

2 Read each sentence. Repeat as needed.
- Dan is learning facts about <u>deserts</u>.
- An <u>arid</u> climate has almost no rainfall.
- It is <u>vital</u> for a cactus to store its water.
- Dan <u>continued</u> to study after dinner.
- He is a <u>dutiful</u> student and gets good grades.

3 If assigned, dictate Extra Challenge Words.

4 Score the test, counting each misspelled word as an error. Correct the dictation sentences by grading only the spelling words or grading the complete sentences.

Student Spelling Support
Cont. from page 20

and compile into a booklet. Have students include facts such as if the cactus is edible, has medicinal uses, is used in building materials, or has other practical uses.

6. Write this week's words, categorize the Pattern, Content, and Vocabulary Words, and attach them to the Word Wall.

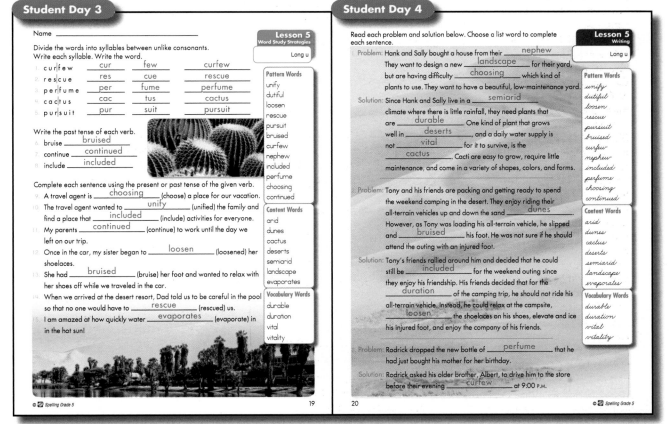

Student Day 3

Name _____

Lesson 5
Word Study Strategies
Long u

Divide the words into syllables between unlike consonants. Write each syllable. Write the word.

1. cur|few   cur   few   curfew
2. res|cue   res   cue   rescue
3. per|fume   per   fume   perfume
4. cac|tus   cac   tus   cactus
5. pur|suit   pur   suit   pursuit

Write the past tense of each verb.
6. bruise _____ bruised
7. continue _____ continued
8. include _____ included

Complete each sentence using the present or past tense of the given verb.
9. A travel agent is _____ choosing _____ (choose) a place for our vacation.
10. The travel agent wanted to _____ unify _____ (unified) the family and find a place that _____ included _____ (include) activities for everyone.
11. My parents _____ continued _____ (continue) to work until the day we left on our trip.
12. Once in the car, my sister began to _____ loosen _____ (loosened) her shoelaces.
13. She had _____ bruised _____ (bruise) her foot and wanted to relax with her shoes off while we traveled in the car.
14. When we arrived at the desert resort, Dad told us to be careful in the pool so that no one would have to _____ rescue _____ (rescued) us.
15. I am amazed at how quickly water _____ evaporates _____ (evaporate) in in the hot sun!

Pattern Words
unify
dutiful
loosen
rescue
pursuit
bruised
curfew
nephew
included
perfume
choosing
continued

Content Words
arid
dunes
cactus
deserts
semiarid
landscape
evaporates

Vocabulary Words
durable
duration
vital
vitality

© Spelling Grade 5   19

Student Day 4

Read each problem and solution below. Choose a list word to complete each sentence.

Lesson 5
Writing
Long u

Problem: Hank and Sally bought a house from their _____ nephew _____. They want to design a new _____ landscape _____ for their yard, but are having difficulty _____ choosing _____ which kind of plants to use. They want to have a beautiful, low-maintenance yard.

Solution: Since Hank and Sally live in a _____ semiarid _____ climate where there is little rainfall, they need plants that are _____ durable _____. One kind of plant that grows well in _____ deserts _____, and a daily water supply is not _____ vital _____ for it to survive, is the _____ cactus _____. Cacti are easy to grow, require little maintenance, and come in a variety of shapes, colors, and forms.

Problem: Tony and his friends are packing and getting ready to spend the weekend camping in the desert. They enjoy riding their all-terrain vehicles up and down the sand _____ dunes _____. However, as Tony was loading his all-terrain vehicle, he slipped and _____ bruised _____ his foot. He was not sure if he should attend the outing with an injured foot.

Solution: Tony's friends rallied around him and decided that he could still be _____ included _____ for the weekend outing since they enjoy his friendship. His friends decided that for the _____ duration _____ of the camping trip, he should not ride his all-terrain vehicle. Instead, he could relax at the campsite, _____ loosen _____ the shoelaces on his shoes, elevate and ice his injured foot, and enjoy the company of his friends.

Problem: Rodrick dropped the new bottle of _____ perfume _____ that he had just bought his mother for her birthday.

Solution: Rodrick asked his older brother, Albert, to drive him to the store before their evening _____ curfew _____ at 9:00 P.M.

Pattern Words
unify
dutiful
loosen
rescue
pursuit
bruised
curfew
nephew
included
perfume
choosing
continued

Content Words
arid
dunes
cactus
deserts
semiarid
landscape
evaporates

Vocabulary Words
durable
duration
vital
vitality

20   © Spelling Grade 5

Student Pages
Pages 21–24

Lesson Materials

T-5
BLM SP5-06A
BLM SP5-06B
BLM SP5-06C
3" × 5" Index cards
BLM SP5-06D
BLMs SP5-06E–F
BLM SP5-06G
BLM SP5-06H

Day 1 Short Vowels

Objective
The students will spell, identify, and sort words according to **short vowels**.

Introduction
Teacher Note: This week's lesson incorporates the Pattern, Content, and Vocabulary Words taught in Lessons 1–5 using a variety of activities such as sorting, a crossword puzzle, filling in the correct answer circle, a word search, riddles, shape boxes, and adding or subtracting letters to form words.

Display **T-5 Lessons 1–5 Study Sheet** on the overhead to review Lesson 1 words in unison, following this technique: say the word, spell the word, say the word. Challenge students to identify the **short vowels** found in Lesson 1 Pattern Words. Circle each short vowel using a transparency pen.

Directed Instruction

1 Write the following Pattern Words from Lesson 1 on the board: chilly, pattern, common, puppetry. Select a student to syllabicate each word, dividing between double consonants. Explain that *puppetry* has a second division between the unlike consonants *t* and *r*. (**pup|pet|ry**) Encourage students to use syllabication as a technique to assist in spelling words correctly.

2 Proceed to page 21. Explain that the box contains all the Pattern, Content, and Vocabulary Words in Lessons 1–5. These lists are a review tool and contain the same words that were previously reviewed on the overhead transparency. Allow students to complete the page independently.

3 Distribute a copy of **BLM SP5-06A Lessons 1–5 Study Sheet** to each student to take home for study. Each review lesson includes a study sheet for student use.

4 Homework suggestion: Distribute a copy of **BLM SP5-06B Lesson 6 Homework I** to each student to practice with **short vowels, long a, long e,** and **long i and long o.**

Day 2 Long a and Long e

Objective
The students will spell and write **long a** words in a crossword puzzle. They will select the appropriate answer circle to indicate if words with **long e** are spelled correctly or incorrectly, and correctly write each word.

Introduction
Display **T-5 Lessons 1–5 Study Sheet.** Give the following clues to **long a** words and invite students to state the correct word that is described: goods to be shipped by rail (**freight**); followed a command, complied (**obeyed**); acting like a friendly neighbor (**neighborly**); an expression of dissatisfaction (**complaint**); loyal (**faithful**).

Directed Instruction

1 Refer to **T-5 Lessons 1–5 Study Sheet** to review Lessons 2–3 words in unison, using the say-spell-say technique.

2 Write and draw the following on the board:

85 pts

Correct Incorrect

acheive ○ ○ (incorrect; achieve)
territory ○ ○ (correct; territory)
vollyball ○ ○ (incorrect; volleyball)

Read each word and ask students to identify if each word is spelled correctly or incorrectly. Fill in each appropriate answer circle. Write each word correctly.

3 Proceed to page 22. Allow students to read the directions and complete the page independently. Provide assistance as needed.

4 Homework suggestion: Distribute a copy of **BLM SP5-06C Lesson 6 Homework II** to each student to practice with **long u**, Content Words, and Vocabulary Words.

Day 3 Long i and Long o and Long u

Objective

The students will find and circle words with **long i and long o** in a word search. They will write words with **long u** to answer riddles.

Introduction

Select a few Lesson 4 Pattern Words from **T-5 Lessons 1–5 Study Sheet** to draw a mini word search on the board. Choose words that contain similar patterns or letters. Position words across, down, diagonally, and backwards. Challenge students to find all of the selected Pattern Words.

Directed Instruction

1 Display **T-5 Lessons 1–5 Study Sheet** to review Lessons 4–5 words in unison, using the say-spell-say technique.

2 To provide practice with riddles, ask students to supply an answer to each of the following, using Pattern Words found in Lesson 5:

- Which word is <u>a substance that gives a pleasant scent</u>? (**perfume**)
- Which word means <u>to have maintained without an interruption</u>? (**continued**)
- Which word is the opposite of <u>to separate into many parts</u>? (**unify**)

3 Proceed to page 23. Assist students as needed as they complete the page.

Day 4 Content Words and Vocabulary Words

Objective

The students will write content words in shape boxes. They will add or subtract letters to write vocabulary words.

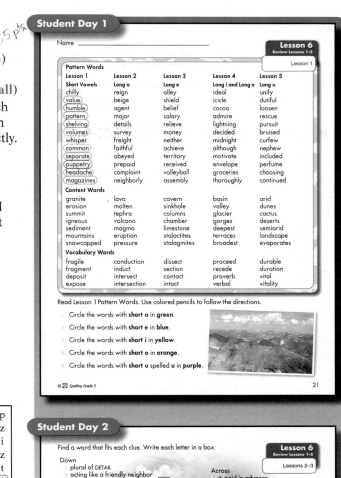

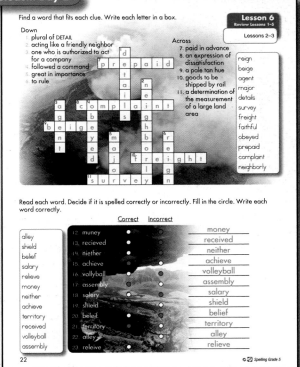

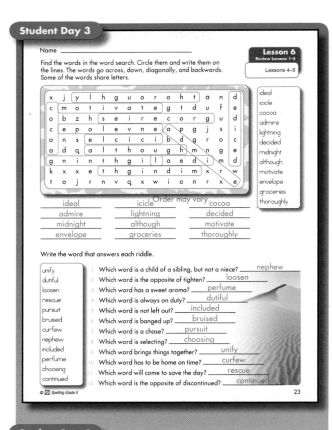

Name _____

Find the words in the word search. Circle them and write them on the lines. The words go across, down, diagonally, and backwards. Some of the words share letters.

Lesson 6
Review Lessons 1–5

Lessons 4–5

Word list: ideal, icicle, cocoa, admire, lightning, decided, midnight, although, motivate, envelope, groceries, thoroughly

Order may vary.

ideal	icicle	cocoa
admire	lightning	decided
midnight	although	motivate
envelope	groceries	thoroughly

Write the word that answers each riddle.

Word bank: unify, dutiful, loosen, rescue, pursuit, bruised, curfew, nephew, included, perfume, choosing, continued

1. Which word is a child of a sibling, but not a niece? __nephew__
2. Which word is the opposite of tighten? __loosen__
3. Which word has a sweet aroma? __perfume__
4. Which word is always on duty? __dutiful__
5. Which word is not left out? __included__
6. Which word is banged up? __bruised__
7. Which word is a chase? __pursuit__
8. Which word is selecting? __choosing__
9. Which word brings things together? __unify__
10. Which word has to be home on time? __curfew__
11. Which word will come to save the day? __rescue__
12. Which word is the opposite of discontinued? __continued__

© Spelling Grade 5

23

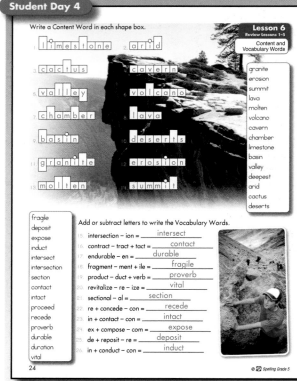

Write a Content Word in each shape box.

Lesson 6
Review Lessons 1–5

Content and Vocabulary Words

1. limestone
2. arid
3. cactus
4. cavern
5. valley
6. volcano
7. chamber
8. lava
9. basin
10. deserts
11. granite
12. erosion
13. molten
14. summit

Word list: granite, erosion, summit, lava, molten, volcano, cavern, chamber, limestone, basin, valley, deepest, arid, cactus, deserts

Add or subtract letters to write the Vocabulary Words.

Word bank: fragile, deposit, expose, induct, intersect, intersection, section, contact, intact, proceed, recede, proverb, durable, duration, vital

15. intersection – ion = __intersect__
16. contract – tract + tact = __contact__
17. endurable – en = __durable__
18. fragment – ment + ile = __fragile__
19. product – duct + verb = __proverb__
20. revitalize – re – ize = __vital__
21. sectional – al = __section__
22. re + concede – con = __recede__
23. in + contact – con = __intact__
24. ex + compose – com = __expose__
25. de + reposit – re = __deposit__
26. in + conduct – con = __induct__

24

© Spelling Grade 5

Introduction

Write *lava* and *arid* on the board. Draw a shape box around each letter—lava, arid. Ask students to study the shape boxes of the two words and to state whether the words have identical or different shape boxes. (**The words have different shape boxes.**) Studying the configuration of words helps develop visual memory.

Directed Instruction

1 Display **T-5 Lessons 1–5 Study Sheet** to review Content and Vocabulary Words in unison, using the say-spell-say technique.

2 Write the following prefixes, roots, and suffixes on 3" × 5" INDEX CARDS: con-, ex-, in-. inter-, ceed, duct, sect, tact, -ion, -ment. Distribute the cards randomly to several students. Call out the prefix *con-* and ask the student with that card to come to the front. Have the student refer to the Vocabulary Words on the overhead and state the words that have the prefix *con-*. (**conduction, contact**) Continue with the remaining cards. (*ex-*: expose; *in-*: induct, intact; *inter-*: intersect, intersection; *ceed*: proceed; *duct*: conduction, induct; *sect*: intersect, intersection, dissect, section; *tact*: contact, intact; *-ion*: conduction, intersection, section; *ment*: fragment)

3 Proceed to page 24. Answer any questions before allowing students to complete the page independently.

4 Homework suggestion: Distribute a copy of **BLM SP5-06D Lessons 1–5 Test Prep** to each student to practice with many of the words that may appear on the Assessment. Prepare for the Assessment by studying the words on **BLM SP5-06A Lessons 1–5 Study Sheet** that was sent home on Day 1.

Day 5 Assessment

Objective

The students will accurately select the appropriate answer within the context of a sentence. They will fill in the corresponding answer circle.

Introduction

Teacher Note: The Test makes provision for Differentiated Instruction. The first twelve sentences include the words assigned to students with shortened lists. Encourage these students to try all the sentences, but only grade the first twelve sentences. The Test is found on two blackline masters.

Distribute a copy of **BLMs SP5-06E–F Lessons 1–5 Test I** and **II** to each student. Duplicate **BLM SP5-06G Student Answer Form** and cut apart. Distribute one answer form to each student. Remind students to fill in each answer circle completely and to erase completely if they wish to change an answer.

© Spelling Grade 5

Directed Assessment

1 Instruct students to listen as you dictate the following Sample:

Sample

One <u>secktion</u> of the <u>chamber</u> was no longer <u>intact</u>. <u>All correct</u>

      A   B   C   D

Say, "Are any of the first three underlined words misspelled?" Pause for replies. Inform students that the letter *A* is below the underlined word that is misspelled. (**section**) Guide students to the answer form that was previously distributed. Lead students to find the Sample box and fill in the appropriate answer circle containing the same letter. Say, "You will continue in the same way. You will read each sentence, choose the word that you think is misspelled, and fill in the corresponding circle on the answer form. If all the words are spelled correctly, fill in the fourth circle, labeled *D*, for *All correct*."

2 Assist students as needed while they read the sentences and complete the Test on their own.

1. Lava poured from the summit of the volcano.
2. It was quite chilly in the cavern made of limestone.
3. Steady erosion continued to expose the bedrock.
4. Can any cactus survive without water in arid deserts?
5. The agent received a high salary for his difficult job.
6. The deepest layers of sediment are under the greatest pressure.
7. Lori decided to paint a landscape of the lovely valley.
8. Tom's nephew found an ideal spot to view the lightning during the storm.
9. Al thoroughly obeyed the rules when climbing the steep wall of granite.
10. When Joe bruised his arm, he used a beige ice pack to relieve swelling.
11. I heard a proverb in an assembly that helped me to be more humble.
12. An envelope with fragile contents was part of the freight in the mail car.
13. The territory contained several ranges of snowcapped mountains.
14. Neither Kim nor Ava could stay up until midnight, although they tried.
15. A major volcanic eruption can threaten the vital balance of nature.
16. Stalagmites and stalactites form columns in some caves.
17. A neighborly handshake provided contact that served to unify everyone.
18. Water quickly evaporates in semiarid gorges and canyons.
19. The dunes receive a repeated deposit of sand over a duration of time.
20. The sack of groceries included a canister of powdered cocoa.
21. Was the police pursuit down that alley meant to rescue a victim?
22. Igneous rock was once molten magma.
23. The boys are choosing to read two volumes about puppetry.
24. We read the details about the conduction of tephra by strong winds.
25. I prepaid the money needed to see the girls play volleyball.

3 Refer to **BLM SP5-06H Lessons 1–5 Answer Key** when correcting the Test.

Words with y

Student Pages

Pages 25–28

Lesson Materials

BLM SP5-07A
BLM SP5-07B
3" × 5" Index cards
BLM SP5-07C

Created Wonders

Lessons 7–11 utilize the theme of plants. The theme of this lesson is seeds. Seeds are God's plan for reproduction in many plants. The seed contains the embryo and starchy food for the young plant. Seeds may be monocot seeds that initially produce a single leaf, such as corn, or dicot seeds with two leaves, such as beans.

Day 1 Pretest

Objective

The students will accurately spell and write **words with y**. They will spell and write content, vocabulary, and challenge words.

Introduction

Before class, select Challenge Words for numbers 24 and 25 from a cross-curricular subject, words misspelled on previous assignments, or words that interest your students. The word *rhythm* has the **short i** sound for **y** and is suggested for number 24. Explain that they are to attempt to write all the spelling words.

Directed Instruction

1 Say each word, use it in a sentence, and then repeat the word.

Pattern Words

1. Lily had a necklace made of <u>crystal</u>.
2. Were you <u>rhyming</u> the words to make a poem?
3. If we confess our sins, Jesus will <u>purify</u> our hearts.
4. A fever can be a <u>symptom</u> of the flu.
5. Reproductive <u>systems</u> in some plants produce seeds.
6. Alex took a class in <u>physics</u> last year.
7. We played basketball in the <u>gymnasium</u>.
8. It is a <u>mystery</u> to me how desert seeds grow with little water.
9. The <u>typist</u> used the computer keyboard to enter the notes.
10. An animal's <u>youthfulness</u> can be seen by looking at its teeth.
11. Wildflower seeds were scattered throughout the <u>canyon</u>.
12. <u>Recycle</u> your newspapers instead of discarding them.

Content Words

13. Some seeds can be <u>dormant</u> for a long time.
14. Warm soil and water are often <u>favorable</u> conditions for plant growth.
15. Ken grew a sunflower <u>seedling</u> in potting soil.
16. Pumpkin seeds take about four days to <u>germinate</u>.
17. <u>Absorption</u> of water through the seed coat is necessary for growth.
18. <u>Adequate</u> water will help the seed grow.
19. If you open a bean seed, you can see the <u>embryo</u>.

Vocabulary Words

20. Birds <u>transport</u> seeds from one place to another.
21. Much <u>progress</u> has been made in understanding how seeds grow.
22. I will be <u>reporting</u> on science news for our school paper.
23. A major forest fire caused a <u>regression</u> in the growth of the forest.

Challenge Words

24. _____
25. _____

2 Allow students to self-correct their Pretest. Write each word on the board. Point out the following sounds for **y**: the consonant sound /y/ as in *yellow*, **long e**, **long i**, and **short i**. Remind students that each Vocabulary Word is made up of a root and an affix(es). Note the roots *gress* and *port* in the Vocabulary Words.

3 As a class, read, spell, and read each word. Direct students to circle misspelled words with a colored pencil and rewrite them correctly.

4 Proof each student's Pretest. This becomes an individualized study sheet that can be used at school or at home.

5 Homework suggestion: Distribute a copy of **BLM SP5-07A Lesson 7 Words and Phrases** to each student.

Day 2 Word Analysis and Vocabulary

Objective
The students will sort **words with y** and complete sentences with content words. They will use a table to write vocabulary words, match definitions, and complete sentences. They will choose the best meaning for the underlined words.

Introduction
Remind students of the following sounds for the letter *y*: the consonant sound /y/ as in *yellow*, the **long e** sound, the **long i** sound, and the **short i** sound. Invite students to refer to the list words, found on page 25, and ask students to give examples of Pattern Words that contain each sound. (**consonant y—canyon, youthfulness; long e—mystery; long i—typist, purify, recycle, rhyming; short i—crystal, physics, systems, mystery, symptom, gymnasium**) Reinforce the two different sounds for *y* in *mystery* by asking students to state whether the first or second *y* has the **short i** or **long i**.

Directed Instruction

1 Select volunteers to look up the words *embryo, germinate,* and *absorption* in their Spelling Dictionary and read each definition aloud. Invite the volunteers to use each word in a sentence of their own.

2 Proceed to page 25. Say, spell, and say each Pattern, Content, and Vocabulary Word. Provide this week's Challenge Words and have students write them in the spaces provided. Assist students as needed to complete the page.

3 Proceed to page 26. Remind students that each Vocabulary Word contains a root and one or more affixes. Build each Vocabulary Word, orally or on the board, before students proceed to the exercises on the page. For example, the prefix *trans-* goes with the root *port* to build

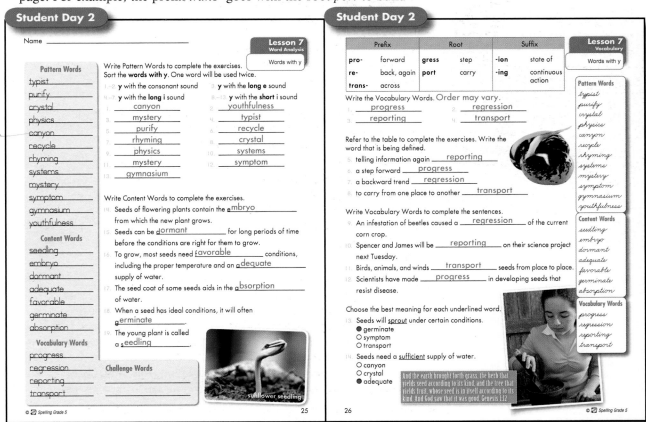

Student Spelling Support

1. Use **BLM SP5-01A A Spelling Study Strategy** in instructional groups to provide assistance with some or all of the words.

2. Duplicate **BLMs SP5-07D–E Lesson 7 Spelling Words I** and **II** on CARD STOCK for students to use as flash cards at school or at home. Another option is to use **BLM SP5-01G Flash Cards Template** or 3"× 5" INDEX CARDS for students to write their own flash cards to use as a study aid.

3. Invite students to write the Challenge Words, numbers 24 and 25, in the Word Bank, in the back of their textbook.

4. Read Genesis 1:12: "And the earth brought forth grass, the herb that yields seed according to its kind, and the tree that yields fruit, whose seed is in itself according to its kind. And God saw that it was good." Relate that the harvest that is produced depends on what kind of seed is sown. Plants are given to us for food, shelter, and pleasure by God.

5. Jesus utilized agricultural connections when teaching spiritual principles. Invite students to read the Parable of the Sower in Matthew 13. Ask students to describe how agricultural concepts are spiritual metaphors for growth and maturity.

Cont. on page 29

the word *transport*. Remind students that knowing the meaning of the roots and affixes is helpful in defining the words. Allow students to complete the page, providing assistance as needed. Select a student to read Genesis 1:12 and discuss plant growth from seeds.

4 Homework suggestion: Distribute a copy of **BLM SP5-07B Lesson 7 Phrases and Sentences** to each student.

Day 3 Word Study Strategies

Objective
The students will categorize and alphabetize list words. They will write list words that would appear on the same dictionary page as sample guide words.

Introduction
Before class, write the following incomplete word lists on the board, leaving blanks as indicated:

• office worker, clerk, secretary, _____ (**typist**)
• gem, mineral, quartz, _____ (**crystal**)
• library, cafeteria, auditorium, _____ (**gymnasium**)

Explain that the words in each list have common characteristics, forming a category. A *category* is a group or set of things that are classified together. Invite students to refer to the list words, found on page 27, as you choose volunteers to select a list word that belongs in each category. Have volunteers state the category and why they chose each word before filling in the blank.

Directed Instruction

1 To review alphabetizing to the fourth or fifth letter, write the following words on 3" × 5" INDEX CARDS: abstract, absolve, absorption. Distribute the cards to three students. Invite the students to come to the front of the room, hold the cards for the class to see, and arrange themselves in alphabetical order. (**absolve, absorption, abstract**) Ask students to name the letters that they needed to use to alphabetize the list. (**abso_l_ve, abso_r_ption, abs_t_ract**)

2 Remind students that *guide words* are two words at the top of the page in a dictionary. These two words are the first and last words defined on a page. Write the following sample guide words on the board: accept, custom. Encourage students to find list words from page 27 that would be found, as entry words, on the same page as the two sample guide words. Write the words on the board in random order. Challenge students to alphabetize the entry words. Choose one student to come to the board and number the words in alphabetical order. (**1—adequate, 2—canyon, 3—crystal**)

3 Proceed to page 27. Invite students to complete the page independently.

Day 4 Writing

Objective
The students will correctly number note cards that represent procedures used in a science experiment. They will find and write list words.

Introduction
Teacher Note: The informative domain is the focus for the writing pages in Lessons 7–11.

Hold a discussion about science projects. Note the various aspects of an experiment that a student might conduct for his or her project, including a hypothesis—a prediction as to the outcome of the experiment, the procedures, and the results. Explain that the procedures are the ordered list of the steps that they did to test their prediction. Ask students to provide examples of steps that they would take to conduct a simple experiment.

Directed Instruction

1 Proceed to page 28 and choose a student to read the information at the top of the page. Remind students that the procedures for an experiment follow a logical order. Students need to read each note card on the page before numbering the cards in order. When complete, choose a volunteer to state the correct order of each note card and read the information on each note card orally.

2 Homework suggestion: Distribute a copy of **BLM SP5-07C Lesson 7 Test Prep** to each student.

Day 5 Posttest

Objective
The students will correctly write dictated spelling words and sentences.

Introduction
Review by using flash cards noted in Student Spelling Support, number 2.

Directed Assessment

1 Dictate the list words by using the Pretest sentences or developing original ones. Reserve *dormant*, *recycle*, *seedling*, *progress*, and *canyon* for the dictation sentences.

2 Read each sentence. Repeat as needed.
- The corn seeds were <u>dormant</u> before we planted them.
- We chose to <u>recycle</u> milk cartons to use as planters.
- Each seed grew into a <u>seedling</u>.
- We measured the <u>progress</u> of each plant.
- Then we planted the corn in the <u>canyon</u>.

3 If assigned, dictate Extra Challenge Words.

4 Score the test, counting each misspelled word as an error. Correct the dictation sentences by grading only the spelling words or grading the complete sentences.

Student Spelling Support
Cont. from page 28

6. Write this week's words, categorize the Pattern, Content, and Vocabulary Words, and attach them to the Word Wall.

7. As a cross-curricular connection, invite students to attempt to grow LIMA BEAN SEEDS under different conditions, including DIFFERENT TYPES OF SOIL (clay, sand, potting mix), varying amounts of light (darkness, black light, sunlight), or with different amounts of water (no water, one teaspoon, one cup). Have students chart the growth of each seedling and report on the results of their experiments.

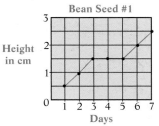

Bean Seed #1

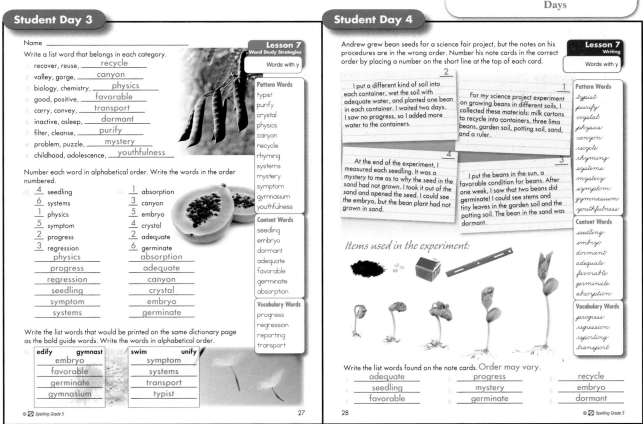

Words with /ȯ/

Student Pages
Pages 29–32

Lesson Materials
BLM SP5-08A
BLM SP5-08B
BLM SP5-08C

Created Wonders

The theme of this lesson is flowering plants. The seeds, or fruit that flowering plants produce, sustain the lives of living things. Plants are the beginning of the food chain, and they are an intricate part of God's design for the web of life. Botanists estimate that there are over 240,000 species of flowering plants. Other uses of plants are perfumes, clothes, and lumber.

Day 1 Pretest

Objective
The students will accurately spell and write **words with /ȯ/**. They will spell and write content, vocabulary, and challenge words.

Introduction
Before class, select Challenge Words for numbers 24 and 25 from a cross-curricular subject, words misspelled on previous assignments, or words that interest your students. The word *automobile* has **/ȯ/** spelled *au* and is suggested for number 24. Explain that they are to attempt to write all the spelling words.

Directed Instruction

1 Say each word, use it in a sentence, and then repeat the word.

Pattern Words
1. The <u>naughty</u> child asked the Lord for forgiveness.
2. Jeannie enjoys drinking <u>coffee</u> with cream and sugar.
3. One <u>ought</u> to put fresh cut flowers in water.
4. Cindi drew a butterfly and a flower on her <u>chalkboard</u>.
5. Shirley and Gerron <u>alternate</u> turns watering the flower garden.
6. A mother cat will <u>foster</u> her new kittens.
7. The sale rack was filled with <u>flawed</u> items.
8. The recipe directions said to <u>scald</u> the milk, then let it cool.
– 9. Deborah <u>recalled</u> that she needed to bring flowers to the party.
10. Jason <u>sought</u> his neighbor's help to find his lost puppy.
11. Grandma Butler let me use her floral cup and <u>saucer</u>.
12. Are you <u>cautious</u> when you ride your bicycle?

Content Words
13. A rose has more than one <u>stamen</u>.
14. The <u>foliage</u> in the flower garden is very colorful.
15. The bee landed on the <u>pistil</u> with its feet.
16. As the flower bud opened, the <u>sepals</u> unfurled.
17. A hummingbird can <u>pollinate</u> a flower.
18. A <u>botanist</u> discovered many uses for the peanut plant.
19. The lavender plant has a lovely <u>fragrance</u> and is used in perfume.

Vocabulary Words
20. A wedding is a <u>formal</u> occasion.
21. Our school experienced a <u>revival</u> during Spiritual Emphasis Week.
22. The doctors were able to <u>revive</u> the victims of the accident.
23. Mr. Smith will <u>inform</u> Mrs. Smith that he will be late for dinner.

Challenge Words
24. _____
25. _____

2 Allow students to self-correct their Pretest. Write each word on the board. Point out the following **/ȯ/** spellings: *a* before *l*, augh, au, aw, ough, o. Note the roots *form* and *viv* in the Vocabulary Words.

3 As a class, read, spell, and read each word. Direct students to circle misspelled words with a colored pencil and rewrite them correctly.

4 Proof each student's Pretest. This becomes an individualized study sheet that can be used at school or at home.

5 Homework suggestion: Distribute a copy of **BLM SP5-08A Lesson 8 Words and Phrases** to each student.

© *Spelling Grade 5*

Day 2 Word Analysis and Vocabulary

Objective
The students will accurately sort **words with /ȯ/**. They will write content words to complete sentences and use a table to correctly write vocabulary words. They will choose the best meaning for a given word.

Introduction
Write the following **/ȯ/** patterns on the board: *a before l, augh, au, aw, ough, o*. Invite students to refer to the list words, found on page 29, for this activity. Read each Pattern Word and select volunteers to state the **/ȯ/** pattern within each word.

Directed Instruction

1 Explain that this week's Content Words relate to the theme of flowering plants. Although *foliage* is sometimes pronounced /ˈfō lij/, the most common pronunciation and the usage in this lesson is /ˈfō lē ij/. Explain that *foliage* means *leaves, flowers,* and *branches*. Ask students which Content Word relates to a person. (**botanist**) Teach that the suffix *-ist* indicates a person. Relate that a *botanist* is *a person who studies botany. Botany* is *plant life.* Ask students to name other words ending with *-ist*. (**Possible answers: scientist, pianist, soloist**) Review the definitions of any other unfamiliar words by having students look them up in the Spelling Dictionary and using them in a sentence.

2 Proceed to page 29. Say, spell, and say each Pattern, Content, and Vocabulary Word. Provide this week's Challenge Words and have students write them in the spaces provided. Instruct students to complete the page. Select a student to read Isaiah 40:8 and discuss that God's Word is eternal.

3 Proceed to page 30. Remind students to use the table to assist in building each Vocabulary Word. Build each Vocabulary Word with the class. For example, the prefix *in-* goes with the root *form* to get the word *inform*.

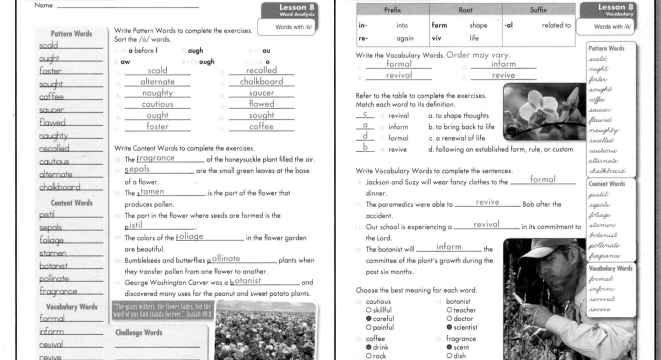

Student Day 2 (page 29)

Lesson 8 — Word Analysis — Words with /ȯ/

Pattern Words: scald, ought, foster, sought, coffee, saucer, flawed, naughty, recalled, cautious, alternate, chalkboard

Content Words: pistil, sepals, foliage, stamen, botanist, pollinate, fragrance

Vocabulary Words: formal, inform, revival, revive

Write Pattern Words to complete the exercises. Sort the /ȯ/ words.

1–4 a before l, 5 augh, 6–7 au, 8 aw, 9–10 ough, 11–12 o

1. scald
2. recalled
3. alternate
4. chalkboard
5. naughty
6. saucer
7. cautious
8. flawed
9. ought
10. sought
11. foster
12. coffee

Write Content Words to complete the exercises.

13. The _fragrance_ of the honeysuckle plant filled the air.
14. _Sepals_ are the small green leaves at the base of a flower.
15. The _stamen_ is the part of the flower that produces pollen.
16. The part in the flower where seeds are formed is the _pistil_.
17. The colors of the _foliage_ in the flower garden are beautiful.
18. Bumblebees and butterflies _pollinate_ plants when they transfer pollen from one flower to another.
19. George Washington Carver was a _botanist_ and discovered many uses for the peanut and sweet potato plants.

"The grass withers, the flower fades, but the word of our God stands forever." Isaiah 40:8

Challenge Words

29

Student Day 2 (page 30)

Lesson 8 — Vocabulary — Words with /ȯ/

Prefix		Root		Suffix	
in-	into	form	shape	-al	related to
re-	again	viv	life		

Write the Vocabulary Words. Order may vary.

1. formal
2. inform
3. revival
4. revive

Refer to the table to complete the exercises. Match each word to its definition.

_c_ 5. revival   a. to shape thoughts
_a_ 6. inform   b. to bring back to life
_d_ 7. formal   c. a renewal of life
_b_ 8. revive   d. following an established form, rule, or custom

Write Vocabulary Words to complete the sentences.

9. Jackson and Suzy will wear fancy clothes to the _formal_ dinner.
10. The paramedics were able to _revive_ Bob after the accident.
11. Our school is experiencing a _revival_ in its commitment to the Lord.
12. The botanist will _inform_ the committee of the plant's growth during the past six months.

Choose the best meaning for each word.

13. cautious
- ○ skillful
- ● careful
- ○ painful

14. botanist
- ○ teacher
- ○ doctor
- ● scientist

15. coffee
- ● drink
- ○ rock
- ○ sandwich

16. fragrance
- ● scent
- ○ dish
- ○ leaves

Pattern Words: scald, ought, foster, sought, coffee, saucer, flawed, naughty, recalled, cautious, alternate, chalkboard

Content Words: pistil, sepals, foliage, stamen, botanist, pollinate, fragrance

Vocabulary Words: formal, inform, revival, revive

30

58 pts.

4 Homework suggestion: Distribute a copy of **BLM SP5-08B Lesson 8 Phrases and Sentences** to each student.

Student Spelling Support Materials

BLM SP5-01A
BLMs SP5-08D–E
Card stock
BLM SP5-01G
3" x 5" Index cards

Student Spelling Support

1. Use **BLM SP5-01A A Spelling Study Strategy** in instructional groups to provide assistance with some or all of the words.

2. Duplicate **BLMs SP5-08D–E Lesson 8 Spelling Words I** and **II** on CARD STOCK for students to use as flash cards at school or at home. Another option is to use **BLM SP5-01G Flash Cards Template** or 3" x 5" INDEX CARDS for students to write their own flash cards to use as a study aid.

3. Invite students to write the Challenge Words, numbers 24 and 25, in the Word Bank, in the back of their textbook.

4. Read Isaiah 40:8: "The grass withers, the flower fades, but the word of our God stands forever." Discuss with the students that for generation after generation, God's Word has not changed, unlike grass and flowers which have withered, faded, and died. God and His Word are the same yesterday, today, and for all eternity. We can rest in the truth that our God is the everlasting God.

5. Have students pretend they are botanists. Instruct them to research a plant such as the Venus flytrap or the giant rafflesia flower, write a report using as many spelling words as possible, and share their findings with the class.

Cont. on page 33

Day 3 Word Study Strategies

Objective

The students will utilize dictionary skills by writing the answers to questions about the different components of a dictionary. They will write list words to complete sentences.

Introduction

Instruct students to find the word *cautious* in their Spelling Dictionary. Write the following dictionary components of the word *cautious* on the board and select volunteers to name them:

• Guide Words (**broadest and centennial**)
• Pronunciation (/ˈkȯ shəs/)
• Part of Speech (**adjective**)
• Definition (**being alert to watch for danger; careful**)
• Sample Sentence (**Are you cautious when you ride your bicycle?**)

Directed Instruction

1 Review how to use context clues. Write the words *scald*, *ought*, and *saucer* in one area of the board. In another area, write the following cloze sentences:
  • The new set of china was missing a _____. (**saucer**)
  • We _____ to think of others more than ourselves. (**ought**)
  • Eddie was careful to not _____ his hands when he put the noodles in the boiling water. (**scald**)
  Select a volunteer to complete each sentence correctly.

2 Proceed to page 31. Instruct students to complete the page independently.

Day 4 Writing

Objective

The students will read an encyclopedia article about flowering plants in the context of a cloze activity. They will write the missing content words.

Introduction

Ask the students to name the number of the day of creation on which God created plants. (**Day 3**) Read Genesis 1:11–13: "Then God said, 'Let the earth bring forth grass, the herb that yields seed, and the fruit tree that yields fruit according to its kind, whose seed is in itself, on the earth'; and it was so. And the earth brought forth grass, the herb that yields seed according to its kind, and the tree that yields fruit, whose seed is in itself according to its kind. And God saw that it was good. So the evening and the morning were the third day."

Directed Instruction

1 When God created flowering plants, He made a way for each to produce seeds and continue its own life cycle. To sustain our lives, we depend on food, such as fruits, vegetables, and nuts, which are grown from flowering plants. Each flower must have a stamen and/or a pistil and be pollinated for the life cycle to continue. Some flowering plants are simply for enjoyment. Ask students to identify all the flowering plants they can in their neighborhood.

2 Proceed to page 32. Direct the students' attention to the diagram, noting the labeled parts of the flower. Read the sentences at the top of the page before students complete the page. Allow students to complete the page.

3 Homework suggestion: Distribute a copy of **BLM SP5-08C Lesson 8 Test Prep** to each student.

Day 5 Posttest

Objective
The students will correctly write dictated spelling words and sentences.

Introduction
Review by using flash cards noted in Student Spelling Support, number 2.

Directed Assessment

1 Dictate the list words by using the Pretest sentences or developing original ones. Reserve *naughty, recalled, stamen, sepals,* and *formal* for the dictation sentences.

2 Read each sentence. Repeat as needed.
- The <u>naughty</u> boy picked some flowers for his mother.
- He <u>recalled</u> that she liked roses.
- He was careful not to touch the <u>stamen</u>.
- He noticed some buds were still covered by <u>sepals</u>.
- He put the vase of flowers on the <u>formal</u> dining room table.

3 If assigned, dictate Extra Challenge Words.

4 Score the test, counting each misspelled word as an error. Correct the dictation sentences by grading only the spelling words or grading the complete sentences.

Student Spelling Support
Cont. from page 32

6. Write this week's words, categorize the Pattern, Content, and Vocabulary Words, and attach them to the Word Wall.

7. Invite students to research Christian ministries and their use of seeds to minister to third world countries. Invite students to describe why "seed planting" is important to the sustainability of the nations (physically and spiritually).

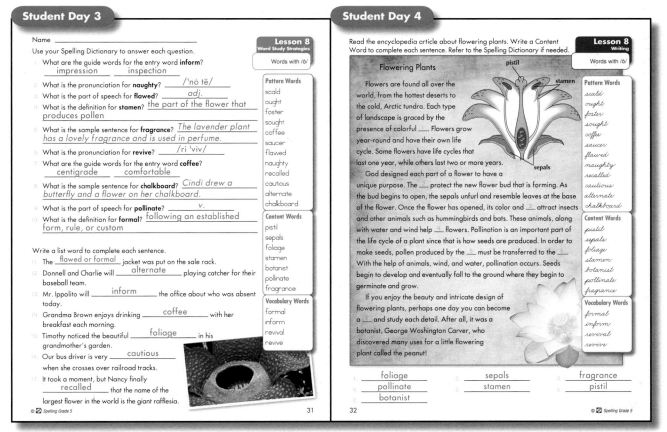

Student Pages
Pages 33–36

Lesson Materials
BLM SP5-09A
BLM SP5-09B
T-6
BLM SP5-09C
BLM SP5-09D

Created Wonders

The theme of this lesson is forests. Forests are areas of vegetation that occupy an extensive area of land. These areas are mainly covered with a dense grouping of trees. The treetops form a ceiling, also known as a canopy. The topography, soil, and climate of the region determine the characteristics of trees in the forest.

Day 1 Pretest

Objective

The students will accurately spell and write words with **diphthongs**. They will spell and write content, vocabulary, and challenge words.

Introduction

Before class, select Challenge Words for numbers 24 and 25 from a cross-curricular subject, words misspelled on previous assignments, or words that interest your students. The word *noisiness* has the **diphthong oi** and is suggested for number 24. Explain that they are to attempt to write all the spelling words.

Directed Instruction

1 Say each word, use it in a sentence, and then repeat the word.

Pattern Words
1. Pollution can <u>destroy</u> the natural habitat of a forest.
2. The <u>crowded</u> campground contained numerous motor homes.
3. It was an <u>enjoyable</u> day to see God's creation in the forest.
4. In the newness of the morning, many leaves were full of <u>moisture</u>.
5. Raymond was given a travel <u>allowance</u> for his vacation.
6. Amber will <u>avoid</u> hiking off the main forest trail.
7. Seth and Logan ventured <u>outdoors</u> for an adventure.
8. The committee will <u>appoint</u> Lucas to the forest ranger department.
9. Professor Ruthe gave an <u>account</u> of the diverse forest vegetation.
10. Reagan found <u>employment</u> with the national park system.
11. Have you seen the <u>royal</u> sequoias in California?
12. It is <u>doubtful</u> that the tourists will take the entire forest tour.

Content Words
13. The <u>evergreen</u> forest was blanketed in snow.
14. The strong <u>lumberjack</u> used a chain saw to cut down a tree.
15. The forest <u>canopy</u> was very dense.
16. Since we hiked past the <u>timberline</u>, there were no trees.
17. <u>Temperate</u> forests are not too hot and not too cold.
18. The old <u>conifer</u> was one hundred feet tall.
19. The <u>deciduous</u> tree had leaves of yellow and red.

Vocabulary Words
20. Since Abi had a good <u>memory</u>, she was asked to lead the forest tour.
21. New trees were planted as a <u>memorial</u> to the brave firemen.
22. The environmental report went through a <u>revision</u> last month.
23. Kelly will <u>revise</u> her report about trees in the forest.

Challenge Words
24. _____
25. _____

2 Allow students to self-correct their Pretest. Write each word on the board. Point out the following vowel spellings in the Pattern Words: oi, oy, ou, ow. These vowel spellings are diphthongs. A *diphthong* is <u>two or more vowels that glide together in one syllable, moving from the position of one vowel sound to the next</u>. Note the roots *memori*, *memor*, and *vis* in the Vocabulary Words.

3 As a class, read, spell, and read each word. Direct students to circle misspelled words with a colored pencil and rewrite them correctly.

4 Proof each student's Pretest. This becomes an individualized study sheet that can be used at school or at home.

5 Homework suggestion: Distribute a copy of **BLM SP5-09A Lesson 9 Words and Phrases** to each student.

Day 2 Word Analysis and Vocabulary

Objective
The students will sort and write words with **diphthongs**. They will complete sentences with content words. They will use a table to write vocabulary words, match definitions, and complete sentences.

Introduction
Write the following on the board: oi = 1, oy = 2, ou = 3, ow = 4. Invite students to refer to the list words, found on page 33, for this activity. Dictate each Pattern Word and direct students to hold up the correct number of fingers that corresponds to the vowel spelling in each dictated word.

Directed Instruction

1 Challenge students to quickly count how many Pattern Words contain the diphthong *oi* (3), the diphthong *oy* (4), the diphthong *ou* (3), and the diphthong *ow* (2).

2 Proceed to page 33. Say, spell, and say each Pattern, Content, and Vocabulary Word. Provide this week's Challenge Words and have students write them in the spaces provided. Students independently complete the page.

3 Proceed to page 34. Select students to build each Vocabulary Word. For example, the prefix *re-* goes with the root *vis* and the suffix *-ion* to get the word *revision*. Note that in *revise*, the silent *e* is not in the original root spelling for *vis*. Provide assistance as the page is independently completed. Chorally read exercises 9–15 when complete.

4 Homework suggestion: Distribute a copy of **BLM SP5-09B Phrases and Sentences** to each student.

Differentiated Instruction

- For students who spelled all the words correctly on the Pretest, select and assign Extra Challenge Words from the following list: dynamic, Macedonia, discrimination, emergency, paraphrase, subsystems.

- For students who spelled less than half correctly, assign the following Pattern, Content, and Vocabulary Words: appoint, doubtful, moisture, outdoors, crowded, enjoyable, conifer, canopy, evergreen, temperate, memory, revise. On the Posttest, evaluate these students on the twelve words assigned; however, encourage them to attempt to spell all the list words to the best of their ability. They are also responsible for writing the dictated sentences.

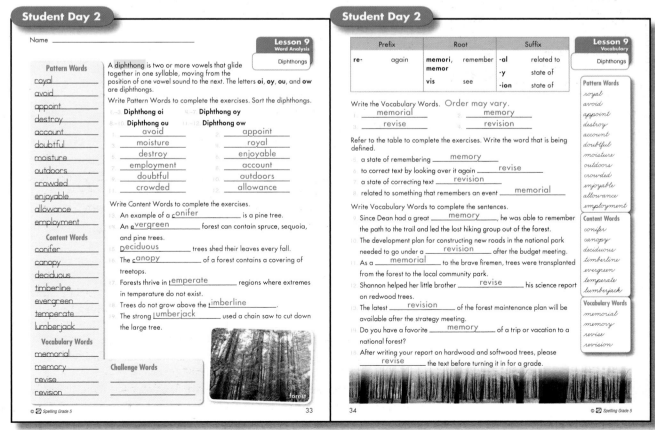

Cont. on page 37

Day 3 Word Study Strategies

Objective

The students will write list words that are related forms of given words. They will complete sentences with list words.

Introduction

Write *royal* and *moisture* on the board and challenge students to identify any related words that contain *royal* or *moisture*. (**Possible answers: royalty, royally, royalist; moisturize, moisturizer, moisturizing**)

Directed Instruction

1 Write the following incomplete sentences on the board:
   - If a tree loses its leaves in the fall, it is _____. (**deciduous**)
   - If you receive some money, it could be your _____. (**allowance**)
   - If the climate is not too hot or cold, it is a _____ climate. (**temperate**)
   - If you are trying to ignore a problem, you are trying to _____ it. (**avoid**)

   Write *allowance, avoid, deciduous,* and *temperate* on the board. Have students silently read each sentence and choose the correct list word that completes each sentence. Invite four volunteers to the board to write in the missing word and read each completed sentence aloud.

2 Proceed to page 35. Students will independently complete the page. When complete, have volunteers read exercises 12–23 aloud. Select a student to read Genesis 2:9 and discuss God's creation of trees.

Day 4 Writing

Objective

The students will use proofreading marks to identify mistakes on an informative poster for forest fire prevention. They will correctly write misspelled words.

Introduction

Display **T-6 Proofreading an Informative Poster** on the overhead, keeping the bottom portion of the transparency covered. Remind students that the marks in the Proofreading Marks box will be used to identify mistakes found on the poster. Read the text aloud and challenge students to raise their hand every time a mistake is reached in the reading process. Have students identify each mark that needs to be written. Correct the identified mistakes using the appropriate proofreading marks. Use **BLM SP5-09C T-6 Answer Key** as a guide. Uncover the bottom of the transparency and read the corrected version of text.

Directed Instruction

1 Proceed to page 36 and read the sentences at the top of the page. Assist students as needed while they independently proofread the poster on the page. Review all the necessary proofreading marks and corrections. (**12 misspellings; 3 capital letters needed; 2 periods needed; 1 delete; 2 add something—*with, a*; 2 small letters needed; 1 new paragraph**)

2 Homework suggestion: Distribute a copy of **BLM SP5-09D Lesson 9 Test Prep** to each student.

Day 5 Posttest

Objective
The students will correctly write dictated spelling words and sentences.

Introduction
Review by using flash cards noted in Student Spelling Support, number 2.

Directed Assessment

1 Dictate the list words by using the Pretest sentences or developing original ones. Reserve *outdoors*, *evergreen*, *temperate*, *memory*, and *enjoyable* for the dictation sentences.

2 Read each sentence. Repeat as needed.
- Vacationing <u>outdoors</u> is a fun thing to do.
- Hiking through an <u>evergreen</u> forest is exciting.
- <u>Temperate</u> forests contain many types of trees.
- What is your favorite vacation <u>memory</u>?
- Did you have an <u>enjoyable</u> time?

3 If assigned, dictate Extra Challenge Words.

4 Score the test, counting each misspelled word as an error. Correct the dictation sentences by grading only the spelling words or grading the complete sentences.

Student Spelling Support
Cont. from page 36

7. For a science connection, students may research forest menaces that threaten the forest environment. Possible examples are invading insects, diseases of trees, deforestation, or fire.

8. Trees are used in Scripture as a metaphor for healthy spiritual growth. Invite students to read Psalm 1:1–3, draw a diagram, and write a paragraph, reflecting on this botanical spiritual metaphor.

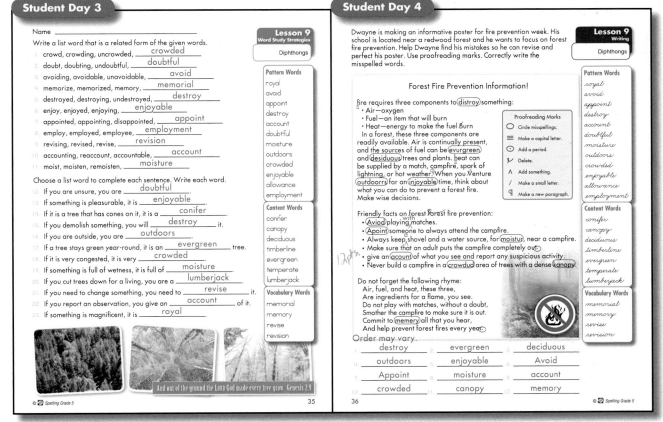

Schwa l and Schwa n

Student Pages

Pages 37–40

Lesson Materials

BLM SP5-10A
BLM SP5-10B
BLM SP5-10C
Newspaper
BLM SP5-10D

Created Wonders

The theme of this lesson is the woodlands. Woodlands differ from forests in that tall trees are much sparser in the woodlands, allowing sunlight to penetrate to ground level. Shrubs and grasses are abundant. The climate of the woodlands is generally semiarid with mild, wet winters and dry summers. Extremely dry conditions make wildfires a constant threat.

Day 1 Pretest

Objective

The students will accurately spell and write words with **schwa l and schwa n**. They will spell and write content, vocabulary, and challenge words.

Introduction

Before class, select Challenge Words for numbers 24 and 25 from a cross-curricular subject, words misspelled on previous assignments, or words that interest your students. The word *journalist* has **schwa l** and is suggested for number 24. Explain that they are to attempt to write all the spelling words.

Directed Instruction

1 Say each word, use it in a sentence, and then repeat the word.

Pattern Words

1. We took a <u>recent</u> field trip to learn about woodland animals.
2. It is the duty of every eligible <u>citizen</u> to vote.
3. Nicole pushed aside the <u>curtain</u> to see the view from her window.
4. God will protect us from every <u>evil</u> scheme of the enemy.
5. It is useful to study a <u>foreign</u> language in school.
6. <u>Human</u> beings need to be careful to protect the woodland ecosystem.
7. The <u>legend</u> of Big Foot is often told around the campfire.
8. Did Rachael tear her <u>linen</u> shirt on a manzanita branch?
9. I often <u>marvel</u> at the beauty of God's creation.
10. The gold miners found precious <u>metal</u> in the woodland streams.
11. Andrea studies <u>musical</u> theory in college.
12. One <u>raisin</u> dropped from the bag of trail mix.

Content Words

13. Many woodland ecosystems have a semiarid <u>climate</u>.
14. Woodland <u>shrubs</u> can provide food for animals.
15. Extremely tall trees are <u>sparse</u> in the woodland areas.
16. It was difficult to hike through the <u>dense</u> clumps of bushes.
17. A deer was caught by its antlers in a <u>thicket</u>.
18. The <u>vegetation</u> in the area included many old olive trees.
19. Erin enjoyed the field trip to the <u>woodlands</u>.

Vocabulary Words

20. We plan to <u>convert</u> our patio into a greenhouse.
21. Our <u>assignment</u> was to transplant plants into larger containers.
22. Davit put the potted shrub into his <u>convertible</u> car.
23. Hot, dry weather and high winds are <u>signals</u> of fire danger.

Challenge Words

24. _____
25. _____

2 Allow students to self-correct their Pretest. Write each word on the board. Explain that the target of the lesson is the schwa sound. A *schwa* is <u>a vowel sound identical to *short u*</u>. <u>The symbol ə represents the schwa in the pronunciation shown in the Spelling Dictionary</u>. Point out the following letter or letters with the schwa sound before *l* or *n* in each Pattern Word: *a* in *metal*, *human*, and *musical*; *ai* in *curtain*; *e* in *linen*, *citizen*, *legend*, *recent*, and *marvel*; *eig* in *foreign*; *i* in *evil* and *raisin*. Note that the letter *g* in *foreign* is silent. The roots in the Vocabulary Words are *sign* and *vert*.

3 As a class, read, spell, and read each word. Direct students to circle

misspelled words with a colored pencil and rewrite them correctly.

4 Proof each student's Pretest. This becomes an individualized study sheet that can be used at school or at home.

5 Homework suggestion: Distribute a copy of **BLM SP5-10A Lesson 10 Words and Phrases** to each student.

Day 2 Word Analysis and Vocabulary

Objective

The students will sort words with **schwa l and schwa n** and complete sentences with content words. They will use a table to write vocabulary words, match given definitions in context, and choose the best meaning for the underlined words.

Introduction

Before class, duplicate a copy of **BLM SP5-10B Schwa Sorting Cards** for each student. Explain that the pronunciation given on each card shows the schwa sound /ə/ before either an *l* or *n*. Remind students that the schwa sound is a vowel sound that is identical to the *short u* sound. The schwa sound can be spelled with many different vowel spellings. It often occurs in unstressed syllables. An *unstressed syllable* is a syllable that is pronounced with less emphasis than the stressed syllable in the word. There is no accent mark on an unstressed syllable. The schwa spelling in each word must be memorized. Instruct students to cut on the dotted lines and then make two piles of cards on their desktop, one pile with words having the schwa sound before *l* and a second pile having the schwa sound before *n*. (**schwa l cards: evil, metal, marvel, musical; schwa n cards: linen, raisin, citizen, legend, human, recent, curtain, foreign**) Save the cards for later use in Student Spelling Support, number 7.

Directed Instruction

1 Referring to the sorting cards from the lesson Introduction, ask students to state the various spellings for the schwa sound in each Pattern Word. (*a in metal, human,* and *musical; ai in curtain;*

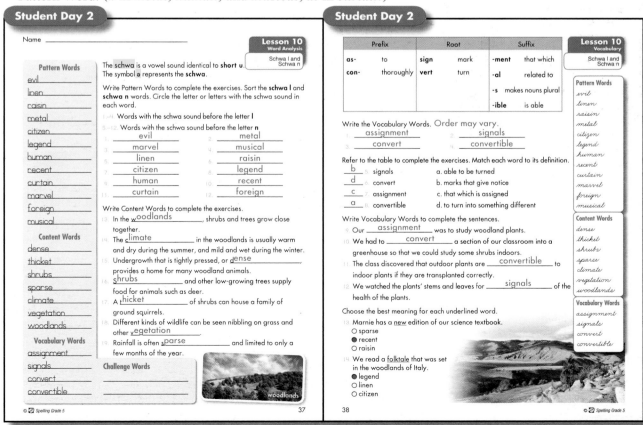

Student Spelling Support Materials

BLM SP5-01A
BLMs SP5-10E–F
Card stock
BLM SP5-01G
3" × 5" Index cards
BLM SP5-10B

Student Spelling Support

1. Use **BLM SP5-01A A Spelling Study Strategy** in instructional groups to provide assistance with some or all of the words.

2. Duplicate **BLMs SP5-10E–F Lesson 10 Spelling Words I** and **II** on CARD STOCK for students to use as flash cards at school or at home. Another option is to use **BLM SP5-01G Flash Cards Template** or 3" × 5" INDEX CARDS for students to write their own flash cards to use as a study aid.

3. Invite students to write the Challenge Words, numbers 24 and 25, in the Word Bank, in the back of their textbook.

4. Read Luke 11:4: "And forgive us our sins, for we also forgive everyone who is indebted to us. And do not lead us into temptation, but deliver us from the **evil** one." In this section of the Lord's Prayer, Jesus reminds us to pray for deliverance from the evil schemes of the enemy. God desires that we have nothing to do with **evil** practices and instead seek His protection and guidance.

5. Challenge students to research the climate in your area, using the Internet. Invite students to choose an aspect of the climate, such as the annual precipitation or average monthly temperatures, and make a line graph showing the

Cont. on page 41

e in *linen, citizen, legend, recent,* and *marvel; eig* in *foreign; i* in *evil* and *raisin*) Select volunteers to look at the accent mark found in the pronunciation, tell which syllable in each word is stressed, and state the type of syllable that is most likely to contain a schwa spelling in any word. (**The schwa spellings are found in the unstressed syllables in each word.**)

2 Proceed to page 37. Say, spell, and say each Pattern, Content, and Vocabulary Word. Provide this week's Challenge Words and have students write them in the spaces provided before completing the page.

3 Proceed to page 38. Remind students that each Vocabulary Word contains a root and an affix or affixes. Build each Vocabulary Word. For example, the root *sign* goes with the suffixes *-al* and *-s* to build the word *signals*. Refer to *assignment* and point out a unique aspect of the prefix *a-* in *as-*. The letter *s* is attached to the prefix *a-* because *a-* takes on the first letter of the root it is attached to—*sign*. This forms the double consonant pattern. This consonant doubling pattern only occurs when the prefix *a-* means *to* or *toward*. Students complete the page.

4 Homework suggestion: Distribute a copy of **BLM SP5-10C Lesson 10 Phrases and Sentences** to each student.

Day 3 Word Study Strategies

Objective

The students will write list words that are nouns or adjectives to replace underlined words.

Introduction

Write the following sentences on the board, underlining as shown:
- Beth ate a <u>sweet</u>, <u>sun-dried grape</u>. (**raisin**)
- Min had <u>a task</u> to complete. (**assignment**)
- Belle played an instrument that is <u>related to music</u>. (**musical**)
- Some native plants are <u>able to be turned</u> into house plants. (**convertible**)

Explain that the underlined words can be replaced with list words that are either nouns or adjectives. Review that a noun is a person, place, thing, or idea. Teach students that an *adjective* is <u>a word that describes a noun</u>. Invite volunteers to refer to the list words, found on page 39, to replace the underlined words with list words. Have students tell the part of speech for each word in the context of the sentence on the board. (*Raisin, assignment*—nouns; *musical, convertible*—adjectives)

Directed Instruction

1 Challenge students to locate the following words in their Spelling Dictionary and state the part of speech: evil, metal, recent, vegetation. (**evil**—*adj.*; **metal**—*n.*; **recent**—*adj.*; **vegetation**—*n.*) Inform students that a word's part of speech depends on its use in context.

2 Proceed to page 39. Allow students to read the directions and complete the page. When complete, select a volunteer to substitute a list word for each set of underlined words and read the page aloud.

Day 4 Writing

Objective

The students will read a newspaper article about a woodland fire. They will write list words that could replace the bold words in the article.

Introduction

Display a news article from a NEWSPAPER. Demonstrate how the newspaper text is arranged in columns. Newspaper articles report recent events. Ask students to list different types of articles that they have read in the newspaper. (**Possible answers: sports stories, human interest stories, political news, weather, financial news, fashion, film/theater**)

Directed Instruction

1 Explain that the activity in today's lesson involves an article about a wildfire. Although the article on the page is fiction, the type and format of the article are similar to an actual newspaper.

2 Proceed to page 40. Encourage students to read the entire article before listing words that have the same meaning as the bold words in the article. When complete, have a volunteer read the article, replacing the bold words with list words.

3 Homework suggestion: Distribute a copy of **BLM SP5-10D Lesson 10 Test Prep** to each student.

Day 5 Posttest

Objective
The students will correctly write dictated spelling words and sentences.

Introduction
Review by using flash cards noted in Student Spelling Support, number 2.

Directed Assessment

1 Dictate the list words by using the Pretest sentences or developing original·ones. Reserve *assignment*, *marvel*, *dense*, *thicket*, and *metal* for the dictation sentences.

2 Read each sentence. Repeat as needed.
- Kent's <u>assignment</u> was to study woodland plants.
- He began to <u>marvel</u> at the many different plants that God created.
- Kent saw small animals in the <u>dense</u> brush.
- He noticed a deer eating the leaves from a <u>thicket</u>.
- Kent picked up a scrap of old rusty <u>metal</u> that littered the ground.

3 If assigned, dictate Extra Challenge Words.

4 Score the test, counting each misspelled word as an error. Correct the dictation sentences by grading only the spelling words or grading the complete sentences.

Student Spelling Support
Cont. from page 40

inches of rainfall or the monthly temperatures during a specified time period. Assign a brief written report of their findings.

6. Write this week's words, categorize the Pattern, Content, and Vocabulary Words, and attach them to the Word Wall.

7. For auditory and visual learners, have students pair up and work together with the sorting cards found on **BLM SP5-10B Schwa Sorting Cards**. Cut the cards so that the pronunciation is separated from the list word. Place the pronunciations in one pile and the words in another pile. Shuffle the cards. Have one student read a list word aloud as the other student searches through the pronunciation cards to locate the card that has the pronunciation of the dictated word. Allow students to switch roles until all the words have been read.

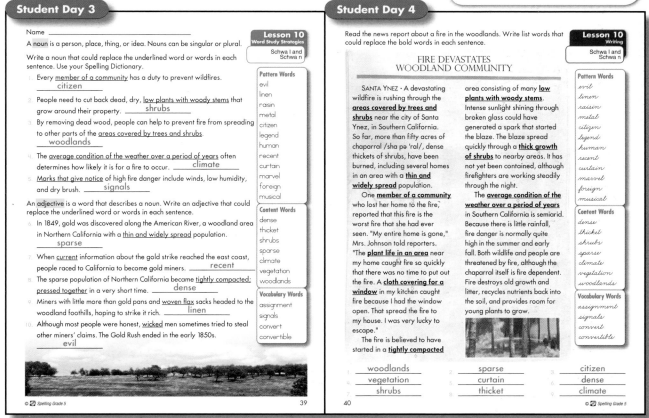

Schwa in Unstressed Syllables

Student Pages

Pages 41–44

Lesson Materials

BLM SP5-11A
BLM SP5-11B
Science textbook
History textbook
BLM SP5-11C

Created Wonders

The theme of this lesson is the tundra. Tundra is an area of land where tree growth is hindered by the following factors: extremely cold temperatures, little precipitation, a short growing season. Tundra is categorized into the following two groups: Arctic and Antarctic tundra, Alpine tundra. Arctic and Antarctic tundra occur at the earth's poles and contain a layer of permafrost. Alpine tundra occurs at high altitudes.

Day 1 Pretest

Objective

The students will accurately spell and write words with **schwa in unstressed syllables**. They will spell and write content, vocabulary, and challenge words.

Introduction

Before class, select Challenge Words for numbers 24 and 25 from a cross-curricular subject, words misspelled on previous assignments, or words that interest your students. The word *sympathy* has a **schwa in the unstressed syllable**, spelled *a*, and is suggested for number 24. Explain that they are to attempt to write all the spelling words.

Directed Instruction

1 Say each word, use it in a sentence, and then repeat the word.

Pattern Words
1. They will <u>televise</u> the tundra documentary tomorrow evening.
2. The <u>scientist</u> conducted a survey about the tundra's flora and fauna.
3. Jonathan did a <u>satisfactory</u> job in preparing for the tundra tour.
4. A <u>parallel</u> feature of tundra biomes is the hindrance of tree growth.
5. A short growing season is an <u>ordinary</u> occurrence on the tundra.
6. Will was asked to lead the <u>management</u> of the tundra expedition.
7. Jesus was <u>innocent</u>, yet He chose to take our sins upon Himself.
8. Can you <u>identify</u> the flora and fauna of the tundra landscape?
9. Experts <u>estimate</u> that the north tundra covers twenty percent of Earth.
10. The <u>diamond</u> is the hardest of all known minerals.
11. The <u>atmosphere</u> is categorized into five different layers.
12. An <u>anonymous</u> author wrote a poem about the desolate tundra.

Content Words
13. The <u>terrain</u> of most tundra contains grasses, shrubs, and moss.
14. A herd of <u>reindeer</u> was seen grazing on the tundra.
15. A distinctive feature of most tundra soil is its <u>permafrost</u>.
16. <u>Lichen</u> can be found growing on trees, rocks, and other surfaces.
17. <u>Arctic</u> tundra occurs on or around the North Pole.
18. <u>Antarctic</u> tundra does not contain large animals.
19. <u>Alpine</u> tundra contains no trees because of the high altitude.

Vocabulary Words
20. Rhiana told her <u>version</u> of the story to her parents.
21. Did the tundra biome lecture <u>reverse</u> your ideas for your project?
22. Did Lea <u>refuse</u> to believe the results of the tundra study?
23. Brody is <u>refusing</u> to study for his test on the tundra terrain.

Challenge Words
24. _____
25. _____

2 Allow students to self-correct their Pretest. Write each word on the board. Remind students that a schwa is a vowel sound identical to *short u*. Point out that the schwa sound occurs in the unaccented syllable or syllables of each Pattern Word. Note the roots *fus* and *vers* in the Vocabulary Words.

3 As a class, read, spell, and read each word. Direct students to circle misspelled words with a colored pencil and rewrite them correctly.

4 Proof each student's Pretest. This becomes an individualized study sheet that can be used at school or at home.

5 Homework suggestion: Distribute a copy of **BLM SP5-11A Lesson 11 Words and Phrases** to each student.

Day 2 Word Analysis and Vocabulary

Objective

The students will read pronunciations, identify, and circle letters that make the schwa sound in unstressed syllables. They will complete sentences with content words, use a table to write vocabulary words, and complete sentences.

Introduction

Reinforce the following definitions by writing them on the board:

• A schwa is a vowel sound identical to *short u*. The symbol ə represents the schwa.

• An unstressed syllable is a syllable that is pronounced with less emphasis than the stressed syllable in the word. There is no accent mark on an unstressed syllable.

Remind students that the schwa sound can be spelled with many different vowel spellings, and this often occurs in unstressed syllables. Because the schwa sound has many different spellings, the schwa spelling in each word must be memorized. Randomly select a few Pattern Words, locate them in the Spelling Dictionary, and write the diacritical marks for each word on the board. Invite students to refer to the list words, found on page 41, for this activity. Challenge students to find a list word that corresponds to each pronunciation on the board. When correctly identified, write out the Pattern Word and point out the stressed syllable, unstressed syllables, and vowel spelling(s) for each schwa. For example, /ˈdī ə mənd/ is the pronunciation for *diamond*. The first syllable /ˈdī/ is the stressed syllable, and the last two syllables /ə mənd/ are unstressed. The vowels *a* and *o* would be circled because they each make the schwa sound in *diamond*.

Student Day 2

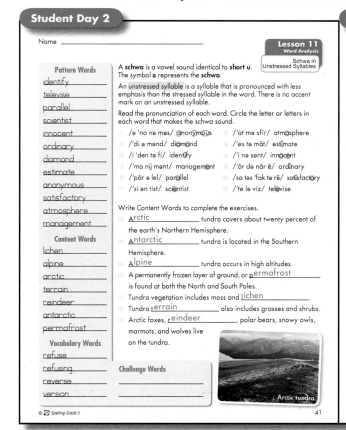

Student Day 2

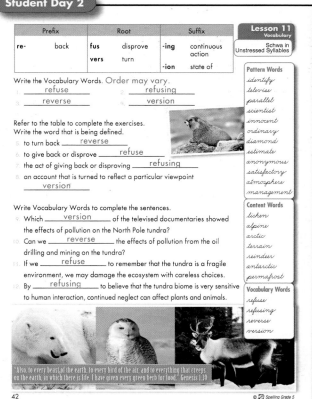

72 pts

Directed Instruction

1 Inform students that the theme for this lesson is the *tundra*. Define *tundra* as *an area of land where tree growth is hindered by very cold temperatures, little precipitation, and a short growing season.* Point out the following to clarify Content Words:
- Arctic tundra is located in the Northern Hemisphere.
- Antarctic tundra is located in the Southern Hemisphere.
- Alpine tundra is located at high altitudes in mountainous areas.

2 Proceed to page 41. Say, spell, and say each Pattern, Content, and Vocabulary Word. Provide this week's Challenge Words and have students write them in the spaces provided. Complete exercises 1–12 together as a class. Insure that all vowels that make the schwa sound are correctly circled. Students independently complete exercises 13–19.

3 Proceed to page 42. Select students to build each Vocabulary Word. For example, the prefix *re-* goes with the root *vers* to get the word *reverse* and silent *e* is not in the original root spelling. Provide assistance as the page is independently completed. Chorally read exercises 9–12 when complete. Select a volunteer to read Genesis 1:30 and discuss how God provides food for all creatures.

4 Homework suggestion: Distribute a copy of **BLM SP5-11B Lesson 11 Phrases and Sentences** to each student.

Day 3 Word Study Strategies

Objective

The students will sort and write list words according to the number of syllables. They will make inferences to complete sentences.

Introduction

Invite students to refer to their list words, found on page 43, for this activity. Chorally read and tap out the syllables in each list word. Challenge students to quickly count how many list words contain two syllables (**8**), three syllables (**11**), four syllables (**3**), and five syllables (**1**).

Directed Instruction

1 Write the following definition on the board: An *inference* is <u>a conclusion reached by looking at facts</u>. Read the following sentences, and then ask students to use the facts to infer, or conclude, which activity is being described:
- Rick wrote a note, put it in an envelope, and quietly walked onto the porch. He quickly placed the note on the screen door and ran back to his car to wait. He wanted to surprise his grandmother, so he didn't sign his note. (**Inference: Rick wanted to remain anonymous so he could surprise his grandmother.**)
- Tina enjoyed helping others. She had a talent for solving problems and bringing teams of people together. She decided to apply for the new leadership position. (**Inference: Tina decided to apply for a position of management.**)

Reread each sentence and ask students to state some facts that led them to each inference. (**Possible facts: didn't sign his note; apply for the new leadership position**)

2 Proceed to page 43. Students independently complete the page. When complete, select volunteers to read exercises 5–10 aloud.

Day 4 Writing

Objective

The students will complete an informative nonfiction book report by selecting and writing the correct list word in a sentence.

Introduction

Display a SCIENCE TEXTBOOK and HISTORY TEXTBOOK. Remind students that these are nonfiction books. Nonfiction books contain factual information about particular topics. Select a passage from one of the chapters, read it aloud, and challenge students to brainstorm ideas for a summary. Write ideas on the board and compile a brief synopsis.

Directed Instruction

1 Proceed to page 44. Students will read and complete the page independently. Select volunteers to read the page orally.

2 Homework suggestion: Distribute a copy of **BLM SP5-11C Lesson 11 Test Prep** to each student.

Day 5 Posttest

Objective

The students will correctly write dictated spelling words and sentences.

Introduction

Review by using flash cards noted in Student Spelling Support, number 2.

Directed Assessment

1 Dictate the list words by using the Pretest sentences or developing original ones. Reserve *terrain*, *arctic*, *identify*, *scientist*, and *refuse* for the dictation sentences.

2 Read each sentence. Repeat as needed.
- The <u>terrain</u> of the tundra is very different.
- <u>Arctic</u> tundra contains unique plants and animals.
- Can you <u>identify</u> any tundra plants or animals?
- The <u>scientist</u> was invited to study the tundra.
- Did he <u>refuse</u> the invitation?

3 If assigned, dictate Extra Challenge Words.

4 Score the test, counting each misspelled word as an error. Correct the dictation sentences by grading only the spelling words or grading the complete sentences.

Cont. from page 44

Student Spelling Support

of flora and fauna should be covered. Students add their research to their progressive journals that were begun in Lesson 1, Student Spelling Support, number 5.

6. Write this week's words, categorize the Pattern, Content, and Vocabulary Words, and attach them to the Word Wall.

7. Challenge students to brainstorm a tundra setting for a fictional short story, including sights, sounds, smells, and textures. Then, encourage students to write drafts of their "Tundra Tales" and share with their classmates.

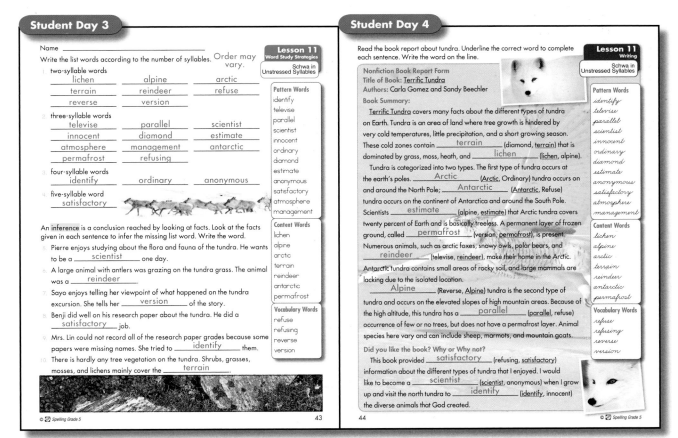

Day 1 Words with y

Objective
The students will spell, identify, and sort **words with y** according to the sound heard in each word.

Introduction
Teacher Note: This week's lesson incorporates the Pattern, Content, and Vocabulary Words taught in Lessons 7–11 using a variety of activities such as sorting, decoding words, a crossword puzzle, a word search, filling in the correct answer circle, shape boxes, and unscrambling words.

Display **T-7 Lessons 7–11 Study Sheet** on the overhead to review Lesson 7 words in unison, using the say, spell, say technique. Challenge students to identify the sounds of the letter *y* found in Lesson 7 Pattern Words. Use a different color transparency pen to circle each of the different sounds for the letter *y* in the Pattern Words. (consonant *y* in *canyon* and *youthfulness*; long e in *mystery*; long i in *typist, purify, recycle,* and *rhyming*; short i in *crystal, physics, systems, mystery, symptom,* and *gymnasium*) *Mystery* will be circled in two different colors.

Directed Instruction

1 Write the following Pattern Words from Lesson 7 on the board: crystal, canyon, rhyming. Select a student to syllabicate *crystal* and *canyon* between unlike consonants. (**crys|tal, can|yon**) Choose a second student to syllabicate *rhyming* before the suffix *-ing*. (**rhym|ing**) Encourage students to use syllabication as a technique to assist them in spelling words correctly.

2 Proceed to page 45. Explain that the box contains all the Pattern, Content, and Vocabulary Words in Lessons 7–11. This list is the same list of words that was previously displayed on the overhead. Encourage students to use this list as a review tool. Instruct students to read the directions and independently complete the page.

3 Distribute a copy of **BLM SP5-12A Lessons 7–11 Study Sheet** to each student to take home for study.

4 Homework suggestion: Distribute a copy of **BLM SP5-12B Lesson 12 Homework I** to each student to practice with **words with y, words with /ȯ/, diphthongs,** and **schwa l and schwa n.**

Day 2 Words with /ȯ/ and Diphthongs

Objective
The students will use a code box to decode **words with /ȯ/.** They will spell and write words with **diphthongs** in a crossword puzzle.

Introduction
Display **T-7 Lessons 7–11 Study Sheet**. Write the following Pattern Words from Lesson 8 on the board, inserting the symbols as shown:

- s c ▲ l d
- fl ▮ e d
- ⬭ t
- n ⬡ t y
- f ☆ s t e r
- c ◆ t i o u s

Make a key for each symbol by drawing each shape and indicating its spelling as follows: triangle—*a* before *l*; oval— *ough*; star—*o*; rectangle—*aw*; hexagon—*augh*; diamond—*au*. Invite volunteers to decode and write each Pattern Word below the word on the board.

(scald, ought, foster, flawed, naughty, cautious)

Directed Instruction

1 Display **T-7 Lessons 7–11 Study Sheet** to review Lessons 8–9 words in unison, using the say-spell-say technique. Have students refer to the transparency as you give the following clues to Lesson 9 Pattern Words and invite students to state the correct word that is being described: to stay away from (**avoid**), to ruin (**destroy**), unlikely (**doubtful**), capable of taking pleasure or satisfaction in (**enjoyable**), wetness (**moisture**).

2 Proceed to page 46. Allow students to read the directions and complete the page independently. Provide assistance as needed.

3 Homework suggestion: Distribute a copy of **BLM SP5-12C Lesson 12 Homework II** to each student to practice with **schwa in unstressed syllables**, Content Words, and Vocabulary Words.

Day 3 Schwa l and Schwa n and Schwa in Unstressed Syllables

Objective

The students will find and circle words with **schwa l and schwa n** in a word search. They will select the appropriate answer circle to indicate if words with **schwa in unstressed syllables** are spelled correctly or incorrectly, and correctly write each word.

Introduction

Select a few Lesson 10 Pattern Words from **T-7 Lessons 7–11 Study Sheet** to draw a mini word search on the board. Choose words that contain similar patterns or letters. Position words across, down, diagonally, and backwards. Challenge students to find all of the selected Pattern Words.

```
r e c e n t
d o g e i l
i b n n s j
o i m g i p
l e v r a m
d l v w r n
```

Directed Instruction

1 Display **T-7 Lessons 7–11 Study Sheet** to review Lessons 10–11 words in unison, using the say-spell-say technique.

2 Write and draw the following on the board:

	Correct	Incorrect	
televise	○	○	(correct; televise)
parrelel	○	○	(incorrect; parallel)
ordinery	○	○	(incorrect; ordinary)

Read each word and ask students to identify if each word is spelled correctly or incorrectly. Fill in each appropriate answer circle. Write each word correctly.

3 Proceed to page 47. Allow students to read the directions and complete the page independently. Provide assistance as needed.

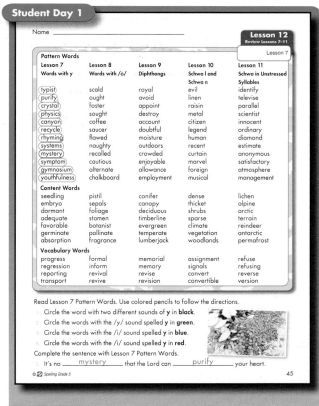

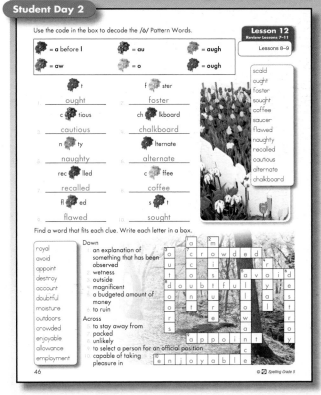

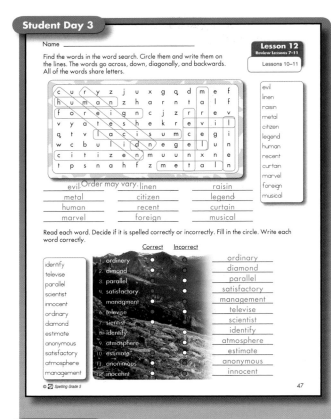

Student Day 3

Name _____

Lesson 12
Review Lessons 7–11
Lessons 10–11

Find the words in the word search. Circle them and write them on the lines. The words go across, down, diagonally, and backwards. All of the words share letters.

| c u r y z j u x g q d m e f |
| h u m a n z h a r n t a l f |
| f o r e i g n c j z r r e v |
| v y a t e s h e k r e v i l |
| q t v l a c i s u m c e g i |
| w c b u l i d n e g e l u n |
| c i t i z e n m u u n x n e |
| t p s n a h f z m e t a l n |

evil
linen
raisin
metal
citizen
legend
human
recent
curtain
marvel
foreign
musical

Order may vary.

evil	linen	raisin
metal	citizen	legend
human	recent	curtain
marvel	foreign	musical

Read each word. Decide if it is spelled correctly or incorrectly. Fill in the circle. Write each word correctly.

identify
televise
parallel
scientist
innocent
ordinary
diamond
estimate
anonymous
satisfactory
atmosphere
management

	Correct	Incorrect	
1. ordinary	○	○	ordinary
2. dimond	○	○	diamond
3. parallel	○	○	parallel
4. satisfactory	○	○	satisfactory
5. managment	○	○	management
6. televise	○	○	televise
7. sientist	○	○	scientist
8. identify	○	○	identify
9. atmosphere	○	○	atmosphere
10. estimate	○	○	estimate
11. anonimous	○	○	anonymous
12. inocehnt	○	○	innocent

© Spelling Grade 5

47

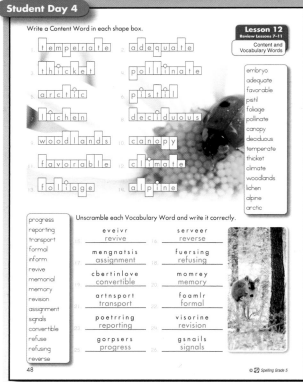

Student Day 4

Write a Content Word in each shape box.

Lesson 12
Review Lessons 7–11
Content and Vocabulary Words

1. temperate   2. adequate
3. thicket   4. pollinate
5. arctic   6. pistil
7. lichen   8. deciduous
9. woodlands   10. canopy
11. favorable   12. climate
13. foliage   14. alpine

embryo
adequate
favorable
pistil
foliage
pollinate
canopy
deciduous
temperate
thicket
climate
woodlands
lichen
alpine
arctic

Unscramble each Vocabulary Word and write it correctly.

progress
reporting
transport
formal
inform
revive
memorial
memory
revision
assignment
signals
convertible
refuse
refusing
reverse

15. eveivr — revive
16. serveer — reverse
17. mengnatsis — assignment
18. fuersing — refusing
19. cbertinlove — convertible
20. momrey — memory
21. artnsport — transport
22. foamlr — formal
23. poetrring — reporting
24. visorine — revision
25. gorpsers — progress
26. gsnails — signals

48

© Spelling Grade 5

Day 4 Content Words and Vocabulary Words

Objective

The students will write content words in shape boxes. They will unscramble letters to write vocabulary words.

Introduction

Write *embryo* and *canopy* on the board. Draw a shape box around each letter—embryo, canopy. Ask students to count the number of letters in each word (**6**), study the shape boxes of the words, state whether the words have an equal or unequal number of letters (**equal number of letters**), and tell if the words have identical or different shape boxes (**different shape boxes**).

Directed Instruction

1 Display **T-7 Lessons 7–11 Study Sheet** to review Content and Vocabulary Words in unison, using the say-spell-say technique.

2 Have the students refer to the Vocabulary Words on the overhead, state, and spell the words that use the prefix *con-* (**convert, convertible**), the prefix *re-* (**regression, reporting, revival, revive, revise, revision, refuse, refusing, reverse**), the root *form* (**formal, inform**), the root *vert, vers* (**convert, convertible, reverse, version**), the suffix *-al* (**formal, revival, memorial, signals**), and the suffix *-ing* (**reporting, refusing**).

3 Proceed to page 48. Assist students as needed to complete the page.

4 Homework suggestion: Distribute a copy of **BLM SP5-12D Lessons 7–11 Test Prep** to each student to practice many of the words that may appear on the Assessment. Prepare for the Assessment by studying the words on **BLM SP5-12A Lessons 7–11 Study Sheet** that was sent home on Day 1.

Day 5 Assessment

Objective

The students will accurately select the appropriate answer within the context of a sentence. They will fill in the corresponding answer circle.

Introduction

Teacher Note: The Test makes provision for Differentiated Instruction. The first twelve sentences include the words assigned to students with shortened lists. Encourage these students to try all the sentences, but only grade the first twelve sentences. The Test is found on two blackline masters.

Distribute a copy of **BLMs SP5-12E–F Lessons 7–11 Test I** and **II** to each student. Duplicate **BLM**

© Spelling Grade 5

SP5-06G Student Answer Form and cut apart. Distribute one answer form to each student. Remind students to fill in each answer circle completely and to erase completely if they wish to change an answer.

Directed Assessment

1 Instruct students to listen as you dictate the following Sample:
Sample

It is <u>enjoyable</u> to <u>marvel</u> at the scenic <u>terain</u> that God created. <u>All correct</u>
      A   B   C   D

Say, "Are any of the first three underlined words misspelled?" Pause for replies. Inform students that the letter *C* is below the underlined word that is misspelled. (**terrain**) Guide students to the answer form that was previously distributed. Lead students to find the Sample box and fill in the appropriate answer circle containing the same letter. Say, "You will continue in the same way. You will read each sentence, choose the word that you think is misspelled, and fill in the corresponding circle on the answer form. If all the words are spelled correctly, fill in the fourth circle, labeled *D*, for *All correct*."

2 Assist students as needed while they read the sentences and complete the Test on their own.
1. Bees transport pollen from the stamen to the pistil of flowers.
2. An embryo will sprout into a seedling after it receives moisture.
3. The innocent citizen walked into the crowded courtroom.
4. The server spilled coffee on the saucer during the formal banquet.
5. Bo recalled that he needed to appoint the cast for the musical play.
6. The play was held outdoors in the temperate climate.
7. The canopy of evergreen trees in a dense forest blocks the sunlight.
8. A good jeweler can identify a flawed diamond.
9. A scientist will study the mystery of a dormant seed.
10. The typist will revise her assignment.
11. The naughty boy will refuse to make progress in his classes.
12. If hiking in a canyon, one ought to bring an adequate water supply.
13. The legend of the talking raisin caused the lumberjack to laugh.
14. The botanist labeled the sepals in the diagram on the chalkboard.
15. The station will televise the recent news to inform its viewers.
16. Dawn has favorable employment as a teacher of physics.
17. The fragrance of lichen and other foliage is pleasant.
18. Lorraine will convert the linen fabric into a lovely curtain.
19. The absorption of water helps seeds to germinate into vegetation.
20. Cameron is not refusing to visit the foreign memorial.
21. The management sought to alternate its meetings each week.
22. The parallel stoplight signals are made of sturdy metal.
23. Deciduous trees and shrubs are planted outside the gymnasium.
24. Can you estimate how many bees pollinate ordinary plants?
25. It is doubtful that all human beings recycle their trash.

3 Refer to **BLM SP5-12G Lessons 7–11 Answer Key** when correcting the Test.

Student Pages
Pages 49–52

Lesson Materials
BLM SP5-13A
T-8
P-4
P-5
BLM SP5-13B
Newspaper page
BLM SP5-13C

Created Wonders
Lessons 13–17 utilize the theme of oceans. The theme of this lesson is algae. Algae are also known as seaweed and kelp. Large kelp forests grow in the ocean and provide shelter for marine life. Algae are not true plants although they have a resemblance. The leaflike structure is called a blade, the stalk is the stipe, and the base of the plant is the holdfast. Algae do not have a true root system.

Day 1 Pretest

Objective
The students will accurately spell and write words that are **homophones**. They will spell and write content, vocabulary, and challenge words.

Introduction
Before class, select Challenge Words for numbers 24 and 25 from a cross-curricular subject, words misspelled on previous assignments, or words that interest your students. The word *aisle* is a **homophone** for *isle* and *I'll* and is suggested for number 24. Administer the Pretest.

Directed Instruction
1 Say each word, use it in a sentence, and then repeat the word.

Pattern Words
1. <u>Sweet</u> foods such as syrup and ice cream contain algae.
2. The Barker family stayed in a <u>suite</u> at the hotel for their vacation.
3. Laura <u>missed</u> the field trip to the aquarium because she was ill.
4. We hurried home in the <u>mist</u> before the heavy rain began to fall.
5. Algae can be a nutritional supplement for the hooves of a <u>horse</u>.
6. Mr. Manning's voice was <u>hoarse</u> because he had a sore throat.
7. Do you think the <u>prophet</u> Jonah saw algae inside the great fish?
8. Fishermen make a <u>profit</u> selling fish and algae.
9. The <u>presence</u> of algae in the ocean is vital to marine life.
10. One of Trisha's <u>presents</u> was a book about marine plants and animals.
11. Mario incorrectly <u>guessed</u> that green is the only color of algae.
→ 12. A <u>guest</u> from La Jolla Aquarium spoke at the assembly today.

Content Words
13. Algae are part of the ocean's <u>ecosystem</u>.
14. Flies like to swarm around <u>kelp</u> that washes up onto the beach.
15. Algae are <u>plantlike</u> organisms that lack a root system.
16. Some <u>seaweed</u> can grow to be three hundred feet tall.
17. Algae are types of <u>aquatic</u> organisms.
18. Most algae make their own food through <u>photosynthesis</u>.
19. Each cell in algae contains a <u>nucleus</u>.

Vocabulary Words
20. A <u>fraction</u> of the algae plant was floating atop the water.
21. The game warden ticketed Ed for the <u>infraction</u> of littering the lake.
22. The new ramp at Moonlight Shores makes the beach easily <u>accessible</u>.
23. Because of disagreements, ten members of the club decided to <u>secede</u>.

Challenge Words
24. _____
25. _____

2 Allow students to self-correct their Pretest. Write each word on the board. Point out that this week's list contains **homophones**. Teach that *homophones* are <u>words that sound the same but have different meanings and spellings</u>. Note the roots *cess*, *cede*, and *fract* in the Vocabulary Words.

3 As a class, read, spell, and read each word. Direct students to circle misspelled words with a colored pencil and rewrite them correctly.

4 Proof each student's Pretest. This becomes an individualized study sheet that can be used at school or at home.

5 Homework suggestion: Distribute a copy of **BLM SP5-13A Lesson 13 Words and Phrases** to each student.

Day 2 Word Analysis and Vocabulary

Objective

The students will sort and write **homophones** according to the number of syllables and complete sentences with content words. They will use a table to write vocabulary words, select words to match definitions, and complete sentences in context. They will choose words to match given definitions.

Introduction

Display **T-8 Lesson 13 Homophones** to review **homophones** in context. Select a volunteer to read the definition of **homophones** at the top of the transparency. Randomly select a set of homophone sentences to be read aloud and invite a volunteer to identify and correctly spell each homophone used. As a challenge, have students identify the part of speech for each homophone. Direct students to their Spelling Dictionary if needed.

Directed Instruction

1 Refer to **P-4** and **P-5 Homophones** to review **homophones**, some of which are in this lesson, and some are not.

2 Explain that this week's Content Words relate to the theme of algae. Teach that the word *algae* is the plural form of the word *alga*. Two Content Words, *kelp* and *seaweed*, are types of algae.

3 Proceed to page 49. Say, spell, and say each Pattern, Content, and Vocabulary Word. Provide this week's Challenge Words and have students write them in the spaces provided. To reinforce syllables, have students identify how many are in each word. Instruct students to complete the page.

4 Proceed to page 50. Remind students that each Vocabulary Word contains a root and an affix(es). Build each Vocabulary Word before

Differentiated Instruction

- For students who spelled all the words correctly on the Pretest, select and assign Extra Challenge Words from the following list: integration, idolatry, honorary, exercise, recurring, retrieval.

- For students who spelled less than half correctly, assign the following Pattern, Content, and Vocabulary Words: mist, sweet, guest, prophet, horse, presents, kelp, nucleus, plantlike, ecosystem, accessible, fraction. On the Posttest, evaluate these students on the twelve words assigned; however, encourage them to attempt to spell all the list words to the best of their ability. They are also responsible for writing the dictated sentences.

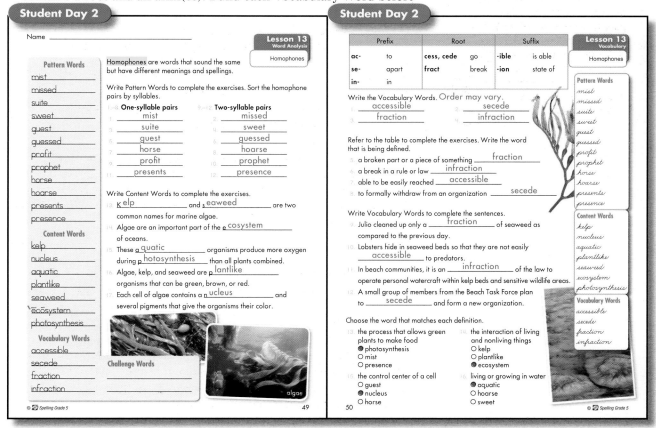

Student Spelling Support Materials

BLM SP5-01A
BLMs SP5-13D–E
Card stock
BLM SP5-01G
3" × 5" Index cards

Student Spelling Support

1. Use **BLM SP5-01A A Spelling Study Strategy** in instructional groups to provide assistance with some or all of the words.

2. Duplicate **BLMs SP5-13D–E Lesson 13 Spelling Words I** and **II** on CARD STOCK for students to use as flash cards at school or at home. Another option is to use **BLM SP5-01G Flash Cards Template** or 3" × 5" INDEX CARDS for students to write their own flash cards to use as a study aid.

3. Invite students to write the Challenge Words, numbers 24 and 25, in the Word Bank, in the back of their textbook.

4. Read Mark 8:36: "For what will it **profit** a man if he gains the whole world, and loses his own soul?" Discuss that the meaning of *profit* in this verse is *benefit*. Help students understand that there is absolutely no benefit to our lives if we achieve fame and fortune and reject God's salvation. Pose the question, "Is having fame and fortune on Earth worth losing our soul and not going to Heaven for all eternity?" (**Absolutely not.**)

5. Have students research and write about different forms of algae. They can illustrate each type and make a booklet.

6. Write this week's words, categorize the Pattern, Content, and Vocabulary Words, and attach them to

Cont. on page 53

students complete the page. For example, the prefix *ac-* goes with the root *cess* and the suffix *-ible* to get the word *accessible*. Review the unique function of the prefix *a-* in *ac-*. The letter *c* is attached to the prefix *a-* because it takes on the first letter of the root it is attached to—*cess*. This forms the double consonant pattern *cc*. Allow students to independently complete the page. Assist as needed.

5 Homework suggestion: Distribute a copy of **BLM SP5-13B Lesson 13 Phrases and Sentences** to each student.

Day 3 Word Study Strategies

Objective

The students will complete sentences by writing **homophones**. They will use the Spelling Dictionary to find the correct usage of each homophone pair.

Introduction

Write the words *suite* and *sweet* on the board. In another area of the board, write the following sentences:

• Perry is a _____ person. (**sweet**)
• The hotel _____ overlooks the ocean. (**suite**)
• A chocolate candy bar is a _____ treat. (**sweet**)

Have students refer to their Spelling Dictionary. Select one volunteer to read the definition(s) and state the part of speech for *suite* and a second volunteer to do the same with the word *sweet*. (**suite—a group of rooms, noun; sweet—tasting like sugar, adjective; sweet—kind, adjective**) Ask students if they notice a difference between the words. (*Suite* **has one definition and** *sweet* **has two.**) Select volunteers to write the correct homophone in each sentence.

Directed Instruction

1 Solicit volunteers to correctly use *guest* and *guessed* in sentences. Check for understanding by asking students to spell the word correctly in the context it is used.

2 Proceed to page 51. Check for accuracy as students complete the page. Ensure that students refer to the Spelling Dictionary.

Day 4 Writing

Objective

The students will complete a cloze activity in the context of a letter to the editor.

Introduction

Teacher Note: The persuasive domain is the focus for the writing pages in Lessons 13–17.

Display a NEWSPAPER PAGE featuring letters to the editor. Read a letter that is appropriate and discuss possible reasons as to why that person wrote the letter. Ask the students to state a purpose for writing a letter to the newspaper editor. (**Possible answers: to report a good deed, to give an opinion, to disagree with an article**)

Directed Instruction

1 Explain that today's assignment consists of completing a letter to the editor about the problem of pollution on beaches. Ask students if they have visited a beach that had trash and dead seaweed scattered around. Relate that it is not very pleasant because trash and dead seaweed attract flies and other insects and have a bad odor. Remind the class that God has created a beautiful world and we all should work together to take care of it. Teach the students that the word *wrack* in the letter means *dried seaweed*.

2 Proceed to page 52. Instruct students to complete the page independently. Assist as needed.

3 Homework suggestion: Distribute a copy of **BLM SP5-13C Lesson 13 Test Prep** to each student.

Day 5 Posttest

Objective
The students will correctly write dictated spelling words and sentences.

Introduction
Review by using flash cards noted in Student Spelling Support, number 2.

Directed Assessment

1 Dictate the list words by using the Pretest sentences or developing original ones. Reserve *sweet*, *ecosystem*, *guest*, *kelp*, and *accessible* for the dictation sentences.

2 Read each sentence. Repeat as needed.
- Aunt Mary is a <u>sweet</u> lady.
- She is a scientist who studies the ocean's <u>ecosystem</u>.
- This weekend Aunt Mary will be our <u>guest</u>.
- She enjoys collecting seashells and <u>kelp</u> that are on the beach.
- The beach is <u>accessible</u> by opening the gate in our backyard.

3 If assigned, dictate Extra Challenge Words.

4 Score the test, counting each misspelled word as an error. Correct the dictation sentences by grading only the spelling words or grading the complete sentences.

Student Spelling Support
Cont. from page 52

the Word Wall.

7. Invite students to explore how trash or pollution or other factors can interrupt God's design for various ecosystems. Have students select an ecosystem, for example, tidal pool, estuary, desert, forest, or mountain and research how human presence has committed infractions against this ecosystem. Challenge students to take action from a stewardship perspective, such as create a poster on stewardship and organize a trash clean-up day, write an editorial, or prepare a guest presentation for a younger class.

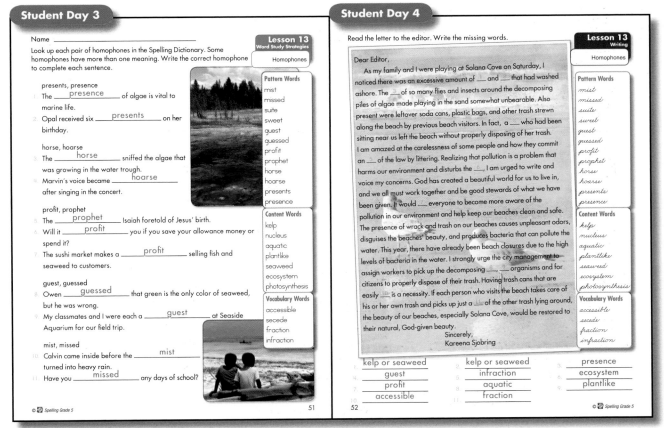

Homophones

Student Pages
Pages 53–56

Lesson Materials
BLM SP5-14A
T-9
P-4
P-5
BLM SP5-14B
BLM SP5-14C

Created Wonders

The theme of this lesson is tidal pools. Tidal pools can also be referred to as tide or rock pools. Along a coastline, these rocky areas can be filled with trapped seawater as the tide recedes. These pools of water can also be fed by the nearby spray of waves or rain. Tidal pools contain many unique species of flora and fauna that are amazingly adaptable to the unique and constantly changing environment.

Day 1 Pretest

Objective
The students will accurately spell and write words that are **homophones**. They will spell and write content, vocabulary, and challenge words.

Introduction
Before class, select Challenge Words for numbers 24 and 25 from a cross-curricular subject, words misspelled on previous assignments, or words that interest your students. The word *foreword* is a **homophone** for *forward* and is suggested for number 24. Administer the Pretest.

Directed Instruction

1 Say each word, use it in a sentence, and then repeat the word.

Pattern Words

1. Have you <u>heard</u> about our field trip to the tidal pools?
2. A <u>herd</u> of sheep grazed near the ocean cliff.
3. What will you see when you <u>peer</u> into the tidal pool?
4. The students will walk on the <u>pier</u> after exploring the tidal pools.
5. The fisherman securely <u>tied</u> his boat to the dock.
6. Clams migrate with the <u>tide</u> to evade preying birds.
7. Our class will write friendly notes to the nursing home <u>patients</u>.
8. One must have <u>patience</u> while waiting for tides to recede.
9. Randy's key <u>ring</u> fell into the tidal pool while he was exploring.
10. Kristen will <u>wring</u> out the wet bathing suits after the beach outing.
11. The cloud <u>ceiling</u> at the beach was very low.
12. The barnacle was <u>sealing</u> itself as the tide lowered.

Content Words

13. As you move inland, an estuary's water <u>salinity</u> decreases.
14. Starfish and algae are examples of <u>organisms</u> found in tidal pools.
15. The <u>intertidal</u> zone is an important part of the ocean's ecosystem.
16. The <u>fluctuation</u> of tides is an integral part of life in a tidal pool.
17. There are many tidal pools up and down the <u>coastline</u>.
18. How many <u>barnacles</u> did you count in the tidal pool?
19. The <u>anemone</u> used its tentacles to attach itself to the rock.

Vocabulary Words

20. The <u>extraction</u> of starfish from tidal pools is illegal.
21. The human heart alternates between <u>contraction</u> and expansion.
22. Your heart's <u>intention</u> should be to share Jesus with others.
23. The students were <u>attentive</u> to the message in chapel.

Challenge Words

24. _____
25. _____

2 Allow students to self-correct their Pretest. Write each word on the board. Point out that this week's list contains **homophones**. Review that **homophones** are words that sound the same but have different meanings and spellings. Note the roots *tent* and *tract* in the Vocabulary Words.

3 As a class, read, spell, and read each word. Direct students to circle misspelled words with a colored pencil and rewrite them correctly.

4 Proof each student's Pretest. This becomes an individualized study sheet that can be used at school or at home.

5 Homework suggestion: Distribute a copy of **BLM SP5-14A Lesson 14 Words and Phrases** to each student.

Day 2 Word Analysis and Vocabulary

Objective
The students will sort and write homophone pairs according to the number of syllables and complete sentences with content words. They will use a table to write vocabulary words, match given definitions in context, and choose the best meaning for the underlined words.

Introduction
Display **T-9 Lesson 14 Homophones** to review **homophones** in context. Read the sentences at the top of the page aloud and select volunteers to read each homophone and the corresponding sentence. For reinforcement, students may follow along in their Spelling Dictionary and locate **homophones** and identify their part(s) of speech.

Directed Instruction

1 Refer to **P-4** and **P-5 Homophones** to review other **homophones** that are not lesson specific.

2 Proceed to page 53. Say, spell, and say each Pattern, Content, and Vocabulary Word. Provide this week's Challenge Words and have students write them in the spaces provided. Students independently complete the page. To reinforce Content Word meanings, select volunteers to read exercises 13–19 aloud when complete.

3 Proceed to page 54. Remind students that each Vocabulary Word contains a root and affixes. Build each Vocabulary Word before students complete the page. For example, the root *tent* goes with the prefix *at-* and the suffix *-ive* to get the word *attentive*. Review the unique function of the prefix *a-* in *at-*. The letter *t* is attached to the prefix *a-* because it takes on the first letter of the root it is attached to—*tent*. This forms the double consonant pattern *tt*. Provide assistance as needed. Select a volunteer to read exercises 9–12 when complete. Select a student to read Genesis 1:10 and discuss how God created unique environments, such as the land and sea, for specific purposes.

Student Day 2

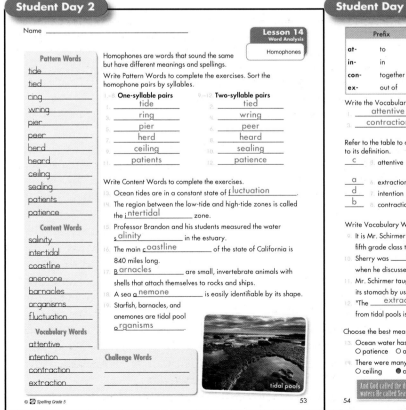

Lesson 14 Word Analysis — Homophones

65 pts.

Pattern Words
tide
tied
ring
wring
pier
peer
herd
heard
ceiling
sealing
patients
patience

Homophones are words that sound the same but have different meanings and spellings.

Write Pattern Words to complete the exercises. Sort the homophone pairs by syllables.

1–8 One-syllable pairs
1. tide
3. ring
5. pier
7. herd
9. ceiling
11. patients

9–12 Two-syllable pairs
2. tied
4. wring
6. peer
8. heard
10. sealing
12. patience

Content Words
salinity, intertidal, coastline, anemone, barnacles, organisms, fluctuation

Write Content Words to complete the exercises.
13. Ocean tides are in a constant state of fluctuation.
14. The region between the low-tide and high-tide zones is called the intertidal zone.
15. Professor Brandon and his students measured the water salinity in the estuary.
16. The main coastline of the state of California is 840 miles long.
17. Barnacles are small, invertebrate animals with shells that attach themselves to rocks and ships.
18. A sea anemone is easily identifiable by its shape.
19. Starfish, barnacles, and anemones are tidal pool organisms.

Vocabulary Words
attentive, intention, contraction, extraction

Challenge Words

tidal pools

© Spelling Grade 5   53

Student Day 2

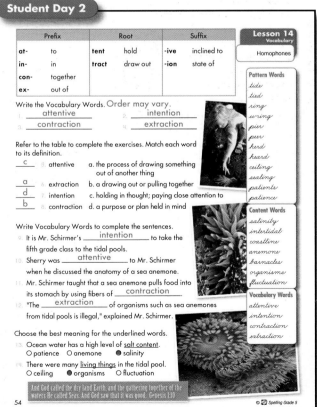

Lesson 14 Vocabulary — Homophones

Prefix		Root		Suffix	
at-	to	tent	hold	-ive	inclined to
in-	in	tract	draw out	-ion	state of
con-	together				
ex-	out of				

Write the Vocabulary Words. Order may vary.
1. attentive
2. intention
3. contraction
4. extraction

Refer to the table to complete the exercises. Match each word to its definition.
- c 5. attentive   a. the process of drawing something out of another thing
- a 6. extraction   b. a drawing out or pulling together
- d 7. intention   c. holding in thought; paying close attention to
- b 8. contraction   d. a purpose or plan held in mind

Write Vocabulary Words to complete the sentences.
9. It is Mr. Schirmer's intention to take the fifth grade class to the tidal pools.
10. Sherry was attentive to Mr. Schirmer when he discussed the anatomy of a sea anemone.
11. Mr. Schirmer taught that a sea anemone pulls food into its stomach by using fibers of contraction.
12. "The extraction of organisms such as sea anemones from tidal pools is illegal," explained Mr. Schirmer.

Choose the best meaning for the underlined words.
13. Ocean water has a high level of salt content.
   ○ patience ○ anemone ● salinity
14. There were many living things in the tidal pool.
   ○ ceiling ● organisms ○ fluctuation

Pattern Words
tide, tied, ring, wring, pier, peer, herd, heard, ceiling, sealing, patients, patience

Content Words
salinity, intertidal, coastline, anemone, barnacles, organisms, fluctuation

Vocabulary Words
attentive, intention, contraction, extraction

And God called the dry land Earth, and the gathering together of the waters He called Seas, and God saw that it was good. Genesis 1:10

54   © Spelling Grade 5

**Student Spelling
Support Materials**

BLM SP5-01A
BLMs SP5-14D–E
Card stock
BLM SP5-01G
3" × 5" Index cards

**Student
Spelling Support**

1. Use **BLM SP5-01A A
   Spelling Study Strategy**
   in instructional groups to
   provide assistance with
   some or all of the words.
2. Duplicate **BLMs
   SP5-14D–E Lesson 14
   Spelling Words I** and **II**
   on CARD STOCK for students
   to use as flash cards at
   school or at home. Another
   option is to use **BLM
   SP5-01G Flash Cards
   Template** or 3" × 5" INDEX
   CARDS for students to write
   their own flash cards to use
   as a study aid.
3. Invite students to write the
   Challenge Words, numbers
   24 and 25, in the Word
   Bank, in the back of their
   textbook.
4. For a Bible connection, read
   Genesis 1:10: "And God
   called the dry land Earth,
   and the gathering together
   of the waters He called Seas.
   And God saw that it was
   good." Discuss how the Lord
   created everything to function
   in a specific and orderly way.
   The unique flora and fauna
   of tidal pools are remarkably
   able to survive in a constantly
   changing environment.
5. Challenge students to
   research a sea animal that
   makes the tidal pool its
   habitat. Invite students to write
   riddles about their selected
   sea animal and add riddles
   to their progressive journals
   from Lesson 1, Student
   Spelling Support, number 5.
   A possible riddle could be the
   following: I look like a flower,
   but I can devour! What am I?
   (**a sea anemone**)

Cont. on page 57

4 Homework suggestion: Distribute a copy of **BLM SP5-14B Lesson 14
Phrases and Sentences** to each student.

Day 3 Word Study Strategies

Objective
The students will correctly write **homophones** according to sentence
usage. They will choose and write **homophones** to complete sentences.

Introduction
Invite students to look up the **homophones** *tide* and *tied* in their Spelling
Dictionary for this activity. Have students silently read and study each
homophone as you write the following on the board:
- tide: the systematic rise and fall of ocean water, generally occurring
  every six hours
- tied: past tense of TIE; to have fastened or attached by knotting

Read the definitions aloud. Select volunteers to answer the following
questions as you point to each corresponding homophone on the board:
- What part of speech does *tide* have? (*n.*)
- What is the sample sentence for *tide*? (**Clams migrate with the tide to
  evade preying birds.**)
- Does the sample sentence match the definition? (**Yes.**)
- What part of speech does *tied* have? (*v.*)
- What is the sample sentence for *tied*? (**The fisherman securely tied his
  boat to the dock.**)
- Does the sample sentence match the definition? (**Yes.**)

Directed Instruction
1 Repeat the preceding activity with the **homophones** *ring* and *wring*.
Ask students to identify something unique about the entry word *ring*
before completing the activity. (***Ring* has two definitions and two
parts of speech.**)

2 Proceed to page 55. Check for accuracy as students independently
complete the page.

Day 4 Writing

Objective
The students will correctly write **homophones** according to sentence usage
in a brochure. They will locate and write content and vocabulary Words.

Introduction
Read the following sentences with mixed-up homophone usage aloud:
- Did you pier over the edge of the ocean peer?
- Many of the patience had to have patients when the electricity went out.

Ask students if the sentences made sense. (**Yes.**) Write the sentences on
the board. Challenge students to silently read each sentence and to locate
the **homophones** in each sentence. Invite volunteers to the board to circle
and identify the mixed-up **homophones** in each sentence. (**pier, peer;
patience, patients**) Correct each sentence by rearranging the mixed-up
homophones. (**peer, pier; patients, patience**)

Directed Instruction
1 Brainstorm sentences using the following **homophones** correctly: tied,
ring, heard, ceiling. Write sentences on the board.

2 Proceed to page 56. Students independently read the sentences at the
top of the page and complete the exercises. Assist as needed.

3 Homework suggestion: Distribute a copy of **BLM SP5-14C Lesson 14
Test Prep** to each student.

Day 5 Posttest

Objective
The students will correctly write dictated spelling words and sentences.

Introduction
Review by using flash cards noted in Student Spelling Support, number 2.

Directed Assessment

1 Dictate the list words by using the Pretest sentences or developing original ones. Reserve *coastline, pier, intertidal, attentive,* and *tide* for the dictation sentences.

2 Read each sentence. Repeat as needed.
- Carol wanted to get a good view of the <u>coastline</u>.
- She visited a tour company on the ocean <u>pier</u>.
- The tour guide pointed out the <u>intertidal</u> zone.
- Carol was <u>attentive</u> to the tour guide.
- Carol watched the <u>tide</u> rise and fall.

3 If assigned, dictate Extra Challenge Words.

4 Score the test, counting each misspelled word as an error. Correct the dictation sentences by grading only the spelling words or grading the complete sentences.

Student Spelling Support
Cont. from page 56

6. Write this week's words, categorize the Pattern, Content, and Vocabulary Words, and attach them to the Word Wall.

7. For visual and auditory learners, distribute six 3" × 5" INDEX CARDS to each student. Students will write a homophone from this lesson on one side of the card and its matching homophone on the other side of the card. For example, write *tide* on one side and *tied* on the other side. Pair students and instruct them to exchange card sets to ensure that each homophone pair was written correctly. Pick one student from the pair to recite a sentence using one of the **homophones**. Each partnered student must listen carefully to the sentence context and show the correct homophone to his or her partner. Students take turns reciting sentences and correctly identifying **homophones**.

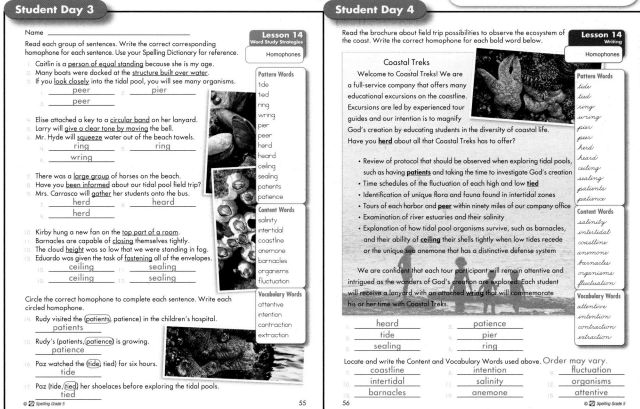

Homographs

Day 1 Pretest

Objective

The students will accurately spell and write words that are **homographs**. They will spell and write content, vocabulary, and challenge words.

Introduction

Before class, select Challenge Words for numbers 24 and 25 from a cross-curricular subject, words misspelled on previous assignments, or words that interest your students. The word *convict* /kən 'vikt/ or /'kon vikt/ is a **homograph** and is suggested for number 24. Administer the Pretest.

Directed Instruction

1 Say each word, use it in a sentence, and then repeat the word.

Pattern Words

1. Our science teacher will <u>address</u> the subject of currents.
2. Is your apartment <u>complex</u> near the shore?
3. Calista's <u>conduct</u> was a reflection of her love for the Lord.
4. The small sailboat was in <u>conflict</u> with the strong current.
5. We used our computer game <u>console</u> to play a DVD about the ocean.
6. The <u>contract</u> for the purchase was signed by both buyer and seller.
7. Mrs. Gonzales will <u>excuse</u> her class from an assignment.
8. Currents <u>increase</u> the nutrients in ocean water.
9. The expired coupon was <u>invalid</u>.
10. Our teacher will <u>produce</u> a map of the Gulf Stream.
11. We will <u>record</u> the science program to view later.
12. The sailor's foot received a <u>wound</u> from a sharp splinter.

Content Words

13. A rip current pulled a swimmer past the <u>continuous</u> line of waves.
14. The moon exerts a <u>gravitational</u> pull on the tides.
15. The course of a current can undergo <u>periodic</u> changes.
16. The swimmer was in close <u>proximity</u> to the shore.
17. A current's direction is caused by the <u>rotation</u> of the earth.
18. We were surprised by the <u>strength</u> of the current.
19. A red sailboat bobbed up and down on the water's <u>surface</u>.

Vocabulary Words

20. Rip currents are <u>invisible</u>, but dangerous to swimmers.
21. Cargo is <u>transportable</u> by ship.
22. Mrs. Milano is <u>transporting</u> the students' science fair projects.
23. Linda can <u>envision</u> herself swimming in an ocean current.

Challenge Words

24. _____
25. _____

2 Allow students to self-correct their Pretest. Write each word on the board. Point out that the Pattern Words in this lesson are **homographs**. *Homographs* are <u>words that are spelled alike but have different meanings</u>. <u>They may also be pronounced differently</u>. The pronunciation of the homograph depends upon the way the word is used in context. Note the roots *port* and *vis* in the Vocabulary Words.

3 As a class, read, spell, and read each word. Direct students to circle misspelled words with a colored pencil and rewrite them correctly.

Student Pages

Pages 57–60

Lesson Materials

BLM SP5-15A
T-10
P-6
P-7
BLM SP5-15B
T-11
BLM SP5-15C
BLM SP5-15D

Created Wonders

The theme of this lesson is currents. Ocean currents are streams of water having their own force and direction within the larger body of water. Sailors and explorers discovered that currents were very useful in navigation. One of the best-known currents is the Gulf Stream, located off the east coast of the United States.

4 Proof each student's Pretest. This becomes an individualized study sheet that can be used at school or at home.

5 Homework suggestion: Distribute a copy of **BLM SP5-15A Lesson 15 Words and Phrases** to each student.

Day 2 Word Analysis and Vocabulary

Objective
The students will correctly write words that are **homographs** below corresponding pronunciations. They will write content words to complete sentences. The students will use a table to write vocabulary words, match given definitions, and to complete sentences.

Introduction
Teacher Note: The Pattern Words for this lesson are all **homographs**. One of each of the **homographs** is illustrated in the Pretest sentences. A homograph for each Pattern Word is shown on **T-10 Homographs**. The Spelling Dictionary lists each homograph as a separate entry word.

Display **T-10 Homographs** to teach the meanings and pronunciations of the Pattern Words. Cover the answers at the bottom of the transparency. Read each sentence and the two pronunciations listed for the underlined word, repeating the pronunciations as needed. Select a volunteer to pronounce and circle the pronunciation that matches the pronunciation of the underlined word, using a transparency pen.

Directed Instruction

1 Referring to the transparency, choose a volunteer to read the pronunciation that was not circled and generate an original sentence. Invite students to check the definition in the Spelling Dictionary as needed. Display **P-6** and **P-7 Homographs**.

2 Proceed to page 57. Say, spell, and say each Pattern, Content, and Vocabulary Word. Provide this week's Challenge Words and have students write them in the spaces provided. Encourage students to look up any unfamiliar Content Words before completing the page.

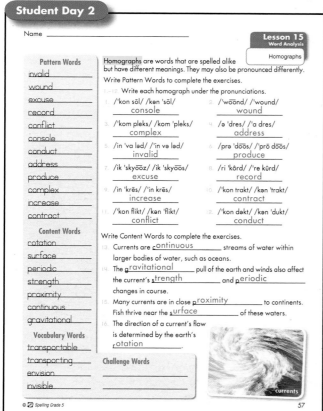

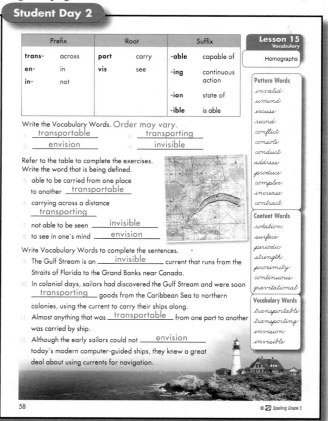

Student Spelling Support

1. Use **BLM SP5-01A A Spelling Study Strategy** in instructional groups to provide assistance with some or all of the words.

2. Duplicate **BLMs SP5-15E–F Lesson 15 Spelling Words I** and **II** on CARD STOCK for students to use as flash cards at school or at home. Another option is to use **BLM SP5-01G Flash Cards Template** or 3" × 5" INDEX CARDS for students to write their own flash cards to use as a study aid.

3. Invite students to write the Challenge Words, numbers 24 and 25, in the Word Bank, in the back of their textbook.

4. For a Bible connection, read James 1:5–6: "If any of you lacks wisdom, let him ask of God ... and it will be given to him. But let him ask in faith, with no doubting, for he who doubts is like a wave of the sea driven and tossed by the wind." Remind students that God is interested in giving us the wisdom we need to make good decisions.

5. Invite students to turn to page 58 and look at the map of the current called the Gulf Stream. This drawing was made by Benjamin Franklin over two hundred years ago. Challenge students to draw a map showing the location and physical features of an interesting place. Invite

Cont. on page 61

3 Proceed to page 58. Encourage students to use the table as an aid in building each Vocabulary Word. For example, the prefix *trans-* goes with the root *port* and the suffix *-ing* to build the word *transporting*. To conclude the lesson, ask students to state additional words that have the roots *port* and *vis*. (**Possible answers: export, portable, provision, visual**) Allow students to complete the page independently.

4 Homework suggestion: Distribute a copy of **BLM SP5-15B Lesson 15 Phrases and Sentences** to each student.

Day 3 Word Study Strategies

Objective

The students will choose the correct meaning for underlined **homographs** according to the context of the sentence. They will choose and write **homographs** to complete sentences and circle the correct pronunciation.

Introduction

Invite students to find the **homographs** *wound, wound, console,* and *console* in their Spelling Dictionary. Remind students to read the definitions for both entries for each homograph silently and study each homograph. Write the following on the board:

• When I fell, I received a <u>wound</u> on my knee. (**entry word number one**)
• Nathan <u>wound</u> the clock before setting the time. (**entry word number two**)
• Andrew will <u>console</u> his friend. (**entry word number two**)
• The computer game <u>console</u> was in need of repair. (**entry word number one**)

Choose volunteers to pronounce each word and to write the number of the entry word that has a definition that matches the way the word is used in each sentence.

Directed Instruction

1 Write the following sentences and pronunciations on the board:
• We can _____ the program and watch it later. /ri 'kôrd/ /'re kûrd/ (**record, /ri 'kôrd/**)
• Our school expects an _____ in enrollment. /in 'krēs/ /'in krēs/ (**increase, /'in krēs/**)

Invite students to turn to page 59 and refer to the list words. Call for volunteers to complete each sentence and circle the pronunciation that matches the homograph they wrote.

2 Proceed to page 59. Allow students to read the directions and complete the page. Select a student to read James 1:5–6 and discuss that believers can ask God for wisdom in making decisions so they are not tossed about.

Day 4 Writing

Objective

The students will use proofreading marks to identify mistakes in a persuasive article. They will correctly write misspelled words.

Introduction

Display **T-11 Proofreading a Persuasive Article** on the overhead, keeping the bottom portion of the transparency covered. Explain that this article is an example of persuasive writing. Read the article and challenge students to state what the author is trying to influence the reader to consider. (**Possible answer: to stay safe from severe storms that follow the Kuroshio Current**) Remind students that the marks in the Proofreading Marks box will be used to identify mistakes found in the article. Slowly read the text aloud and challenge students to raise their hand when they notice an error, and identify each mark that needs to be written in order to correct the text. Correct the identified mistakes using the appropriate proofreading marks. Use **BLM SP5-15C T-11 Answer Key** as a guide. Uncover the bottom of the transparency and choose a volunteer to read the corrected version of the text.

© Spelling Grade 5

Directed Instruction

1 The article in today's lesson is an example of persuasive writing. Remind students that persuasive writing is written to try to persuade the reader to agree with the author's opinion.

2 Proceed to page 60. Allow students to proofread the text, assisting students as needed to make sure that all errors are corrected. (9 misspellings; 2 capital letters needed; 2 periods needed; 2 deletes; 2 add something—*the*, *of*; 2 small letters needed; 1 new paragraph)

3 Homework suggestion: Distribute a copy of **BLM SP5-15D Lesson 15 Test Prep** to each student.

Day 5 Posttest

Objective
The students will correctly write dictated spelling words and sentences.

Introduction
Review by using flash cards noted in Student Spelling Support, number 2.

Directed Assessment

1 Dictate the list words by using the Pretest sentences or developing original ones. Reserve *record*, *increase*, *surface*, *strength*, and *transporting* for the dictation sentences.

2 Read each sentence. Repeat as needed.
- Sailors made maps to <u>record</u> the location of useful currents.
- Knowledge of currents began to <u>increase</u> in the 1500s.
- Sailors found that waters on the <u>surface</u> of the current were warmer.
- They also learned that the <u>strength</u> of the current was changeable.
- Soon ships began <u>transporting</u> cargo around the world.

3 If assigned, dictate Extra Challenge Words.

4 Score the test, counting each misspelled word as an error. Correct the dictation sentences by grading only the spelling words or grading the complete sentences.

Student Spelling Support
Cont. from page 60

students to write a persuasive paragraph encouraging their classmates to visit.

6. Write this week's words, categorize the Pattern, Content, and Vocabulary Words, and attach them to the Word Wall.

7. For a cross-curricular connection, allow students to experiment with generating water currents using wind power. Fill a shallow DISHPAN about one third of the way full with clean water. Provide DRINKING STRAWS to three students at a time and invite them to blow softly across the surface of the water, observing the ripples formed. Change variables such as the distance from the straw to the water, the force with which air is blown, or the direction of the air flow. Challenge students to predict what will happen if any of the variables change.

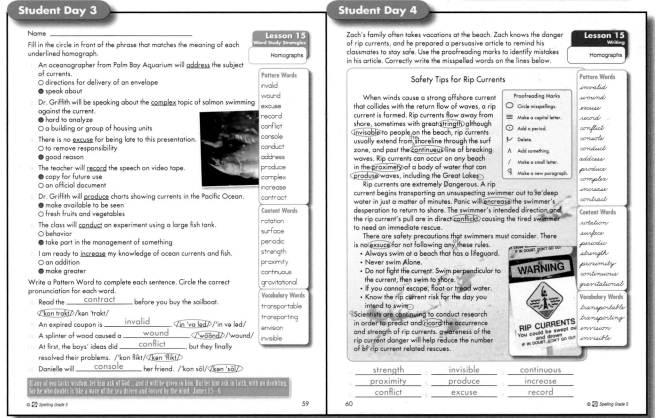

Endings

Lesson Materials

BLM SP5-16A
BLM SP5-16B
T-12
BLM SP5-16C

Created Wonders

The theme of this lesson is coral reefs. Coral reefs are known as "the beautiful gardens of the sea." The beauty of the underwater colonies rivals the most beautiful places on land. The coral reef community is one of the most diverse ecosystems in the world. Fringing reefs, barrier reefs, and atolls are the three types of coral reefs.

Day 1 Pretest

Objective

The students will accurately spell and write words with various **endings**. They will spell and write content, vocabulary, and challenge words.

Introduction

Before class, select Challenge Words for numbers 24 and 25 from a cross-curricular subject, words misspelled on previous assignments, or words that interest your students. The word *preference* has the ending **ence** and is suggested for number 24. Administer the Pretest.

Directed Instruction

1 Say each word, use it in a sentence, and then repeat the word.

Pattern Words
1. Do you know the <u>difference</u> between tree coral and brain coral?
2. Coral is not <u>indestructible</u> since it can be damaged by storms.
3. <u>Sensible</u> scuba divers always dive with a buddy.
4. Diving and exploring a coral reef is a <u>pleasant</u> adventure.
5. Scuba divers wear <u>comfortable</u> wet suits to keep their bodies warm.
6. Divers must be <u>reasonable</u> and not spend long periods underwater.
7. God gave each one of us the <u>intelligence</u> to learn about Him.
8. A <u>convenient</u> way to learn about coral is to read a book.
9. It is <u>important</u> to protect our environment.
10. The Lord wants us to be <u>obedient</u> to His Word.
11. We have <u>deliverance</u> through Jesus Christ from the evil one.
12. The <u>entrance</u> to the dive shop is on the west side of the building.

Content Words
13. Coral reefs are only located in warm, <u>tropical</u> waters.
14. A <u>polyp</u> will float in the water and attach itself to a rock.
15. Corals receive <u>nutrients</u> from the algae that live in them.
16. Polyps produce <u>calcium</u> that helps to form the base of a reef.
17. A <u>barrier</u> reef is like a long wall that is parallel to a coastline.
18. The largest <u>atoll</u> in land area is Christmas Island.
19. A <u>skeletal</u> base provides protection for polyps from predators.

Vocabulary Words
20. Some divers are <u>corrupting</u> reefs by taking pieces of coral.
21. Pollution in the ocean causes a <u>disruption</u> in the reef's ecosystem.
22. Max began to <u>exclaim</u> in order to get everyone's attention.
23. The teacher's <u>proclamation</u> about the field trip excited the class.

Challenge Words
24. _____
25. _____

2 Allow students to self-correct their Pretest. Write each word on the board. Point out that this week's list contains Pattern Words with the **endings** *able, ance, ant, ence, ent, ible*. Note the roots *claim, clam,* and *rupt* in the Vocabulary Words.

3 As a class, read, spell, and read each word. Direct students to circle misspelled words with a colored pencil and rewrite them correctly.

4 Proof each student's Pretest. This becomes an individualized study sheet that can be used at school or at home.

5 Homework suggestion: Distribute a copy of **BLM SP5-16A Lesson 16 Words and Phrases** to each student.

Day 2 Word Analysis and Vocabulary

Objective
The students will sort and write words with **endings** and complete sentences with content words. They will use a table to write vocabulary words, select words to match definitions, and complete sentences in context.

Introduction
Write the following **endings** on the board: able, ance, ant, ence, ent, ible. Invite students to refer to the list words, found on page 61, for this activity. Read each Pattern Word and select a volunteer to state and spell the **ending** of the word.

Directed Instruction

1 Explain that this week's Content Words relate to the theme of coral reefs. Teach about the following kinds of reefs—atoll, barrier, and fringing. An *atoll* is a circular coral reef surrounding a lagoon; a *barrier reef* lies farther out in the ocean, is parallel to the coastline, and has a lagoon that separates the reef from the shore; a *fringing reef* lies close to the coastline and does not have a lagoon between it and the shore. Point out that *atoll* and *barrier* are Content Words.

2 Proceed to page 61. Say, spell, and say each Pattern, Content, and Vocabulary Word. Provide this week's Challenge Words and have students write them in the spaces provided. Instruct students to complete the page.

3 Proceed to page 62. Remind students that each Vocabulary Word contains a root and an affix(es). Build each Vocabulary Word before students complete the page. For example, the prefix *ex-* goes with the root *claim* to get the word *exclaim*. Allow students to independently complete the page. Assist as needed.

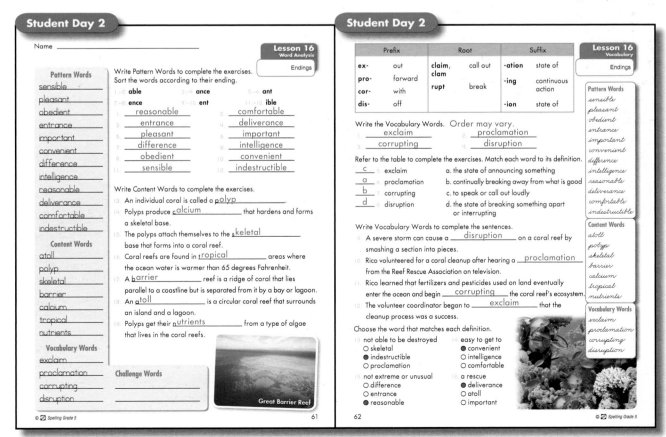

Student Day 2

67 pts.

Name _____

Lesson 16 Word Analysis — Endings

Pattern Words
sensible
pleasant
obedient
entrance
important
convenient
difference
intelligence
reasonable
deliverance
comfortable
indestructible

Content Words
atoll
polyp
skeletal
barrier
calcium
tropical
nutrients

Vocabulary Words
exclaim
proclamation
corrupting
disruption

Write Pattern Words to complete the exercises. Sort the words according to their ending.

1–2 **able**   3–4 **ance**   5–6 **ant**
7–8 **ence**   9–10 **ent**   11–12 **ible**

1. reasonable   2. comfortable
3. entrance   4. deliverance
5. pleasant   6. important
7. difference   8. intelligence
9. obedient   10. convenient
11. sensible   12. indestructible

Write Content Words to complete the exercises.
13. An individual coral is called a polyp _____.
14. Polyps produce calcium _____ that hardens and forms a skeletal base.
15. The polyps attach themselves to the skeletal _____ base that forms into a coral reef.
16. Coral reefs are found in tropical _____ areas where the ocean water is warmer than 65 degrees Fahrenheit.
17. A barrier _____ reef is a ridge of coral that lies parallel to a coastline but is separated from it by a bay or lagoon.
18. An atoll _____ is a circular coral reef that surrounds an island and a lagoon.
19. Polyps get their nutrients _____ from a type of algae that lives in the coral reefs.

Challenge Words

Great Barrier Reef

© Spelling Grade 5   61

Student Day 2

	Prefix		Root		Suffix	
ex-	out	claim, clam	call out	-ation	state of
pro-	forward			-ing	continuous action
cor-	with	rupt	break		
dis-	off			-ion	state of

Lesson 16 Vocabulary — Endings

Write the Vocabulary Words. Order may vary.
1. exclaim   2. proclamation
3. corrupting   4. disruption

Refer to the table to complete the exercises. Match each word to its definition.
c 5. exclaim   a. the state of announcing something
a 6. proclamation   b. continually breaking away from what is good
b 7. corrupting   c. to speak or call out loudly
d 8. disruption   d. the state of breaking something apart or interrupting

Write Vocabulary Words to complete the sentences.
9. A severe storm can cause a disruption _____ on a coral reef by smashing a section into pieces.
10. Rico volunteered for a coral cleanup after hearing a proclamation _____ from the Reef Rescue Association on television.
11. Rico learned that fertilizers and pesticides used on land eventually enter the ocean and begin corrupting _____ the coral reef's ecosystem.
12. The volunteer coordinator began to exclaim _____ that the cleanup process was a success.

Choose the word that matches each definition.
13. not able to be destroyed
○ skeletal
● indestructible
○ proclamation
14. easy to get to
● convenient
○ intelligence
○ comfortable
15. not extreme or unusual
○ difference
○ entrance
● reasonable
16. a rescue
● deliverance
○ atoll
○ important

Pattern Words
sensible
pleasant
obedient
entrance
important
convenient
difference
intelligence
reasonable
deliverance
comfortable
indestructible

Content Words
atoll
polyp
skeletal
barrier
calcium
tropical
nutrients

Vocabulary Words
exclaim
proclamation
corrupting
disruption

62   © Spelling Grade 5

Student Spelling Support Materials

BLM SP5-01A
BLMs SP5-16D–E
Card stock
BLM SP5-01G
3" × 5" Index cards

Student Spelling Support

1. Use **BLM SP5-01A A Spelling Study Strategy** in instructional groups to provide assistance with some or all of the words.

2. Duplicate **BLMs SP5-16D–E Lesson 16 Spelling Words I** and **II** on CARD STOCK for students to use as flash cards at school or at home. Another option is to use **BLM SP5-01G Flash Cards Template** or 3" × 5" INDEX CARDS for students to write their own flash cards to use as a study aid.

3. Invite students to write the Challenge Words, numbers 24 and 25, in the Word Bank, in the back of their textbook.

4. Read Proverbs 16:24: "**Pleasant** words are like a honeycomb, sweetness to the soul and health to the bones." Discuss with the students how kind words are much more beneficial than harsh words, even in times of conflict. Brainstorm a list of **pleasant** words and phrases titled, "Ways to Praise." Write the words and phrases on a poster board and display it in your classroom. Challenge students to refer to the poster when they feel the urge to say words that are unkind and negative, encouraging them to replace their harsh words with kind and pleasant words.

Cont. on page 65

Day 3 Word Study Strategies

Objective

The students will write list words to complete analogies. They will write list words that are related forms of groups of words.

Introduction

Instruct students to refer to the list words on page 63 for today's activities. Write the following incomplete analogies on the board:
- Square is to a box as circle is to an _____. (**atoll**)
- A person is to a citizen as a wall is to a _____. (**barrier**)
- Incomplete is to unfinished as unbreakable is to _____. (**indestructible**)

Read the first analogy and ask a volunteer to state how the words *square* and *box* are related. (**Possible answer: A** *square* **is the shape of a** *box*.) Apply the same relationship to the second part of the analogy by asking students which list word has a circular shape. (**an atoll**) In the next analogy, assist students in understanding the relationship between *person* and *citizen*. (*Person* **and** *citizen* **are synonyms.**) Apply the same relationship to *wall*. (**barrier**) Continue with the third bulleted analogy.

Directed Instruction

1 Write the following related words on the board:
- inconveniences, inconvenient, conveniences, _____ (**convenient**)
- obey, obediently, obedience, _____ (**obedient**)

Read the first group of words and have a volunteer state a list word that is a related form of the given words. Repeat the process for the second group of related words. As a challenge, select volunteers to make their own list of related words for the following:
- cooperate (**Possible answers: cooperates, cooperating, cooperated**)
- possible (**Possible answers: possibility, impossible, impossibility**)

2 Proceed to page 63. Allow students to read the directions and complete the page independently. Select volunteers to read the exercises and provide the answers.

Day 4 Writing

Objective

The students will write list words that are synonyms for given words within the context of an invitation.

Introduction

Display **T-12 Coral Reef** on the overhead. Ask students if they are interested in scuba diving and would like to visit a coral reef someday. Have them describe the things they might see. Ask students why it is critical to be obedient to the directions of a scuba instructor. (**Possible answers: A scuba instructor knows more, including safety issues.**) Brainstorm others to whom it is important for students to be obedient (**Possible answers: God, father, mother, teacher**) and why (**Possible answer: Ephesians 6:1–2 says: "Children, obey your parents in the Lord, for this is right. 'Honor your father and mother,' which is the first commandment with promise."**).

Directed Instruction

1 Explain that today's assignment has to do with synonyms. Remind students that a synonym is a word that means the same or almost the same as another word. Select a volunteer to state a synonym for *hot*. (**Possible answer: tropical**) As a challenge, select volunteers to name several synonyms and write them on the board.

2 Proceed to page 64. Select a student to read the sentences at the top of the page. Allow students to work independently, assisting as needed. When finished, invite a volunteer to read the invitation orally, inserting the synonyms in place of the given words.

3 Homework suggestion: Distribute a copy of **BLM SP5-16C Lesson 16 Test Prep** to each student.

Day 5 Posttest

Objective
The students will correctly write dictated spelling words and sentences.

Introduction
Review by using flash cards noted in Student Spelling Support, number 2.

Directed Assessment

1 Dictate the list words by using the Pretest sentences or developing original ones. Reserve *entrance*, *important*, *atoll*, *tropical*, and *disruption* for the dictation sentences.

2 Read each sentence. Repeat as needed.
- Lee walked through the <u>entrance</u> to the library.
- He had an <u>important</u> science project to do.
- Lee wanted to make a model of an <u>atoll</u>.
- He needed to learn about this type of <u>tropical</u> coral reef.
- Lee was quiet and did not cause a <u>disruption</u> for the librarian.

3 If assigned, dictate Extra Challenge Words.

4 Score the test, counting each misspelled word as an error. Correct the dictation sentences by grading only the spelling words or grading the complete sentences.

Student Spelling Support
Cont. from page 64

5. Challenge students to write several paragraphs about an undersea diving adventure at the Great Barrier Reef near Australia. Have students write about what they would see, touch, hear, taste, and or smell. Encourage students to use several spelling words.

6. Write this week's words, categorize the Pattern, Content, and Vocabulary Words, and attach them to the Word Wall.

7. For visual learners, write the Pattern Words on one set of twelve 3" × 5" INDEX CARDS, omitting the **endings**. On a second set of twelve 3" × 5" INDEX CARDS, write each ending twice—*able*, *ance*, *ant*, *ence*, *ent*, and *ible*. Allow students to match the beginning part of each word to its ending. Students may refer to the list of words in their spelling book to check for accuracy.

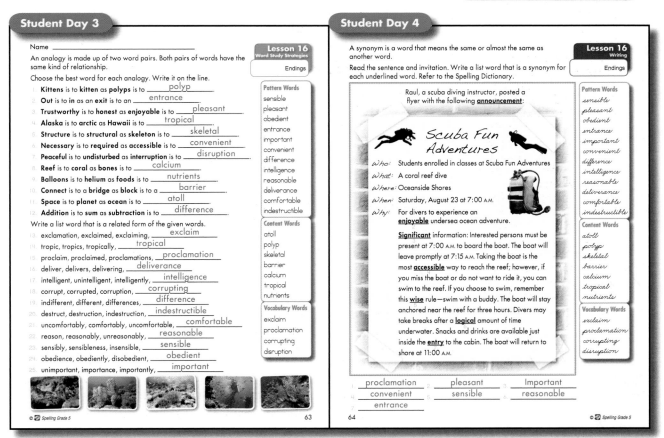

Student Day 3

Name _____

An analogy is made up of two word pairs. Both pairs of words have the same kind of relationship.

Choose the best word for each analogy. Write it on the line.
1. Kittens is to kitten as polyps is to _____ polyp
2. Out is to in as an exit is to an _____ entrance
3. Trustworthy is to honest as enjoyable is to _____ pleasant
4. Alaska is to arctic as Hawaii is to _____ tropical
5. Structure is to structural as skeleton is to _____ skeletal
6. Necessary is to required as accessible is to _____ convenient
7. Peaceful is to undisturbed as interruption is to _____ disruption
8. Reef is to coral as bones is to _____ calcium
9. Balloons is to helium as foods is to _____ nutrients
10. Connect is to a bridge as block is to a _____ barrier
11. Space is to planet as ocean is to _____ atoll
12. Addition is to sum as subtraction is to _____ difference

Write a list word that is a related form of the given words.
13. exclamation, exclaimed, exclaiming, _____ exclaim
14. tropic, tropics, tropically, _____ tropical
15. proclaim, proclaimed, proclamations, _____ proclamation
16. deliver, delivers, delivering, _____ deliverance
17. intelligent, unintelligent, intelligently, _____ intelligence
18. corrupt, corrupted, corruption, _____ corrupting
19. indifferent, different, differences, _____ difference
20. destruct, destruction, indestruction, _____ indestructible
21. uncomfortably, comfortably, uncomfortable, _____ comfortable
22. reason, reasonably, unreasonably, _____ reasonable
23. sensibly, sensibleness, insensible, _____ sensible
24. obedience, obediently, disobedient, _____ obedient
25. unimportant, importance, importantly, _____ important

Lesson 16
Word Study Strategies
Endings

Pattern Words
sensible
pleasant
obedient
entrance
important
convenient
difference
intelligence
reasonable
deliverance
comfortable
indestructible

Content Words
atoll
polyp
skeletal
barrier
calcium
tropical
nutrients

Vocabulary Words
exclaim
proclamation
corrupting
disruption

© Spelling Grade 5   63

Student Day 4

A synonym is a word that means the same or almost the same as another word.

Read the sentence and invitation. Write a list word that is a synonym for each underlined word. Refer to the Spelling Dictionary.

Raul, a scuba diving instructor, posted a flyer with the following **announcement**:

Scuba Fun Adventures

Who: Students enrolled in classes at Scuba Fun Adventures
What: A coral reef dive
Where: Oceanside Shores
When: Saturday, August 23 at 7:00 A.M.
Why: For divers to experience an **enjoyable** undersea ocean adventure.

Significant information: Interested persons must be present at 7:00 A.M. to board the boat. The boat will leave promptly at 7:15 A.M. Taking the boat is the most **accessible** way to reach the reef; however, if you miss the boat or do not want to ride it, you can swim to the reef. If you choose to swim, remember this **wise** rule—swim with a buddy. The boat will stay anchored near the reef for three hours. Divers may take breaks after a **logical** amount of time underwater. Snacks and drinks are available just inside the **entry** to the cabin. The boat will return to shore at 11:00 A.M.

1. proclamation   2. pleasant   3. Important
4. convenient   5. sensible   6. reasonable
7. entrance

Lesson 16
Writing
Endings

Pattern Words
sensible
pleasant
obedient
entrance
important
convenient
difference
intelligence
reasonable
deliverance
comfortable
indestructible

Content Words
atoll
polyp
skeletal
barrier
calcium
tropical
nutrients

Vocabulary Words
exclaim
proclamation
corrupting
disruption

64   © Spelling Grade 5

Student Pages

Pages 65–68

Lesson Materials

BLM SP5-17A
BLM SP5-17B
Newspaper
BLM SP5-17C

Created Wonders

The theme of this lesson is trenches. Trenches are deep, narrow, underwater depressions that are formed by the subduction of a tectonic plate. The Mariana Trench in the Pacific Ocean near the Mariana Islands contains the deepest point on Earth, the Challenger Deep, which is estimated to be 36,198 feet deep.

Day 1 Pretest

Objective

The students will accurately spell and write words with various **endings**. They will spell and write content, vocabulary, and challenge words.

Introduction

Before class, select Challenge Words for numbers 24 and 25 from a cross-curricular subject, words misspelled on previous assignments, or words that interest your students. The word *conscious* has the ending **cious** and is suggested for number 24. Administer the Pretest.

Directed Instruction

1 Say each word, use it in a sentence, and then repeat the word.

Pattern Words

1. <u>Commercial</u> fishing boats often use sonar to detect schools of fish.
2. Jesus showed His <u>compassion</u> by dying on the cross for sinners.
3. Two divers engaged in <u>conversation</u> before exploring the trench.
4. The oceanographers reached a <u>decision</u> about where to dive.
5. The fresh tuna was <u>delicious</u>.
6. The encyclopedia contains a <u>description</u> of how trenches are formed.
7. The oceanographer had a <u>partial</u> list of the fish he wished to study.
8. The <u>physician</u> checked the patient's pulse before allowing her to dive.
9. Our governor has been a life-long <u>politician</u>.
10. Natural pearls are <u>precious</u> gems.
11. Mr. and Mrs. Garcia met at a <u>social</u> function.
12. The crew received <u>substantial</u> information about the ocean floor.

Content Words

13. Trenches are deep, narrow, underwater <u>depressions</u>.
14. Trenches extend into the <u>lithosphere</u>.
15. The <u>Mariana</u> Trench is the deepest seafloor trench in the world.
16. The <u>Pacific</u> Ocean is home to many species of fish.
17. Trenches are formed by the <u>subduction</u> of tectonic plates.
18. Daron consulted a <u>topographic</u> map of the ocean floor before diving.
19. <u>Undersea</u> exploration is advancing our knowledge of trenches.

Vocabulary Words

20. Shallow Caribbean waters may be <u>aquamarine</u> in color.
21. The divers will <u>circumscribe</u> an area on the map for today's dive.
22. The <u>submarine</u> explored the deep trench.
23. Can you <u>describe</u> what you saw while exploring the trench?

Challenge Words

24. _____
25. _____

2 Allow students to self-correct their Pretest. Write each word on the board. Point out the following Pattern Word **endings**: cial, cian, cious, sion, tial, tion. Explain that the letters *ci*, *si*, and *ti* have either the /sh/ or the /zh/ sound in the **endings** in this lesson. The words *Pacific* and *Mariana* are proper adjectives and are capitalized. Note the roots *aqua*, *mar*, *circum*, and *scrib* in the Vocabulary Words. Words may have more than one root as in *aquamarine* and *circumscribe*.

3 As a class, read, spell, and read each word. Direct students to circle misspelled words with a colored pencil and rewrite them correctly.

4 Proof each student's Pretest. This becomes an individualized study sheet that can be used at school or at home.

5 Homework suggestion: Distribute a copy of **BLM SP5-17A Lesson 17 Words and Phrases** to each student.

Day 2 Word Analysis and Vocabulary

Objective

The students will sort and write words with **endings**. They will complete sentences with content words. They will use a table to write vocabulary words, match definitions, and complete sentences. Students will choose the best meaning for underlined words.

Introduction

Write the following **endings** on the board: cial, cian, cious, sion, tial, tion. Choose a volunteer to pronounce each ending. Remind students that the letters *ci, si,* and *ti* have either the /sh/ or the /zh/ sound in the **endings** in this lesson. Invite students to turn to the list words, found on page 65, and identify the words that have each ending. (**cial—social, commercial; cian—politician, physician; cious—delicious, precious; sion—decision, compassion; tial—partial, substantial; tion—description, conversation**)

Directed Instruction

1 Inform students that the theme of this lesson is trenches. Define *trenches* as *undersea depressions that form where two tectonic plates collide, and one plate is pushed below the other in the process of subduction.* Point out the following to clarify the Content Words:

- The *lithosphere* is the solid part of the earth consisting of the crust and the upper mantle. The lithosphere consists of a number of plates that move independently over the mantle of the earth.
- *Subduction* occurs when two oceanic plates or an oceanic plate and a continental plate collide, forcing one plate to slide beneath the other. A trench is formed at the lowest point.

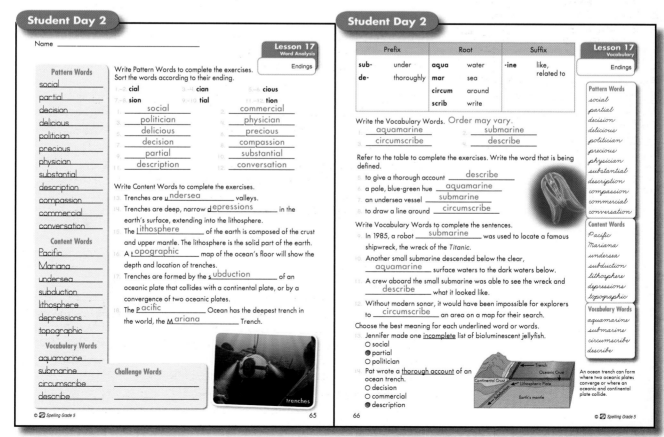

Student Day 2

60 pts.

Name _____

Lesson 17
Word Analysis
Endings

Pattern Words
social
partial
decision
delicious
politician
precious
physician
substantial
description
compassion
commercial
conversation

Content Words
Pacific
Mariana
undersea
subduction
lithosphere
depressions
topographic

Vocabulary Words
aquamarine
submarine
circumscribe
describe

Write Pattern Words to complete the exercises. Sort the words according to their ending.

| 1–2 **cial** | 3–4 **cian** | 5–6 **cious** |
| 7–8 **sion** | 9–10 **tial** | 11–12 **tion** |

1. social
2. commercial
3. politician
4. physician
5. delicious
6. precious
7. decision
8. compassion
9. partial
10. substantial
11. description
12. conversation

Write Content Words to complete the exercises.
13. Trenches are undersea valleys.
14. Trenches are deep, narrow depressions in the earth's surface, extending into the lithosphere.
15. The lithosphere of the earth is composed of the crust and upper mantle. The lithosphere is the solid part of the earth.
16. A topographic map of the ocean's floor will show the depth and location of trenches.
17. Trenches are formed by the subduction of an oceanic plate that collides with a continental plate, or by a convergence of two oceanic plates.
18. The Pacific Ocean has the deepest trench in the world, the Mariana Trench.

Challenge Words
_____
_____

trenches

© Spelling Grade 5   65

Student Day 2

	Prefix		Root		Suffix
sub-	under	aqua	water	-ine	like, related to
de-	thoroughly	mar	sea		
		circum	around		
		scrib	write		

Lesson 17
Vocabulary
Endings

Write the Vocabulary Words. Order may vary.
1. aquamarine
2. submarine
3. circumscribe
4. describe

Refer to the table to complete the exercises. Write the word that is being defined.
5. to give a thorough account — describe
6. a pale, blue-green hue — aquamarine
7. an undersea vessel — submarine
8. to draw a line around — circumscribe

Write Vocabulary Words to complete the sentences.
9. In 1985, a robot submarine was used to locate a famous shipwreck, the wreck of the *Titanic*.
10. Another small submarine descended below the clear, aquamarine surface waters to the dark waters below.
11. A crew aboard the small submarine was able to see the wreck and describe what it looked like.
12. Without modern sonar, it would have been impossible for explorers to circumscribe an area on a map for their search.

Choose the best meaning for each underlined word or words.
13. Jennifer made one incomplete list of bioluminescent jellyfish.
○ social
● partial
○ politician
14. Pat wrote a thorough account of an ocean trench.
○ decision
○ commercial
○ description

Pattern Words
social
partial
decision
delicious
politician
precious
physician
substantial
description
compassion
commercial
conversation

Content Words
Pacific
Mariana
undersea
subduction
lithosphere
depressions
topographic

Vocabulary Words
aquamarine
submarine
circumscribe
describe

An ocean trench can form where two oceanic plates converge or where an oceanic and continental plate collide.

Trench
Oceanic Crust
Continental Crust
Lithospheric Plate
Subduction
Earth's mantle

66   © Spelling Grade 5

Student Spelling Support Materials

BLM SP5-01A
BLMs SP5-17D–E
Card stock
BLM SP5-01G
3" × 5" Index cards

Student Spelling Support

1. Use **BLM SP5-01A A Spelling Study Strategy** in instructional groups to provide assistance with some or all of the words.

2. Duplicate **BLMs SP5-17D–E Lesson 17 Spelling Words I** and **II** on CARD STOCK for students to use as flash cards at school or at home. Another option is to use **BLM SP5-01G Flash Cards Template** or 3" × 5" INDEX CARDS for students to write their own flash cards to use as a study aid.

3. Invite students to write the Challenge Words, numbers 24 and 25, in the Word Bank, in the back of their textbook.

4. Read Psalm 135:6: "Whatever the LORD pleases He does, in heaven and in earth, in the seas and in all deep places." Psalm 135 tells of the great and awesome power of God. Remind students that God is not only all-powerful, but that He is always present. Even if we journey to the very deepest part of the sea, God is there!

5. Challenge students to write a fictional account of an undersea journey into a deep ocean trench. Have students include details such as the color of the water, bioluminescent marine life, or the depth to which they dive. Ask students to use several list words in their fictional account.

Cont. on page 69

2 Proceed to page 65. Say, spell, and say each Pattern, Content, and Vocabulary Word. Provide this week's Challenge Words and have students write them in the spaces provided. Students independently complete the page. Assist as needed.

3 Proceed to page 66. Select students to build each Vocabulary Word. For example, the prefix *sub-* goes with the root *mar* and the suffix *-ine* to build the word *submarine*. *Aquamarine* has two roots, *aqua* and *mar*. *Circumscribe* also has two roots, *circum* and *scrib*. Silent *e* is not in the original root spelling of *scrib*. Provide assistance as the page is independently completed.

4 Homework suggestion: Distribute a copy of **BLM SP5-17B Lesson 17 Phrases and Sentences** to each student.

Day 3 Word Study Strategies
Objective
The students will write list words that are related forms of given words. They will use given pronunciations and sentence context to complete sentences with list words.

Introduction
Before class, write the following on the board:
- society, sociable, _____ (<u>soci</u>al)
- aquatic, aquarium, _____ (<u>aqua</u>marine)
- delicacy, delicatessen, _____ (<u>delic</u>ious)
- substantially, substantiality, _____ (<u>sub</u>stantial)

Inform students that the words listed are related forms of list words. Invite students to reference the list words, found on page 67, to select related words. Select volunteers to underline the portion of each given word that helped them to determine which list word to choose as the related form.

Directed Instruction
1 Write the following pronunciations on the board and select volunteers to write the matching list word:
- /'pre shəs/ (**precious**)
- /kə 'mûr shəl/ (**commercial**)
- /po lə 'ti shən/ (**politician**)
- /'sō shəl/ (**social**)

Invite students to check their responses by using the pronunciations shown in their Spelling Dictionary.

2 Proceed to page 67. Allow students to complete exercises 1–9 on their own. Choose students to read sentences 10–18, substituting the correct list word for each pronunciation. Ask a volunteer to read Psalm 135:6 and discuss the power of God over all creation.

Day 4 Writing
Objective
The students will read an advertisement for oceanographers. They will write list words that could replace the bold words in the advertisement.

Introduction
Display an advertisement for an open job from your local NEWSPAPER. Read the advertisement aloud. Ask students to list the requirements for someone seeking the job and what a job seeker should do if he or she wishes to apply for the position.

Directed Instruction
1 Explain that the activity in today's lesson involves an advertisement for *oceanographers*. Define *oceanographer* as *a scientist who is involved in the study of the ocean, including its physical, chemical, and biological aspects.* Discuss things that oceanographers do in their line of work. (**Possible answers: sample ocean water, examine marine life, study the topography of the ocean floor**) Brainstorm a list

© Spelling Grade 5

of requirements that an oceanographer needs to meet to be able to be employed. (**Possible answers: have a college degree, be able to work underwater, be familiar with equipment for diving**)

2 Proceed to page 68. Encourage students to read the entire advertisement before listing words that have the same meaning as the bold words in the text. When complete, have a volunteer read the advertisement, replacing the bold words with list words.

3 Homework suggestion: Distribute a copy of **BLM SP5-17C Lesson 17 Test Prep** to each student.

Day 5 Posttest

Objective
The students will correctly write dictated spelling words and sentences.

Introduction
Review by using flash cards noted in Student Spelling Support, number 2.

Directed Assessment

1 Dictate the list words by using the Pretest sentences or developing original ones. Reserve *decision, description, undersea, depressions,* and *describe* for the dictation sentences.

2 Read each sentence. Repeat as needed.
- Jill prayed before making a <u>decision</u> to become a scientist.
- Her first job would be to write a <u>description</u> of an underwater trench.
- Jill was greatly interested in <u>undersea</u> trenches.
- Trenches and other <u>depressions</u> contain interesting fish and animals.
- Jill was able to <u>describe</u> fish that live in total darkness.

3 If assigned, dictate Extra Challenge Words.

4 Score the test, counting each misspelled word as an error. Correct the dictation sentences by grading only the spelling words or grading the complete sentences.

Student Spelling Support
Cont. from page 68

6. Write this week's words, categorize the Pattern, Content, and Vocabulary Words, and attach them to the Word Wall.

7. To assist kinesthetic and visual learners, duplicate **BLMs SP5-17D–E Lesson 17 Spelling Words I** and **II** on CARD STOCK and cut the **endings** cial, cian, cious, sion, tial, and tion from the Pattern Words, using scissors. Mix up the **endings** and invite students to reconnect each ending with its beginning to make a Pattern Word. Have students tape the words together and write the words on the back of the flash cards when complete.

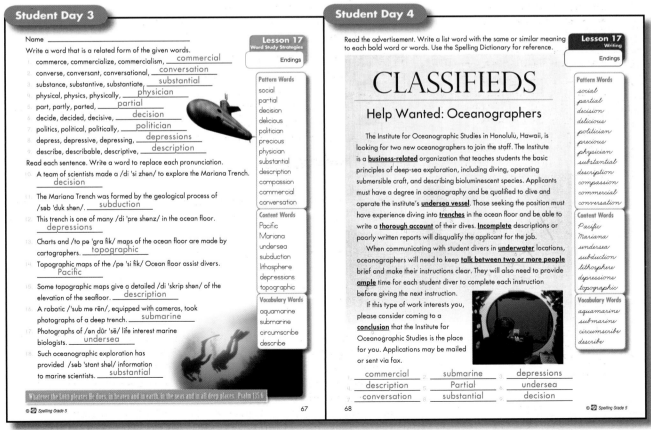

Lesson 18 Review Lessons 13–17

Student Pages
Pages 69–72

Lesson Materials

T-13
BLM SP5-18A
BLM SP5-18B
T-14
BLM SP5-18C
3" × 5" Index cards
BLM SP5-18D
BLMs SP5-18E–F
BLM SP5-06G
BLM SP5-18G

Day 1 Homophones

Objective

The students will spell, identify, and sort **homophones** according to the number of syllables. They will complete sentences with the correct homophone.

Introduction

Teacher Note: This week's lesson incorporates the Pattern, Content, and Vocabulary Words taught in Lessons 13–17 using a variety of activities such as sorting, a word search, shape boxes, decoding words, filling in the correct answer circle, unscrambling words, and filling in missing affixes or roots.

Display **T-13 Lessons 13–17 Study Sheet** on the overhead to review Lesson 13 words in unison using the say-spell-say technique. Remind students that **homophones** are words that sound the same but have different meanings and spellings. Challenge students to identify the difference in spellings for each homophone pair in Lesson 13.

Directed Instruction

1 Invite volunteers to identify and circle the one-syllable and two-syllable homophone pairs. Use two different colors of transparency pens for this activity.

2 Proceed to page 69. Explain that the box contains all the Pattern, Content, and Vocabulary Words in Lessons 13–17. This list is the same list of words that was previously displayed on the overhead. Encourage students to use this list as a review tool. Instruct students to read the directions and independently complete the page.

3 Distribute a copy of **BLM SP5-18A Lessons 13–17 Study Sheet** to each student to take home for study.

4 Homework suggestion: Distribute a copy of **BLM SP5-18B Lesson 18 Homework I** to each student to practice with **homophones**, **homographs**, and words with different **endings**.

Day 2 Homophones and Homographs

Objective

The students will find and circle **homophones** in a word search. They will write **homographs** in shape boxes that are shaded in to indicate the accented syllables.

Introduction

Write the following Pattern Words from Lesson 14 on the board: tied, ring, peer, heard, ceiling. Select a volunteer to make a mini word search on **T-14 Mini Word Search Grid**, using the words on the board. Assist the volunteer in positioning the words across, down, diagonally, and backwards. Fill in each remaining square on the grid with a letter. When complete, display the transparency on the overhead and challenge students to find the Pattern Words from the board. An example mini word search is shown.

Directed Instruction

1 Display **T-13 Lessons 13–17 Study Sheet** to review Lessons 14–15 words in unison, using the say-spell-say technique.

© Spelling Grade 5

2 Invite a volunteer to the board to write the homograph *contract* on the board two times. Remind students that **homographs** are words that are spelled alike but have different meanings. They may also be pronounced differently. Select another volunteer to draw a shape box around each letter—c|o|n|t|r|a|c|t, c|o|n|t|r|a|c|t. Ask students to pronounce *contract* two different ways by accenting the first or second syllable. Lightly shade in the boxes that represent the accented syllable in each pronunciation. Provide the two definitions of *contract*. (c|o|n|t|r|a|c|t—**a written agreement**, c|o|n|t|r|a|c|t—**to become less in size**)

3 Proceed to page 70. Invite students to read the directions silently and complete the page individually. When complete, select volunteers to correctly read the **homographs** at the bottom of the page by accenting the first or second syllable.

4 Homework suggestion: Distribute a copy of **BLM SP5-18C Lesson 18 Homework II** to each student to practice words with different **endings**, Content Words, and Vocabulary Words.

Day 3 Endings

Objective
The students will use a code to spell and write words with different **endings**. They will select the appropriate answer circle to indicate if words with different **endings** are spelled correctly or incorrectly, and correctly write each word.

Introduction
Write the following incomplete words on the board:
- obedi_____ (**obedient**)
- entr_____ (**entrance**)
- import_____ (**important**)
- differ_____ (**difference**)
- comfort_____ (**comfortable**)
- indestruct_____ (**indestructible**)

Review the following **endings** from Lesson 16 by writing them on the board: able, ance, ant, ence, ent, ible. Invite volunteers to complete each word by writing in the correct missing ending in each word as you dictate the following: obedient, entrance, important, difference, comfortable, indestructible.

Directed Instruction
1 Display **T-13 Lessons 13–17 Study Sheet** to review Lessons 16–17 words in unison, using the say-spell-say technique.

2 Select three volunteers to come to the board and write the following:
- s o s h u l (**incorrect; social**)
- d i s i s i o n (**incorrect; decision**)
- c o n v e r s a t i o n (**correct; conversation**)

Dictate each word and invite students to identify whether each dictated word was spelled correctly or incorrectly. Instruct the three volunteers to

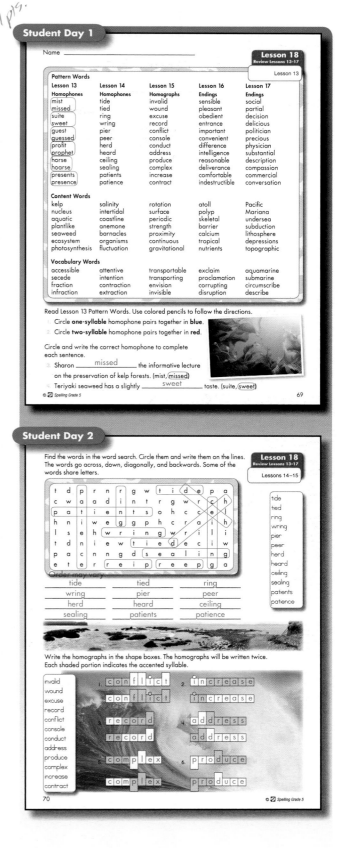

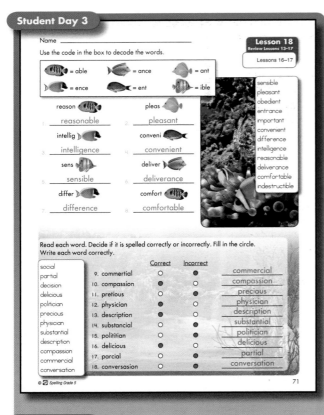

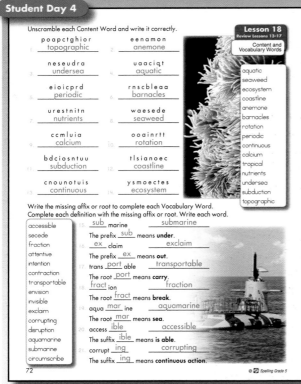

correct the spelling of their word or leave it as is.

3 Proceed to page 71. Students complete the page independently. Assist as needed.

Day 4 Content Words and Vocabulary Words

Objective

The students will unscramble and write content words. They will write missing affixes or roots and write vocabulary words.

Introduction

Display **T-13 Lessons 13–17 Study Sheet** to review Content Words in unison, using the say-spell-say technique. Write the following Content Words on 3" × 5" INDEX CARDS and pass them out to five volunteers: nucleus, intertidal, proximity, tropical, lithosphere. Invite the volunteers to come to the board and have them scramble and write their word on the board. Challenge students to unscramble the Content Words. When correctly identified, have each volunteer correctly write his or her word next to the scrambled word.

Directed Instruction

1 Continue to refer to **T-13 Lessons 13–17 Study Sheet** to review Vocabulary Words in unison, using the say-spell-say technique. Select volunteers to circle the following affixes or roots in the Vocabulary Words as you dictate them: ac, in, fract, vis, able, ation. (**ac**—accessible; **in**—infraction, intention, invisible; **fract**—fraction, infraction; **vis**—envision, invisible; **able**—transportable; **ation**—proclamation)

2 Review the following meanings for the dictated affixes and roots:
- *ac* means *to*
- *fract* means *break*
- *able* means *capable of*
- *in* means *in* or *not*
- *vis* means *see*
- *ation* means *state of*

3 Proceed to page 72. Students independently complete the page. When complete, select volunteers to read exercises 15–21 aloud to reinforce the definitions of affixes and roots.

4 Homework suggestion: Distribute a copy of **BLM SP5-18D Lessons 13–17 Test Prep** to each student to practice with many of the words that may appear on the Assessment. Prepare for the Assessment by studying the words on **BLM SP5-18A Lessons 13–17 Study Sheet** that was sent home on Day 1.

Day 5 Assessment

Objective

The students will accurately select the appropriate answer within the context of a sentence. They will fill in the corresponding answer circle.

Introduction

Teacher Note: The Test makes provision for Differentiated Instruction. The first twelve sentences include the words assigned to students with shortened lists. Encourage these students to try all the sentences, but only grade the first twelve sentences. The Test is found on two blackline masters.

Duplicate a copy of **BLMs SP5-18E–F Lessons 13–17 Test I** and **II** and distribute to each student. Duplicate **BLM SP5-06G Student Answer Form** and cut apart. Distribute one answer form to each student. Remind students to fill in each answer circle completely and to erase completely if they wish to change an answer.

Directed Assessment

1 Instruct students to listen as you dictate the following Sample:
Sample
      Tameka was <u>atentive</u> as she watched the <u>tide</u> from the <u>pier</u>. <u>All correct</u>
                A   B   C   D
Say, "Are any of the first three underlined words misspelled?" Pause for replies. Inform students that the letter *A* is below the underlined word that is misspelled. (**attentive**) Guide students to the answer form that was previously distributed. Lead students to find the Sample box and fill in the appropriate answer circle containing the same letter. Say, "You will continue in the same way. You will read each sentence, choose the word that you think is misspelled, and fill in the corresponding circle on the answer form. If all the words are spelled correctly, fill in the fourth circle, labeled *D*, for *All correct*."

2 Assist students as needed while they read the sentences and complete the Test on their own.
  1. The palomino horse was sweet and obedient.
  2. Have you heard about the organisms in the intertidal zone?
  3. Kelp is an important part of an ocean's ecosystem.
  4. Does this road have an accessible entrance to the coastline?
  5. The topographic map showed numerous undersea depressions.
  6. Aquamarine water surrounded the tropical island's atoll.
  7. Can you describe the color of the plantlike anemone?
  8. Please give a partial description of the lithosphere in your report.
  9. We will record the periodic movement of continuous currents.
10. The jeweler is transporting a substantial number of precious jewels.
11. Floyd made the sensible decision to have patience during the chaos.
12. The comfortable guest was engaged in a lively conversation.
13. An invalid address was printed on the new contract.
14. The pleasant physician visited her sick patients.
15. Hal missed the speech on the gravitational pull and fluctuation of tides.
16. The submarine was bound for the Mariana Trench in the Pacific Ocean.
17. Commercial harvesting of seaweed brings in a large profit.
18. Calcium is one of the essential nutrients for a healthy skeletal system.
19. Rhonda had compassion on her peer Leila and chose to console her.
20. The presence of photosynthesis is rampant in aquatic regions.
21. A politician should possess intelligence and proficient social skills.
22. Gil has the intention of buying delicious produce at the local market.
23. The surface of the indestructible barrier was made of a new material.
24. Lavonne wound and tied ribbon around the birthday presents.
25. Stefan will conduct a complex experiment on water salinity.

3 Refer to **BLM SP5-18G Lessons 13–17 Answer Key** when correcting the Test.

VCCV and VCCCV Spelling Patterns

Student Pages

Pages 73–76

Lesson Materials

BLM SP5-19A
3" × 5" Index cards
BLM SP5-19B
BLM SP5-19C

Created Wonders

Lessons 19–23 utilize the theme of living things. Lesson 19 begins with people. Our glorious Creator made us and created our bodies to function in specific and remarkable ways. Each of our senses, organs, muscles, and bones are unique attributes of how the Lord carefully crafted us. Psalm 139:14 reads, "I will praise You, for I am fearfully and wonderfully made." The Lord has uniquely designed us, and we should praise Him continually!

Day 1 Pretest

Objective

The students will accurately spell and write words with **VCCV and VCCCV spelling patterns**. They will spell and write content, vocabulary, and challenge words.

Introduction

Before class, select Challenge Words for numbers 24 and 25 from a cross-curricular subject, words misspelled on previous assignments, or words that interest your students. The word *suggestion* has the **VCCV pattern** and is suggested for number 24. Administer the Pretest.

Directed Instruction

1 Say each word, use it in a sentence, and then repeat the word.

Pattern Words
1. *Loving* is an <u>adjective</u> that perfectly describes Jae's personality.
2. Scratching a mosquito bite will <u>aggravate</u> it.
3. The <u>apostrophe</u> in the word *wouldn't* replaces the letter *o* in *not*.
4. Annie exercises six times a week and is a serious <u>athlete</u>.
5. Porter will <u>attempt</u> to run a marathon next year.
6. Mr. Agustin will <u>congratulate</u> his students after their chapel skit.
7. Philippians 4:8 exhorts us to <u>entertain</u> thoughts that are pure.
8. Ling-Mei has <u>freckles</u> on her cheeks and nose.
9. What kind of <u>journey</u> will God lead you on?
10. Oliver visited the <u>orchard</u> and picked a basket of peaches.
11. The cardiologist studied a medical <u>sculpture</u> of a human heart.
12. The arm at the <u>shoulder</u> is a freely movable joint.

Content Words
13. <u>Anatomy</u> is a basic area of study for doctors during medical school.
14. <u>Circulation</u> is a function of the cardiovascular system in a body.
15. Trent stretched his leg <u>muscles</u> before the track-and-field meet.
16. Shawn became a pathologist to study diseased <u>organs</u>.
17. Doctors should be familiar with the <u>physical</u> structure of the body.
18. <u>Senses</u> enable people to experience the world around them.
19. The bones in a human <u>skeleton</u> are connected by ligaments.

Vocabulary Words
20. The surgeon will examine the X-rays for <u>fusion</u> of the broken bones.
21. Reiko received a fluid <u>transfusion</u> during her hospital stay.
22. Bret eventually <u>resigned</u> that the weather was not going to clear up.
23. Nala displayed no signs of <u>resignation</u> when asked to combine teams.

Challenge Words
24. _____
25. _____

2 Allow students to self-correct their Pretest. Write each word on the board. Point out the following spelling patterns in the Pattern Words: VCCV (vowel-consonant|consonant-vowel as in <u>a|tt|e</u>mpt), VCCCV vowel-consonant|consonant-consonant-vowel as in <u>o|rch|a</u>rd). Note the roots *fus* and *sign* in the Vocabulary Words.

3 As a class, read, spell, and read each word. Direct students to circle misspelled words with a colored pencil and rewrite them correctly.

4 Proof each student's Pretest. This becomes an individualized study sheet that can be used at school or at home.

5 Homework suggestion: Distribute a copy of **BLM SP5-19A Lesson 19 Words and Phrases** to each student.

Day 2 Word Analysis and Vocabulary

Objective
The students will sort and write words with **VCCV and VCCCV spelling patterns**. They will complete sentences with content words, use a table to write vocabulary words, and complete sentences.

Introduction
Write the spelling pattern VCCV on one side and VCCCV on the other side of 3" × 5" INDEX CARDS. Use a black marker for each *V* and a red marker for each *C*. Pass out a card to each student. Write the following words on the board:
- journey (**VCCV**) • orchard (**VCCCV**) • attempt (**VCCV**)
- freckles (**VCCCV**) • sculpture (**VCCCV**) • athlete (**VCCCV**)

Read each word aloud. Have students raise the appropriate card side that identifies the spelling pattern in each word.

Directed Instruction

1 Point out that *entertain* and *adjective* each have more than one VCCV spelling pattern. Note that *apostrophe* contains both a VCCCV and VCCV spelling pattern.

2 Challenge students to identify words from previous lessons—possibly from the Word Wall—that follow the **VCCV and VCCCV spelling patterns**. (**Possible answers: barrier, describe**)

3 Proceed to page 73. Say, spell, and say each Pattern, Content, and Vocabulary Word. Provide this week's Challenge Words and have students write them in the spaces provided. Students independently complete the page. Select volunteers to read exercises 13–19 when complete.

4 Proceed to page 74. Select students to build each Vocabulary Word. For example, the prefix *trans-* goes with the root *fus* and the

---

Student Day 2

Name _____

Lesson 19
Word Analysis
VCCV and VCCCV Spelling Patterns

63 pts.

Pattern Words
athlete
journey
freckles
attempt
orchard
shoulder
entertain
adjective
sculpture
aggravate
apostrophe
congratulate

Content Words
senses
organs
physical
muscles
skeleton
anatomy
circulation

Vocabulary Words
fusion
transfusion
resignation
resigned

Write Pattern Words to complete the exercises.
Sort the words with VCCV and VCCCV spelling patterns.

1. Both VCCCV and VCCV spelling patterns

2–6 VCCV spelling pattern only   7–12 VCCCV spelling pattern only
1. apostrophe   2. journey
3. attempt   4. shoulder
5. entertain   6. adjective
7. athlete   8. freckles
9. orchard   10. sculpture
11. aggravate   12. congratulate

Write Content Words to complete the exercises.
13. The unique physical structure of people was designed by God, and we are made in His image.
14. The five senses that God gave to us are hearing, sight, smell, taste, and touch.
15. The human skeleton of an infant contains over 300 bones.
16. Medical doctors must study anatomy to familiarize themselves with the structure of the human body.
17. God created the organs in our bodies, such as the heart and liver, to perform specific functions.
18. God designed muscles to move the bones, line the organs, and pump the heart.
19. The heart, blood, and blood vessels all make up the cardiovascular system, which transports materials throughout the body by the process of circulation.

Challenge Words
_____
_____
_____

people

© *Spelling Grade 5*   73

Student Day 2

74

Lesson 19
Vocabulary
VCCV and VCCCV Spelling Patterns

Prefix		Root		Suffix	
trans-	across	fus	melt, pour	-ion	state of
re-	against	sign	sign	-ation	state of
				-ed	makes verbs past tense

Write the Vocabulary Words. Order may vary.
1. fusion   2. transfusion
3. resignation   4. resigned

Refer to the table to complete the exercises. Write the word that is being defined.
5. to have shown signs of accepting something reluctantly resigned
6. a state or process of transferring fluid into a vein or artery transfusion
7. a state of accepting something reluctantly against your desired position resignation
8. a state of putting or melting together fusion

Write Vocabulary Words to complete the sentences.
9. Jacqueline did not have a single resignation when she felt the Lord leading her to become a doctor.
10. Even though Jacqueline studied diligently, she eventually resigned herself to the fact that no amount of studying would enable her to learn everything at once.
11. One thing Jacqueline learned was that the transfusion of fluids during surgical procedures was very important.
12. The natural fusion of broken bones intrigued Jacqueline so she decided to become an orthopedist, a bone doctor.

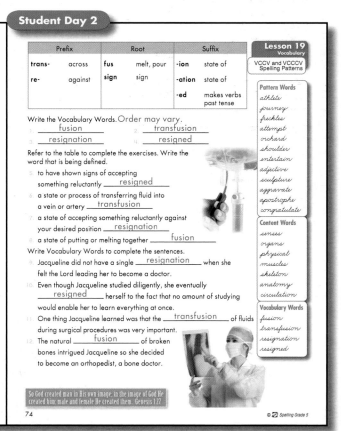

Pattern Words
athlete
journey
freckles
attempt
orchard
shoulder
entertain
adjective
sculpture
aggravate
apostrophe
congratulate

Content Words
senses
organs
physical
muscles
skeleton
anatomy
circulation

Vocabulary Words
fusion
transfusion
resignation
resigned

So God created man in His own image, in the image of God He created him: male and female He created them. Genesis 1:27

© *Spelling Grade 5*

Cont. on page 77

suffix *-ion* to get the word *transfusion*. Provide assistance as the page is independently completed. Chorally read exercises 9–12 when complete. Select a volunteer to read Genesis 1:27 and discuss that every person has been created in the image of God.

5 Homework suggestion: Distribute a copy of **BLM SP5-19B Phrases and Sentences** to each student.

Day 3 Word Study Strategies

Objective
The students will divide words with **VCCV and VCCCV spelling patterns**. They will alphabetize list words.

Introduction
Write the following words on the board: shoulder, adjective, attempt. Read the following aloud: Divide VCCV words into syllables between consonants. Each syllable should contain a vowel sound. Select volunteers to come to the board to syllabicate the VCCV words. (shoul|der, ad|jec|tive, at|tempt)
     vc|cv   vc|cvc|cv   vc|cv

Directed Instruction
1 Read the following definitions aloud:
- A *consonant blend* is <u>a group of two or three consecutive consonants in a syllable where each consonant sound is heard</u>.
- A *consonant digraph* is <u>a group of two consecutive consonants in a syllable that stands for a single sound</u>.

Write the following words on the board and select volunteers to identify the consonant blend or consonant digraph in each word:
- aggravate (**consonant blend *gr***)
- athlete (**consonant digraph *th***)
- congratulate (**consonant blend *gr***)
- apostrophe (**consonant blend *str***)
- orchard (**consonant digraph *ch***)

Remind students of the following: Divide VCCCV words into syllables between consonants. Do not split consonant digraphs. Assist students in syllabicating each word.
(ag|gra|vate, ath|lete, con|gra|tu|late, a|pos|tro|phe, or|chard)

2 Select a volunteer to alphabetize the VCCCV words on the board. (**aggravate, apostrophe, athlete, congratulate, orchard**)

3 Proceed to page 75. Students independently complete the page. Assist as needed.

Day 4 Writing

Objective
The students will complete a narrative biography in the context of a cloze activity using pattern, content, and vocabulary words.

Introduction
Teacher Note: The narrative domain is the focus for the writing pages in Lessons 19–23.

Review the following definition: A *biography* is <u>a written account of someone's life</u>. Inform students that most biographies start off as written work but can be adapted into movies, plays, or television shows. Select a student to narrate a brief biography about a classmate or peer.

Directed Instruction
1 Inform students that they will be reading a biography about a Christian missionary doctor named Paul White in today's lesson. Dr. White dedicated his life to serving the Lord and helping people in the jungles of Tanzania. Show Tanzania on a map or a globe. Discuss

how the Lord has a perfect plan for each of us and the importance of following His calling upon our lives. God created each person with unique gifts to serve Him and help one another.

2 Proceed to page 76 and select a volunteer to read the sentences at the top of the page. Instruct students to silently read the biography and to complete the cloze activity independently. Chorally read the completed biography.

3 Homework suggestion: Distribute a copy of **BLM SP5-19C Lesson 19 Test Prep** to each student.

Day 5 Posttest

Objective
The students will correctly write dictated spelling words and sentences.

Introduction
Review by using flash cards noted in Student Spelling Support, number 2.

Directed Assessment

1 Dictate the list words by using the Pretest sentences or developing original ones. Reserve *entertain, attempt, resignation, anatomy,* and *skeleton* for the dictation sentences.

2 Read each sentence. Repeat as needed.
- Mrs. Park asked us to <u>entertain</u> thoughts of being doctors.
- Kate said she wanted to <u>attempt</u> to become a physician.
- She did not have one <u>resignation</u> after praying about it.
- Mrs. Park told Kate she would have to study <u>anatomy</u>.
- Kate was excited to learn about the human <u>skeleton</u>.

3 If assigned, dictate Extra Challenge Words.

4 Score the test, counting each misspelled word as an error. Correct the dictation sentences by grading only the spelling words or grading the complete sentences.

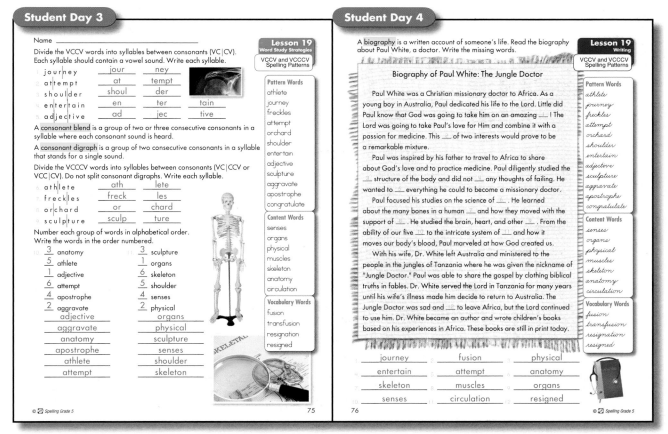

R-Controlled Vowels

Student Pages

Pages 77–80

Lesson Materials

BLM SP5-20A
BLM SP5-20B
T-15
BLM SP5-20C
BLM SP5-20D

Created Wonders

The theme of this lesson is mammals. Mammals are vertebrate animals that nourish their babies with milk. Most mammals have either hair or fur, and they exhibit specialized teeth for cutting and chewing food. Mammals have highly developed nervous systems and are among the most intelligent animals on Earth.

Day 1 Pretest

Objective

The students will accurately spell and write words with **r-controlled vowels**. They will spell and write content, vocabulary, and challenge words.

Introduction

Before class, select Challenge Words for numbers 24 and 25 from a cross-curricular subject, words misspelled on previous assignments, or words that interest your students. The word *manufacture* has the **r-controlled vowel** sound /ûr/ and is suggested for number 24. Administer the Pretest.

Directed Instruction

1 Say each word, use it in a sentence, and then repeat the word.

Pattern Words

1. The boys can <u>afford</u> to pay their entrance into the zoo.
2. The <u>calendar</u> shows days on which the zoo is closed.
3. One of Isabel's <u>chores</u> is to feed her dog.
4. The <u>courtroom</u> was quiet before the trial.
5. It is possible to see the <u>internal</u> organs of baby flying squirrels.
6. The young zoologist felt <u>nervous</u> when entering the lion's enclosure.
7. It is <u>normal</u> for baby mammals to stay near their mother.
8. House cats often prefer a <u>particular</u> type of cat food.
9. Steve's <u>purpose</u> in going to the zoo was to study mammals.
10. The lion was <u>searching</u> the grasslands for prey.
11. Jesus' atonement on the cross is the <u>source</u> of our faith.
12. The <u>squirrel</u> climbed high into the tree.

Content Words

13. Each <u>carnivore</u> at the zoo receives a daily ration of meat.
14. A reindeer's <u>habitat</u> is the tundra.
15. An animal that primarily eats plants is an <u>herbivore</u>.
16. A kangaroo is a <u>marsupial</u>.
17. Newborn opossums are <u>nourished</u> inside their mother's pouch.
18. Arctic animals are able to <u>tolerate</u> cold temperatures.
19. Are all mammals, including bats, <u>vertebrates</u>?

Vocabulary Words

20. After buying a ticket, Alexis received <u>admittance</u> into the zoo.
21. When I threw the ball to my friend, my dog tried to <u>intercept</u> it.
22. Danae tried to <u>recapture</u> her hamster.
23. The zoo receipt showed the amount of the <u>remittance</u>.

Challenge Words

24. _____
25. _____

2 Allow students to self-correct their Pretest. Write each word on the board. Point out that each Pattern Word contains an r-controlled vowel spelling pattern. *R-controlled vowels* are <u>vowels or combinations of vowels that precede *r* or *rr*. The letter *r* affects the sound of the vowel(s).</u> The vowel sounds /ôr/ heard in *afford* and /ûr/ heard in *purpose* are in this week's lesson. Note the roots *capt*, *cept*, and *mit* in the Vocabulary Words. The letter *t* is doubled in the root *mit* because the suffix *-ance* begins with a vowel.

3 As a class, read, spell, and read each word. Direct students to circle

misspelled words with a colored pencil and rewrite them correctly.

4 Proof each student's Pretest. This becomes an individualized study sheet that can be used at school or at home.

5 Homework suggestion: Distribute a copy of **BLM SP5-20A Lesson 20 Words and Phrases** to each student.

Day 2 Word Analysis and Vocabulary

Objective

The students will sort and write words with **r-controlled vowels**. They will complete sentences with content words. They will use a table to write vocabulary words, match definitions, complete sentences, and choose the best meaning for underlined words.

Introduction

Remind students of the following r-controlled vowel sounds in the lesson: /ôr/, /ûr/. Write the sounds on the board and list the spellings below the sounds as follows: /ôr/—or, ore, our; /ûr/—ar, ear, er, irr, ur. Invite students to refer to the list words, found on page 77, and ask students to give examples of Pattern Words that contain each sound. (/ôr/—aff**or**d, s**our**ce, ch**or**es, n**or**mal, c**our**troom; /ûr/—int**er**nal, squ**irr**el, n**er**vous, p**ur**pose, cal**e**ndar, s**ear**ching, p**ar**ticular) Reinforce the spellings for each sound by asking students to state the spellings for the r-controlled vowel sound in each word.

Directed Instruction

1 Inform students that the theme of this lesson is *mammals*. Mammals are warm-blooded vertebrate animals that provide milk to nourish their babies, breathe with lungs, and have some hair. *Marsupials* are a class of mammals in which the female has a pouch or fold of skin on its abdomen. A marsupial baby is born in an underdeveloped state and spends much of its early life in its mother's pouch. Kangaroos, wallabies, opossums, and bilbies are examples of marsupials.

2 Proceed to page 77. Say, spell, and say each Pattern, Content, and

65 pts.

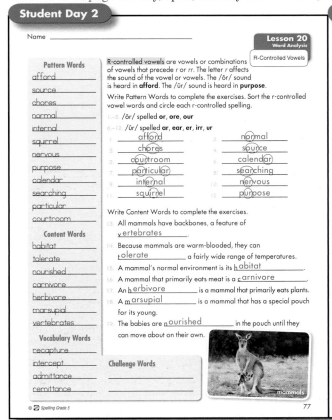

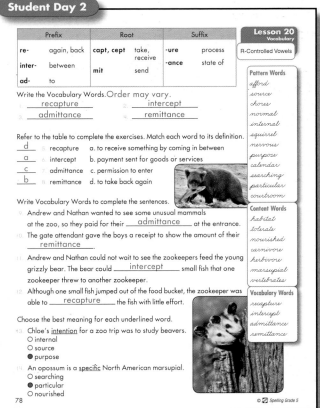

Student Spelling Support Materials

BLM SP5-01A
BLMs SP5-20E–F
Card stock
BLM SP5-01G
3" × 5" Index cards

Student Spelling Support

1. Use **BLM SP5-01A A Spelling Study Strategy** in instructional groups to provide assistance with some or all of the words.

2. Duplicate **BLMs SP5-20E–F Lesson 20 Spelling Words I** and **II** on CARD STOCK for students to use as flash cards at school or at home. Another option is to use **BLM SP5-01G Flash Cards Template** or 3" × 5" INDEX CARDS for students to write their own flash cards to use as a study aid.

3. Invite students to write the Challenge Words, numbers 24 and 25, in the Word Bank, in the back of their textbook.

4. For a Bible connection, read Proverbs 12:10: "A righteous man regards the life of his animal." Discuss with students the need to take responsibility for animals that are entrusted to their care, including exercising, feeding, and grooming.

5. Challenge students to write a personal essay about an experience that they have had observing a mammal in its native habitat, or at the zoo. Students should include the animal's description, diet, activities, and habits. Encourage students to include what unique aspects of God's design they appreciated and what characteristics fascinated them most.

6. Write this week's words, categorize the Pattern,

Cont. on page 81

Vocabulary Word. Provide this week's Challenge Words and have students write them in the spaces provided. Encourage students to look up any unfamiliar Content Words in their Spelling Dictionary before completing the exercises on the page independently.

3 Proceed to page 78. Explain that the roots *capt* and *cept* have the same meaning. Build each Vocabulary Word before students complete the page. For example, the prefix *re-* goes with the root *capt* and the suffix *-ure* to build the word *recapture*. Students complete the page.

4 Homework suggestion: Distribute a copy of **BLM SP5-20B Lesson 20 Phrases and Sentences** to each student.

Day 3 Word Study Strategies

Objective

The students will write list words to form alliterative sentences. They will utilize dictionary skills by answering questions about the different components of a dictionary entry.

Introduction

Write the following alliterative tongue twisters on the board:

- Sally sells seashells by the seashore.
- Peter Piper picked a peck of pickled peppers. How many pickled peppers did Peter Piper pick?

Select a volunteer to read each tongue twister and to underline the repeated initial consonant spelling in each sentence. Explain that these tongue twisters are examples of alliteration. *Alliteration* is a repetition of consonant sounds at the beginning of several words in a phrase. Alliteration is used in tongue twisters, rhymes, and poetry. Alliteration adds interest and fun to creative writing.

Directed Instruction

1 To practice dictionary skills, invite students to find the word *internal* in their Spelling Dictionary. Select volunteers to name the following dictionary components of the word *internal*:
- Guide Words (**instructor and kelp**) • Pronunciation (**/in 'tûr nəl/**)
- Part of Speech (**adjective**) • Definition (**inner; interior**)
- Sample Sentence (**It is possible to see the internal organs of baby flying squirrels.**)

2 Proceed to page 79. Allow students to complete the page independently. Conclude the lesson by asking volunteers to suggest alliterative phrases or sentences using list words that were not used.

Day 4 Writing

Objective

The students will use proofreading marks to identify mistakes in a personal essay. They will correctly write misspelled words.

Introduction

Display **T-15 Proofreading a Personal Essay** on the overhead, keeping the bottom portion of the transparency covered. Explain that this essay is a *narrative*, writing that tells a story, often from the author's point of view. In many narratives, the author recounts a personal experience. Read the essay and challenge students to tell why this is an example of a narrative. (**The author tells the story from his or her own experience.**) Remind students that the marks in the Proofreading Marks box will be used to identify mistakes found in the article. Slowly read the text aloud and challenge students to raise their hand when they notice an error, and identify each mark that needs to be written in order to correct the text. Correct the identified mistakes using the appropriate proofreading marks. Use **BLM SP5-20C T-15 Answer Key** as a guide. Uncover the bottom of the transparency and choose a volunteer to read the corrected version of the text.

Directed Instruction

1 Remind students that the narrative in today's lesson is a type of writing in which the author tells a personal story.

2 Proceed to page 80. Assist students as needed while they independently proofread the personal essay on the page. Review all the necessary proofreading marks and corrections. (12 misspellings; 2 capital letters needed; 2 periods needed; 2 deletes; 2 add something—*of*, *to*; 1 small letter needed; 1 new paragraph)

3 Homework suggestion: Distribute a copy of **BLM SP5-20D Lesson 20 Test Prep** to each student.

Day 5 Posttest

Objective
The students will correctly write dictated spelling words and sentences.

Introduction
Review by using flash cards noted in Student Spelling Support, number 2.

Directed Assessment

1 Dictate the list words by using the Pretest sentences or developing original ones. Reserve *normal*, *purpose*, *habitat*, *herbivore*, and *recapture* for the dictation sentences.

2 Read each sentence. Repeat as needed.
- It is <u>normal</u> for young beavers to spend time with their mother.
- The beaver uses its front teeth for the <u>purpose</u> of cutting wood.
- Most beavers live in a forest <u>habitat</u>.
- Because it eats leaves, twigs, and bark, a beaver is an <u>herbivore</u>.
- Zookeepers had to <u>recapture</u> a beaver that had escaped.

3 If assigned, dictate Extra Challenge Words.

4 Score the test, counting each misspelled word as an error. Correct the dictation sentences by grading only the spelling words or grading the complete sentences.

Student Spelling Support
Cont. from page 80

Content, and Vocabulary Words, and attach them to the Word Wall.

7. For two visual learners to work as partners, provide a list of this week's Pattern Words. Duplicate two sets of flash cards found on **BLMs SP5-20E–F Lesson 20 Spelling Words I** and **II**. Cover the r-controlled vowel spelling in each word by taping paper to the flash card. Invite one student to read the Pattern Words from the list as the second student finds the word and writes the missing r-controlled spelling onto the taped paper. Invite students to reverse roles, using the second set of flash cards.

8. Challenge students to write an "Animal Antics" alliterative book utilizing this week's spelling words. For example, Bilbo the Buck bantered with an **herbivore** about the bales of hay.

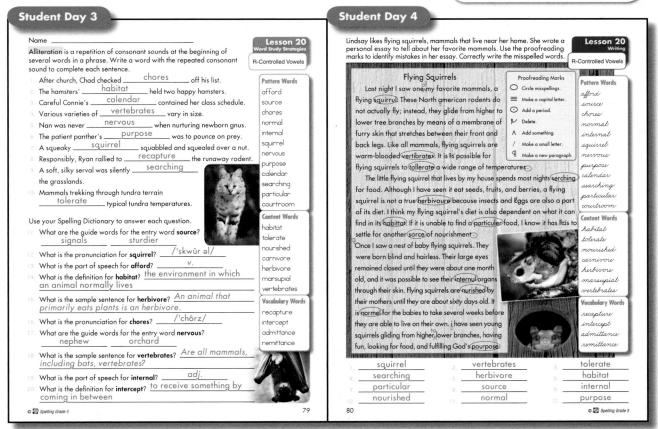

© Spelling Grade 5   79

80   © Spelling Grade 5

Student Pages

Pages 81–84

Lesson Materials

BLM SP5-21A
BLM SP5-21B
BLM SP5-21C

Created Wonders

The theme of this lesson is birds. Birds are the only animals with feathers. Approximately 10,000 kinds of birds exist in the world. Humans are intrigued and inspired by God's wondrous design of birds, their capabilities of flight, and their musical calls. Birding is a worldwide hobby with many organizations and publications.

Day 1 Pretest

Objective

The students will accurately spell and write words with **r-controlled vowels**. They will spell and write content, vocabulary, and challenge words.

Introduction

Before class, select Challenge Words for numbers 24 and 25 from a cross-curricular subject, words misspelled on previous assignments, or words that interest your students. The word *tartar* has two **r-controlled vowels**—/är/ in the first syllable and /ûr/ in the second syllable. *Tartar* is suggested for number 24. Administer the Pretest.

Directed Instruction

1 Say each word, use it in a sentence, and then repeat the word.

Pattern Words
1. The red <u>parrot</u> began to sing, "Row, row, row your boat."
2. Monique will <u>cherish</u> the necklace her grandmother gave to her.
3. Enrique read an interesting <u>article</u> about owls in the newspaper.
4. Ivan was <u>sincere</u> when he asked the Lord into his heart.
5. Most people are <u>irritable</u> when they are tired.
6. A secretary bird looks like it is <u>wearing</u> a shirt and pants.
7. The finches sang in <u>harmony</u> with each other.
8. I did not want to leave the zoo even though I was <u>weary</u>.
9. Mom will <u>prepare</u> turkey and stuffing for dinner tonight.
10. It is <u>apparent</u> that Isaiah has a bird since he brought it on Pet Day.
11. Miguel and his <u>guardian</u> vacationed in the Canary Islands.
12. John Audubon was an <u>artist</u> who enjoyed drawing birds.

Content Words
13. Tropical birds have brightly colored <u>plumage</u>.
14. Birds use their bill or beak and their feet when <u>preening</u>.
15. Geese <u>migrate</u> south every winter and return north each spring.
16. Most <u>songbirds</u> are perching birds.
17. Most birds lose their <u>feathers</u> every year and grow new ones.
18. A crane <u>nestling</u> can fly when it is ten weeks old.
19. Is an ostrich a <u>lightweight</u> bird since it can weigh up to 345 pounds?

Vocabulary Words
20. Four birds <u>performed</u> tricks they had learned.
21. Mr. Cavender built an <u>aviary</u> for his ten birds.
22. Leon checked out books about helicopters, jets, and <u>aviation</u>.
23. While at the zoo, our class attended a <u>performance</u> featuring birds.

Challenge Words
24. _____
25. _____

2 Allow students to self-correct their Pretest. Write each word on the board. Point out that this week's lesson contains more words with **r-controlled vowels**—/är/ heard in *artist*, /âr/ heard in *parrot*, and /îr/ heard in *weary*. Note the roots *avi* and *form* in the Vocabulary Words.

3 As a class, read, spell, and read each word. Direct students to circle misspelled words with a colored pencil and rewrite them correctly.

4 Proof each student's Pretest. This becomes an individualized study sheet that can be used at school or at home.

Day 2 Word Analysis and Vocabulary

Objective

The students will sort and write words according to r-controlled vowel sounds and complete sentences with content words. They will use a table to write vocabulary words, complete sentences in context, and select words to match definitions.

Introduction

Write the following pronunciations on the board and pronounce each one: /är/, /âr/, /îr/. Teach the students that in this lesson, the r-controlled vowel sound /är/ has one spelling, but /âr/ and /îr/ have multiple spellings. Provide the following clue word for each pronunciation to solidify the different spellings for the r-controlled vowels:

• *are* for /är/   • *air* for /âr/   • *ear* for /îr/

Invite students to refer to the list words found on page 81. Pronounce a word and have students identify the r-controlled pronunciation and spelling.

/är/	/âr/	/îr/
artist	parrot	weary
article	cherish	sincere
guardian	wearing	irritable
harmony	prepare	
	apparent	

Directed Instruction

1 Explain that this week's Content Words relate to the theme of birds. Teach that two words in the list are synonyms—*plumage* and *feathers*. Write *nestling* on the board and underline *nest*. Teach that a *nestling* is *a baby bird that is not ready to leave the nest.*

2 Proceed to page 81. Say, spell, and say each Pattern, Content, and Vocabulary Word. Provide this week's Challenge Words and have

Differentiated Instruction

• For students who spelled all the words correctly on the Pretest, select and assign Extra Challenge Words from the following list: palindrome, animosity, nobility, chronic, metaphor, application.

• For students who spelled less than half correctly, assign the following Pattern, Content, and Vocabulary Words: artist, weary, parrot, cherish, sincere, harmony, nestling, feathers, preening, songbirds, aviation, performed. On the Posttest, evaluate these students on the twelve words assigned; however, encourage them to attempt to spell all the list words to the best of their ability. They are also responsible for writing the dictated sentences.

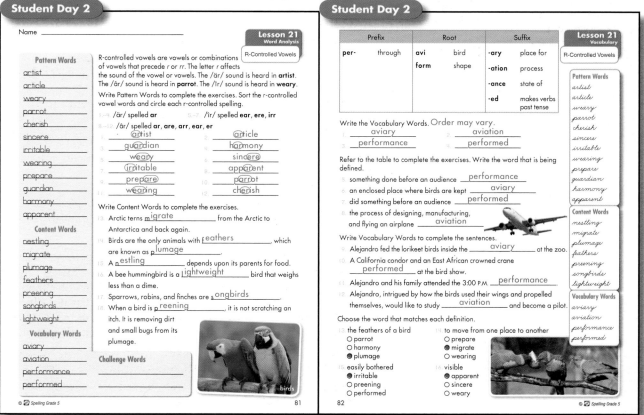

students write them in the spaces provided. Instruct students to complete the page.

3 Proceed to page 82. Explain that the Vocabulary Words contain the roots *avi* and *form*. Build each Vocabulary Word before students complete the page. For example, the root *avi* goes with the suffix *-ary* to form the word *aviary*. Allow students to independently complete the page. Assist as needed.

4 Homework suggestion: Distribute a copy of **BLM SP5-21B Lesson 21 Phrases and Sentences** to each student.

Day 3 Word Study Strategies

Objective

The students will make inferences to complete sentences. They will correctly write list words to match pronunciations.

Introduction

Remind students that an inference is a conclusion reached by looking at facts. Read the following sentences and invite students to infer the missing word:

- Stuart is wearing his swimming trunks and is carrying a towel and goggles. Stuart is ready to go _____ . (**Possible answers: swimming, to the beach**)
- Neva is studying the names of countries and their capital cities. She is locating the countries on a blank map. She needs to know them by tomorrow because in geography class she is having a _____ . (**Possible answers: test, quiz**)

Directed Instruction

1 Discuss the facts in each scenario that helped students come to the appropriate conclusion.
   - **Stuart was wearing swimming trunks and was carrying a towel and goggles. These items are used when swimming in a pool or splashing in the waves at the beach.**
   - **Neva was studying the names of countries and their capital cities. She must know them by tomorrow. A test may be approaching.**

2 Write the following pronunciations on the board:
   - /pri ˈpâr/ (**prepare**)
   - /ˈär tist/ (**artist**)
   - /ˈā vē âr ē/ (**aviary**)
   - /ˈmī grāt/ (**migrate**)

   Invite students to state the words from the pronunciations. Write each word on the board next to its pronunciation.

3 Proceed to page 83. Check for accuracy as students complete the page. When finished, select volunteers to read exercises 1–8. Select a student to read Genesis 1:20 and discuss the creation of water and air animals.

Day 4 Writing

Objective

The students will unscramble words in a narrative story about birds.

Introduction

Solicit students to share about a pet bird or interesting facts they know about birds. For example, a hummingbird can flap its wings 22–78 times per second; some albatross can live to be more than 60 years old; the sooty tern, a type of seabird, can fly for years by taking shorts naps that last a few seconds; pelicans do not have any feathers at birth.

Directed Instruction

1 Invite students to turn to page 84 and refer to the lists words. Write the following scrambled words on the board and solicit students to identify each word:

- **t a v n o i i a** (aviation)   - **r t p r a o** (parrot)
- **c s r e e i n** (sincere)   - **g n s b o i d s r** (songbirds)

Remind students to look for r-controlled vowel spellings in the Pattern Words, the theme of birds in the Content Words, and the root *avi* or *form* in the Vocabulary Words. Provide a clue about which category each word is located in.

2 Proceed to page 84. Instruct students to complete the page independently. Assist as needed.

3 Homework suggestion: Distribute a copy of **BLM SP5-21C Lesson 21 Test Prep** to each student.

Day 5 Posttest

Objective

The students will correctly write dictated spelling words and sentences.

Introduction

Review by using flash cards noted in Student Spelling Support, number 2.

Directed Assessment

1 Dictate the list words by using the Pretest sentences or developing original ones. Reserve *performed*, *songbirds*, *harmony*, *parrot*, and *preening* for the dictation sentences.

2 Read each sentence. Repeat as needed.
- Four birds <u>performed</u> in a show.
- Two <u>songbirds</u> sang a song.
- They did not sing in <u>harmony</u> so the trainer made them sing again.
- A <u>parrot</u> told a funny joke.
- A dove began <u>preening</u> instead of doing its trick.

3 If assigned, dictate Extra Challenge Words.

4 Score the test, counting each misspelled word as an error. Correct the dictation sentences by grading only the spelling words or grading the complete sentences.

Cont. from page 84

Student Spelling Support

6. Write this week's words, categorize the Pattern, Content, and Vocabulary Words, and attach them to the Word Wall.

7. As a cross-curricular connection, have students visit the library and find books about John Audubon. John spent years exploring areas of the United States and drawing birds. His fascination with birds led to an organization being named after him. The Audubon Society is an organization for people who enjoy watching and learning about birds as a hobby. This hobby is called birding.

8. Challenge students to write a humorous narrative from the perspective of their favorite bird. Encourage the use of list words in context.

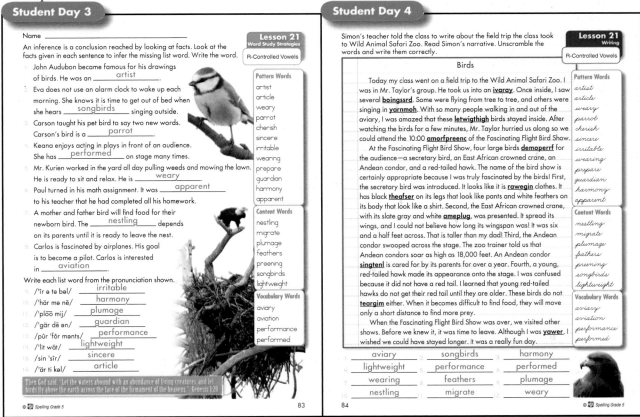

Student Pages
Pages 85–88

Lesson Materials
BLM SP5-22A
BLM SP5-22B
BLM SP5-22C

Created Wonders

The theme of this lesson is fish. Fish are unique creatures that live and breathe in water. Fish live in almost every underwater habitat—arctic waters, hot springs, freshwater lakes, tropical ponds, and oceans. Most fish have protective scales, streamlined bodies, and fins for swimming. God created fish to live successfully in the water habitat.

Day 1 Pretest

Objective
The students will accurately spell and write words with **prefixes**. They will spell and write content, vocabulary, and challenge words.

Introduction
Before class, select Challenge Words for numbers 24 and 25 from a cross-curricular subject, words misspelled on previous assignments, or words that interest your students. The word *complaining* has the **prefix com-** and is suggested for number 24. Administer the Pretest.

Directed Instruction

1 Say each word, use it in a sentence, and then repeat the word.

Pattern Words
1. Roberto had a <u>compound</u> fracture in his arm after he fell.
2. To stop a wound from bleeding, you should <u>compress</u> the area.
3. Keisha drove to the <u>discount</u> supply store for aquarium filters.
4. <u>Conforming</u> to the rules during an ocean expedition is important.
5. Deena will <u>deactivate</u> the alarm to the laboratory in the morning.
6. Kenji decided to <u>configure</u> his fish tank after the one at school.
7. Ray was <u>dissatisfied</u> with his science test grade so he studied harder.
8. Choose a <u>design</u> for your aquarium before you go to the store.
9. The two scientists <u>conversed</u> about the many different species of fish.
10. The <u>discovery</u> of a new fish species excited the scientists.
11. There was a traffic <u>detour</u> near the marina.
12. A <u>concave</u> hideout in a rock or coral is beneficial to aquarium fish.

Content Words
13. Sharks have skeletons that are made of bendable <u>cartilage</u>.
14. <u>Fisheries</u> are a vital source of food for people who live on the coast.
15. The <u>marine</u> biologist enjoyed his job immensely.
16. Did you know that gill <u>membranes</u> are designed to help fish breathe?
17. God designed fish with protective <u>scales</u>.
— 18. The deep-sea anglerfish lives near the dark <u>seafloor</u>.
19. Fish bodies are <u>streamlined</u> for swimming efficiency.

Vocabulary Words
20. The <u>luminous</u> school of fish reflected vivid colors.
21. Schools of fish in coral reefs can <u>illuminate</u> the waters.
22. The community was in <u>opposition</u> to coastal land development.
23. Is it an <u>imposition</u> for you to meet five times in a week?

Challenge Words
24. _____
25. _____

2 Allow students to self-correct their Pretest. Write each word on the board. Point out the following **prefixes** in the Pattern Words: com-, con-, de-, dis-. Note the roots *lumin* and *posit* in the Vocabulary Words.

3 As a class, read, spell, and read each word. Direct students to circle misspelled words with a colored pencil and rewrite them correctly.

4 Proof each student's Pretest. This becomes an individualized study sheet that can be used at school or at home.

5 Homework suggestion: Distribute a copy of **BLM SP5-22A Lesson 22 Words and Phrases** to each student.

Day 2 Word Analysis and Vocabulary

Objective

The students will sort words by prefix, and complete sentences with content words. They will use a table to write vocabulary words, match given definitions in context, and complete sentences.

Introduction

Review the following definition: A *prefix* is <u>a word part that is added to the beginning of a root or a root with a suffix</u>. <u>A prefix is also known as an</u> *affix*. <u>Affixes expand the meaning or function of a word</u>. Invite students to refer to the list words, found on page 85, for this activity. Dictate each Pattern Word while omitting the prefix. Challenge students to search their word list for the missing prefix that correlates with the dictated ending word, raise their hand, and identify the missing prefix. For example, dictate *press* for *compress* (**com-**), *cave* for *concave* (**con-**), *sign* for *design* (**de-**), and *count* for *discount* (**dis-**).

Directed Instruction

1 Select four Pattern Words to write on the board. Invite a volunteer to come to the board and circle the prefix in each word. Point out that when **prefixes** are added to the beginning of a root or root with a suffix, no spelling change occurs.

2 Proceed to page 85. Say, spell, and say each Pattern, Content, and Vocabulary Word. Provide this week's Challenge Words and have students write them in the spaces provided. Students independently complete the page. To reinforce Content Word meanings, select volunteers to read exercises 13–19 aloud when complete.

3 Proceed to page 86. Build each Vocabulary Word before students complete the page. For example, the prefix *il-* goes with the root *lumin* and the suffix *-ate* to get the word *illuminate*. Provide assistance as needed. Select a volunteer to read exercises 9–13 when complete. Select a student to read Genesis 1:20 and lead a short discussion about

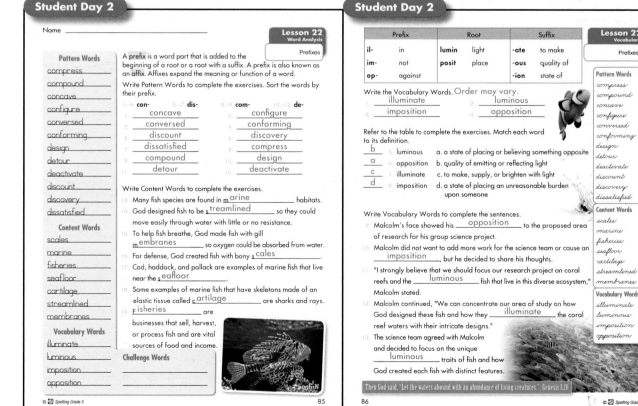

4 Homework suggestion: Distribute a copy of **BLM SP5-22B Lesson 22 Phrases and Sentences** to each student.

Day 3 Word Study Strategies

Objective

The students will write list words that are related forms of given words, write words to match definitions, and syllabicate words after prefixes.

Introduction

Dictate the following words and invite students to refer to the list words, found on page 87, for this activity:

- activated, actively, deactivation (**deactivate**)
- satisfaction, satisfy, dissatisfaction (**dissatisfied**)
- position, reposition, deposition (**imposition, opposition**)

Instruct students to scan the list of words and to raise their hand when a related form(s) of the dictated word is found. Write the related word form(s) adjacent to the correct trio of words.

Directed Instruction

1 Remind students that a prefix is a word part that is added to the beginning of a root or a root with a suffix. A prefix is also known as an affix. Affixes expand the meaning or function of a word. Inform students that prefixes can have more than one meaning. Review the following prefixes and some of their meanings:

- com- = with, together, thoroughly
- con- = with, together, thoroughly
- de- = thoroughly, from, reverse
- dis- = not, off, apart

2 Write the following words on the board and assist students in syllabicating multisyllable words:

- compress (**com|press**)
- configure (**con|fig|ure**)
- conforming (**con|form|ing**)
- deactivate (**de|act|i|vate**)
- discovery (**dis|cov|er|y**)
- dissatisfied (**dis|sat|is|fied**)

3 Proceed to page 87. Students will independently complete the page. Encourage students to use their Spelling Dictionary. Assist as needed.

Day 4 Writing

Objective

The students will correctly write list words that have the same meanings as words used in narrative paragraphs.

Introduction

Invite students to refer to the list words, found on page 88, for this activity. Slowly read the following narrative paragraph aloud:

Fish are wonderful creatures that were created by God. His **plan** (**design**) for them is very unique and amazing. God designed fish to be **contoured** (**streamlined**) so they could be efficient swimmers. God also gave fish the unique ability to breathe underwater. He placed **layers of tissue** (**membranes**) over the fish's gills so oxygen could be absorbed. God also placed protective **rigid covering plates** (**scales**) on most fish. Doesn't God's creation astound you?

While reading, raise your hand as each bold word or words is dictated. Invite students to watch for your hand, scan their word list, and locate a list word that could replace the indicated word or words.

Directed Instruction

1 Reread the paragraph with the correct list words inserted into the text.

2 Proceed to page 88 and choose a volunteer to read the sentences at the top of the page. Invite students to collaborate in groups as they complete the page. When complete, select volunteers to read the

---

Student Spelling Support Materials

BLM SP5-01A
BLMs SP5-22D–E
Card stock
BLM SP5-01G
3" × 5" Index cards

Student Spelling Support

1. Use **BLM SP5-01A A Spelling Study Strategy** in instructional groups to provide assistance with some or all of the words.

2. Duplicate **BLMs SP5-22D–E Lesson 22 Spelling Words I** and **II** on CARD STOCK for students to use as flash cards at school or at home. Another option is to use **BLM SP5-01G Flash Cards Template** or 3" × 5" INDEX CARDS for students to write their own flash cards to use as a study aid.

3. Invite students to write the Challenge Words, numbers 24 and 25, in the Word Bank, in the back of their textbook.

4. Read Genesis 1:20: "Then God said, 'Let the waters abound with an abundance of living creatures.'" Discuss how the Lord spoke the creatures that live in water habitats into existence when He created the earth. The Lord specifically designed these sea creatures, like fish, to live and breathe in the unique water environment. The Lord created the earth in a very orderly way.

5. Challenge students to research and write a one-page report on a specific species of fish, whether from freshwater lakes or from the ocean. Students should include information on unique abilities and habitat.

6. Write this week's words, categorize the Pattern,

Cont. on page 89

information aloud, replacing each bold word or words with a list word.

3 Homework suggestion: Distribute a copy of **BLM SP5-22C Lesson 22 Test Prep** to each student.

Day 5 Posttest

Objective

The students will correctly write dictated spelling words and sentences.

Introduction

Review by using flash cards noted in Student Spelling Support, number 2.

Directed Assessment

1 Dictate the list words by using the Pretest sentences or developing original ones. Reserve *conversed*, *discovery*, *marine*, *seafloor*, and *luminous* for the dictation sentences.

2 Read each sentence. Repeat as needed.
- The young scientists <u>conversed</u> in excited tones.
- A recent <u>discovery</u> of a new fish thrilled them.
- A <u>marine</u> magazine article described the fish.
- The new fish was discovered near the <u>seafloor</u>.
- God created the fish with <u>luminous</u> abilities.

3 If assigned, dictate Extra Challenge Words.

4 Score the test, counting each misspelled word as an error. Correct the dictation sentences by grading only the spelling words or grading the complete sentences.

Student Spelling Support
Cont. from page 88

Content, and Vocabulary Words, and attach them to the Word Wall.

7. For visual learners, instruct each student to use colored pencils to write the Pattern Words from this lesson. Students use a different color for each prefix and ending word. The following are some examples: **compress**, **conforming**, **design**, **dissatisfied**. For an extra challenge, students may repeat the process with Vocabulary Words from this lesson, focusing on the affixes and roots. For example, **illuminate**, **opposition**.

8. For a cross-curricular connection, students research fish classification. Classification is the process of arranging animals or other things into groups, according to their characteristics. Students should include the scientific name for their fish.

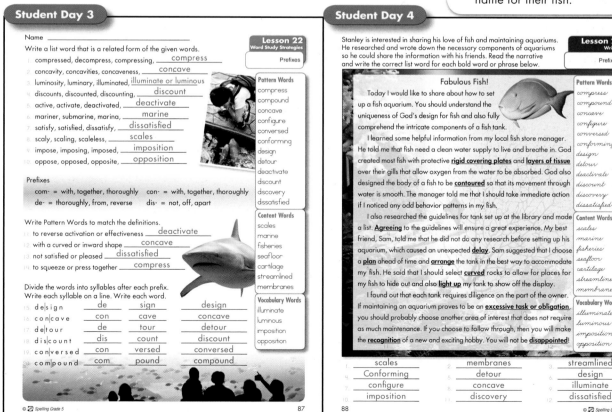

Student Day 3

Name _____

Write a list word that is a related form of the given words.

1. compressed, decompress, compressing, ___ **compress**
2. concavity, concavities, concaveness, ___ **concave**
3. luminosity, luminary, illuminated, ___ **illuminate or luminous**
4. discounts, discounted, discounting, ___ **discount**
5. active, activate, deactivated, ___ **deactivate**
6. mariner, submarine, marina, ___ **marine**
7. satisfy, satisfied, dissatisfy, ___ **dissatisfied**
8. scaly, scaling, scaleless, ___ **scales**
9. impose, imposing, imposed, ___ **imposition**
10. oppose, opposed, opposite, ___ **opposition**

Prefixes
com- = with, together, thoroughly   con- = with, together, thoroughly
de- = thoroughly, from, reverse   dis- = not, off, apart

Write Pattern Words to match the definitions.
11. to reverse activation or effectiveness ___ **deactivate**
12. with a curved or inward shape ___ **concave**
13. not satisfied or pleased ___ **dissatisfied**
14. to squeeze or press together ___ **compress**

Divide the words into syllables after each prefix. Write each syllable on a line. Write each word.
15. de|sign — de — sign — design
16. con|cave — con — cave — concave
17. de|tour — de — tour — detour
18. dis|count — dis — count — discount
19. con|versed — con — versed — conversed
20. com|pound — com — pound — compound

Lesson 22
Word Study Strategies
Prefixes

Pattern Words
compress
compound
concave
configure
conversed
conforming
design
detour
deactivate
discount
discovery
dissatisfied

Content Words
scales
marine
fisheries
seafloor
cartilage
streamlined
membranes

Vocabulary Words
illuminate
luminous
imposition
opposition

© Spelling Grade 5   87

Student Day 4

Stanley is interested in sharing his love of fish and maintaining aquariums. He researched and wrote down the necessary components of aquariums so he could share the information with his friends. Read the narrative and write the correct list word for each bold word or phrase below.

Lesson 22
Writing
Prefixes

Fabulous Fish!

Today I would like to share about how to set up a fish aquarium. You should understand the uniqueness of God's design for fish and also fully comprehend the intricate components of a fish tank.

I learned some helpful information from my local fish store manager. He told me that fish need a clean water supply to live and breathe in. God created most fish with protective **rigid covering plates** and **layers of tissue** over their gills that allow oxygen from the water to be absorbed. God also designed the body of a fish to be **contoured** so that its movement through water is smooth. The manager told me that I should take immediate action if I noticed any odd behavior patterns in my fish.

I also researched the guidelines for tank set up at the library and made a list. **Agreeing** to the guidelines will ensure a great experience. My best friend, Sam, told me that he did not do any research before setting up his aquarium, which caused an unexpected **delay**. Sam suggested that I choose a **plan** ahead of time and **arrange** the tank in the best way to accommodate my fish. He said that I should select **curved** rocks to allow for places for my fish to hide out and also **light up** my tank to show off the display.

I found out that each tank requires diligence on the part of the owner. If maintaining an aquarium proves to be an **excessive task or obligation**, you should probably choose another area of interest that does not require as much maintenance. If you choose to follow through, then you will make the **recognition** of a new and exciting hobby. You will not be **disappointed**!

Pattern Words
compress
compound
concave
configure
conversed
conforming
design
detour
deactivate
discount
discovery
dissatisfied

Content Words
scales
marine
fisheries
seafloor
cartilage
streamlined
membranes

Vocabulary Words
illuminate
luminous
imposition
opposition

1. scales
2. membranes
3. streamlined
4. Conforming
5. detour
6. design
7. configure
8. concave
9. illuminate
10. imposition
11. discovery
12. dissatisfied

88   © Spelling Grade 5

Prefixes

Student Pages
Pages 89–92

Lesson Materials
BLM SP5-23A
BLM SP5-23B
BLM SP5-23C

Created Wonders

The theme of this lesson is insects. Insects can be both helpful and harmful. Helpful insects eat other insects that destroy plants as well as get rid of wastes and dead plants and animals. Harmful insects bite, sting, carry diseases, or destroy crops. Tropical rainforests are home to more insects than any other place in the world.

Day 1 Pretest

Objective

The students will accurately spell and write words with **prefixes**. They will spell and write content, vocabulary, and challenge words.

Introduction

Before class, select Challenge Words for numbers 24 and 25 from a cross-curricular subject, words misspelled on previous assignments, or words that interest your students. The word *nonchalant* has the **prefix non**- and is suggested for number 24. Administer the Pretest.

Directed Instruction

1 Say each word, use it in a sentence, and then repeat the word.

Pattern Words

1. The Philippines exports butterflies to museums in the United States.
2. The United States imports insects from other countries.
3. Metamorphosis for a butterfly is incomplete at the pupa stage.
4. The encyclopedia of insects contains informative details.
5. Insects are incapable of living at the North and South Poles.
6. Moths are inactive during the day and active at night.
7. Our teacher warned us not to be impolite while at the museum.
8. Ty's facial expression was comical when he saw the giant beetle.
9. Ross and Wes decided to exchange the souvenirs they purchased.
10. The crack in the insect model was an imperfection.
11. The most important nonfiction book is God's Word, the Bible.
12. It is nonsense to believe that God's Word is untrue.

Content Words

13. An insect has three segmented body parts.
14. Did you know that an antenna also has three parts?
15. The insect is the only invertebrate that has wings.
16. There are over twelve thousand species of ants.
17. An insect's wings and legs are attached to the thorax.
18. The abdomen of a scorpion fly can curve over its back.
19. All of an insect's soft body parts are protected by an exoskeleton.

Vocabulary Words

20. The contortion of a butterfly can be seen as it leaves its chrysalis.
21. Will a dragonfly distort itself when it molts?
22. A mayfly has bilateral wings on its body.
23. Wings are not unilateral since they are on both sides of the body.

Challenge Words

24. _____
25. _____

2 Allow students to self-correct their Pretest. Write each word on the board. Point out the following **prefixes** in the Pattern Words: ex-, im-, in-, non-. Note the roots *later* /'la tûr/ and *tort* in the Vocabulary Words.

3 As a class, read, spell, and read each word. Direct students to circle misspelled words with a colored pencil and rewrite them correctly.

4 Proof each student's Pretest. This becomes an individualized study sheet that can be used at school or at home.

5 Homework suggestion: Distribute a copy of **BLM SP5-23A Lesson 23 Words and Phrases** to each student.

Day 2 Word Analysis and Vocabulary

Objective
The students will sort and write words with **prefixes** and complete sentences with content words. They will use a table to write vocabulary words, complete sentences in context, and select words to match definitions.

Introduction
Remind students that a prefix is a word part that is added to the beginning of a root or a root with a suffix. A prefix is also known as an affix. Affixes expand the meaning or function of a word. Randomly read each Pattern Word aloud and select a volunteer to identify and spell the prefix.

Directed Instruction

1 Explain that this week's Content Words relate to the theme of insects. Teach that the word *antenna* is often confused with its plural form, *antennae*.

2 Proceed to page 89. Say, spell, and say each Pattern, Content, and Vocabulary Word. Provide this week's Challenge Words and have students write them in the spaces provided. Instruct students to complete the page.

3 Proceed to page 90. Explain that the Vocabulary Words contain the roots *later* /'la tûr/ and *tort*. Build each Vocabulary Word before students complete the page. For example, the prefix *bi-* goes with the root *later* and the suffix *-al* to get the word *bilateral*. Allow students to independently complete the page. Assist as needed.

4 Homework suggestion: Distribute a copy of **BLM SP5-23B Lesson 23 Phrases and Sentences** to each student.

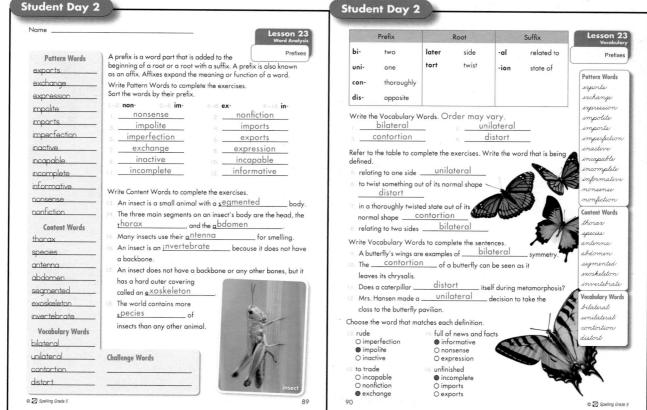

Day 3 Word Study Strategies

Objective

The students will write list words that are antonyms for given words, match definitions, and identify idioms.

Introduction

Write the word *impolite* on the board and ask a volunteer to state a word that is the opposite. (**polite**) Solicit a volunteer to name the word that means the opposite of another word. (**antonym**) Teach that an *antonym* is a word that means the opposite of another word.

Directed Instruction

1 Teach the meaning of the prefixes in the Pattern Words by writing the following on the board:
- ex- = out, from, away
- im- = not, into
- in- = in, not, into
- non- = not

Have students refer to the list words on page 91 for this activity. State the following definitions and select volunteers to name the appropriate Pattern Word:
- not active (**inactive**)
- not sensible (**nonsense**)
- not perfection (**imperfection**)
- sends things out from one country into another country (**exports**)

Ask students to suggest other words with these **prefixes**.

2 Write *talkative* and *gave away a secret* on one area of the board. On another area, write the following sentences:
- Aunt Lois has the gift of gab. (**talkative**)
- She let the cat out of the bag about the surprise party. (**gave away a secret**)

Read the sentences and explain that the underlined phrases are idioms. *Idioms* are fun ways to talk about everyday things. Select a volunteer to state the meaning of each underlined idiom.

3 Proceed to page 91. Check for accuracy as students complete the page. As a challenge, have students underline the part of the sentence that is an idiom in exercises 13–18. (**let the grass grow under their feet; half-baked; get under someone's skin; a deadpan look; in the know; dropped the ball**)

Day 4 Writing

Objective

The students will complete a narrative story by writing list words in sentences.

Introduction

Briefly share about a trip to a museum that you have taken and describe the interesting things that you saw. Be sure to tell it in a narrative form.

Directed Instruction

1 Proceed to page 92. Explain that this is a fictional narrative story. Relate that museums do have *docents*. Define *docent* as *a tour guide for groups at a museum*. Instruct students to complete the page. Assist as needed. When complete, select a volunteer to read the narrative story aloud.

2 Homework suggestion: Distribute a copy of **BLM SP5-23C Lesson 23 Test Prep** to each student.

Day 5 Posttest

Objective
The students will correctly write dictated spelling words and sentences.

Introduction
Review by using flash cards noted in Student Spelling Support, number 2.

Directed Assessment

1 Dictate the list words by using the Pretest sentences or developing original ones. Reserve *nonfiction*, *species*, *invertebrate*, *bilateral*, and *informative* for the dictation sentences.

2 Read each sentence. Repeat as needed.
- Mora read a <u>nonfiction</u> book about insects.
- There was a chapter for each of ten different insect <u>species</u>.
- She learned that a grasshopper is an <u>invertebrate</u>.
- Its body displays <u>bilateral</u> symmetry.
- Mora enjoyed reading the very <u>informative</u> book.

3 If assigned, dictate Extra Challenge Words.

4 Score the test, counting each misspelled word as an error. Correct the dictation sentences by grading only the spelling words or grading the complete sentences.

Student Spelling Support
Cont. from page 92

features, and life cycle. Have students illustrate their paragraph, labeling the body parts. Encourage students to use as many spelling words as possible in their paragraph and illustration.

6. Write this week's words, categorize the Pattern, Content, and Vocabulary Words, and attach them to the Word Wall.

7. For visual and kinesthetic learners, provide colored pencils and 3" × 5" INDEX CARDS. Instruct students to write each Pattern Word on the index card using one color for the prefix, a second color for the root, and a third color for the suffix. For example, **exports**. Verify if a Pattern Word has a prefix, root, or suffix before allowing students to write in color.

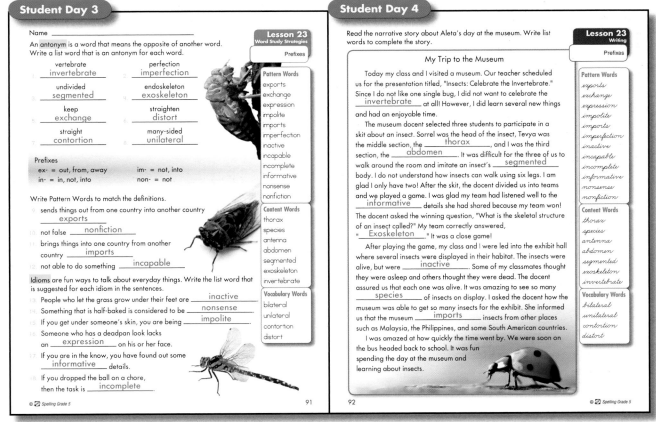

Student Pages
Pages 93–96

Lesson Materials

T-16
BLM SP5-24A
BLM SP5-24B
BLM SP5-24C
T-14
3" × 5" Index cards
BLM SP5-24D
BLMs SP5-24E–F
BLM SP5-06G
BLM SP5-24G

Day 1 VCCV and VCCCV Spelling Patterns

Objective
The students will spell, identify, and sort words with **VCCV and VCCCV spelling patterns** according to the type of pattern contained in each word.

Introduction
Teacher Note: This week's lesson incorporates the Pattern, Content, and Vocabulary Words taught in Lessons 19–23 using a variety of activities such as sorting, decoding words, a crossword puzzle, a word search, filling in the correct answer circle, shape boxes, and adding or subtracting letters to form words.

Display **T-16 Lessons 19–23 Study Sheet** on the overhead to review Lesson 19 words in unison using the say-spell-say technique. Remind students that VCCV and VCCCV words have vowel-consonant-consonant-vowel or vowel-consonant-consonant-consonant-vowel spelling patterns. Challenge students to identify the spelling patterns for each Pattern Word in Lesson 19.

Directed Instruction

1 Continue to use **T-16 Lessons 19–23 Study Sheet** and invite volunteers to identify and circle the **VCCV and VCCCV spelling patterns** in Lesson 19 words. Use two different colors of transparency pens for this activity, one for each spelling pattern. The words *entertain* and *adjective* each have more than one VCCV spelling pattern. *Apostrophe* has both a VCCCV and a VCCV spelling pattern.

2 Proceed to page 93. Explain that the box contains all the Pattern, Content, and Vocabulary Words in Lessons 19–23. This list is the same list of words that was previously displayed on the overhead. Encourage students to use this list as a review tool. Instruct students to read the directions and independently complete the page.

3 Distribute a copy of **BLM SP5-24A Lessons 19–23 Study Sheet** to each student to take home for study.

4 Homework suggestion: Distribute a copy of **BLM SP5-24B Lesson 24 Homework I** to each student to practice with **VCCV and VCCCV spelling patterns**, **r-controlled vowels**, and words with **prefixes**.

Day 2 R-Controlled Vowels

Objective
The students will use a code to spell and write words with **r-controlled vowels**. They will spell and write words in a crossword puzzle.

Introduction
Display **T-16 Lessons 19–23 Study Sheet**. Write the following Pattern Words from Lesson 20 on the board, inserting the symbols as shown:

- calend ▲
- s ⬭ ching
- n ☆ vous
- ch ▢ s
- s ⬡ ce
- p ◆ pose

Make a key for each symbol by drawing each shape and indicating its spelling as follows:

▲—ar; ⬭— ear; ☆—er; ▢—ore; ⬡—our; ◆—ur. Invite volunteers to decode and write each Pattern Word below the word on the board. (**calendar, searching, nervous, chores, source, purpose**) Encourage students to pronounce each word they have written on the board, and challenge students to generate an example of another word with the same **r-controlled vowel** spelling.

Directed Instruction

1 Refer to **T-16 Lessons 19–23 Study Sheet** to review Lessons 20–21 words in unison, using the say-spell-say technique.

2 Read the following riddles and challenge students to find a word from Lesson 21 to fit each riddle:
- I may appear in a magazine, but I am not a celebrity. (**article**)
- I am as protective as a shepherd, but I do not tend sheep. (**guardian**)

3 Proceed to page 94. Invite students to read the directions silently and complete the page individually. Encourage students to use their Spelling Dictionary to ~~crossword puzzle.~~

4 Homework suggestion
SP5-24C Lesson 24 H
to practice words with
and Vocabulary Word

Day 3 Prefix

Objective

The students will find an
in a word search. They w
answer circle to indicate
spelled correctly or incor
each word.

Introduction

Using **T-14 Mini Word S**
to write the following Pa
in the squares of the grid: compress, concave, design, detour. Assist the volunteer in positioning the words across, down, diagonally, and backwards. Fill in each remaining square on the grid with a letter. When complete, display the transparency on the overhead and challenge students to find the Pattern Words that are being reflected on the board. Have students refer to the list words at the top of page 95. Circle each word as it is found. An example mini word search is shown.

```
x d e r s m y s
r u o t e d s u
i g a l i e t r
c v q l r s a s
k z i p v i w x
t x m n z g v q
r o x r p n z o
c o n c a v e b
```

Directed Instruction

1 Display **T-16 Lessons 19–23 Study Sheet** to review Lessons 22–23 words in unison, using the say-spell-say technique.

2 Review the following **prefixes** from Lessons 22–23 by writing them on the board: com-, con-, de-, dis-, ex-, im-, in-, non-. Remind students that a prefix is a word part that is added to the beginning of a root or a root with a suffix. A prefix is also known as an affix. Affixes expand the meaning or

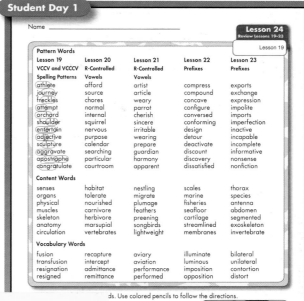

Name _____

Lesson 24
Review Lessons 19–23

Pattern Words				
Lesson 19 VCCV and VCCCV Spelling Patterns	**Lesson 20** R-Controlled Vowels	**Lesson 21** R-Controlled Vowels	**Lesson 22** Prefixes	**Lesson 23** Prefixes
athlete	afford	artist	compress	exports
journey	source	article	compound	exchange
freckles	chores	weary	concave	expression
attempt	normal	parrot	configure	impolite
orchard	internal	cherish	conversed	imports
shoulder	squirrel	sincere	conforming	imperfection
entertain	nervous	irritable	design	inactive
adjective	purpose	wearing	detour	incapable
sculpture	calendar	prepare	deactivate	incomplete
aggravate	searching	guardian	discount	informative
apostrophe	particular	harmony	discovery	nonsense
congratulate	courtroom	apparent	dissatisfied	nonfiction

Content Words				
senses	habitat	nestling	scales	thorax
organs	tolerate	migrate	marine	species
physical	nourished	plumage	fisheries	antenna
muscles	carnivore	feathers	seafloor	abdomen
skeleton	herbivore	preening	cartilage	segmented
anatomy	marsupial	songbirds	streamlined	exoskeleton
circulation	vertebrates	lightweight	membranes	invertebrate

Vocabulary Words				
fusion	recapture	aviary	illuminate	bilateral
transfusion	intercept	aviation	luminous	unilateral
resignation	admittance	performance	imposition	contortion
resigned	remittance	performed	opposition	distort

ds. Use colored pencils to follow the directions.

vord that make up the **VCCV**
here may be more than one
a word.

word that make up the **VCCCV**
e.

CCV spelling pattern and a
Write the word with both spelling patterns. _____apostrophe_____

93

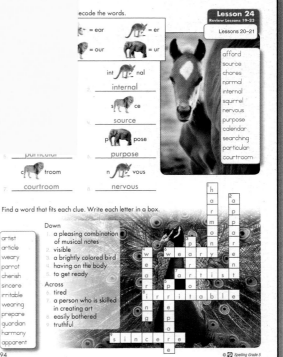

Handwritten note: Note the directions for pg. 93 - Circle the letters not the words!

Lesson 24
Review Lessons 19–23

Lessons 20–21

= ear   = er
= our   = ur

int ___ nal
internal
s___ce
source
p___pose
purpose
c___troom
courtroom
n___vous
nervous

afford
source
chores
normal
internal
squirrel
nervous
purpose
calendar
searching
particular
courtroom

Find a word that fits each clue. Write each letter in a box.

artist
article
weary
parrot
cherish
sincere
irritable
wearing
prepare
guardian
harmony
apparent

Down
1. a pleasing combination of musical notes
2. visible
3. a brightly colored bird
4. having on the body
5. to get ready

Across
6. tired
7. a person who is skilled in creating art
8. easily bothered
9. truthful

94

© Spelling Grade 5

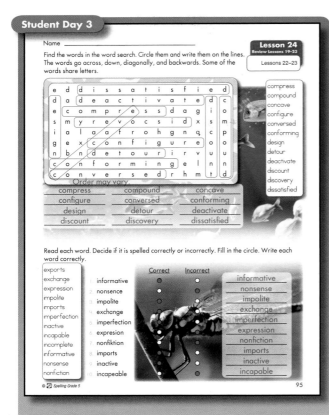

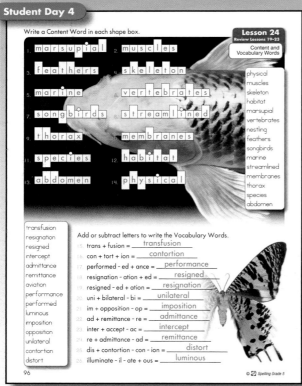

function of a word. Invite volunteers to circle each prefix in Lessons 22–23, using a different colored transparency pen.

3 Proceed to page 95. Students complete the page independently. Assist as needed.

Day 4 Content Words and Vocabulary Words

Objective

The students will write content words in shape boxes. They will add or subtract letters to write vocabulary words.

Introduction

Display **T-16 Lessons 19–23 Study Sheet** to review Content Words in unison, using the say-spell-say technique. Write the following Content Words on the board: physical, marsupial, lightweight, scales, species. Invite the volunteers to the board to draw shape boxes around each word. Challenge students to find words that are longer, shorter, have more tall letters, or have more tail letters than the word that the volunteer has just written.

Directed Instruction

1 Refer to **T-16 Lessons 19–23 Study Sheet** to review Vocabulary Words in unison, using the say-spell-say technique.

2 Write the following Vocabulary Words on 3" × 5" INDEX CARDS and pass them out to ten volunteers: fusion, resignation, intercept, admittance, aviary, performance, illuminate, imposition, unilateral, contortion. Read the following affixes or roots and invite the students with the card containing that affix or root to come to the board and write their word.

- *fus* means *melt, pour*
- *cept* means *receive*
- *avi* means *bird*
- *lumin* means *light*
- *uni-* means *one*
- *sign* means *sign*
- *ad-* means *to*
- *form* means *shape*
- *posit* means *place*
- *tort* means *twist*.

3 Proceed to page 96. Students independently complete the page. When complete, select volunteers to read exercises 15–26 aloud to reinforce the spelling of the Vocabulary Words.

4 Homework suggestion: Distribute a copy of **BLM SP5-24D Lessons 19–23 Test Prep** to each student to practice with many of the words that may appear on the Assessment. Prepare for the Assessment by studying the words on **BLM SP5-24A Lessons 19–23 Study Sheet** that was sent home on Day 1.

Day 5 Assessment

Objective

The students will accurately select the appropriate answer within the context of a sentence. They will fill in the corresponding answer circle.

Introduction

Teacher Note: The Test makes provision for Differentiated Instruction. The first twelve sentences include the words assigned to students with shortened lists. Encourage these students to try all the sentences, but only grade the first twelve sentences. The Test is found on two blackline masters.

Duplicate a copy of **BLMs SP5-24E–F Lessons 19–23 Test I** and **II** and distribute to each student. Duplicate **BLM SP5-06G Student Answer Form** and cut apart. Distribute one answer form to each student. Remind students to fill in each answer circle completely and to erase completely if they wish to change an answer.

Directed Assessment

1 Instruct students to listen as you dictate the following Sample:
Sample

> The <u>athelete</u> injured one of her <u>shoulder</u> <u>muscles</u>. <u>All correct</u>
>   A   B   C   D

Say, "Are any of the first three underlined words misspelled?" Pause for replies. Inform students that the letter *A* is below the underlined word that is misspelled. (**athlete**) Guide students to the answer form that was previously distributed. Lead students to find the Sample box and fill in the appropriate answer circle containing the same letter. Say, "You will continue in the same way. You will read each sentence, choose the word that you think is misspelled, and fill in the corresponding circle on the answer form. If all the words are spelled correctly, fill in the fourth circle, labeled *D*, for *All correct*."

2 Assist students as needed while they read the sentences and complete the Test on their own.

1. The owner was searching the finch's habitat for the nestling.
2. Has the parrot with green feathers performed yet?
3. The discount coupon allowed us to afford the price of admittance.
4. We will attempt to recapture one of the missing songbirds.
5. The normal diet for a carnivore depends upon its species.
6. The streamlined bodies of marine animals have a useful purpose.
7. The discovery of the prehistoric fish skeleton fascinated the artist.
8. We read an informative, nonfiction report about fusion of broken bones.
9. Dad imports and exports goods to provide us with a source of income.
10. The harmony of the choir served to entertain the weary traveler.
11. A fossilized exoskeleton of an invertebrate was found on the seafloor.
12. The scientist conversed about his journey to study a particular bird.
13. It was apparent that his circulation improved after the transfusion.
14. I read an article that told how a marsupial nourished its baby.
15. Dissatisfied, Lynn decided to exchange what she was wearing.
16. The internal organs of a baby squirrel are visible through the skin.
17. Clark felt nervous as he began to prepare for the performance.
18. Sharks are vertebrates that have lightweight cartilage instead of bones.
19. Victor did the chores in the orchard with a pleasant expression.
20. The incapable witness seemed to aggravate everyone in the courtroom.
21. The insect model shows the thorax, antenna, and abdomen.
22. Mrs. Baxter was sincere in her opposition to incomplete reports.
23. Birds that migrate rely on their senses, not the calendar.
24. Impolite remarks about her freckles made Traci irritable.
25. The artist's design for a sculpture requires him to compress the clay.

3 Refer to **BLM SP5-24G Lessons 19–23 Answer Key** when correcting the Test.

Student Pages

Pages 97–100

Lesson Materials

BLM SP5-25A
BLM SP5-25B
BLM SP5-25C

Created Wonders

Lessons 25–29 utilize the theme of seasons. The theme of this lesson is summer. Summer falls between spring and autumn, from June to August in the northern hemisphere. It is the season with the highest average daytime temperatures and the greatest number of hours of daylight. The summer solstice, on or about June 22, is the longest day of the year.

Day 1 Pretest

Objective

The students will accurately spell and write words with **suffixes**. They will spell and write content, vocabulary, and challenge words.

Introduction

Before class, select Challenge Words for numbers 24 and 25 from a cross-curricular subject, words misspelled on previous assignments, or words that interest your students. The word *compromised* has the **suffix -ed** and is suggested for number 24. Administer the Pretest.

Directed Instruction

1 Say each word, use it in a sentence, and then repeat the word.

Pattern Words

1. The chipmunks were <u>actively</u> storing food for the winter.
2. It is <u>advisable</u> to wear sunscreen when playing outdoors.
3. The hero acted in a <u>courageous</u> manner.
4. It is <u>definitely</u> warmer in the summer.
5. May <u>delicately</u> added a tower to her sand castle.
6. Tristan invented an <u>imaginary</u> land for a story.
7. That sunburn on your shoulders is quite <u>noticeable</u>.
8. Our team <u>practiced</u> softball all summer long.
9. Jesus <u>purchased</u> our salvation through His death on the cross.
10. Melanie's <u>refusal</u> to give in to temptation was a sign of her faith.
11. Animals' <u>survival</u> in the winter often depends on summer foraging.
12. That gold ring looks <u>valuable</u>.

Content Words

13. A <u>centigrade</u> scale is divided into 100 degrees.
14. An <u>equinox</u> occurs during spring and fall.
15. Water freezes at thirty-two degrees <u>Fahrenheit</u>.
16. The summer <u>solstice</u> occurs on or about June 22.
17. Outdoor activities are often done during the <u>summertime</u>.
18. The <u>temperature</u> during the summer months is usually warm.
19. Have you decided what to do during your <u>vacation</u>?

Vocabulary Words

20. Without a microphone, the speaker's voice was <u>inaudible</u>.
21. The ceremony of <u>promotion</u> was held at the beginning of the summer.
22. The <u>audience</u> clapped for the graduates.
23. There was quite a <u>commotion</u> when our pet hamster escaped.

Challenge Words

24. _____
25. _____

2 Allow students to self-correct their Pretest. Write each word on the board. Point out the following **suffixes** in the Pattern Words: -able, -al, -ary, -ed, -ly, -ous. The following spelling generalization applies to the Pattern Words in this lesson: Drop silent *e* when adding a suffix that begins with a vowel. Keep silent *e* after *c* or *g* when the suffix begins with *a* or *o*. The word *Fahrenheit* is always capitalized because it is derived from Daniel G. Fahrenheit, the inventor of the scale used as the customary unit of measurement of temperature. Note the roots *audi*, *aud*, and *mot* in the Vocabulary Words.

3 As a class, read, spell, and read each word. Direct students to circle

misspelled words with a colored pencil and rewrite them correctly.

4 Proof each student's Pretest. This becomes an individualized study sheet that can be used at school or at home.

5 Homework suggestion: Distribute a copy of **BLM SP5-25A Lesson 25 Words and Phrases** to each student.

Day 2 Word Analysis and Vocabulary

Objective
The students will sort and write words with **suffixes**. They will complete sentences with content words. They will use a table to write vocabulary words, match definitions, complete sentences, and choose the best meaning for underlined words.

Introduction
Write the following on the board: -able = 1, -al = 2, -ary = 3, -ed = 4, -ly = 5, -ous = 6. Invite students to refer to the list words, found on page 97, for this activity. Dictate each Pattern Word and direct students to hold up the correct number of fingers that correspond to the suffix in each dictated word. Ask students to tell you which **suffixes** begin with vowels (**-able, -al, -ary, -ed, -ous**) and which suffix begins with a consonant (**-ly**). Explain that each Pattern Word originally ended in silent *e*. Silent *e* is dropped when adding a suffix that begins with a vowel. Silent *e* is retained in words ending in *ce* or *ge* when adding a suffix beginning with *a* or *o*. This is done to maintain the soft sound of the *c* or *g*.

Directed Instruction
1 Challenge students to quickly count how many Pattern Words drop **silent e** before the suffix (**7**) and how many do not drop **silent e** (**5**).

2 Proceed to page 97. Say, spell, and say each Pattern, Content, and Vocabulary Word. Provide this week's Challenge Words and have students write them in the spaces provided. Students independently complete the page.

Differentiated Instruction

- For students who spelled all the words correctly on the Pretest, select and assign Extra Challenge Words from the following list: publicity, apostles, society, counseling, hyperbole, copyright.

- For students who spelled less than half correctly, assign the following Pattern, Content, and Vocabulary Words: refusal, actively, valuable, purchased, imaginary, courageous, solstice, vacation, summertime, temperature, audience, promotion. On the Posttest, evaluate these students on the twelve words assigned; however, encourage them to attempt to spell all the list words to the best of their ability. They are also responsible for writing the dictated sentences.

Student Day 2

Name _____

Lesson 25
Word Analysis

Suffixes

Pattern Words
refusal
survival
actively
definitely
delicately
valuable
advisable
noticeable
practiced
purchased
imaginary
courageous

Content Words
solstice
equinox
vacation
Fahrenheit
centigrade
summertime
temperature

Vocabulary Words
audience
inaudible
commotion
promotion

A **suffix** is a word part that is added to the ending of a root or a root with a prefix.

Drop **silent e** when adding a suffix that begins with a vowel. Keep **silent e** after *c* or *g* when the suffix begins with *a* or *o*.

Write Pattern Words to complete the exercises. Sort the words according to their spelling. The suffixes are *-able, -al, -ary, -ed, -ly,* and *-ous.*

1.–7. Words that drop **silent e** before the suffix
8.–12. Words that do not drop **silent e** before the suffix

1. refusal	2. survival
3. valuable	4. advisable
5. practiced	6. purchased
7. imaginary	8. actively
9. definitely	10. delicately
11. noticeable	12. courageous

Write Content Words to complete the exercises.

13. When the northern hemisphere tilts toward the sun, the season is called summer or summertime.

14. The longest day of the year, the summer solstice, occurs on or about June 22.

15. An equinox, the two days of the year when day and night are the same length, occurs during spring and fall.

16. Celsius temperature is measured using the centigrade scale.

17. Water boils at 212 degrees Fahrenheit.

18. In the summer, you may take a vacation.

Challenge Words
_____
_____
_____

© Spelling Grade 5   97

Student Day 2

Prefix		Root		Suffix	
in-	not	audi, aud	hear	-ence	state of
com-	with	mot	move	-ible	is able
pro-	forward			-ion	state of

Lesson 25
Vocabulary

Suffixes

Write the Vocabulary Words. Order may vary.
1. audience   2. inaudible
3. commotion   4. promotion

Refer to the table to complete the exercises. Write the word that is being defined.

5. not able to be heard inaudible
6. a state of confusion with much movement commotion
7. those who come to see and hear a program audience
8. a forward advancement in a job, grade, or position promotion

Write Vocabulary Words to complete the sentences.

9. On June 23, we had a ceremony of promotion for all of the graduates of our sixth grade class.

10. The principal spoke, but the microphone did not work at first, so the speech was inaudible.

11. The audience tried to hear what our principal had to say.

12. Without any commotion, the parent of a student readjusted the microphone, and we were able to hear the speech.

Choose the best meaning for each underlined word.

13. Annette gingerly handled the blown-glass sand castle.
   ○ purchased
   ○ definitely
   ● delicately

14. The brave lifeguard rescued the struggling swimmer.
   ○ noticeable
   ● courageous
   ○ practiced

Pattern Words
refusal
survival
actively
definitely
delicately
valuable
advisable
noticeable
practiced
purchased
imaginary
courageous

Content Words
solstice
equinox
vacation
Fahrenheit
centigrade
summertime
temperature

Vocabulary Words
audience
inaudible
commotion
promotion

While the earth remains, seedtime and harvest, cold and heat, winter and summer, and day and night shall not cease. Genesis 8:22

98   © Spelling Grade 5

Student Spelling Support

1. Use **BLM SP5-01A A Spelling Study Strategy** in instructional groups to provide assistance with some or all of the words.

2. Duplicate **BLMs SP5-25D–E Lesson 25 Spelling Words I** and **II** on CARD STOCK for students to use as flash cards at school or at home. Another option is to use **BLM SP5-01G Flash Cards Template** or 3" × 5" INDEX CARDS for students to write their own flash cards to use as a study aid.

3. Invite students to write the Challenge Words, numbers 24 and 25, in the Word Bank, in the back of their textbook.

4. For a Bible connection, read Genesis 8:22: "While the earth remains, seedtime and harvest, cold and heat, winter and summer, and day and night shall not cease." Invite students to discuss God's marvelous creation, including the creation of the seasons and how they are important to life on Earth. Extend the discussion by inviting students to make a poster illustrating this verse.

5. Challenge students to write two paragraphs describing an outdoor experience that they have had during the summer. Encourage them to use as many sensory descriptions as possible, including sights, sounds, smells, and textures.

Cont. on page 101

3 Proceed to page 98. Select students to build each Vocabulary Word. For example, the prefix *in-* goes with the root *aud* and the suffix *-ible* to build the word *inaudible*. Remind students that the roots *audi* and *aud* have identical meanings. Provide assistance as the page is completed. Select a student to read Genesis 8:22 and reinforce the creativity of God.

4 Homework suggestion: Distribute a copy of **BLM SP5-25B Lesson 25 Phrases and Sentences** to each student.

Day 3 Word Study Strategies

Objective

The students will write words with **suffixes** to match definitions. They will complete sentences by adding **suffixes** to adjectives to form adverbs and adding **suffixes** to verbs to form adjectives.

Introduction

Remind students that a *suffix* is a word part that is added to the ending of a root or a root with a prefix. A suffix is also known as an *affix*. Affixes expand the meaning or function of a word. Inform students that suffixes can have more than one meaning. Review the following **suffixes** and meanings:

- -able = capable of, is
- -ary = related to
- -ly = characteristic of, forms an adverb from an adjective
- -ous = quality of
- -al = related to
- -ed = makes verbs past tense

Directed Instruction

1 Write the following incomplete sentences on the board.
- Jana (active, actively) participated in summer sports. (**actively**)
- She (definitely, definite) preferred swimming. (**definitely**)
- Jana will (proud, proudly) represent her country in the Olympics. (**proudly**)

Invite a volunteer to identify the verb in the first sentence (**participated**), then ask *how, when, where, why,* or *to what extent* is the action done in the sentence, and choose one of the words in parentheses that answers the question (**actively**). Explain that the part of speech for *actively* is an adverb. An *adverb* is a word that modifies a verb, an adjective, or another adverb. An adverb tells how, when, where, why, or to what extent something is done. Choose volunteers to follow the same procedure to complete the other sentences.

2 Proceed to page 99. Students independently complete the page.

Day 4 Writing

Objective

The students will complete a cloze activity in the context of a quatrain poem.

Introduction

Teacher Note: The descriptive writing domain is the focus for Lessons 25–29. Write the following quatrain poem on the board:

> When it's summertime,
> The temperature soars.
> I'll soon be playing
> Anyplace outdoors.

Select a volunteer to read the poem aloud. Explain that this four-line poem is called a *quatrain*. Note that, in this quatrain example, the second and fourth lines of the poem rhyme, an ABCB rhyme scheme.

Directed Instruction

1 Introduce students to a *cinquain*, a five-line, unrhymed form of poetry. This type of poem uses various parts of speech. The format for a cinquain is as follows:
- Line 1: the subject of the poem
- Line 2: two adjectives that describe the subject

- Line 3: three action verbs that relate to the subject
- Line 4: a sentence about the subject
- Line 5: a synonym of the subject

2 Proceed to page 100 and read the definition of a quatrain at the top of the page. Have students write the missing words on the lines.

3 Review the example of a cinquain poem. Invite students to write a poem.

4 Homework suggestion: Distribute a copy of **BLM SP5-25C Lesson 25 Test Prep** to each student.

Day 5 Posttest

Objective
The students will correctly write dictated spelling words and sentences.

Introduction
Review by using flash cards noted in Student Spelling Support, number 2.

Directed Assessment

1 Dictate the list words by using the Pretest sentences or developing original ones. Reserve *actively*, *purchased*, *vacation*, *summertime*, and *audience* for the dictation sentences.

2 Read each sentence. Repeat as needed.
- During the summer, Don and Kyle played <u>actively</u> outdoors.
- They <u>purchased</u> a new swimming pool.
- The boys took a <u>vacation</u> to visit their grandparents.
- In the <u>summertime</u>, the boys went to a concert in the park.
- They sat in the <u>audience</u> and enjoyed the show.

3 If assigned, dictate Extra Challenge Words.

4 Score the test, counting each misspelled word as an error. Correct the dictation sentences by grading only the spelling words or grading the complete sentences.

Student Spelling Support
Cont. from page 100

6. Write this week's words, categorize the Pattern, Content, and Vocabulary Words, and attach them to the Word Wall.

7. Challenge students to write and illustrate quatrains and cinquains on "God's Marvelous Creation." Students write poetry related to the seasons, light, or nature as they reflect on Genesis' creation record. Compile the poetry into a permanent class collection.

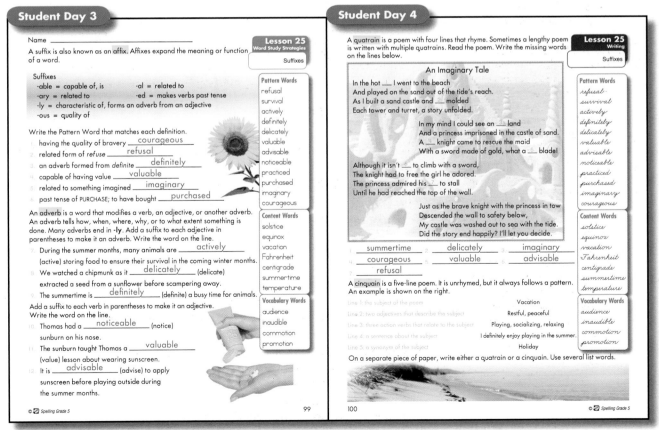

Student Day 3

Name _____

A suffix is also known as an affix. Affixes expand the meaning or function of a word.

Lesson 25
Word Study Strategies
Suffixes

Suffixes
-able = capable of, is   -al = related to
-ary = related to   -ed = makes verbs past tense
-ly = characteristic of, forms an adverb from an adjective
-ous = quality of

Write the Pattern Word that matches each definition.
1. having the quality of bravery ___courageous___
2. related form of *refuse* ___refusal___
3. an adverb formed from *definite* ___definitely___
4. capable of having value ___valuable___
5. related to something imagined ___imaginary___
6. past tense of PURCHASE; to have bought ___purchased___

An adverb is a word that modifies a verb, an adjective, or another adverb. An adverb tells how, when, where, why, or to what extent something is done. Many adverbs end in -ly. Add a suffix to each adjective in parentheses to make it an adverb. Write the word on the line.
7. During the summer months, many animals are ___actively___ (active) storing food to ensure their survival in the coming winter months.
8. We watched a chipmunk as it ___delicately___ (delicate) extracted a seed from a sunflower before scampering away.
9. The summertime is ___definitely___ (definite) a busy time for animals.

Add a suffix to each verb in parentheses to make it an adjective. Write the word on the line.
10. Thomas had a ___noticeable___ (notice) sunburn on his nose.
11. The sunburn taught Thomas a ___valuable___ (value) lesson about wearing sunscreen.
12. It is ___advisable___ (advise) to apply sunscreen before playing outside during the summer months.

Pattern Words
refusal
survival
actively
definitely
delicately
valuable
advisable
noticeable
practiced
purchased
imaginary
courageous

Content Words
solstice
equinox
Fahrenheit
centigrade
summertime
temperature

Vocabulary Words
audience
inaudible
commotion
promotion

© *Spelling Grade 5*   99

Student Day 4

A quatrain is a poem with four lines that rhyme. Sometimes a lengthy poem is written with multiple quatrains. Read the poem. Write the missing words on the lines below.

Lesson 25
Writing
Suffixes

An Imaginary Tale

In the hot __ I went to the beach
And played on the sand out of the tide's reach.
As I built a sand castle and __ molded
Each tower and turret, a story unfolded

In my mind I could see an __ land
And a princess imprisoned in the castle of sand.
A __ knight came to rescue the maid
With a sword made of gold, what a __ blade!

Although it isn't __ to climb with a sword,
The knight had to free the girl he adored.
The princess admired his __ to stall
Until he had reached the top of the wall.

Just as the brave knight with the princess in tow
Descended the wall to safety below,
My castle was washed out to sea with the tide.
Did the story end happily? I'll let you decide.

1. summertime   2. delicately   3. imaginary
4. courageous   5. valuable   6. advisable
7. refusal

A cinquain is a five-line poem. It is unrhymed, but it always follows a pattern. An example is shown on the right.

Line 1: the subject of the poem — Vacation
Line 2: two adjectives that describe the subject — Restful, peaceful
Line 3: three action verbs that relate to the subject — Playing, socializing, relaxing
Line 4: a sentence about the subject — I definitely enjoy playing in the summer.
Line 5: a synonym of the subject — Holiday

On a separate piece of paper, write either a quatrain or a cinquain. Use several list words.

Pattern Words
refusal
survival
actively
definitely
delicately
valuable
advisable
noticeable
practiced
purchased
imaginary
courageous

Content Words
solstice
equinox
vacation
Fahrenheit
centigrade
summertime
temperature

Vocabulary Words
audience
inaudible
commotion
promotion

100   © *Spelling Grade 5*

Student Pages

Pages 101–104

Lesson Materials

BLM SP5-26A
BLM SP5-26B
T-17
BLM SP5-26C
BLM SP5-26D

Created Wonders

The theme of this lesson is fall. Fall, also called autumn, begins on or about September 23 in the northern hemisphere and on or about March 21 in the southern hemisphere. These dates coincide with the equinoxes that occur two times each year. Harvesting crops and attending festivals are common activities during the fall season.

Day 1 Pretest

Objective

The students will accurately spell and write words with **suffixes**. They will spell and write content, vocabulary, and challenge words.

Introduction

Before class, select Challenge Words for numbers 24 and 25 from a cross-curricular subject, words misspelled on previous assignments, or words that interest your students. The word *noisiest* has the **suffix -est** and is suggested for number 24. Administer the Pretest.

Directed Instruction

1 Say each word, use it in a sentence, and then repeat the word.

Pattern Words

1. The <u>heaviest</u> pumpkin weighed fifty pounds.
2. Farms are <u>supplying</u> consumers with vegetables.
3. Some farmers are busy <u>applying</u> pesticides to their crops.
4. Falling leaves are quickly <u>multiplying</u> as the gentle breeze blows.
5. Jesus fills our lives with <u>happiness</u>.
6. The <u>scratchiness</u> of my throat disappeared after drinking water.
7. Are you <u>easily</u> distracted when doing your work?
8. The <u>hardiness</u> of the old tree was evident during the strong winds.
9. Grandpa's new ladder is <u>sturdier</u> than his old one.
10. Some crops are not <u>necessarily</u> ripe enough when they are harvested.
11. Are brown leaves <u>crunchier</u> than green leaves when you step on them?
12. The <u>marriage</u> of my grandparents spanned fifty-seven years.

Content Words

13. <u>Autumn</u> is the season for harvesting crops.
14. The crops are picked by <u>harvesters</u>.
15. Farmers enjoy having an <u>abundance</u> of crops to sell.
16. Many <u>festivals</u> occur during the fall season.
17. A <u>cornucopia</u> is a decoration often seen during fall months.
18. The <u>pigment</u> in maple leaves changes during the fall.
19. Do all green leaves contain <u>chlorophyll</u>?

Vocabulary Words

20. Football is a sport that begins at the <u>conclusion</u> of summer.
21. There was an <u>exclusion</u> of certain players on the football team.
22. Her scientific <u>cognition</u> was astounding.
23. Do you <u>recognize</u> the leaves from an oak tree?

Challenge Words

24. _____
25. _____

2 Allow students to self-correct their Pretest. Write each word on the board. Point out the following **suffixes**: -age, -er, -est, -ing, -ly, -ness. Note the roots *clus*, *cogni*, and *cogn* in the Vocabulary Words.

3 As a class, read, spell, and read each word. Direct students to circle misspelled words with a colored pencil and rewrite them correctly.

4 Proof each student's Pretest. This becomes an individualized study sheet that can be used at school or at home.

5 Homework suggestion: Distribute a copy of **BLM SP5-26A Lesson 26 Words and Phrases** to each student.

Day 2 Word Analysis and Vocabulary

Objective
The students will sort and write words with **suffixes** and complete sentences with content words. They will use a table to write vocabulary words, select words to match definitions, and complete sentences in context. They will choose the best meanings for given words.

Introduction
Write the following words in a column on the board: easy, sturdy, apply, heavy, marry, hardy. Ask students to state the letter that is common in each word. (**y**) Challenge students to identify the sound of y in each word. (/ē/—easy, sturdy, heavy, marry, hardy; /ī/—apply) Keep the column of words on the board for use in the Directed Instruction.

Directed Instruction

1 Teach students to change *y* to *i* when a word ends in a consonant *y* pattern, except when the suffix begins with *i*. Refer back to the column of words on the board from the Introduction. Next to each word, write the following Pattern Words that change *y* to *i* when adding the suffix: easily, sturdier, heaviest, marriage, hardiness.

2 Teach students that in the word *apply*, the *y* is not changed before adding the suffix *-ing*. Write the Pattern Word *applying* next to the word *apply* in the column of words on the board.

3 Have students refer to the list words on page 101. Challenge students to identify the total number of words that change *y* to *i* when adding a suffix (**9**) and how many keep the letter *y* when adding the suffix (**3**). Pronounce each Pattern Word and invite students to pronounce the original word that is heard before the suffix is added.

4 Proceed to page 101. Say, spell, and say each Pattern, Content, and Vocabulary Word. Provide this week's Challenge Words and have students write them in the spaces provided. Instruct students to complete the page.

Student Day 2

68 pts.

Name _____

Lesson 26 Word Analysis
Suffixes

Pattern Words
easily
necessarily
sturdier
crunchier
applying
supplying
multiplying
heaviest
marriage
hardiness
happiness
scratchiness

Content Words
autumn
festivals
pigment
chlorophyll
harvesters
abundance
cornucopia

Vocabulary Words
conclusion
exclusion
cognition
recognize

A suffix is a word part that is added to the ending of a root or a root with a prefix.

Change **y** to **i** when a word ends in a consonant **y** pattern. Do not change **y** to **i** when the suffix begins with **i**.

Write Pattern Words to complete the exercises. Sort the words according to their spelling. The suffixes are *-age, -er, -est, -ing, -ly,* and *-ness.*

1–9 Words that change **y** to **i** before the suffix
10–12 Words that do not change **y** to **i** before the suffix

1. easily
2. necessarily
3. sturdier
4. crunchier
5. heaviest
6. marriage
7. hardiness
8. happiness
9. scratchiness
10. applying
11. supplying
12. multiplying

Write Content Words to complete the exercises.

13. In the northern hemisphere when Earth reaches the halfway point between the summer and winter solstices, it is the season called fall, also known as ___autumn___.
14. Many ___festivals___ occur during autumn.
15. In the fall, crops are ready to be picked by ___harvesters___.
16. ___abundance___ of crops were grown this season.
17. Leaves and stems on crops and plants contain a green ___pigment___, known as ___chlorophyll___.
18. A ___cornucopia___ represents an abundance of harvested fruits, vegetables, and grains.

Challenge Words
_____
_____

© *Spelling Grade 5*   101

Student Day 2

Prefix		Root		Suffix	
con-	thoroughly	clus	close, shut	-ion	state of
ex-	out	cogni, cogn	know	-tion	state of
re-	again			-ize	to act

Lesson 26 Vocabulary
Suffixes

Write the Vocabulary Words. Order may vary.
1. conclusion
2. exclusion
3. cognition
4. recognize

Refer to the table to complete the exercises. Match each word to its definition.

b 5. conclusion — a. the state of knowing; awareness
d 6. exclusion — b. thoroughly coming to a close or end
a 7. cognition — c. the act of knowing someone or something again
c 8. recognize — d. the state of being left out

Write Vocabulary Words to complete the sentences.
9. Autumn begins at the ___conclusion___ of summer.
10. Do you ___recognize___ the signs of autumn?
11. The ___cognition___ that autumn is beginning usually happens when the leaves start changing colors.
12. We planned for the ___exclusion___ of deciduous trees in the yard, so there would be no leaves to rake.

Choose the best meaning for each word.

13. hardiness
   ○ the quality of being irritating
   ○ the quality of being glad
   ● the quality of withstanding harsh conditions

14. sturdier
   ● more solid
   ○ less solid
   ○ not solid

15. autumn
   ○ the season between winter and summer
   ○ the season between fall and spring
   ● the season between summer and winter

16. supplying
   ○ the action of increasing
   ● the action of providing
   ○ the action of needing

Pattern Words
easily
necessarily
sturdier
crunchier
applying
supplying
multiplying
heaviest
marriage
hardiness
happiness
scratchiness

Content Words
autumn
festivals
pigment
chlorophyll
harvesters
abundance
cornucopia

Vocabulary Words
conclusion
exclusion
cognition
recognize

102   © *Spelling Grade 5*

5 Proceed to page 102. Select students to build each Vocabulary Word. For example, the prefix *con-* goes with the root *clus* and the suffix *-ion* to build the word *conclusion*. Remind students that the roots *cogni* and *cogn* have the same meaning, *know*. Provide assistance as students complete the page.

6 Homework suggestion: Distribute a copy of **BLM SP5-26B Lesson 26 Phrases and Sentences** to each student.

Day 3 Word Study Strategies

Objective

The students will write words with **suffixes** to match definitions. They will write list words that are related forms of given words.

Introduction

Write the following **suffixes** and meanings on the board:

- -age = state of
- -est = most
- -er = more
- -ing = continuous action
- -ly = characteristic of, forms an adverb from an adjective
- -ness = quality of

Remind students that **suffixes** have different meanings and review the meaning of each one listed.

Directed Instruction

1 Have students refer to the list of words found on page 103. Invite students to identify Pattern Words that match the following definitions:

- the action of providing (**supplying**)
- more sturdy (**sturdier**)
- the quality of being irritating (**scratchiness**)

2 Write the following words and invite students to identify the list word that is a related form:

- happy, happier, happiest (**happiness**)
- marry, marries, married (**marriage**)
- multiply, multiples, multiplied (**multiplying**)

3 Proceed to page 103. Check for accuracy as students complete the page. Encourage students to refer to the Spelling Dictionary.

Day 4 Writing

Objective

The students will use proofreading marks to identify mistakes in a descriptive journal entry. They will correctly write misspelled words.

Introduction

Display **T-17 Proofreading a Descriptive Journal Entry** on the overhead, keeping the bottom portion covered. Explain that this journal entry is an example of descriptive writing. Read the journal entry and challenge students to identify what is being described. (**Possible answers: the season of autumn; a beautiful fall day; cool, breezy days of autumn; apples, pumpkins, corn, and grains that are ready for harvest; busy harvesters that are picking crops; leaves that are changing colors; cornucopia that is filled with fruit, vegetables, and grains**) Orally read the text again and challenge students to locate the mistakes. Correct the mistakes on the overhead using the appropriate proofreading mark. Use **BLM SP5-26C T-17 Answer Key** as a guide. Uncover the bottom of the transparency, so students can see a corrected version.

Directed Instruction

1 Proceed to page 104. Select a student to read the sentences at the top of the page. Allow students to work independently, assisting as needed to ensure each error is corrected. Encourage students to edit their papers using the proofreading marks. (9 misspellings; 3 capital letters needed; 2 periods needed; 2 deletes; 3 add something—comma, *the*, *an*; 2 small letters needed; 1 new paragraph)

2 Homework suggestion: Distribute a copy of **BLM SP5-26D Lesson 26 Test Prep** to each student.

Day 5 Posttest

Objective
The students will correctly write dictated spelling words and sentences.

Introduction
Review by using flash cards noted in Student Spelling Support, number 2.

Directed Assessment

1 Dictate the list words by using the Pretest sentences or developing original ones. Reserve *autumn*, *harvesters*, *heaviest*, *crunchier*, and *recognize* for the dictation sentences.

2 Read each sentence. Repeat as needed.
- During <u>autumn</u> there are plenty of apples.
- <u>Harvesters</u> pick the ripe apples and other crops.
- Clayton carried the <u>heaviest</u> bushel of apples to the truck.
- Ripe apples are <u>crunchier</u> than cooked ones.
- Do you know how to <u>recognize</u> a ripe apple?

3 If assigned, dictate Extra Challenge Words.

4 Score the test, counting each misspelled word as an error. Correct the dictation sentences by grading only the spelling words or grading the complete sentences.

Student Spelling Support
Cont. from page 104

Instruct students to write a paragraph describing why it is their favorite dish.

6. Write this week's words, categorize the Pattern, Content, and Vocabulary Words, and attach them to the Word Wall.

7. Using **BLM SP5-01G Flash Cards Template**, have auditory, visual, and kinesthetic learners write each Pattern Word on one side of the flash card and the related word on the other side. For example, write *easily* on one side and *easy* on the other side. Have students quietly read each related word and recall the generalization—change *y* to *i* when a word ends in a consonant *y* pattern, except when the suffix begins with *i*. Students write the Pattern Word on another piece of paper, then flip the flash card over to self-check the written word.

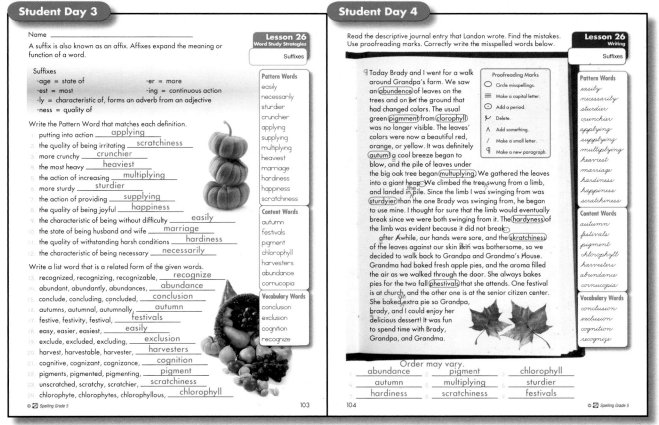

Student Pages
Pages 105–108

Lesson Materials
BLM SP5-27A
BLM SP5-27B
Photographs
BLM SP5-27C

Created Wonders

The theme of this lesson is winter. Winter is one of the four seasons created by God. Seasons are primarily determined by the tilt of the earth's axis. During the winter, snow can be a common occurrence in some places. Snowflakes are usually made up of several ice crystals. Snow is actually transparent, but reflection from many sides of its crystals gives it the appearance of being opaque white. God created each snowflake uniquely. There are no two snowflakes alike!

Day 1 Pretest

Objective

The students will accurately spell and write words with **suffixes**. They will spell and write content, vocabulary, and challenge words.

Introduction

Before class, select Challenge Words for numbers 24 and 25 from a cross-curricular subject, words misspelled on previous assignments, or words that interest your students. The word *transmitted* has the **suffix -ed** and is suggested for number 24. Administer the Pretest.

Directed Instruction

1 Say each word, use it in a sentence, and then repeat the word.

Pattern Words
1. Have you become <u>accustomed</u> to cold temperatures?
2. Sandy was <u>admitting</u> that she forgot to turn the heater off.
3. Denny used an <u>electrical</u> heater to provide warmth to the cabin.
4. Jasmine was <u>frightened</u> when she heard about the avalanche danger.
5. Can you describe what is <u>happening</u> when water turns into snow?
6. When the avalanche <u>occurred</u>, many people volunteered to help.
7. The judge is <u>pardoning</u> the criminal in the courtroom.
8. Mason <u>preferred</u> the black coat over the blue one.
9. A <u>seasonal</u> storm is a common occurrence during winter.
10. Reina was <u>straightening</u> up the skis in her closet.
11. Raji was <u>submitting</u> his video essay on seasons and climate.
12. When Jorge heard the <u>upsetting</u> news, he went to the Lord in prayer.

Content Words
13. The meteorologist used a <u>barometer</u> to assist him in his forecast.
14. The powerful <u>blizzard</u> lasted for three days.
15. Bears are one example of animals that <u>hibernate</u> during the winter.
16. Goose down is used to <u>insulate</u> winter vests and jackets.
17. Many <u>subzero</u> temperatures were reported throughout the region.
18. The <u>thermometer</u> broke and did not show an accurate reading.
19. Miranda bought a new <u>toboggan</u> for her winter vacation.

Vocabulary Words
20. During a winter storm, snow can <u>accumulate</u> in massive piles.
21. The winter storms had a <u>cumulative</u> effect on the road conditions.
22. An <u>incredible</u> amount of snow fell in the mountains.
23. Ashley gave an <u>incredulous</u> stare when she saw the snowflake crystal.

Challenge Words
24. _____
25. _____

2 Allow students to self-correct their Pretest. Write each word on the board. Point out the following **suffixes** in the Pattern Words: -al, -ed, -ing. The suffix -*en* appears in *straightening* and *frightened*, but the target **suffixes** are -*ing* and -*ed*. Note the roots *cred* and *cumul* in the Vocabulary Words.

3 As a class, read, spell, and read each word. Direct students to circle misspelled words with a colored pencil and rewrite them correctly.

4 Proof each student's Pretest. This becomes an individualized study sheet that can be used at school or at home.

5 Homework suggestion: Distribute a copy of **BLM SP5-27A Lesson 27 Words and Phrases** to each student.

Day 2 Word Analysis and Vocabulary

Objective
The students will sort and write words with **suffixes** and complete sentences with content words. They will use a table to write vocabulary words and complete sentences, and choose the best meaning for underlined words.

Introduction
Invite students to refer to the list words, found on page 105, for this activity. Challenge students to locate the three different **suffixes** found in the Pattern Words. (-al, -ed, -ing) Remind students that the suffix -en is not a lesson target. Dictate each Pattern Word while omitting the target **suffixes**. Challenge students to search their word list for the missing suffix that correlates with the dictated word, raise their hand, and identify the missing suffix. For example, dictate *season* for *seasonal* (-al).

Directed Instruction

1 Write the following words on the board:
- **sea**son (<u>season</u>)
- e**lec**tric (<u>electric</u>)
- up**set** (<u>upset</u>)
- **par**don (<u>pardon</u>)
- pre**fer** (<u>prefer</u>)
- ac**cus**tom (<u>accustom</u>)

Dictate each word while emphasizing the stressed syllable, shown in bold, in each multisyllable word. Teach the following generalization: When a multisyllable word ends in a stressed CVC pattern, and the suffix begins with a vowel, double the final consonant. Select volunteers to come to the board and underline the stressed syllable. Students then add a suffix to each word to make a list word. (**seasonal, electrical, upsetting, pardoning, preferred, accustomed**)

2 Challenge students to identify which words do not double the final consonant before adding the suffix (**seasonal, electrical, pardoning, accustomed**) and the words that do double the final consonant before adding the suffix (**upsetting, preferred**).

3 Proceed to page 105. Say, spell, and say each Pattern, Content, and Vocabulary Word. Provide this week's Challenge Words and have students write them in the spaces provided. Students complete the page.

Student Day 2

Name _____

Lesson 27
Word Analysis

Suffixes

Pattern Words
seasonal
electrical
upsetting
admitting
pardoning
happening
submitting
straightening
occurred
frightened
preferred
accustomed

Content Words
insulate
blizzard
subzero
toboggan
hibernate
barometer
thermometer

Vocabulary Words
incredible
incredulous
accumulate
cumulative

A suffix is a word part that is added to the ending of a root or a root with a prefix.

When a multisyllable word ends in a stressed CVC pattern, and the suffix begins with a vowel, double the final consonant.

Write Pattern Words to complete the exercises. Sort the words according to their spelling. The suffixes are -al, -ed, and -ing.

1.–5. Words that double the final consonant before the suffix
6.–12. Words that do not double the final consonant before the suffix

1. upsetting
2. admitting
3. submitting
4. occurred
5. perferred
6. seasonal
7. electrical
8. pardoning
9. happening
10. straightening
11. frightened
12. accustomed

Write Content Words to complete the exercises.

13. During the winter, it is not uncommon for subzero temperatures to be reflected on a thermometer.

14. Special materials are used to insulate winter jackets so a person can stay warm.

15. A barmoeter is an instrument that is used to assist meteorologists in weather forecasting.

16. The winter blizzard left five feet of snow!

17. A toboggan is a sled with a flat bottom that is used to coast down slopes of snow.

18. Many animals become inactive and hibernate during the winter season.

Challenge Words

winter

© Spelling Grade 5   105

Student Day 2

Lesson 27
Vocabulary

Suffixes

Prefix		Root		Suffix	
in-	not	cred	believe	-ible	is able
ac-	to	cumul	heap	-ulous	quality of
				-ate	to make
				-ative	inclined to

Write the Vocabulary Words. Order may vary.

1. incredible
2. incredulous
3. accumulate
4. cumulative

Refer to the table to complete the exercises. Write the word that is being defined.

5. having a quality of unbelieving incredulous
6. not able to believe; amazing incredible
7. to make a heap or pile accumulate
8. inclined to gradually heap up, build, or amass cumulative

Write Vocabulary Words to complete the sentences.

9. Talia heard on the news that c u m u l a t i v e total of snowfall from the blizzard was measured to be seven feet!

10. Talia was unbelieving and gave an i n c r e d u l o u s stare as she looked at her driveway after the blizzard.

11. She was not able to believe that the blizzard had left so much snow and thought that the amount of snow was i n c r e d i b l e.

12. Talia decided to shovel the snow onto her lawn and a c c u m u l a t e it in a pile away from her driveway.

Choose the best meaning for the underlined word or words.

13. The heavy snowstorm lasted two days.
○ electrical ● blizzard ○ incredible

14. Faye used a sled to coast downhill.
○ subzero ○ seasonal ● toboggan

Pattern Words
seasonal
electrical
upsetting
admitting
pardoning
happening
submitting
straightening
occurred
frightened
preferred
accustomed

Content Words
insulate
blizzard
subzero
toboggan
hibernate
barometer
thermometer

Vocabulary Words
incredible
incredulous
accumulate
cumulative

106   © Spelling Grade 5

Cont. on page 109

4 Proceed to page 106. Build each Vocabulary Word before students complete the page. For example, the prefix *ac-* goes with the root *cumul* and the suffix *-ate* to get the word *accumulate*. Review the unique function of the prefix *a-* in *ac-*. The letter *c* is attached to the prefix *a-* because it takes on the first letter of the root it is attached to—*cumul*. This forms the double consonant pattern *cc*. Provide assistance as needed. Select a volunteer to read exercises 9–12 when complete.

5 Homework suggestion: Distribute a copy of **BLM SP5-27B Lesson 27 Phrases and Sentences** to each student.

Day 3 Word Study Strategies

Objective

The students will write words with **suffixes** to match definitions. They will complete sentences with list words that are adjectives and verbs in the past tense.

Introduction

Remind students that a suffix, also known as an affix, expands the meaning or function of a word. Review the following **suffixes** and their meanings:

- -al = related to
- -ing = continuous action
- -ed = makes verbs past tense

Invite students to refer to the list words, found on page 107, for the following activities. Dictate the following definitions: action of making something tidy (**straightening**), related to electricity (**electrical**), past tense of PREFER (**preferred**). Challenge students to locate the correct list word for each definition. Remind them to use the meanings of each suffix to assist them in locating the correct list word.

Directed Instruction

1 Review the following generalization: When a multisyllable word ends in a stressed CVC pattern, and the suffix begins with a vowel, double the final consonant.

2 Write the following incomplete sentence on the board:
- To prepare for a blizzard, or _____ storm, one should have plenty of blankets and canned food. (season) (**seasonal**)

Remind students that an adjective is a word that describes a noun. Students select a suffix to add to the word in parentheses to make an adjective from the list.

3 Remind students that a verb is an action word that can be in the present tense or past tense. The *present tense* <u>describes an action that is happening now</u>. The *past tense* <u>describes an action that has already happened</u>. Write the following verbs, in present tense, on the board: occur, prefer. Select volunteers to write the past tense of each verb. (**occurred, preferred**)

4 Proceed to page 107. Students independently complete the page. Invite a volunteer to read Psalm 74:17 and lead a short discussion about how God created the unique seasons on Earth.

Day 4 Writing

Objective

The students will read captions on a scrapbook page. They will find and write list words.

Introduction

Share a few PHOTOGRAPHS from a vacation experience. Invite students to assist you in collating the photographs and writing caption labels. Display photographs and captions on a large sheet of construction paper.

Directed Instruction

1 Ask students if they have ever designed a scrapbook page. Explain that a scrapbook is a great way of noting memorable events through pictures and captions. Inform students that today's lesson contains a scrapbook page.

2 Proceed to page 108. Select volunteers to read the captions below the photographs aloud. Allow students to work in pairs or trios to reread each caption, find the list words, and write the list words.

3 Homework suggestion: Distribute a copy of **BLM SP5-27C Lesson 27 Test Prep** to each student.

Day 5 Posttest

Objective

The students will correctly write dictated spelling words and sentences.

Introduction

Review by using flash cards noted in Student Spelling Support, number 2.

Directed Assessment

1 Dictate the list words by using the Pretest sentences or developing original ones. Reserve *incredible, occurred, blizzard, seasonal,* and *subzero* for the dictation sentences.

2 Read each sentence. Repeat as needed.
- Last winter, an <u>incredible</u> storm blew into town.
- The storm <u>occurred</u> during the weekend.
- The powerful <u>blizzard</u> lasted for two days.
- These <u>seasonal</u> storms can be very strong.
- We experienced <u>subzero</u> temperatures.

3 If assigned, dictate Extra Challenge Words.

4 Score the test, counting each misspelled word as an error. Correct the dictation sentences by grading only the spelling words or grading the complete sentences.

Student Spelling Support

Cont. from page 108

Content, and Vocabulary Words, and attach them to the Word Wall.

7. For visual, auditory, and kinesthetic learners, invite groups of students to gather around a large piece of WHITE CONSTRUCTION PAPER. Provide a list of this week's Pattern Words and instruct one student to randomly write the Pattern Words on the paper using a BLACK MARKER. The selected student becomes the list word reader. Other students in the group will use DIFFERENT COLORED HIGHLIGHTERS to separately highlight the beginning of each dictated word and suffix. Some words will need to be highlighted with three colors if a consonant is doubled before the ending suffix. Students "race" to see who can highlight the dictated word fastest. The following are some examples: seasonal, pardoning, admitting, occurred.

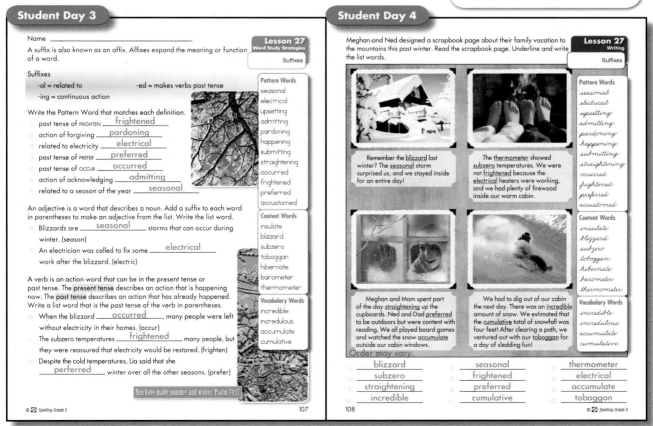

© Spelling Grade 5

Student Pages
Pages 109–112

Lesson Materials
BLM SP5-28A
3" × 5" Index cards
BLM SP5-28B
T-18
BLM SP5-28C

Created Wonders

The theme of this lesson is spring. Spring falls between winter and summer, from mid March to mid June in the northern hemisphere. The vernal equinox, the day when the number of daylight and nighttime hours is almost the same, signals the beginning of spring. Springtime holidays celebrated in the United States include Easter and Mother's Day.

Day 1 Pretest

Objective
The students will accurately spell and write words that are **plural** nouns. They will spell and write content, vocabulary, and challenge words.

Introduction
Before class, select Challenge Words for numbers 24 and 25 from a cross-curricular subject, words misspelled on previous assignments, or words that interest your students. The word *affixes* is **plural** and is suggested for number 24. Administer the Pretest.

Directed Instruction

1 Say each word, use it in a sentence, and then repeat the word.

Pattern Words
1. Three <u>businesses</u> promised to support our school fund-raising drive.
2. The <u>aircraft</u> were taking off from the airport.
3. <u>Countries</u> in the northern hemisphere have spring weather in April.
4. The library contains <u>dictionaries</u> printed by different companies.
5. Nina used sprigs of parsley as <u>garnishes</u> for her salad.
6. The family received the <u>kindnesses</u> of others with joy.
7. The <u>missionaries</u> planted several new churches in Asia.
8. Rabbits may have four or more <u>offspring</u> per litter.
9. <u>Onions</u> grow below the ground.
10. Baseball players need sharp <u>reflexes</u> to make plays quickly.
11. <u>Salmon</u> swim upstream to lay their eggs.
12. Tia made several egg salad <u>sandwiches</u>.

Content Words
13. Is Easter an <u>annual</u> celebration?
14. Followers of <u>Christianity</u> believe that Jesus rose from the dead.
15. Livia enjoys <u>gardening</u> in the spring.
16. April showers provided much needed <u>precipitation</u>.
17. Easter is the celebration of Jesus' <u>resurrection</u>.
18. Daffodils and crocuses bloom in <u>springtime</u>.
19. The <u>vernal</u> equinox occurs during the spring.

Vocabulary Words
20. A <u>juvenile</u> rabbit is called a bunny.
21. The tulips bloomed in <u>vivid</u> shades of red and pink.
22. The spring thaw seemed to <u>rejuvenate</u> the mountain meadow.
23. A <u>vivacious</u> little robin perched on a branch.

Challenge Words
24. _____
25. _____

2 Allow students to self-correct their Pretest. Write each word on the board. Point out that each Pattern Word is a plural noun. Note that most of the plural nouns in this lesson follow a predictable pattern. The irregular **plurals** are *salmon, aircraft,* and *offspring.* The irregular **plurals** have the same spelling in both the singular and plural forms. *Christianity* is always capitalized because it is a proper noun. Note the roots *juven* and *viv* in the Vocabulary Words.

3 As a class, read, spell, and read each word. Direct students to circle misspelled words with a colored pencil and rewrite them correctly.

4 Proof each student's Pretest. This becomes an individualized study

sheet that can be used at school or at home.

5 Homework suggestion: Distribute a copy of **BLM SP5-28A Lesson 28 Words and Phrases** to each student.

Day 2 Word Analysis and Vocabulary

Objective

The students will sort and write words that are **plurals** and complete sentences with content words. They will use a table to write vocabulary words, match definitions, complete sentences, and choose the best meaning for underlined words.

Introduction

Write the singular form of each Pattern Word on one side and the plural form on the other side of 3" × 5" INDEX CARDS. The irregular **plurals**, *salmon*, *aircraft*, and *offspring*, will be the same on both sides. Distribute the cards to twelve students. Write the following generalizations on the board:

- To make most nouns plural, add -*s*. (**onions**)
- To make nouns ending in *ch*, *s*, *sh*, or *x* plural, add -*es*. (**sandwiches, kindnesses, businesses, garnishes, reflexes**)
- To make nouns ending in a consonant *y* pattern plural, change *y* to *i* and add -*es*. (**countries, dictionaries, missionaries**)
- Some irregular plural nouns are spelled alike, whether singular or plural. (**salmon, aircraft, offspring**)

Instruct students to look at both sides of their cards to determine what was done to each singular noun to form the plural noun. Read each generalization aloud. Have students raise their card if they have a word that follows the generalization mentioned. Invite students to spell both the singular and plural forms. Retain the index cards for use in Student Spelling Support, number 7.

Directed Instruction

1 Choose a student to look up the Content Words *vernal* and *precipitation* in their Spelling Dictionary. Invite the student to share the pronunciation,

Differentiated Instruction

- For students who spelled all the words correctly on the Pretest, select and assign Extra Challenge Words from the following list: sonata, ambitious, representative, appendectomy, character, external.
- For students who spelled less than half correctly, assign the following Pattern, Content, and Vocabulary Words: onions, salmon, reflexes, offspring, countries, missionaries, annual, gardening, springtime, resurrection, rejuvenate, vivid. On the Posttest, evaluate these students on the twelve words assigned; however, encourage them to attempt to spell all the list words to the best of their ability. They are also responsible for writing the dictated sentences.

65 pts.

Student Day 2

Name _____

Lesson 28
Word Analysis

Plurals

Pattern Words
onions
salmon
aircraft
reflexes
offspring
countries
garnishes
kindnesses
businesses
dictionaries
sandwiches
missionaries

Content Words
vernal
annual
gardening
springtime
Christianity
precipitation
resurrection

Vocabulary Words
juvenile
rejuvenate
vivacious
vivid

Plural nouns name more than one person, place, thing, or idea.

To make most nouns plural, add -**s**. Add -**es** to nouns ending in *ch*, *s*, *sh*, or *x*. Change **y** to **i** and add -**es** to nouns ending in a consonant **y** pattern.

Irregular plural nouns do not follow regular patterns. These nouns are often spelled alike whether singular or plural.

Write Pattern Words to complete the exercises. Sort the words according to their spelling.

1. Word that adds -**s**   2.–6. Words that add -**es** after *ch*, *s*, *sh*, or *x*
7.–9. Words that change **y** to **i** and add -**es**   10.–12. Irregular plurals

1. onions
2. sandwiches
3. kindnesses
4. businesses
5. garnishes
6. reflexes
7. countries
8. dictionaries
9. missionaries
10. salmon
11. aircraft
12. offspring

Write Content Words to complete the exercises.

13. The season between winter and summer is springtime.
14. Many people enjoy gardening during this season.
15. Springtime in the northern hemisphere often brings light precipitation, providing needed moisture for plants.
16. The vernal equinox occurs in the springtime.
17. Easter Sunday celebrates Christ's resurrection.
18. The annual celebration of Easter is shared by all followers of christianity.

Challenge Words

© Spelling Grade 5   109

Student Day 2

	Prefix		Root		Suffix	
re-	again	juven	young	-ile	related to	
		viv	life	-ate	to make	
				-acious	quality of	
				-id	like	

Lesson 28
Vocabulary

Plurals

Write the Vocabulary Words. Order may vary.
1. juvenile   2. rejuvenate
3. vivacious   4. vivid

Refer to the table to complete the exercises. Match each word to its definition.

d 5. juvenile   a. bright; lifelike
c 6. rejuvenate b. having the quality of liveliness
a 7. vivid   c. to make youthful again
b 8. vivacious   d. young

Write Vocabulary Words to complete the sentences.

9. After a long, cold winter, the meadow seemed to rejuvenate itself in the springtime.
10. The snow had melted, and the animals were perky and vivacious.
11. Flowers were blooming in vivid shades of red, yellow, pink, and purple.
12. Newborn bunnies and other juvenile animals frolicked and scampered about.

Choose the best meaning for the underlined word or words.

13. The ewe nurtured her twin babies.
- ● offspring   ○ missionaries
- ○ garnishes   ○ reflexes

14. We appreciated their kindly acts and generosity.
- ○ salmon   ● kindnesses
- ○ dictionaries ○ missionaries

Pattern Words
onions
salmon
aircraft
reflexes
offspring
countries
garnishes
kindnesses
businesses
dictionaries
sandwiches
missionaries

Content Words
vernal
annual
gardening
springtime
Christianity
precipitation
resurrection

Vocabulary Words
juvenile
rejuvenate
vivacious
vivid

110   © Spelling Grade 5

part of speech, definition, and sample sentence with the class.

2 Proceed to page 109. Say, spell, and say each Pattern, Content, and Vocabulary Word. Provide this week's Challenge Words and have students write them in the spaces provided. Students complete the page.

3 Proceed to page 110. Select students to build each Vocabulary Word. For example, the prefix re- goes with the root *juven* and the suffix -*ate* to build the word *rejuvenate*. Provide assistance as students complete the page independently.

4 Homework suggestion: Distribute a copy of **BLM SP5-28B Lesson 28 Phrases and Sentences** to each student.

Day 3 Word Study Strategies

Objective

The students will write the plural form of singular words. They will write singular or plural possessive nouns to complete phrases.

Introduction

Write the following incomplete phrases on the board, leaving blanks as indicated:

- the flavor of the onion   the _____ flavor (**onion's**)
- the flavor of ten onions   the _____ flavor (**onions'**)
- the customer of the business   the _____ customer (**business'**)
- the customer of ten businesses   the _____ customer (**businesses'**)

Explain that a *possessive noun* <u>shows ownership</u>. Possessive nouns may be singular or plural. To make singular nouns and irregular plural nouns possessive, add an apostrophe and -*s*. Choose a volunteer to fill in the first blank. To make singular nouns ending in *s* and regular plural nouns possessive, add an apostrophe after the *s*. Invite a volunteer to fill in the second, third, and fourth blanks.

Directed Instruction

1 Invite students to turn to the list of Pattern Words, found on page 111, and state the singular form of each plural noun.

2 Proceed to page 111. Remind students to look closely at the singular words shown in exercises 1–12 and to apply the generalizations for forming **plurals** covered in Day 2 Introduction. Select volunteers to spell the plural for each singular noun in exercises 1–12. Students complete the page.

3 Choose a student to read John 11:25. Share how Christ's resurrection has impacted your life.

Day 4 Writing

Objective

The students will read a report about the season of spring. They will write list words that could replace the bold words in the report.

Introduction

Display **T-18 Graphic Organizer** and explain that the diagram is a graphic organizer. A *graphic organizer* is <u>a drawing that shows how words or ideas fit together</u>. Graphic organizers can provide a beginning for a writing assignment. Write the word *springtime* in the oval on the transparency. Brainstorm things that would fall into the categories of sights, smells, tastes, sounds, textures, and activities associated with springtime in the area where you live. Write students' ideas on the board. Invite students to assist you in filling in the boxes in the graphic organizer on the transparency, using a separate box for each category.

Directed Instruction

1 Remind students that the Spelling Dictionary provides definitions for each list word. They may use the Spelling Dictionary as an aid to

defining words and determining synonyms.

2 Proceed to page 112. Encourage students to read the entire report before selecting each word with the same meaning as the bold words in the report. When complete, have a volunteer read the report, replacing the bold words with list words.

3 Invite students to reference the graphic organizer in the lesson Introduction as a framework for writing the suggested paragraph at the bottom of the page.

4 Homework suggestion: Distribute a copy of **BLM SP5-28C Lesson 28 Test Prep** to each student.

Day 5 Posttest

Objective
The students will correctly write dictated spelling words and sentences.

Introduction
Review by using flash cards noted in Student Spelling Support, number 2.

Directed Assessment

1 Dictate the list words by using the Pretest sentences or developing original ones. Reserve *springtime, countries, offspring, annual,* and *vivid* for the dictation sentences.

2 Read each sentence. Repeat as needed.
- Springtime is a season between winter and summer.
- In countries north of the equator, the days grow longer in the spring.
- Many woodland animals give birth to offspring in this season.
- Easter, an annual celebration, is always in the spring.
- Flowers with vivid colors bloom in the spring.

3 If assigned, dictate Extra Challenge Words.

4 Score the test, counting each misspelled word as an error. Correct the dictation sentences by grading only the spelling words or grading the complete sentences.

Student Spelling Support
Cont. from page 112

Content, and Vocabulary Words, and attach them to the Word Wall.

7. Kinesthetic learners will enjoy matching plural nouns with their singular forms. Spread two sets of word cards like those used in Day 2 Introduction in random order on a table, placing one set with the singular words faceup and one set with the plural words faceup. Invite a student to match each singular noun with its plural form quickly while you time the activity using a clock with a second hand. Record the length of time needed to match the cards. Invite a second student to repeat the activity in less time.

8. Challenge students to interview missionaries and then write a description of their ministry setting—both geographically and spiritually. Collect these writings in a class book entitled "Christianity at Work."

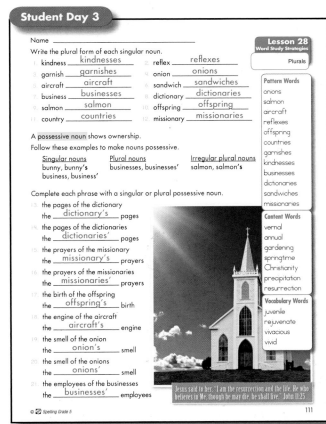

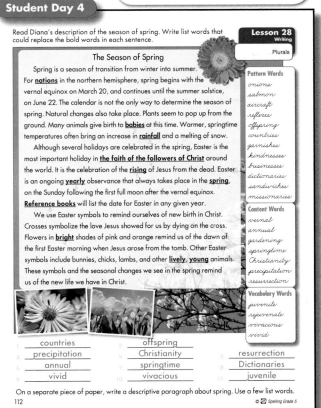

Variant Consonant Spellings

Student Pages
Pages 113–116

Lesson Materials
BLM SP5-29A
BLMs SP5-29B–C
BLM SP5-29D
T-4
BLM SP5-29E

Created Wonders
The theme of this lesson is hemispheres. A hemisphere is a half of a sphere and generally refers to half of the earth. The earth has two hemispheric pairs—the northern and southern hemispheres, and the eastern and western hemispheres. The northern and southern hemispheres are equally divided by the earth's equator. The eastern hemisphere includes Europe, Asia, Africa, and Australia. The western hemisphere contains the Americas and their surrounding waters.

Day 1 Pretest

Objective
The students will accurately spell and write words with **variant consonant spellings**. They will spell and write content, vocabulary, and challenge words.

Introduction
Before class, select Challenge Words for numbers 24 and 25 from a cross-curricular subject, words misspelled on previous assignments, or words that interest your students. The word *chrysanthemum* has the **variant consonant spelling** for the /k/ sound, spelled *ch*, and is suggested for number 24. Administer the Pretest.

Directed Instruction

1 Say each word, use it in a sentence, and then repeat the word.

Pattern Words
1. How does God <u>anchor</u> the earth in the solar system?
2. Caleb read two <u>biographies</u> about Sir George Airy, an astronomer.
3. After the <u>catastrophe</u>, many countries sent relief aid.
4. Simone heard an <u>echo</u> after shouting into the valley.
5. Did you include <u>enough</u> information in your report?
6. Royal Observatory <u>machinery</u> emits a prime meridian laser beam.
7. Reid was <u>measuring</u> the distance on a Mercator projection map.
8. Shantal's <u>parachute</u> opened when she pulled the cord.
9. Mr. Mordue needed <u>roughly</u> two hours for his hemispheres lecture.
10. Colby used <u>scissors</u> to cut out pictures for a project on hemispheres.
11. Dr. Micah ate a <u>sugary</u> treat at the navigational conference.
12. The observatory museum holds a <u>treasury</u> of astronomical tools.

Content Words
13. God created the earth to rotate around an <u>axis</u>.
14. The <u>equator</u> is the line from which latitudes on Earth are measured.
15. The north and south poles are <u>equidistant</u> from the earth's equator.
16. Europe, Asia, Africa, and Australia are in the eastern <u>hemisphere</u>.
17. <u>Latitude</u> identifies locations north and south of the equator.
18. <u>Longitude</u> represents a distance from the prime meridian.
19. The <u>meridians</u> of longitude converge at the earth's poles.

Vocabulary Words
20. To <u>counteract</u> a low test grade, Margot turned in extra credit.
21. An <u>inspection</u> of Earth's divisions showed Abe four hemispheres.
22. There was <u>interaction</u> among twenty-five nations at the conference.
23. "In <u>retrospect</u>, I should have done more research," Cora said.

Challenge Words
24. _____
25. _____

2 Allow students to self-correct their Pretest. Write each word on the board. Point out that each Pattern Word contains a consonant sound that is represented by a variant consonant spelling. A *variant consonant spelling* is an uncommon spelling for a consonant sound. The **variant consonant spellings** are as follows: ch for /k/, ch or s for /sh/, gh or ph for /f/, s for /z/, and s for /zh/. Clearly differentiate between the similar sounds of /sh/ and /zh/. Review each spelling and its sound. Note the roots *act* and *spect* in the Vocabulary Words.

3 As a class, read, spell, and read each word. Direct students to circle

misspelled words with a colored pencil and rewrite them correctly.

4 Proof each student's Pretest. This becomes an individualized study sheet that can be used at school or at home.

5 Homework suggestion: Distribute a copy of **BLM SP5-29A Lesson 29 Words and Phrases** to each student.

Day 2 Word Analysis and Vocabulary

Objective

The students will sort words with **variant consonant spellings** and complete sentences with content words. They will use a table to write vocabulary words and complete sentences.

Introduction

Write the following consonant sounds and **variant consonant spellings** on the board: /k/ spelled ch, /sh/ spelled ch or s, /f/ spelled gh or ph, /z/ spelled s, /zh/ spelled s. Distribute a copy of **BLMs SP5-29B–C Lesson 29 Spelling Words I** and **II** to each student. Leave the copies intact and do not cut apart the cards. Dictate each Pattern Word and the consonant sound that has a unique spelling. Select a volunteer to identify each uncommon spelling that correlates with the consonant sound. Instruct students to underline the variant consonant spelling. For example, for the word *echo*, dictate /ˈe kō/, isolate and say /k/; students should identify *ch* as the variant consonant spelling and underline *ch* on their copies.

Directed Instruction

1 Invite students to refer to the list words on page 113. Challenge seven groups of students to locate the definition of a specified Content Word. Students use their Spelling Dictionary and write the definition of their assigned word on the appropriate flash card from the blackline masters in the Introduction. Each group orally shares the definition of their specified word. Students write the definition of each Content Word. (Note that *latitude* and *longitude* have two definitions each.)

2 Select a volunteer to read the Vocabulary Words from page 113.

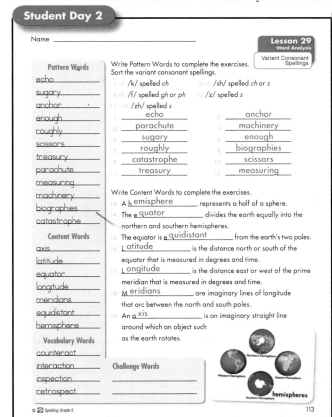

Differentiated Instruction

- For students who spelled all the words correctly on the Pretest, select and assign Extra Challenge Words from the following list: staccato, communion, presidential, protective, conjunction, capacity.

- For students who spelled less than half correctly, assign the following Pattern, Content, and Vocabulary Words: echo, sugary, enough, scissors, measuring, biographies, latitude, equator, longitude, hemisphere, interaction, inspection. On the Posttest, evaluate these students on the twelve words assigned; however, encourage them to attempt to spell all the list words to the best of their ability. They are also responsible for writing the dictated sentences.

Student Day 2

Name _____

Lesson 29
Word Analysis
Variant Consonant Spellings

Pattern Words
echo
sugary
anchor
enough
roughly
scissors
treasury
parachute
measuring
machinery
biographies
catastrophe

Content Words
axis
latitude
equator
longitude
meridians
equidistant
hemisphere

Vocabulary Words
counteract
interaction
inspection
retrospect

Write Pattern Words to complete the exercises. Sort the variant consonant spellings.

1–2 /k/ spelled ch   3–5 /sh/ spelled ch or s
6–9 /f/ spelled gh or ph   10 /z/ spelled s
11–12 /zh/ spelled s

1. echo   2. anchor
3. parachute   4. machinery
5. sugary   6. enough
7. roughly   8. biographies
9. catastrophe   10. scissors
11. treasury   12. measuring

Write Content Words to complete the exercises.
13. A hemisphere represents a half of a sphere.
14. The equator divides the earth equally into the northern and southern hemispheres.
15. The equator is equidistant from the earth's two poles.
16. Latitude is the distance north or south of the equator that is measured in degrees and time.
17. Longitude is the distance east or west of the prime meridian that is measured in degrees and time.
18. Meridians are imaginary lines of longitude that arc between the north and south poles.
19. An axis is an imaginary straight line around which an object such as the earth rotates.

Challenge Words

hemispheres

© Spelling Grade 5   113

Student Day 2

Prefix		Root		Suffix	
counter-	opposite of	act	do	-ion	state of
inter-	among	spect	look		
in-	into				
retro-	back				

Lesson 29
Vocabulary
Variant Consonant Spellings

Write the Vocabulary Words. Order may vary.
1. counteract   2. interaction
3. inspection   4. retrospect

Refer to the table to complete the exercises. Write the word that is being defined.
5. to do the opposite of   counteract
6. a look back to think about or review   retrospect
7. a state of looking into and examining something   inspection
8. a state of communication or collaboration among two or more people   interaction

Write Vocabulary Words to complete the sentences.
9. Ailea took the initative to discuss her project on the earth's hemispheres with her teacher, Mrs. Lim, because Ailea knew that frequent ____interaction____ between students and teachers was important.
10. During her research, Ailea learned that when the northern hemisphere experiences summer, the southern hemisphere is experiencing winter. In her project, she explained that sunscreen could be used as an effective method to ____counteract____ the damaging rays of the sun.
11. Ailea prepared for Mrs. Lim's detailed ____inspection____ of her project. Ailea was glad that she included facts on the northern and southern hemispheres as well as the eastern and western hemispheres.
12. In ____retrospect____, Ailea was happy that she took the time to ask Mrs. Lim some questions, research, and include many pertinent facts about the earth's hemispheres in her project.

The earth is the Lord's, and all its fullness, the world and those who dwell therein. Psalm 24:1

114   © Spelling Grade 5

Pattern Words
echo
sugary
anchor
enough
roughly
scissors
treasury
parachute
measuring
machinery
biographies
catastrophe

Content Words
axis
latitude
equator
longitude
meridians
equidistant
hemisphere

Vocabulary Words
counteract
interaction
inspection
retrospect

Cont. on page 117

Instruct students to underline the roots *act* and *spect* on their flash cards. Students cut apart all of the flash cards and retain them as a reference tool and study aid for this week's lesson.

3 Proceed to page 113. Say, spell, and say each Pattern, Content, and Vocabulary Word. Provide this week's Challenge Words and have students write them in the spaces provided. Students may choose to add the Challenge Words to their flash card study pile. Remind students to use their flash cards to assist them in completing the page.

4 Proceed to page 114. Build each Vocabulary Word before students complete the page. For example, the prefix *inter-* goes with the root *act* and the suffix *-ion* to get the word *interaction*. Provide assistance as needed. Invite a volunteer to read Psalm 24:1 and lead a short discussion about how all of God's creation belongs to Him.

5 Homework suggestion: Distribute a copy of **BLM SP5-29D Lesson 29 Phrases and Sentences** to each student.

Day 3 Word Study Strategies

Objective

The students will write list words to match their pronunciations and identify a word that has the same consonant sound as the underlined letter or letters in a given word. They will utilize dictionary skills by answering questions about the different components of a dictionary entry.

Introduction

Write the following pronunciations on the board: /ˈshoo gə rē/ (**sugary**), /mə ˈri dē ənz/ (**meridians**), /in ˈspek shən/ (**inspection**).
Challenge students to sound out the pronunciations and identify the words.

Directed Instruction

1 Write the following words, with underlined **variant consonant spellings**, on the board: s<u>ug</u>ary, rou<u>gh</u>ly, trea<u>s</u>ury, mea<u>s</u>uring, ma<u>ch</u>inery, catastro<u>ph</u>e. Challenge students to identify pairs of words that contain the same underlined consonant sound. (**sugary and machinery; roughly and catastrophe; treasury and measuring**)

2 Display **T-4 Using the Spelling Dictionary** to quickly review the following parts of a dictionary page: guide words, entry word, pronunciation, part of speech, definition, sample sentence.

3 Proceed to page 115. Students independently complete the page. Assist as needed.

Day 4 Writing

Objective

The students will read two descriptive passages about the earth's hemispheres. They will complete sentences by writing the missing syllable or syllables in each list word.

Introduction

Invite students to refer to the list words, found on page 116, for this activity. Slowly read the following informative passage aloud, while dictating only the first syllable of each underlined list word and completely dictating each sentence:

Did you know that the earth is divided in half by an imaginary circle called the e_____(equator)? The equator is e_____(equidistant) from the earth's poles and divides the world into the northern he_____ (hemisphere) and the southern hemisphere. The earth is also divided into eastern and western hemispheres. The mea_____ (measuring) of the systems of la_____ (latitude) and lon_____ (longitude) enable one to pinpoint a location anywhere in the world.

While reading, raise your hand as you dictate the first syllable only of each incomplete list word. Complete the sentence dictation. Invite students to watch for your hand, scan their word list, and locate the most appropriate list word that completes the dictated first syllable.

Directed Instruction

1 Reread the passage with the completed list words inserted into the text.

2 Proceed to page 116 and choose a volunteer to read the sentences at the top of the page. Invite students to collaborate in groups as they complete the page and read the passages aloud.

3 Homework suggestion: Distribute a copy of **BLM SP5-29E Lesson 29 Test Prep** to each student.

Day 5 Posttest

Objective

The students will correctly write dictated spelling words and sentences.

Introduction

Review by using flash cards noted in Student Spelling Support, number 2.

Directed Assessment

1 Dictate the list words by using the Pretest sentences or developing original ones. Reserve *interaction, hemisphere, equator, scissors,* and *enough* for the dictation sentences.

2 Read each sentence. Repeat as needed.
- The <u>interaction</u> in a group project is very important.
- Pete decided to research the southern <u>hemisphere</u>.
- He mentioned the location of the <u>equator</u> in his report.
- Pete used <u>scissors</u> to cut out maps and drawings.
- He researched <u>enough</u> information for his part of the project.

3 If assigned, dictate Extra Challenge Words.

4 Score the test, counting each misspelled word as an error. Correct the dictation sentences by grading only the spelling words or grading the complete sentences.

Student Spelling Support

Cont. from page 116

6. Write this week's words, categorize the Pattern, Content, and Vocabulary Words, and attach them to the Word Wall.

7. For visual learners, instruct each student to use two different colored pencils to write the Pattern Words from this lesson. Students use one color to write the complete word and then trace over each variant consonant spelling with a different color. The following are some examples: **echo, sugary, enough, treasury**.

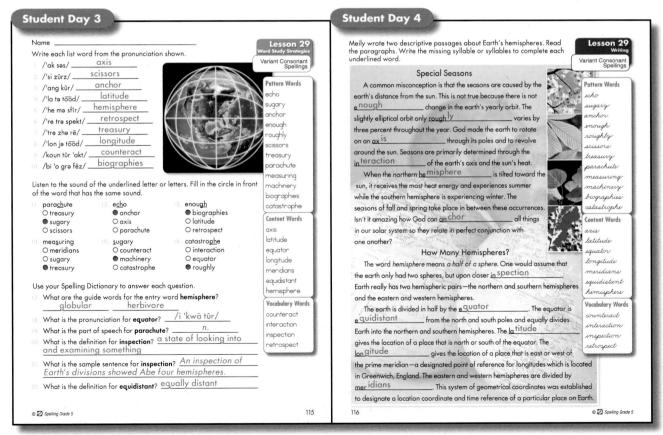

Student Pages
Pages 117–120

Lesson Materials

T-19
BLM SP5-30A
BLM SP5-30B
T-14
BLM SP5-30C
BLM SP5-30D
BLMs SP5-30E–F
BLM SP5-06G
BLM SP5-30G

Day 1 Suffixes

Objective
The students will spell, identify, and sort words that drop silent *e* before **suffixes** are added and words that do not drop silent *e* before **suffixes** are added.

Introduction
Teacher Note: This week's lesson incorporates the Pattern, Content, and Vocabulary Words taught in Lessons 25–29 using a variety of activities such as sorting, a word search, adding or subtracting letters to form words, a crossword puzzle, filling in the correct answer circle, unscrambling words, and shape boxes.

Write the following words and **suffixes** in a column on the board: refuse (-al), survive (-al), active (-ly), definite (-ly), delicate (-ly), value (-able), advise (-able), notice (-able), practice (-ed), purchase (-ed), imagine (-ary), courage (-ous). Select volunteers to write the word with the suffix to form a new word. Have students write the new word next to the word and suffix, forming a new column. For example, *survive* (-al), *survival*. Point out the words that drop silent *e* when adding a suffix and those that do not.

Directed Instruction

1 Remind students that silent *e* is dropped when adding a suffix that begins with a vowel as in *refusal*. However, silent *e* is retained when adding a suffix beginning with an *a* or *o* as in *noticeable* and *courageous*. This is done to maintain the soft sound of the *c* or *g*.

2 Display **T-19 Lessons 25–29 Study Sheet** on the overhead to review Lesson 25 words in unison, using the say-spell-say technique.

3 Proceed to page 117. Explain that the box contains all the Pattern, Content, and Vocabulary Words in Lessons 25–29. This list is the same list of words that was previously displayed on the overhead. Encourage students to use this list as a review tool. Instruct students to read the directions and independently complete the page.

4 Distribute a copy of **BLM SP5-30A Lessons 25–29 Study Sheet** to each student to take home for study.

5 Homework suggestion: Distribute a copy of **BLM SP5-30B Lesson 30 Homework I** to each student to practice words with **suffixes** and **plurals**.

Day 2 Suffixes

Objective
The students will find and circle words with **suffixes** in a word search. They will add or subtract letters to write words with **suffixes**.

Introduction
Before class, select a volunteer to write the following Pattern Words from Lesson 26 in the squares of the **T-14 Mini Word Search Grid**: easily, sturdier, heaviest, marriage. Assist the volunteer in positioning the words across, down, diagonally, and backwards. Fill in each remaining square on the grid with a letter. When complete, display the transparency on the overhead and challenge students

to locate the Pattern Words that are being reflected on the board. Have students refer to the top of page 118 for the list words. Circle each word as it is found. An example of a mini word search is shown.

Directed Instruction

1 Display **T-19 Lessons 25–29 Study Sheet** to review Lesson 26 words in unison, using the say-spell-say technique.

2 Write the following on the board:
- electric + al = _____ (**electrical**)
- straightened – ed + ing = _____ (**straightening**)
- occurring – ing + ed = _____ (**occurred**)

Select volunteers to complete each word.

3 Refer to **T-19 Lessons 25–29 Study Sheet** to review Lesson 27 words in unison, using the say-spell-say technique.

4 Proceed to page 118. Students complete the page independently. Assist as needed.

5 Homework suggestion: Distribute a copy of **BLM SP5-30C Lesson 30 Homework II** to each student to practice words with **variant consonant spellings**, Content Words, and Vocabulary Words.

Day 3 Plurals and Variant Consonant Spellings

Objective

The students will spell and write **plurals** in a crossword puzzle. They will select the appropriate answer circle to indicate if words with **variant consonant spellings** are spelled correctly or incorrectly, and correctly write the word.

Introduction

Display **T-19 Lessons 25–29 Study Sheet** to review Lessons 28–29 words in unison, using the say-spell-say technique.

Directed Instruction

1 Read the following definitions and challenge students to find a word from Lesson 28 that matches each definition:
- automatic responses (**reflexes**)
- vehicles made for traveling through the air (**aircraft**)
- reference books (**dictionaries**)
- babies (**offspring**)

2 Write the following words from Lesson 29 on the board:
- tresury (**incorrect; treasury**)
- biografies (**incorrect; biographies**)
- sugary (**correct; sugary**)

Select volunteers to identify if the word is spelled correctly or incorrectly, and correctly write each word.

3 Proceed to page 119. Invite students to read the directions and complete the page individually. Encourage students to refer to their Spelling Dictionary for assistance in completing the crossword puzzle.

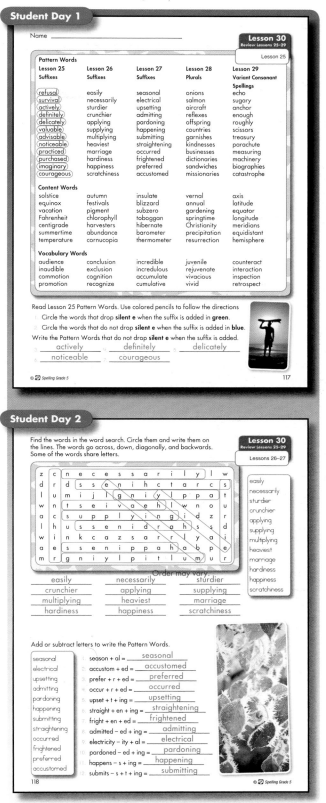

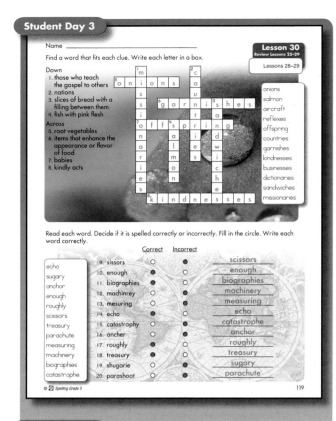

Name _____

Find a word that fits each clue. Write each letter in a box.

Lesson 30
Review Lessons 28–29

Lessons 28–29

Down
1. those who teach the gospel to others
2. nations
3. slices of bread with a filling between them
4. fish with pink flesh

Across
5. root vegetables
6. items that enhance the appearance or flavor of food
7. babies
8. kindly acts

onions
salmon
aircraft
reflexes
offspring
countries
garnishes
kindnesses
businesses
dictionaries
treasury
sandwiches
missionaries

Read each word. Decide if it is spelled correctly or incorrectly. Fill in the circle. Write each word correctly.

		Correct	Incorrect	
echo	9. sissors	○	●	scissors
sugary	10. enough	●	○	enough
anchor	11. biographies	●	○	biographies
enough	12. machinrey	○	●	machinery
roughly	13. mesuring	○	●	measuring
scissors	14. echo	●	○	echo
treasury	15. catastrophy	○	●	catastrophe
parachute	16. ancher	○	●	anchor
measuring	17. roughly	●	○	roughly
machinery	18. treasury	●	○	treasury
biographies	19. shugarie	○	●	sugary
catastrophe	20. parashoot	○	●	parachute

© Spelling Grade 5   119

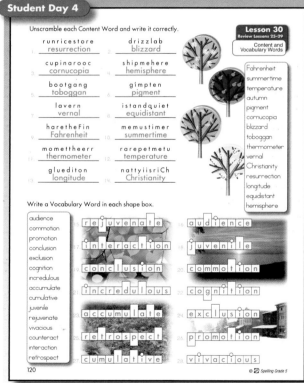

Unscramble each Content Word and write it correctly.

Lesson 30
Review Lessons 25–29

Content and
Vocabulary Words

1. runricestore — resurrection
2. drizzlab — blizzard
3. cupinarooc — cornucopia
4. shipmehere — hemisphere
5. bootgang — toboggan
6. gimpten — pigment
7. lavern — vernal
8. istandquiet — equidistant
9. haretheFin — Fahrenheit
10. memustimer — summertime
11. momettheerr — thermometer
12. rarepetmetu — temperature
13. gluediton — longitude
14. nattyiisriCh — Christianity

Fahrenheit
summertime
temperature
autumn
pigment
cornucopia
blizzard
toboggan
thermometer
vernal
Christianity
resurrection
longitude
equidistant
hemisphere

Write a Vocabulary Word in each shape box.

audience
commotion
promotion
conclusion
exclusion
cognition
incredulous
accumulate
cumulative
juvenile
rejuvenate
vivacious
counteract
interaction
retrospect

15. rejuvenate
16. audience
17. interaction
18. juvenile
19. conclusion
20. commotion
21. incredulous
22. cognition
23. accumulate
24. exclusion
25. retrospect
26. promotion
27. cumulative
28. vivacious

120   © Spelling Grade 5

Day 4 Content Words and Vocabulary Words

Objective

The students will unscramble and write content words. They will write vocabulary words in shape boxes.

Introduction

Display **T-19 Lessons 25–29 Study Sheet** to review Content Words and Vocabulary Words in unison, using the say-spell-say technique.

Directed Instruction

1 Write the following scrambled Content Words on the board:
- n e r l a v (**vernal**)
- t e n g i m p (**pigment**)
- a p e r e r m u t t e (**temperature**)

Challenge students to unscramble the words. Select three volunteers to write the correct spellings on the board.

2 Select volunteers to draw shape boxes for the following words:
- inaudible
- vivid
- inspection

3 Proceed to page 120. Students independently complete the page.

4 Homework suggestion: Distribute a copy of **BLM SP5-30D Lessons 25–29 Test Prep** to each student to practice with many of the words that may appear on the Assessment. Prepare for the Assessment by studying the words on **BLM SP5-30A Lessons 25–29 Study Sheet** that was sent home on Day 1.

Day 5 Assessment

Objective

The students will accurately select the appropriate answer within the context of a sentence. They will fill in the corresponding answer circle.

Introduction

Teacher Note: The Test makes provision for Differentiated Instruction. The first twelve sentences include the words assigned to students with shortened lists. Encourage these students to try all the sentences, but only grade the first twelve sentences. The Test is found on two blackline masters.

Duplicate a copy of **BLMs SP5-30E–F Lessons 25–29 Test I** and **II** and distribute to each student. Duplicate **BLM SP5-06G Student Answer Form** and cut apart. Distribute one answer form to each student. Remind students to fill in each answer circle completely and to erase completely if they wish to change an answer.

© Spelling Grade 5

Directed Assessment

1 Instruct students to listen as you dictate the following Sample:
Sample

     Will you take your <u>anual</u> <u>vacation</u> during the <u>summertime</u>? All <u>correct</u>
               A   B   C   D

Say, "Are any of the first three underlined words misspelled?" Pause for replies. Inform students that the letter *A* is below the underlined word that is misspelled. (**annual**) Guide students to the answer form that was previously distributed. Lead students to find the Sample box and fill in the appropriate answer circle containing the same letter. Say, "You will continue in the same way. You will read each sentence, choose the word that you think is misspelled, and fill in the corresponding circle on the answer form. If all the words are spelled correctly, fill in the fourth circle, labeled *D*, for *All correct*."

2 Assist students as needed while they read the sentences and complete the Test on their own.

1. The thermometer showed a subzero temperature.
2. Some animals hibernate at the conclusion of autumn.
3. The harvesters gathered an abundance of onions.
4. Gardening in the springtime produces enough flowers.
5. Dee is measuring the valuable cloth before cutting it with scissors.
6. Isn't it incredible how salmon swim upstream to produce offspring?
7. Many courageous missionaries live in other countries.
8. We were frightened when the electrical storm occurred.
9. The audience showed its happiness at the business promotion.
10. We recognize the equator as a line of latitude.
11. A seasonal blizzard will cause snow to accumulate.
12. Nan purchased a red vase painted with a vivid pigment.
13. Some aircraft are necessarily equipped with a parachute.
14. Mia delicately placed garnishes next to the sandwiches.
15. The commotion outside the businesses was upsetting.
16. The barometer definitely indicated impending precipitation.
17. Meridians are lines of longitude that extend into each hemisphere.
18. The librarian is straightening the dictionaries and biographies.
19. The heaviest machinery is sturdier than lightweight tools.
20. Christianity celebrates several vernal festivals.
21. Derek preferred centigrade to Fahrenheit scales.
22. The biologist was incredulous at the hardiness of the juvenile mice.
23. In retrospect, the catastrophe left the survival of the mice in doubt.
24. Was it noticeable that the echo was becoming inaudible?
25. We were not accustomed to our new toboggan, so we practiced.

3 Refer to **BLM SP5-30G Lessons 25–29 Answer Key** when correcting the Test.

Student Pages

Pages 121–124

Lesson Materials

BLM SP5-31A
P-2
P-3
BLM SP5-31B
Newspaper
Magazine
BLM SP5-31C

Created Wonders

Lessons 31–35 utilize the theme of the universe. The theme of this lesson is Earth. Earth is the only planet in our solar system capable of sustaining life. Since God placed Earth as the third planet from the sun, it is neither too hot nor too cold. Earth also has plenty of water and an atmosphere that sustains life. God's design is perfect.

Day 1 Pretest

Objective

The students will accurately spell and write words with **Latin roots**. They will spell and write content, vocabulary, and challenge words.

Introduction

Before class, select Challenge Words for numbers 24 and 25 from a cross-curricular subject, words misspelled on previous assignments, or words that interest your students. The word *unpredictable* has the **root dict** and is suggested for number 24. Administer the Pretest.

Directed Instruction

1 Say each word, use it in a sentence, and then repeat the word.

Pattern Words
1. The moon is <u>visible</u> from Earth.
2. <u>Visibility</u> during a blizzard is very limited.
3. Does the moon greatly <u>affect</u> the earth's tides?
4. Exhaust pollutants can <u>effect</u> a change in the quality of air.
5. The globe was <u>defective</u> since it would not rotate.
6. God has great <u>affection</u> toward each of His children.
7. Bryn will <u>supervise</u> the science project for her team.
8. She will kindly <u>dictate</u> each team member's responsibilities.
9. The team's <u>prediction</u> is that they will receive a good grade.
10. Careful <u>supervision</u> of the team made the project run smoothly.
11. Many people <u>contradict</u> the theory of evolution on Earth.
12. The jury returned a not-guilty <u>verdict</u> to the judge.

Content Words
13. The Lord God created the entire <u>universe</u>.
14. <u>Ozone</u> helps protect Earth from the sun's harmful radiation.
15. The thickest layer of the earth is the <u>mantle</u>.
16. Earth's <u>revolution</u> around the sun takes 365.25 days.
17. The <u>orbital</u> path of the earth is an elliptical shape.
18. <u>Inertia</u> is the resistance to a change in motion.
19. The <u>velocity</u> of the moving ball was slowed by friction.

Vocabulary Words
20. In 1976, the United States celebrated its <u>bicentennial</u> birthday.
21. Many people attended the <u>centennial</u> celebration in Philadelphia.
22. Rocket boosters <u>accelerate</u> the space shuttle from Earth into space.
23. A drag chute helps the space shuttle <u>decelerate</u> when it lands.

Challenge Words
24. _____
25. _____

2 Allow students to self-correct their Pretest. Write each word on the board. Point out that the **Latin roots** in the Pattern Words are *dict*, *fect*, and *vis*. Remind students that a root is the part of a word that gives the basic meaning and that some words contain more than one root. Teach that *contradict* and *verdict* each contain two roots—*contra* and *dict*, *ver* and *dict*. The roots in the Vocabulary Words are *celer* and *enni*. Note that *bicentennial* contains two prefixes.

3 As a class, read, spell, and read each word. Direct students to circle misspelled words with a colored pencil and rewrite them correctly.

4 Proof each student's Pretest. This becomes an individualized study

sheet that can be used at school or at home.

5 Homework suggestion: Distribute a copy of **BLM SP5-31A Lesson 31 Words and Phrases** to each student.

Day 2 Word Analysis and Vocabulary

Objective

The students will sort and write words that have **Latin roots** and complete sentences with content words. They will use a table to write vocabulary words, select words to match definitions, complete sentences in context, and choose the best meanings for given words.

Introduction

Display **P-2** and **P-3 Greek and Latin Roots** for students to use as a reference. Instruct students to fold a piece of notebook paper lengthwise into three columns, labeling the first column *prefix*, the second *root*, and the third *suffix*. Invite students to turn to page 121 to use as a reference. Explain that each Pattern and Vocabulary Word has a root and an affix or affixes. Not every word contains all three word parts; some words contain two roots or two prefixes. Note that in *supervise*, the silent *e* is not in the original root spelling for *vis*. Demonstrate how to segment each Pattern and Vocabulary Word. Allow students to complete the activity. Assist as needed.

Prefix	Root	Suffix	Prefix	Root	Suffix
af-	fect			vis	-ible
ef-	fect			vis	-ibility
af-	fect	-ion	super-	vis	
de-	fect	-ive	super-	vis	-ion
	dict	-ate	ac-	celer	-ate
	ver, dict		de-	celer	-ate
pre-	dict	-ion	bi-, cent-	enni	-al
	contra, dict		cent-	enni	-al

Directed Instruction

1 Invite students to refer to their chart to identify the following:

60 pts.

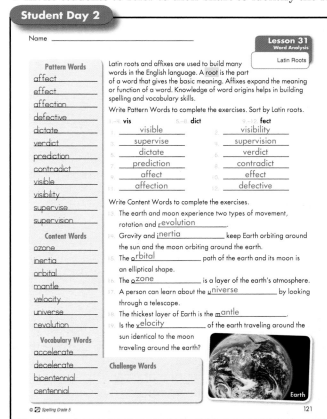

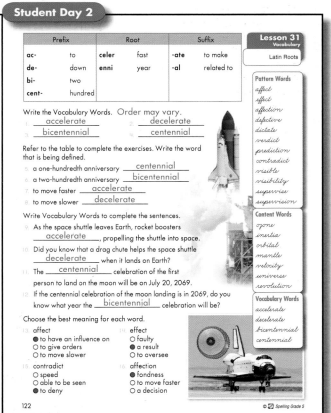

Student Spelling Support

1. Use **BLM SP5-01A A Spelling Study Strategy** in instructional groups to provide assistance with some or all of the words.

2. Duplicate **BLMs SP5-31D–E Lesson 31 Spelling Words I** and **II** on CARD STOCK for students to use as flash cards at school or at home. Another option is to use **BLM SP5-01G Flash Cards Template** or 3" × 5" INDEX CARDS for students to write their own flash cards to use as a study aid.

3. Invite students to write the Challenge Words, numbers 24 and 25, in the Word Bank, in the back of their textbook.

4. Read Psalm 115:15–16: "May you be blessed by the LORD, who made heaven and earth. The heaven, even the heavens, are the LORD's; but the earth He has given to the children of men." Discuss with students that Earth is the planet that God created to sustain life. It was not by accident, but by a purposeful design, that Earth was created to have all living things within it. God then gave the earth to His children. It is our responsibility to be good stewards of what we have been given.

5. Have students write two or three paragraphs stating two or three strategies about how to take care of the earth that God has given us. Encourage students to

Cont. on page 125

- words with two roots (**verdict, contradict**)
- a word with two prefixes (**bicentennial**)
- words without a suffix (**affect, effect, verdict, contradict, supervise**)
- words without a prefix (**dictate, verdict, contradict, visible, visibility**)
- a word with silent *e* added to the root (**supervise**)

2 Proceed to page 121. Say, spell, and say each Pattern, Content, and Vocabulary Word. Provide this week's Challenge Words and have students write them in the spaces provided. Students complete the page.

3 Proceed to page 122. Build each Vocabulary Word before students complete the page. For example, the prefix ac- goes with the root *celer* to build the word *accelerate*. Review that the letter *c* is attached to the prefix *a-* because it takes on the first letter of the root it is attached to—*celer*. Provide assistance as students complete the page.

4 Homework suggestion: Distribute a copy of **BLM SP5-31B Lesson 31 Phrases and Sentences** to each student.

Day 3 Word Study Strategies

Objective

The students will circle common roots in sets of words and write the roots according to their definitions. They will use given roots to complete sentences with list words and correctly use *affect* and *effect* in sentences.

Introduction

Remind students to reference **P-2** and **P-3 Greek and Latin Roots**. Write the following words and incomplete sentences on the board:

- bicentennial, centennial   The root _____ means *year*. (**enni**)
- accelerate, decelerate   The root _____ means *fast*. (**celer**)

Invite volunteers to circle and write the common root in each pair of words.

Directed Instruction

1 Explain that two list words, *affect* and *effect*, are easily confused. Teach that *affect* as a verb means *to have an influence on* and usually involves feelings. *Effect* as a noun means *a result*; as a verb, *effect* means *to bring about* or *to make a change happen*. Write the following sentences on the board and invite volunteers to correctly complete each one using *affect* or *effect*:

- The sun will _____ Chloe's pale skin. (**affect**)
- The _____ will be a sunburn. (**effect**)

2 Proceed to page 123. Students independently complete the page. Invite volunteers to orally read each group of sentences.

Day 4 Writing

Objective

The students will read an essay and write list words that are synonyms of given words in informative paragraphs.

Introduction

Teacher Note: The informative domain is the focus for the writing pages in Lessons 31–35.

Select an essay published in a NEWSPAPER or a MAGAZINE that is appropriate for fifth grade students. Read the essay and discuss what the author is informing the reader about.

Directed Instruction

1 Explain that today's assignment is a student's essay about the universe. The paragraphs contain informative details and facts about protecting Earth's environment.

2 Remind students that a synonym is a word that means the same or almost the same as another word. Invite students to state a few synonyms. (**Possible answers: grateful, thankful; wrong, incorrect**)

3 Proceed to page 124. Select a student to read the sentences at the top of the page. Allow students to complete the page independently.

4 Select a student to read the paragraphs, inserting the list word for the given synonym. Invite another student to read Psalm 115:15–16. Discuss how God has blessed us with a beautiful world and that we need to be good stewards of what He has given us.

5 Homework suggestion: Distribute a copy of **BLM SP5-31C Lesson 31 Test Prep** to each student.

Day 5 Posttest

Objective
The students will correctly write dictated spelling words and sentences.

Introduction
Review by using flash cards noted in Student Spelling Support, number 2.

Directed Assessment

1 Dictate the list words by using the Pretest sentences or developing original ones. Reserve *universe, dictate, orbital, decelerate,* and *defective* for the dictation sentences.

2 Read each sentence. Repeat as needed.
- God created the <u>universe</u>.
- During creation God began to <u>dictate</u> the placement of each thing.
- God set in motion the <u>orbital</u> path of Earth.
- Friction on Earth causes objects to <u>decelerate</u>.
- There is nothing <u>defective</u> about God's creation.

3 If assigned, dictate Extra Challenge Words.

4 Score the test, counting each misspelled word as an error. Correct the dictation sentences by grading only the spelling words or grading the complete sentences.

Student Spelling Support
Cont. from page 124

use several spelling words. Ask for volunteers to read their paragraphs. Display the paragraphs on a bulletin board.

6. Write this week's words, categorize the Pattern, Content, and Vocabulary Words, and attach them to the Word Wall.

7. For visual, auditory, and kinesthetic learners, write each prefix, root, and suffix in the Pattern and Vocabulary Words on 3" × 5" INDEX CARDS. Include a silent *e* card. Students shuffle the cards and then match word parts to make a list word. When a word is formed, students write the word on a piece of paper. Auditory learners may spell the words aloud for memory reinforcement.

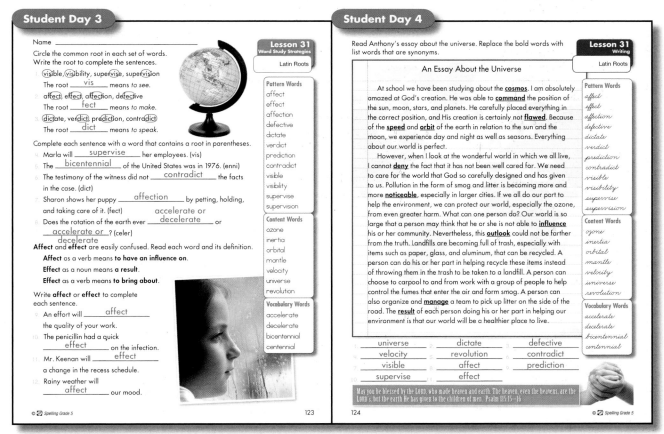

Student Pages
Pages 125–128

Lesson Materials
BLM SP5-32A
P-2
P-3
BLM SP5-32B
BLM SP5-32C

Created Wonders

The theme of this lesson is the sun. God created the sun as a medium-sized star, the closest star to Earth. The sun is a huge mass of hot, glowing gas, producing light and heat energy by nuclear fusion reactions, allowing life to exist on Earth. The intense gravitational pull of the sun keeps the planets in our solar system in orbit.

Day 1 Pretest

Objective

The students will accurately spell and write words with **Latin roots**. They will spell and write content, vocabulary, and challenge words.

Introduction

Before class, select Challenge Words for numbers 24 and 25 from a cross-curricular subject, words misspelled on previous assignments, or words that interest your students. The word *infrastructure* has the **root struct** and is suggested for number 24. Administer the Pretest.

Directed Instruction

1 Say each word, use it in a sentence, and then repeat the word.

Pattern Words
1. The speaker <u>abruptly</u> ended his discussion of the sun's activity.
2. Jesus' will was perfectly <u>conformed</u> to His Father's will.
3. The observatory was <u>constructed</u> in 1957.
4. The collapse of the tripod caused <u>destruction</u> of the telescope's lens.
5. Our teacher told us the <u>format</u> for our research paper.
6. Mrs. Montgomery is a fine <u>instructor</u>.
7. The fire drill caused an <u>interruption</u> in our class schedule.
8. Does that desk <u>obstruct</u> your view of the screen?
9. Overinflating a tire may cause it to <u>rupture</u>.
10. The main <u>structure</u> in the observatory houses the telescope.
11. Copernicus' ideas <u>transformed</u> the way scholars saw the solar system.
12. The <u>uniformity</u> of the scientists' observations supported a theory.

Content Words
13. A lunar <u>eclipse</u> may be total or partial.
14. We will be studying <u>magnetic</u> fields in science today.
15. The sun produces energy by means of <u>nuclear</u> fusion reactions.
16. A picture of the <u>photosphere</u> showed sunspots.
17. An astronomer will explain the <u>prominence</u> shown in the video.
18. Planets in our <u>solar</u> system revolve around the sun.
19. When viewed through a telescope, the sun's <u>corona</u> looks like a crown.

Vocabulary Words
20. Galileo had the <u>determination</u> needed to face opposition.
21. Opponents of Galileo tried to <u>exterminate</u> his teachings.
22. The author added a <u>postscript</u> that listed contributions to the book.
23. Galileo's work became a <u>prescription</u> for later scientific thought.

Challenge Words
24. _____
25. _____

2 Allow students to self-correct their Pretest. Write each word on the board. Point out that each Pattern and Vocabulary Word has a Latin root. Remind students that a root is the part of a word that gives the basic meaning. The **Latin roots** in the Pattern Words are *form*, *rupt*, and *struct*. The roots in the Vocabulary Words are *script* and *termin*.

3 As a class, read, spell, and read each word. Direct students to circle misspelled words with a colored pencil and rewrite them correctly.

4 Proof each student's Pretest. This becomes an individualized study sheet that can be used at school or at home.

5 Homework suggestion: Distribute a copy of **BLM SP5-32A Lesson 32 Words and Phrases** to each student.

Day 2 Word Analysis and Vocabulary

Objective
The students will sort and write words that have **Latin roots** and complete sentences with content words. They will use a table to write vocabulary words, match definitions, complete sentences, and choose the best meaning for underlined words.

Introduction
Display **P-2** and **P-3 Greek and Latin Roots** for students to use as a reference. Instruct students to fold a piece of notebook paper lengthwise into three columns. Invite students to label the first column *prefix*, the second *root*, and the third *suffix*. Direct students to turn to page 125 to refer to the list words. Explain that each Pattern and Vocabulary Word has a root and an affix or affixes. Not every word contains all three word parts. Demonstrate how to segment each Pattern and Vocabulary Word. Allow students to complete the activity. Assist as needed.

Prefix	Root	Suffix	Prefix	Root	Suffix
	form	-at		struct	-ure
uni-	form	-ity	in-	struct	-or
con-	form	-ed	de-	struct	-ion
trans-	form	-ed	con-	struct	-ed
	rupt	-ure	post-	script	
ab-	rupt	-ly	pre-	script	-ion
inter-	rupt	-ion	de-	termin	-ation
ob-	struct		ex-	termin	-ate

Directed Instruction

1 Invite students to refer to the list words on page 125. Pronounce several Pattern, Content, and Vocabulary Words, and have students

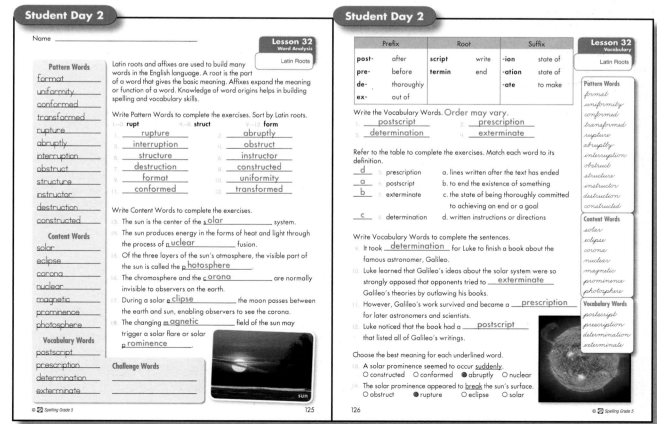

59 pts.

Student Day 2

Name _____

Lesson 32 Word Analysis — Latin Roots

Latin roots and affixes are used to build many words in the English language. A root is the part of a word that gives the basic meaning. Affixes expand the meaning or function of a word. Knowledge of word origins helps in building spelling and vocabulary skills.

Write Pattern Words to complete the exercises. Sort by Latin roots.

1–3. **rupt**
1. rupture
3. interruption
5. structure
7. destruction
9. format
11. conformed

4–8. **struct**
2. abruptly
4. obstruct
6. instructor
8. constructed
10. uniformity
12. transformed

9–12. **form**

Write Content Words to complete the exercises.
13. The sun is the center of the s**olar** system.
14. The sun produces energy in the forms of heat and light through the process of n**uclear** fusion.
15. Of the three layers of the sun's atmosphere, the visible part of the sun is called the p**hotosphere**.
16. The chromosphere and the c**orona** are normally invisible to observers on the earth.
17. During a solar e**clipse** the moon passes between the earth and sun, enabling observers to see the corona.
18. The changing m**agnetic** field of the sun may trigger a solar flare or solar p**rominence**.

Pattern Words
format
uniformity
conformed
transformed
rupture
abruptly
interruption
obstruct
structure
instructor
destruction
constructed

Content Words
solar
eclipse
corona
nuclear
magnetic
prominence
photosphere

Vocabulary Words
postscript
prescription
determination
exterminate

Challenge Words
_____
_____

© Spelling Grade 5   125

Student Day 2

Lesson 32 Vocabulary — Latin Roots

Prefix		Root		Suffix	
post-	after	script	write	-ion	state of
pre-	before	termin	end	-ation	state of
de-	thoroughly			-ate	to make
ex-	out of				

Write the Vocabulary Words. Order may vary.
1. postscript
2. prescription
3. determination
4. exterminate

Refer to the table to complete the exercises. Match each word to its definition.
d 5. prescription
a 6. postscript
b 7. exterminate
c 8. determination

a. lines written after the text has ended
b. to end the existence of something
c. the state of being thoroughly committed to achieving an end or a goal
d. written instructions or directions

Write Vocabulary Words to complete the sentences.
9. It took **determination** for Luke to finish a book about the famous astronomer, Galileo.
10. Luke learned that Galileo's ideas about the solar system were so strongly opposed that opponents tried to **exterminate** Galileo's theories by outlawing his books.
11. However, Galileo's work survived and became a **prescription** for later astronomers and scientists.
12. Luke noticed that the book had a **postscript** that listed all of Galileo's writings.

Choose the best meaning for each underlined word.
13. A solar prominence seemed to occur <u>suddenly</u>.
○ constructed ○ conformed ● abruptly ○ nuclear
14. The solar prominence appeared to <u>break</u> the sun's surface.
○ obstruct ● rupture ○ eclipse ○ solar

Pattern Words
format
uniformity
conformed
transformed
rupture
abruptly
interruption
obstruct
structure
instructor
destruction
constructed

Content Words
solar
eclipse
corona
nuclear
magnetic
prominence
photosphere

Vocabulary Words
postscript
prescription
determination
exterminate

126   © Spelling Grade 5

locate the word in the Spelling Dictionary. Invite students to share the definition of the specified word with the class.

2 Proceed to page 125. Say, spell, and say each Pattern, Content, and Vocabulary Word. Provide this week's Challenge Words and have students write them in the spaces provided. Challenge students to locate the roots *form*, *rupt*, and *struct* in the Pattern Words that they wrote on their paper completed in the lesson Introduction. Instruct students to choose three colored pencils and to underline each Pattern Word containing the root *form* in one color, the root *rupt* in the second color, and the root *struct* in the third color. Provide assistance as students complete the page.

3 Proceed to page 126. Build each Vocabulary Word before students complete the page. For example, the prefix *post-* goes with the root *script* to build the word *postscript*. Allow students to complete the page independently.

4 Homework suggestion: Distribute a copy of **BLM SP5-32B Lesson 32 Phrases and Sentences** to each student.

Day 3 Word Study Strategies

Objective

The students will circle common roots in sets of words and write the roots according to their definitions. They will write pattern words to match definitions and complete sentences with synonyms.

Introduction

Remind students to refer to **P-2** and **P-3 Greek and Latin Roots** as they complete the activity that follows. Write the following sets of words on the board, and select volunteers to underline the root that is common to the words in each set:

- <u>audi</u>tory, <u>audi</u>ence, <u>audi</u>tion (**hear**)
- <u>cred</u>ible, in<u>cred</u>ible, in<u>cred</u>ulous (**believe**)
- con<u>form</u>, trans<u>form</u>, re<u>form</u> (**shape**)

Choose a volunteer to write the root meanings next to the lists of words. Remind students that knowledge of the root meaning is an invaluable aid in determining the definition of a word.

Directed Instruction

1 Review that a synonym is a word that means the same or almost the same as another word. Point out any dictionaries and thesauri in the classroom and relate that they are beneficial sources of synonyms for use in student writing. Knowledge and usage of synonyms strengthen students' vocabulary.

2 Proceed to page 127. Instruct students to use the Spelling Dictionary as an aid in defining the list words. Choose a student to read Genesis 1:16 and hold a brief discussion about God's creation of the sun and moon. Allow students to complete the page independently.

Day 4 Writing

Objective

The students will read a set of directions necessary to complete a science project in the context of a cloze activity. They will write the missing pattern, content, and vocabulary words.

Introduction

Ask students to name various activities that require adherence to a set of ordered steps to be completed successfully. (**Possible answers: baking cookies, constructing a model, making a craft project, performing a science experiment**) Continue the discussion by asking students to tell what might happen if a step was omitted or if the order of any of the steps was changed. Lead students to conclude that many activities require following directions.

Directed Instruction

1 Remind students that the procedures for an experiment or science project follow a logical order. Today's assignment enumerates the steps needed to make a solar oven.

2 Proceed to page 128 and select a volunteer to read the sentences at the top of the page. Instruct students to silently read the report and to complete the cloze activity independently. Choose a different volunteer to read each of the steps orally, replacing each blank with the list word.

3 Homework suggestion: Distribute a copy of **BLM SP5-32C Lesson 32 Test Prep** to each student.

Day 5 Posttest

Objective

The students will correctly write dictated spelling words and sentences.

Introduction

Review by using flash cards noted in Student Spelling Support, number 2.

Directed Assessment

1 Dictate the list words by using the Pretest sentences or developing original ones. Reserve *instructor, structure, solar, eclipse,* and *determination* for the dictation sentences.

2 Read each sentence. Repeat as needed.
- Jeff's <u>instructor</u> took his class on a field trip to learn about the sun.
- He visited a <u>structure</u> that housed a huge telescope.
- It was exciting to view <u>solar</u> activity through the telescope.
- Jeff was thrilled to observe an <u>eclipse</u> of the sun.
- Jeff had the <u>determination</u> needed to become a scientist.

3 If assigned, dictate Extra Challenge Words.

4 Score the test, counting each misspelled word as an error. Correct the dictation sentences by grading only the spelling words or grading the complete sentences.

Student Spelling Support

Cont. from page 128

each student to share the directions with a classmate.

6. Write this week's words, categorize the Pattern, Content, and Vocabulary Words, and attach them to the Word Wall.

7. Invite a pair of visual learners to write the definitions for each list word on the back of each of their flash cards, made in Student Spelling Support, number two. One partner reads a word and the other partner supplies the definition. Turn the cards to the other side and repeat the procedure.

8. As a science connection, invite students to learn more about Copernicus and Galileo by conducting research in an encyclopedia or by using the Internet. Each of these astronomers added immensely to our modern understanding of the nature of the solar system.

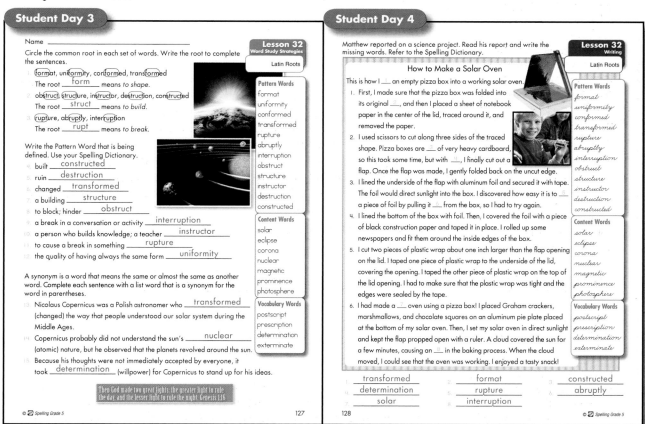

Greek and Latin Roots

Student Pages

Pages 129–132

Lesson Materials

BLM SP5-33A
P-2
P-3
BLMs SP5-33B–C
BLM SP5-33D
Cash register paper tape
Sentence strips
T-20
BLM SP5-33E
BLM SP5-33F

Created Wonders

The theme of this lesson is the moon. The moon is Earth's only natural satellite. From Earth, the moon is the second brightest object in the sky, after the sun, and is very bright because of the reflectivity of the sun's light. The moon moves in an elliptical orbit around the earth and rotates so that the same side is always turned toward Earth. Natural satellites of other planets are also usually referred to as moons.

Day 1 Pretest

Objective

The students will accurately spell and write words with **Greek and Latin roots**. They will spell and write content, vocabulary, and challenge words.

Introduction

Before class, select Challenge Words for numbers 24 and 25 from a cross-curricular subject, words misspelled on previous assignments, or words that interest your students. The word *compression* has the **Latin root press** and is suggested for number 24. Administer the Pretest.

Directed Instruction

1 Say each word, use it in a sentence, and then repeat the word.

Pattern Words

1. Jesus wants us to hold one another <u>accountable</u> in our actions.
2. Each astronaut will be asked to <u>recount</u> mission details.
3. The <u>intended</u> destination of the module was the Sea of Tranquility.
4. The moon has the <u>tendency</u> to orbit Earth in an elliptical path.
5. Buzz Aldrin was <u>expressive</u> while describing the moon's soil.
6. The astronaut's boot left an <u>impression</u> on the lunar soil.
7. Jamison wanted to study <u>aeronautics</u> at the Air Force Academy.
8. Brooke decided to study to become an <u>astronaut</u>.
9. Darrah's favorite area of study was <u>astronomy</u>.
10. Robin was able to get ten <u>autographs</u> on her space center brochure.
11. Neil Armstrong mounted a camera on a <u>tripod</u> to take pictures.
12. Did you know that the study of the moon is called <u>selenology</u>?

Content Words

13. The moon's <u>albedo</u> /al ˈbē dō/ reflected a magnificent glow.
14. The surface of the moon contains numerous <u>craters</u>.
15. The <u>density</u> of an object is determined by dividing mass by volume.
16. The word <u>*mare*</u> /ˈmär ā/ comes from the Latin word for *sea*.
17. The moon goes through many <u>phases</u> as it orbits around Earth.
18. The <u>reflectivity</u> of the moon comes from the sun.
19. The moon is the only natural <u>satellite</u> of Earth.

Vocabulary Words

20. A plaque with an <u>inscription</u> was left on the moon during *Apollo 11*.
21. The mission team reviewed the launch <u>manuscript</u> very carefully.
22. Astronomers used a <u>misnomer</u> when identifying the moon's dark areas.
23. The astronaut accepted the managerial <u>nomination</u> reluctantly.

Challenge Words

24. _____
25. _____

2 Allow students to self-correct their Pretest. Write each word on the board. Point out that the **Greek and Latin roots** in the Pattern Words are *aero, astr, auto, count, graph, naut, nomy, ology, pod, press, selen, tend,* and *tri*. The Latin roots in the Vocabulary Words are *nom, nomin, script,* and *manu*. Point out that *manuscript* is made of two roots. Remind students that a root is the part of a word that gives the basic meaning.

3 As a class, read, spell, and read each word. Direct students to circle misspelled words with a colored pencil and rewrite them correctly.

4 Proof each student's Pretest. This becomes an individualized study sheet that can be used at school or at home.

5 Homework suggestion: Distribute a copy of **BLM SP5-33A Lesson 33 Words and Phrases** to each student.

Day 2 Word Analysis and Vocabulary

Objective

The students will sort words with **Greek and Latin roots** and complete sentences with content words. They will use a table to write vocabulary words, match given definitions in context, and complete sentences.

Introduction

Display **P-2** and **P-3** Greek and Latin Roots. Distribute a copy of **BLMs SP5-33B–C Lesson 33 Spelling Words I** and **II** to each student. Do not cut apart the cards. Dictate each Pattern and Vocabulary Word. Instruct students to underline or highlight each root and affix. Remind students that some words contain two roots. Note that in *astronaut* and *astronomy*, the letter *o* is not part of the original Greek root.

Prefix	Root	Suffix	Prefix	Root	Suffix
re-	count			astr, nomy	
ac-	count	-able		auto, graph	-s
ex-	press	-ive		selen, ology	
im-	press	-ion		tri, pod	
in-	tend	-ed	mis-	nom	-er
	tend	-ency		nomin	-ation
	aero, naut	-ics	in-	script	-ion
	astr, naut			manu, script	

Directed Instruction

1 Invite students to refer to the list words on page 129. Review the pronunciation of *mare* /ˈmär ā/ and *albedo* /al ˈbē dō/. Challenge seven groups of students to locate the definition of a specified Content Word from their Spelling Dictionary. Each group orally shares the definition of their specified word. Students write definitions on the appropriate flash card and cut apart the cards.

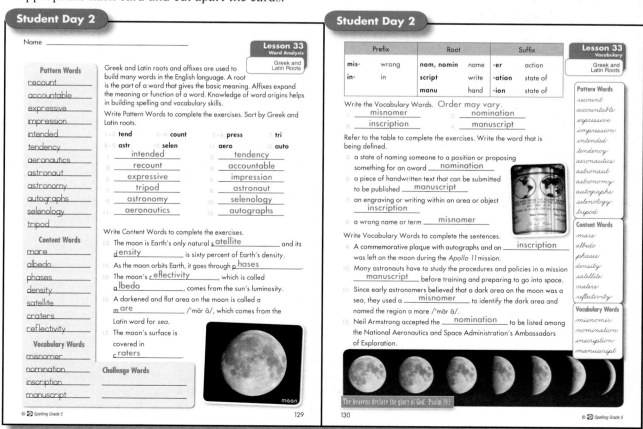

2 Proceed to page 129. Say, spell, and say each Pattern, Content, and Vocabulary Word. Provide this week's Challenge Words and have students write them in the spaces provided. Students may choose to add the Challenge Words to their flash card study pile and use their flash cards as a reference tool when completing the page.

3 Proceed to page 130. Build each Vocabulary Word before students complete the page. For example, the prefix *mis-* goes with the root *nom* and the suffix *-er* to get the word *misnomer*. Provide assistance as needed. Invite a volunteer to read Psalm 19:1 and lead a short discussion about how God's creation displays His glory.

4 Homework suggestion: Distribute a copy of **BLM SP5-33D Lesson 33 Phrases and Sentences** to each student.

Day 3 Word Study Strategies

Objective

The students will identify and circle common Latin roots in pairs of words and write roots to complete sentences. They will use combined Greek root meanings to write list words and write a missing root, affix, or affixes to complete words.

Introduction

Greek and Latin roots are used to build many words in the English language. To differentiate between **Greek and Latin roots**, write the following on the board:
- Latin roots found in Pattern Words: count, press, tend
- Greek roots found in Pattern Words: aero, astr, auto, graph, naut, nomy, ology, pod, selen, tri
- Latin roots found in Vocabulary Words: manu, nom, nomin, script

Students reference **P-2** and **P-3 Greek and Latin Roots** to define each root.

Directed Instruction

1 Have students use the list words on page 131 as a reference. Write the following on the board and select a volunteer to form a list word:
- star (astr) + ship (naut) = _____ (**astronaut**)

2 To challenge students further, write the following on the board and invite a volunteer to complete the exercise:
- air + ship = _____ (**aeronautics**)

3 Write the following and select volunteers to complete the exercises:
- Did you take <u>astro</u>_____ to learn about the moon's craters? (**nomy**)
- What _____<u>press</u>_____ did you get from the moon lecture? (**im-; -ion**)

4 Proceed to page 131. Students complete the page independently.

Day 4 Writing

Objective

The students will use proofreading marks to identify mistakes in an article summary. They will correctly write misspelled words and rewrite a run-on sentence as two complete sentences.

Introduction

Write the following run-on sentence on CASH REGISTER PAPER TAPE or on SENTENCE STRIPS that are taped together and display:
- The astronaut slowly climbed down the stairs of the lunar module he was excited to walk on the moon he felt very thankful to God as he stepped onto the moon's surface

Read the run-on sentence aloud without pausing. Ask students to state what is incorrect grammar. (**The ideas in the sentence are all jumbled together and there are no punctuation marks.**) Define the following: A *run-on sentence* is <u>an incorrect combination of two or more complete sentences</u>. Select a volunteer to reread the sentence, stopping where a complete sentence ends. Cut the tape or sentence strip apart and insert a period at the end of the sentence. Capitalize the first letter of the next word. Select another volunteer to read the run-on. Continue until the run-on sentence is broken into three complete sentences. Chorally read the three complete sentences. (**The astronaut slowly climbed down the stairs of the lunar module. He was excited to walk on the moon. He felt very thankful to God as he stepped onto the moon's surface.**)

Directed Instruction

1 Display **T-20 Proofreading an Informative Summary** on the overhead, keeping the bottom portion of the transparency covered. Read the text aloud. Correct the identified mistakes using the appropriate proofreading marks. Challenge students to identify the run-on sentence. Use **BLM SP5-33E T-20 Answer Key** as a guide. Uncover the bottom of the transparency and read the corrected version of text.

2 Proceed to page 132. Assist students as needed while they independently proofread the summary. Review all the necessary proofreading marks and corrections. (**6 misspellings; 4 capital letters needed; 2 periods needed; 2 deletes; 2 add something—*a*, *the*; 2 small letters needed; 1 new paragraph**)

3 Homework suggestion: Distribute a copy of **BLM SP5-33F Lesson 33 Test Prep** to each student.

Day 5 Posttest

Objective
The students will correctly write dictated spelling words and sentences.

Introduction
Review by using flash cards noted in Student Spelling Support, number 2.

Directed Assessment

1 Dictate the list words by using the Pretest sentences or developing original ones. Reserve *expressive*, *intended*, *craters*, *phases*, and *manuscript* for the dictation sentences.

2 Read each sentence. Repeat as needed.

Paul —
- Sid told an imaginary and <u>expressive</u> story in class.
- His <u>intended</u> story setting was the moon's surface.
- Sid described chocolate <u>craters</u> on the moon in detail.
- He said that the moon's <u>phases</u> were affected by sugar.
- Sid had a <u>manuscript</u> of his silly story published.

3 If assigned, dictate Extra Challenge Words.

4 Score the test, counting each misspelled word as an error. Correct the dictation sentences by grading only the spelling words or grading the complete sentences.

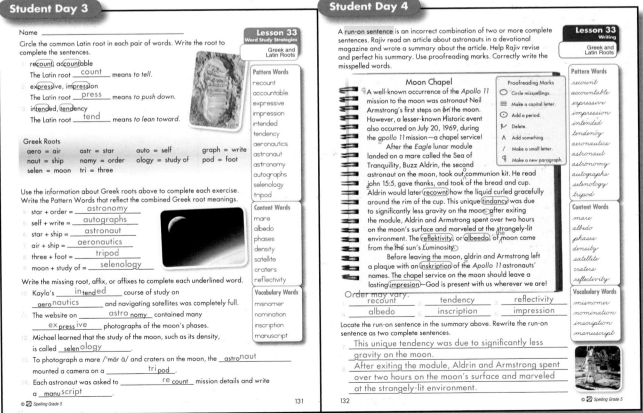

Words from French

Student Pages
Pages 133–136

Lesson Materials
BLM SP5-34A
T-21
BLM SP5-34B
BLM SP5-34C

Created Wonders

The theme of this lesson is stars. God created stars on the fourth day of Creation to give light to the earth. He calls each one by name. Stars continue to form by gravity pulling gas and dust together. Stars can be red, orange, yellow, white, or blue. The cooler stars are reddish while the hotter stars are bluish.

Day 1 Pretest

Objective

The students will accurately spell and write **words from French**. They will spell and write content, vocabulary, and challenge words.

Introduction

Before class, select Challenge Words for numbers 24 and 25 from a cross-curricular subject, words misspelled on previous assignments, or words that interest your students. The word *ballerina* comes from the **French** language and is suggested for number 24. Administer the Pretest.

Directed Instruction

1 Say each word, use it in a sentence, and then repeat the word.

Pattern Words

1. An exploding star forms a <u>bizarre</u> shape.
2. The <u>government</u> funds the research for astronomy.
3. The choral <u>ensemble</u> held a concert outdoors.
4. The <u>traitor</u> ran away under the darkness of the night sky.
5. The observatory committee hired an <u>attorney</u> to represent them.
6. Patsy baked a <u>quiche</u> for the space center's party.
7. Tessa observed the stars from the <u>plateau</u>.
8. Brent won a <u>trophy</u> for his stellar painting.
9. The scientific book was placed on the <u>bureau</u>.
10. Norman read many <u>essays</u> about the universe.
11. NASA employees represent the scientific <u>elite</u>.
12. We have <u>liberty</u> in Jesus Christ our Lord.

Content Words

13. The <u>luminosity</u> of stars is the only source of light in the universe.
14. Some <u>constellations</u> are visible only certain times of the year.
15. An <u>astronomer</u> maps where stars are in the sky.
16. Scientists study the <u>composition</u> of a star's outer layers.
17. A nebula is a cloud of <u>gaseous</u> material from an exploding star.
18. The <u>energy</u> from nuclear fusion causes a star to shine.
19. In 1990, an orbiting <u>telescope</u> was released into space.

Vocabulary Words

20. Astronauts began to <u>renovate</u> the Hubble Space Telescope in 1993.
21. One scientist's <u>innovation</u> led to the development of space telescopes.
22. The telescope was built with a <u>contemporary</u> design.
23. A scientist made an <u>extemporaneous</u> comment about stars.

Challenge Words

24. _____
25. _____

2 Allow students to self-correct their Pretest. Write each word on the board. Point out that some words in the English language have been borrowed from other languages. Each Pattern Word in this lesson comes from the French language. The Content Word *gaseous* is pronounced /ˈga sē əs/. Note the roots *nov* and *tempor* in the Vocabulary Words.

3 As a class, read, spell, and read each word. Direct students to circle misspelled words with a colored pencil and rewrite them correctly.

4 Proof each student's Pretest. This becomes an individualized study sheet that can be used at school or at home.

5 Homework suggestion: Distribute a copy of **BLM SP5-34A Lesson 34 Words and Phrases** to each student.

Day 2 Word Analysis and Vocabulary

Objective

The students will sort **words from French** by the number of syllables and complete sentences with content words. They will use a table to write vocabulary words, select words to match definitions, and complete sentences in context. They will choose the best meaning for given words.

Introduction

Remind students that the Pattern Words in this week's lesson are derived from French words. *Derivation* is <u>the act of determining the source or origin of a word</u>. Studying word origins helps in developing spelling and vocabulary skills. Display **T-21 Words from French** on the overhead. Read the sentences at the top of the transparency. Invite students to share any difference in the spelling of each word in both languages. Explain that an accent mark is a symbol used in some French words. For the next activity, have students refer to the Pattern Words on page 133. Read the sentences and then select students to read, correctly spell each word, and write it on the transparency.

7. liberty   8. traitor   9. trophy   10. quiche
11. plateau   12. elite   13. ensemble   14. attorney
15. government   16. bureau   17. essays   18. bizarre

Directed Instruction

1 Pronounce a few Pattern Words and have students hold up their fingers indicating the number of syllables.

2 Proceed to page 133. Say, spell, and say each Pattern, Content, and Vocabulary Word. Provide this week's Challenge Words and have students write them in the spaces provided. Assist students as needed.

3 Proceed to page 134. Build each Vocabulary Word before students complete the page. For example, the prefix *in-* goes with the root *nov*

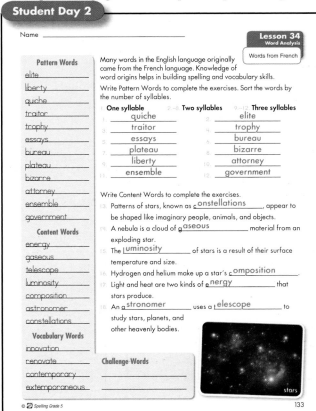

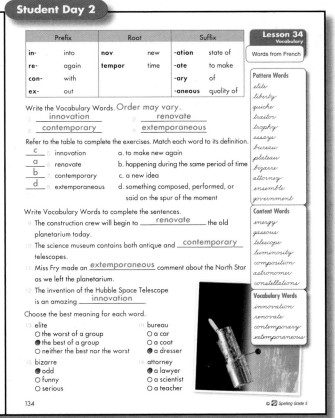

and the suffix *-ation* to build the word *innovation*. Allow students to independently complete the page.

4 Homework suggestion: Distribute a copy of **BLM SP5-34B Lesson 34 Phrases and Sentences** to each student.

Day 3 Word Study Strategies

Objective

The students will use the Spelling Dictionary to find the meanings of pairs of words to correctly complete sentences. They will write list words that belong in categories. The students will write words from pronunciations and the part of speech for given words.

Introduction

Write the words *ensemble* and *quiche* on the board. In another area of the board, write the following sentences:

- The musical _____ sang beautiful hymns during the church service. (**ensemble**)
- Mom fixed a delicious _____ for brunch. (**quiche**)

Have students look up each word in their Spelling Dictionary. Invite volunteers to orally read each definition, name the part of speech, and write the correct words in the sentences.

Directed Instruction

1 Write the following categories of words on the board:
  - effort, power, force, _____ (**energy**)
  - odd, strange, unusual, _____ (**bizarre**)

Read each group of words. Have students refer to the list words on page 135 to find a word that belongs in each category. Solicit volunteers to write the answers.

2 Write the following pronunciations on the board:
  - /ə ˈstro nə mûr/ (**astronomer; noun**)
  - /ˈe sāz/ (**essays; plural noun**)

Select volunteers to read each pronunciation, write the word correctly on the board, and state the part of speech.

3 Proceed to page 135. Provide assistance as students complete the page.

Day 4 Writing

Objective

The students will read an informal time line of the Hubble Space Telescope. They will replace definitions in the sentences with list words.

Introduction

Share the following time line with the students by drawing a line on the board and inserting the important events in the history of air and space exploration at appropriate intervals along the line:

- 1903 - The Wright Brothers flew their aircraft, the *Flyer*.
- 1927 - Charles Lindbergh flew the *Spirit of St. Louis* across the Atlantic Ocean.
- 1969 - The *Apollo 11* mission landed men on the surface of the moon.
- 1981 - The first space shuttle, *Columbia*, was launched.

Explain that today's lesson involves a time line of events regarding the Hubble Space Telescope.

Directed Instruction

1 Write the following definitions on the board:
  - a lawyer (**attorney**)
  - the state of being free (**liberty**)
  - the state of emitting or reflecting light (**luminosity**)

Have students refer to the list words on page 136 and their Spelling Dictionary. Select volunteers to state the list word for each definition.

2 Proceed to page 136. Direct students to refer to their Spelling Dictionary as needed. When complete, select volunteers to read the time line inserting the list word for each definition.

3 Homework suggestion: Distribute a copy of **BLM SP5-34C Lesson 34 Test Prep** to each student.

Day 5 Posttest

Objective

The students will correctly write dictated spelling words and sentences.

Introduction

Review by using flash cards noted in Student Spelling Support, number 2.

Directed Assessment

1 Dictate the list words by using the Pretest sentences or developing original ones. Reserve *essays, innovation, telescope, astronomer,* and *government* for the dictation sentences.

2 Read each sentence. Repeat as needed.
- Many scientists have written essays.
- A rocket scientist wrote about his innovation.
- His new idea was to put a telescope into orbit.
- An astronomer liked the idea.
- Finally, the government helped to launch the invention into space.

3 If assigned, dictate Extra Challenge Words.

4 Score the test, counting each misspelled word as an error. Correct the dictation sentences by grading only the spelling words or grading the complete sentences.

Student Spelling Support
Cont. from page 136

5. Challenge students to write a time line about their life, a historical person, or the development of an object. Have them include as many list words as possible.

6. Write this week's words, categorize the Pattern, Content, and Vocabulary Words, and attach them to the Word Wall.

7. Challenge students to acquire a list of ten French words or phrases and give the literal meaning, for example, *encore* means *again* and *bon voyage* means *good trip.* Invite students to write a paragraph using several French words or phrases and several of their list words.

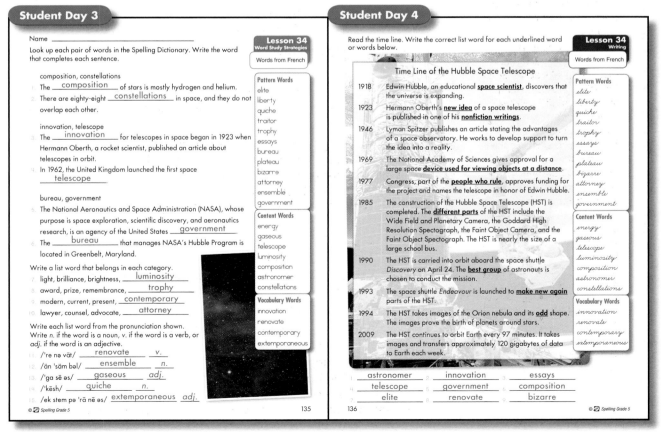

Student Day 3

Name _____

Look up each pair of words in the Spelling Dictionary. Write the word that completes each sentence.

Lesson 34
Word Study Strategies
Words from French

composition, constellations
1. The ___composition___ of stars is mostly hydrogen and helium.
2. There are eighty-eight ___constellations___ in space, and they do not overlap each other.

innovation, telescope
3. The ___innovation___ for telescopes in space began in 1923 when Hermann Oberth, a rocket scientist, published an article about telescopes in orbit.
4. In 1962, the United Kingdom launched the first space ___telescope___.

bureau, government
5. The National Aeronautics and Space Administration (NASA), whose purpose is space exploration, scientific discovery, and aeronautics research, is an agency of the United States ___government___.
6. The ___bureau___ that manages NASA's Hubble Program is located in Greenbelt, Maryland.

Write a list word that belongs in each category.
7. light, brilliance, brightness, ___luminosity___
8. award, prize, remembrance, ___trophy___
9. modern, current, present, ___contemporary___
10. lawyer, counsel, advocate, ___attorney___

Write each list word from the pronunciation shown. Write n. if the word is a noun, v. if the word is a verb, or adj. if the word is an adjective.
11. /ˈre nə vāt/ ___renovate___ v.
12. /än ˈsäm bəl/ ___ensemble___ n.
13. /ˈga sē əs/ ___gaseous___ adj.
14. /ˈkēsh/ ___quiche___ n.
15. /ek stem pə ˈrā nē əs/ ___extemporaneous___ adj.

Pattern Words
elite
liberty
quiche
traitor
trophy
essays
bureau
plateau
bizarre
attorney
ensemble
government

Content Words
energy
gaseous
telescope
luminosity
composition
astronomer
constellations

Vocabulary Words
innovation
renovate
contemporary
extemporaneous

© Spelling Grade 5   135

Student Day 4

Read the time line. Write the correct list word for each underlined word or words below.

Lesson 34
Writing
Words from French

Time Line of the Hubble Space Telescope

1918   Edwin Hubble, an educational **space scientist**, discovers that the universe is expanding.

1923   Hermann Oberth's **new idea** of a space telescope is published in one of his **nonfiction writings**.

1946   Lyman Spitzer publishes an article stating the advantages of a space observatory. He works to develop support to turn the idea into a reality.

1969   The National Academy of Sciences gives approval for a large space **device used for viewing objects at a distance**.

1977   Congress, part of the **people who rule**, approves funding for the project and names the telescope in honor of Edwin Hubble.

1985   The construction of the Hubble Space Telescope (HST) is completed. The **different parts** of the HST include the Wide Field and Planetary Camera, the Goddard High Resolution Spectograph, the Faint Object Camera, and the Faint Object Spectograph. The HST is nearly the size of a large school bus.

1990   The HST is carried into orbit aboard the space shuttle *Discovery* on April 24. The **best group** of astronauts is chosen to conduct the mission.

1993   The space shuttle *Endeavour* is launched to **make new again** parts of the HST.

1994   The HST takes images of the Orion nebula and its **odd** shape. The images prove the birth of planets around stars.

2009   The HST continues to orbit Earth every 97 minutes. It takes images and transfers approximately 120 gigabytes of data to Earth each week.

Pattern Words
elite
liberty
quiche
traitor
trophy
essays
bureau
plateau
bizarre
attorney
ensemble
government

Content Words
energy
gaseous
telescope
luminosity
composition
astronomer
constellations

Vocabulary Words
innovation
renovate
contemporary
extemporaneous

1. astronomer   2. innovation   3. essays
4. telescope   5. government   6. composition
7. elite   8. renovate   9. bizarre

136   © Spelling Grade 5

Words from Spanish

Created Wonders

The theme of this lesson is galaxies. Galaxies are enormous collections of hundreds of millions of stars, all interacting and orbiting about a common center. Galaxies exhibit a variety of forms—elliptical galaxies have a globular shape with a bright nucleus; spiral galaxies have a flattened, disklike shape; irregular galaxies have a disklike shape, but no overall spiral form. Our own galaxy, the Milky Way, is a spiral galaxy.

Day 1 Pretest

Objective
The students will accurately spell and write **words from Spanish**. They will spell and write content, vocabulary, and challenge words.

Introduction
Before class, select Challenge Words for numbers 24 and 25 from a cross-curricular subject, words misspelled on previous assignments, or words that interest your students. The word *burrito* comes from the **Spanish** language and is suggested for number 24. Administer the Pretest.

Directed Instruction

1 Say each word, use it in a sentence, and then repeat the word.

Pattern Words
1. Early Spanish settlers used <u>adobe</u> to construct houses.
2. The <u>avocado</u> was sliced and arranged on a plate.
3. The astronomer used a <u>burro</u> to carry his telescope to the desert.
4. We discussed the science quiz while eating in the <u>cafeteria</u>.
5. Donnie paddled out in his <u>canoe</u> to see the stars one night.
6. A bar of <u>chocolate</u> was named for the Milky Way galaxy.
7. Late at night the boys went on an <u>escapade</u> to view a comet.
8. The <u>hurricane</u> hit the Hawaiian Islands last month.
9. Quentin swatted a large <u>mosquito</u>.
10. The <u>palomino</u> was running in the pasture.
11. Esteban put on his waterproof <u>poncho</u>.
12. The <u>tornado</u> did no damage to the town.

Content Words
13. Do you know the <u>classification</u> for the Andromeda galaxy?
14. <u>Clusters</u> of stars are found within galaxies.
15. Many galaxies are <u>elliptical</u> in shape.
16. The Milky Way has a <u>flattened</u> shape, like a coin.
17. Stars in <u>globular</u> galaxies rotate around a bright nucleus.
18. Galaxies contain not only stars, but complex <u>molecules</u> of gas.
19. The Milky Way is a <u>spiral</u> galaxy.

Vocabulary Words
20. You do not have to <u>convince</u> me that God created galaxies.
21. The committee will <u>nominate</u> a candidate for the prize.
22. Jesus' resurrection from the dead proved that He was <u>invincible</u>.
23. Dr. Salazar will be the <u>nominee</u> for the award in astronomy.

Challenge Words
24. _____
25. _____

2 Allow students to self-correct their Pretest. Write each word on the board. Point out that each Pattern Word is derived from the Spanish language. Review the pronunciation of *globular*, /ˈglo byə lûr/. Note the roots *nomin* and *vinc* in the Vocabulary Words.

3 As a class, read, spell, and read each word. Direct students to circle misspelled words with a colored pencil and rewrite them correctly.

4 Proof each student's Pretest. This becomes an individualized study sheet that can be used at school or at home.

5 Homework suggestion: Distribute a copy of **BLM SP5-35A Lesson 35 Words and Phrases** to each student.

Day 2 Word Analysis and Vocabulary

Objective
The students will sort **words from Spanish** by the number of syllables and complete sentences with content words. They will use a table to write vocabulary words, match given definitions in context, and complete sentences. Students will choose list words to match definitions.

Introduction
Remind students that the Pattern Words in this week's lesson are derived from Spanish words. Derivation is the act of determining the source or origin of a word. Studying word origins helps in developing spelling and vocabulary skills. Invite students to turn to page 137 to refer to the list words. Display **T-22 Words from Spanish** on the overhead. Cover the answers at the bottom. Select a volunteer to complete each clue with a Pattern Word and to write the number of the clue on the line in front of the corresponding picture. Instruct students to look carefully at both the derivation of the word as well as its meaning to determine which Pattern Word to write.

Directed Instruction
1 Inform students that the theme for this lesson is galaxies. Define a *galaxy* as *an enormous collection of hundreds of millions of stars, all interacting and orbiting about a common center. Galaxies are classified by their forms—spiral, elliptical, and irregular.* Point out the following to clarify Content Words and galaxy forms:
  • Elliptical galaxies have a globular shape with a bright nucleus.
  • Spiral galaxies have a flattened, disklike shape.
  • Irregular galaxies have a disklike shape, but with no overall spiral form.

2 Proceed to page 137. Say, spell, and say each Pattern, Content, and Vocabulary Word. Provide this week's Challenge Words and have students write them in the spaces provided. Select a few Pattern Words at random and ask students to tell you the number of syllables in each word.

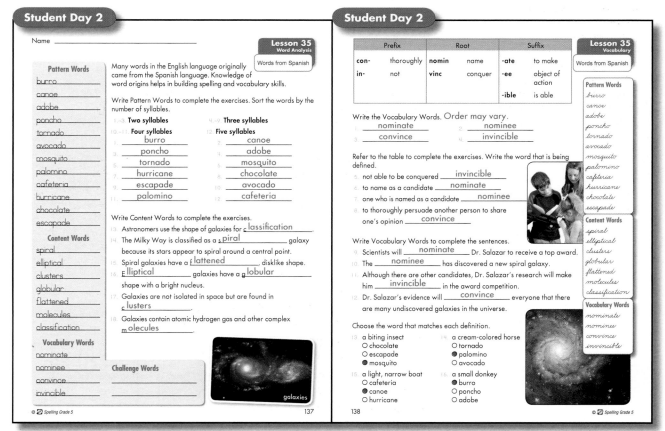

Student Day 2

Name _____

Lesson 35 — Word Analysis
Words from Spanish

Many words in the English language originally came from the Spanish language. Knowledge of word origins helps in building spelling and vocabulary skills.

Write Pattern Words to complete the exercises. Sort the words by the number of syllables.

Pattern Words
burro
canoe
adobe
poncho
tornado
avocado
mosquito
palomino
cafeteria
hurricane
chocolate
escapade

1–3 **Two syllables**   4–9 **Three syllables**
10–11 **Four syllables**   12 **Five syllables**

1. burro   2. canoe
3. poncho   4. adobe
5. tornado   6. mosquito
7. hurricane   8. chocolate
9. escapade   10. avocado
11. palomino   12. cafeteria

Write Content Words to complete the exercises.

Content Words
spiral
elliptical
clusters
globular
flattened
molecules
classification

13. Astronomers use the shape of galaxies for classification
14. The Milky Way is classified as a spiral galaxy because its stars appear to spiral around a central point.
15. Spiral galaxies have a flattened, disklike shape.
16. Elliptical galaxies have a globular shape with a bright nucleus.
17. Galaxies are not isolated in space but are found in clusters.
18. Galaxies contain atomic hydrogen gas and other complex molecules.

Vocabulary Words
nominate
nominee
convince
invincible

Challenge Words
_____
_____

galaxies

137

Student Day 2

Prefix		Root		Suffix	
con-	thoroughly	nomin	name	-ate	to make
in-	not	vinc	conquer	-ee	object of action
				-ible	is able

Lesson 35 — Vocabulary
Words from Spanish

Write the Vocabulary Words. Order may vary.
1. nominate   2. nominee
3. convince   4. invincible

Refer to the table to complete the exercises. Write the word that is being defined.
5. not able to be conquered invincible
6. to name as a candidate nominate
7. one who is named as a candidate nominee
8. to thoroughly persuade another person to share one's opinion convince

Write Vocabulary Words to complete the sentences.
9. Scientists will nominate Dr. Salazar to receive a top award.
10. The nominee has discovered a new spiral galaxy.
11. Although there are other candidates, Dr. Salazar's research will make him invincible in the award competition.
12. Dr. Salazar's evidence will convince everyone that there are many undiscovered galaxies in the universe.

Choose the word that matches each definition.
13. a biting insect
  ○ chocolate
  ○ escapade
  ● mosquito
14. a cream-colored horse
  ○ tornado
  ● palomino
  ○ avocado
15. a light, narrow boat
  ○ cafeteria
  ● canoe
  ○ hurricane
16. a small donkey
  ● burro
  ○ poncho
  ○ adobe

Pattern Words
burro
canoe
adobe
poncho
tornado
avocado
mosquito
palomino
cafeteria
hurricane
chocolate
escapade

Content Words
spiral
elliptical
clusters
globular
flattened
molecules
classification

Vocabulary Words
nominate
nominee
convince
invincible

138

Student Spelling Support

1. Use **BLM SP5-01A A Spelling Study Strategy** in instructional groups to provide assistance with some or all of the words.

2. Duplicate **BLMs SP5-35D–E Lesson 35 Spelling Words I** and **II** on CARD STOCK for students to use as flash cards at school or at home. Another option is to use **BLM SP5-01G Flash Cards Template** or 3" × 5" INDEX CARDS for students to write their own flash cards to use as a study aid.

3. Invite students to write the Challenge Words, numbers 24 and 25, in the Word Bank, in the back of their textbook.

4. For a Bible connection, read Psalm 8:3–4: "When I consider Your heavens, the work of Your fingers, the moon and the stars, which You have ordained, what is man that You are mindful of him, and the son of man that You visit him?" Discuss how the vast expanse of the universe can make one feel insignificant in comparison. However, we have a wonderful, kind, and caring God, who in His love for us, does not consider us to be insignificant at all. He is concerned with every detail of our lives. Invite students to respond to the discussion by listing some awesome creations of God.

5. Challenge students to research three galaxies

Cont. on page 141

---

3 Proceed to page 138. Build each Vocabulary Word before students complete the page. For example, the prefix *con-* goes with the root *vinc* to build the word *convince* and silent *e* is not in the original root spelling. Provide assistance as needed.

4 Homework suggestion: Distribute a copy of **BLM SP5-35B Lesson 35 Phrases and Sentences** to each student.

Day 3 Word Study Strategies

Objective

The students will write words to match definitions, complete analogies with list words, and choose list words to complete alliterative sentences.

Introduction

To practice dictionary skills, instruct students to find the word *escapade* in their Spelling Dictionary. Select volunteers to name the following dictionary components of the entry word *escapade*:

• Pronunciation (**Students locate the diacriticals and pronounce the word.**)
• Part of Speech (**noun**)
• Definition(s) (**an unusually adventurous action; an adventure**)
• Sample Sentence (**Late at night the boys went on an escapade to view a comet.**)

Directed Instruction

1 Remind students that analogies are made up of two word pairs. Both pairs of words have the same kind of relationship. Request an example of an analogy from a volunteer. (**Possible answers:** *Up* is to *down* as *hot* is to *cold*. *Red* is to *apple* as *yellow* is to *banana*.)

2 Review that alliteration is a repetition of consonant sounds at the beginning of several words in a phrase. Choose a volunteer to provide an example of alliteration. (**Possible answers: Peter Piper picked a peck of pickled peppers. A sailor sailed the seven seas to see what he could see.**)

3 Proceed to page 139. Provide assistance as students complete the page independently.

Day 4 Writing

Objective

The students will complete sentences in an informative journal entry with list words that match pronunciations.

Introduction

Hold a discussion about various ways students might demonstrate scientific principles, such as friction, unbalanced forces, or the law of gravity. For example, students may choose to demonstrate how friction produces heat by rubbing their hands together. Pushing a ball across the floor demonstrates unbalanced forces—the force coming from the direction of the push is greater than any other force acting on the ball. Gravity can be demonstrated by dropping a small object from a short distance onto a table or the floor. Explain that the today's writing page contains demonstrations involving the formation of galaxies in space.

Directed Instruction

1 Write the following sentences on the board, including the pronunciations as shown:
  • Raul rode a /ˈbûr ō/_____ to town on market day. (**burro**)
  • He bought an /ä və ˈkä dō/ _____ to make guacamole. (**avocado**)
  • Raul decided to get some /ˈcho kə lət/ _____ for dessert. (**chocolate**)
  Invite students to refer to the list words, found on page 140. Select volunteers to read each sentence aloud, choose a list word that fits both the pronunciation and the sentence context, and write the word.

2 Proceed to page 140. Invite a volunteer to read the information at the

top of the page. Direct students to read the text of the journal entry before deciding which list words to write. Remind students to use both the pronunciations and the sentence context to assist in choosing the correct list words.

3 Homework suggestion: Distribute a copy of **BLM SP5-35C Lesson 35 Test Prep** to each student.

Day 5 Posttest

Objective
The students will correctly write dictated spelling words and sentences.

Introduction
Review by using flash cards noted in Student Spelling Support, number 2.

Directed Assessment

1 Dictate the list words by using the Pretest sentences or developing original ones. Reserve *escapade, canoe, clusters, classification,* and *convince* for the dictation sentences.

2 Read each sentence. Repeat as needed.
- One summer night, we went on an <u>escapade</u>.
- We took our <u>canoe</u> out onto a lake and looked up at the stars.
- <u>Clusters</u> of stars and galaxies were easy to see.
- We knew the <u>classification</u> of several of the galaxies.
- It was easy to <u>convince</u> us that God created the heavens.

3 If assigned, dictate Extra Challenge Words.

4 Score the test, counting each misspelled word as an error. Correct the dictation sentences by grading only the spelling words or grading the complete sentences.

Student Spelling Support

Cont. from page 140

in the universe, using an encyclopedia or the Internet. Invite students to write and illustrate a paragraph about each galaxy.

6. Write this week's words, categorize the Pattern, Content, and Vocabulary Words, and attach them to the Word Wall.

7. For visual and kinesthetic learners, duplicate **BLM SP5-35F Spanish Words**. Provide each student with a set of flash cards, described in Student Spelling Support, number 2. Use only the Pattern Word cards for this activity. Students cut apart the Spanish word cards and match a flash card with each Spanish word card.

8. Challenge students to collect additional English words with Spanish orgins and post on the classroom Word Wall.

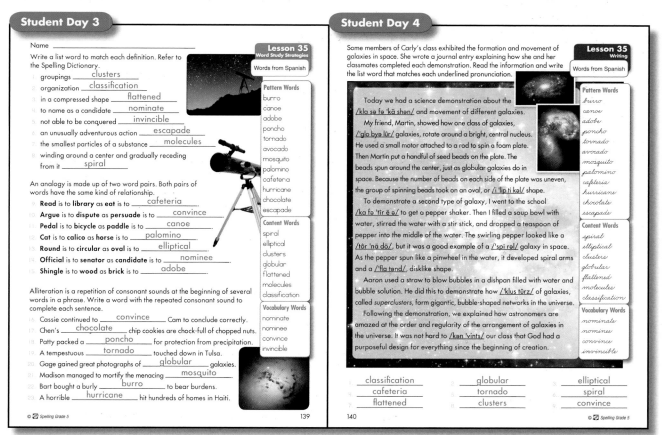

Review Lessons 31–35

Day 1 Latin Roots

Objective

The students will spell, identify, and sort words with **Latin roots**. They will complete sentences with the correct word with a Latin root.

Introduction

Teacher Note: This week's lesson incorporates the Pattern, Content, and Vocabulary Words taught in Lessons 31–35 using a variety of activities such as sorting, a word search, shape boxes, riddles, filling in the correct answer circle, unscrambling words, and decoding words.

Display **T-23 Lessons 31–35 Study Sheet** on the overhead to review Lesson 31 words in unison using the say-spell-say technique. Remind students that a root is the part of a word that gives the basic meaning. Challenge students to identify the **Latin roots** found in Lesson 31 words. (fect, dict, vis)

Directed Instruction

1 Refer to **P-2** and **P-3 Greek and Latin Roots** and select volunteers to locate and review the meaning of each Latin root from Lesson 31. (fect = make; dict = speak; vis = see)

2 Proceed to page 141. Explain that the box contains all the Pattern, Content, and Vocabulary Words in Lessons 31–35. This list is the same list of words that was previously displayed on the overhead. Encourage students to use this list as a review tool. Instruct students to read the directions and independently complete the page.

3 Distribute a copy of **BLM SP5-36A Lessons 31–35 Study Sheet** to each student to take home for study.

4 Homework suggestion: Distribute a copy of **BLM SP5-36B Lesson 36 Homework I** to each student to practice with **Latin roots**, **Greek and Latin roots**, and **words from French**.

Day 2 Latin Roots and Greek and Latin Roots

Objective

The students will find and circle words with **Latin roots** in a word search. They will write words with **Greek and Latin roots** in shape boxes that are shaded in to indicate a specific root.

Introduction

Display **T-23 Lessons 31–35 Study Sheet** to review Lessons 32–33 words in unison, using the say-spell-say technique. Write the following Pattern Words from Lesson 32 on the board: format, uniformity, rupture, obstruct, structure. Challenge students to identify the Latin roots found in Lesson 32 words. (form, rupt, struct) Use **T-14 Mini Word Search Grid** and draw the example mini word search shown. Display the transparency on the overhead and challenge students to find the Pattern Words from the board.

```
f o r m f r u p t s t
r u c t o f o r m r u
o b s t r u c t u r e
p t s t m r u c t f o
r m r u a p t s t r u
c r u p t u r e t f o
r y t i m r o f i n u
```

Directed Instruction

1 Refer to **P-2** and **P-3 Greek and Latin Roots** and select volunteers to

locate and review the meaning of each Latin root from Lesson 32. (**form = shape; rupt = break; struct = build**)

2 Write the following words from Lesson 33 on an overhead transparency sheet: recount, impression, tendency, astronaut, astronomy. Display the words on the overhead and select volunteers to draw shape boxes around each word.

3 Have students refer to **P-2** and **P-3 Greek and Latin Roots** to identify the roots and meanings of each word on the transparency. (**count = tell; press = push down; tend = lean toward; astr = star; naut = ship; nomy = order**) Lightly shade in the boxes that spell out each root. Use a different color, as shown, to differentiate between Greek and Latin roots. In this lesson, Greek roots are shaded in teal, and Latin roots are shaded in pink. A darker shade of teal is used to identify the second Greek root in each word.

(r e c o u n t, i m p r e s s i o n, t e n d e n c y, a s t r o n a u t, a s t r o n o m y)

4 Proceed to page 142. Students read the directions silently and complete the page independently.

5 Homework suggestion: Distribute a copy of **BLM SP5-36C Lesson 36 Homework II** to each student to practice with **Words from Spanish**, Content Words, and Vocabulary Words.

Day 3 Words from French and Words from Spanish

Objective
The students will write **words from French** to answer riddles. They will select the appropriate answer circle to indicate if **words from Spanish** are spelled correctly or incorrectly, and correctly write each word.

Introduction
Display **T-23 Lessons 31–35 Study Sheet** to review Lesson 34 words in unison, using the say-spell-say technique. To provide practice with riddles, ask students to supply an answer to each of the following, using words from Lesson 34:
- Which word is <u>a lawyer</u>? (**attorney**)
- Which word is <u>the best of a group</u>? (**elite**)

Directed Instruction
1 Refer to **T-23 Lessons 31–35 Study Sheet** to review Lesson 35 words in unison, using the say-spell-say technique.

2 Write and draw the following on the board:

	Correct	Incorrect	
buroe	O	O	(**incorrect; burro**)
cafateria	O	O	(**incorrect; cafeteria**)
chocolate	O	O	(**correct; chocolate**)

Read each word and select volunteers to identify if each word is spelled correctly or incorrectly. Fill in each appropriate answer circle. Write each word correctly.

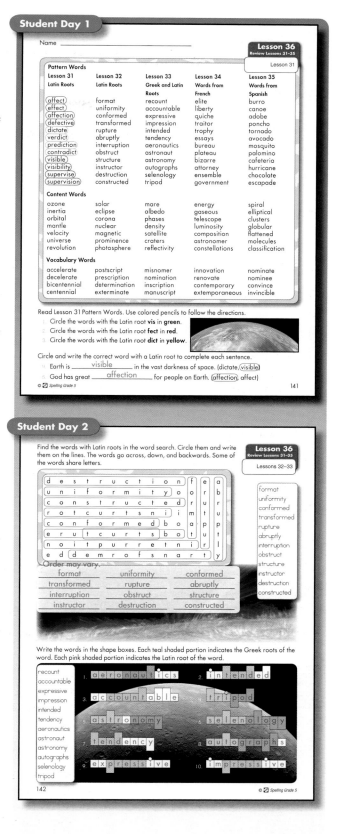

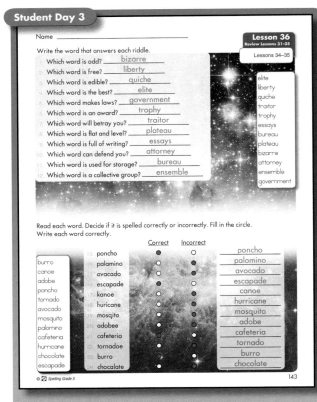

Student Day 3

Name _____

Write the word that answers each riddle.

1. Which word is odd? **bizarre**
2. Which word is free? **liberty**
3. Which word is edible? **quiche**
4. Which word is the best? **elite**
5. Which word makes laws? **government**
6. Which word is an award? **trophy**
7. Which word will betray you? **traitor**
8. Which word is flat and level? **plateau**
9. Which word is full of writing? **essays**
10. Which word can defend you? **attorney**
11. Which word is used for storage? **bureau**
12. Which word is a collective group? **ensemble**

Lesson 36
Review Lessons 31–35
Lessons 34–35

elite
liberty
quiche
traitor
trophy
essays
bureau
plateau
bizarre
attorney
ensemble
government

Read each word. Decide if it is spelled correctly or incorrectly. Fill in the circle. Write each word correctly.

burro
canoe
adobe
poncho
tornado
avocado
mosquito
palomino
cafeteria
hurricane
chocolate
escapade

		Correct	Incorrect	
13	poncho	●	○	poncho
14	palamino	○	●	palomino
15	avacado	○	●	avocado
16	escapade	●	○	escapade
17	kanoe	○	●	canoe
18	huricane	○	●	hurricane
19	mosqito	○	●	mosquito
20	adobee	○	●	adobe
21	cafeteria	●	○	cafeteria
22	tornadoe	○	●	tornado
23	burro	●	○	burro
24	chocalate	○	●	chocolate

© Spelling Grade 5   143

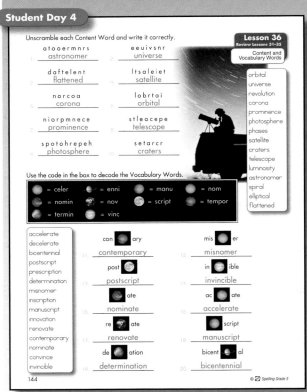

Student Day 4

Unscramble each Content Word and write it correctly.

1. atooermnrs — **astronomer**
2. eeuivsnr — **universe**
3. daftelent — **flattened**
4. ltsaleiet — **satellite**
5. norcoa — **corona**
6. lobrtai — **orbital**
7. niorpmnece — **prominence**
8. stleocepe — **telescope**
9. spotohrepeh — **photosphere**
10. setarcr — **craters**

Lesson 36
Review Lessons 31–35
Content and Vocabulary Words

orbital
universe
revolution
corona
prominence
photosphere
phases
satellite
craters
telescope
luminosity
astronomer
spiral
elliptical
flattened

Use the code in the box to decode the Vocabulary Words.

= celer   = enni   = manu   = nom
= nomin   = nov   = script   = tempor
= termin   = vinc

accelerate
decelerate
bicentennial
postscript
prescription
determination
misnomer
inscription
manuscript
innovation
renovate
contemporary
nominate
convince
invincible

11. con ○ ary — **contemporary**
12. mis ○ er — **misnomer**
13. post ○ — **postscript**
14. in ○ ible — **invincible**
15. ○ ate — **nominate**
16. ac ○ ate — **accelerate**
17. re ○ ate — **renovate**
18. ○ script — **manuscript**
19. de ○ ation — **determination**
20. bicent ○ al — **bicentennial**

144   © Spelling Grade 5

---

3 Proceed to page 143. Students independently complete the page. Encourage students to refer to their Spelling Dictionary for exercises 1–12. Assist as needed.

Day 4 Content Words and Vocabulary Words

Objective

The students will unscramble and write content words. They will use a code to spell and write vocabulary words.

Introduction

Display **T-23 Lessons 31–35 Study Sheet** to review Content Words in unison, using the say-spell-say technique. Write the following Content Words on 3" × 5" INDEX CARDS and pass them out to five volunteers: universe, corona, craters, telescope, spiral. Invite the volunteers to the board, and instruct them to scramble and write their word. Challenge students to unscramble and correctly write the Content Words.

Directed Instruction

1 Continue to refer to **T-23 Lessons 31–35 Study Sheet** to review Vocabulary Words in unison, using the say-spell-say technique. Remind students that a root is the part of a word that gives the basic meaning. Some words contain more than one root. Select volunteers to circle the following roots as you dictate each Vocabulary Word: celer, enni, manu, nom, nomin, nov, script, tempor, termin, vinc. (**celer—accelerate, decelerate; enni—bicentennial, centennial; manu—manuscript; nom—misnomer; nomin—nomination, nominate, nominee; nov—innovation, renovate; script—postscript, prescription, inscription, manuscript; tempor—contemporary, extemporaneous; termin—determination, exterminate; vinc—convince, invincible**)

2 To reinforce root meanings, refer to **P-2** and **P-3 Greek and Latin Roots** and select volunteers to locate and review the meaning of the following roots from the Vocabulary Words:
- *celer* means *fast*
- *enni* means *year*
- *manu* means *hand*
- *nom* means *name*
- *nomin* means *name*
- *nov* means *new*
- *script* means *write*
- *tempor* means *time*
- *termin* means *end*
- *vinc* means *conquer*

3 Proceed to page 144. Students complete the page.

4 Homework suggestion: Distribute a copy of **BLM SP5-36D Lessons 31–35 Test Prep** to each student to practice with many of the words that may appear on the Assessment. Prepare for the Assessment by studying the words on **BLM SP5-36A Lessons 31–35 Study Sheet** that was sent home on Day 1.

Day 5 Assessment

Objective

The students will accurately select the appropriate answer within the context of a sentence. They will fill in the corresponding answer circle.

© Spelling Grade 5

Introduction

Teacher Note: The Test makes provision for Differentiated Instruction. The first twelve sentences include the words assigned to students with shortened lists. Encourage these students to try all the sentences, but only grade the first twelve sentences. The Test is found on two blackline masters.

Duplicate a copy of **BLMs SP5-36E–F Lessons 31–35 Test I** and **II** and distribute to each student. Duplicate **BLM SP5-06G Student Answer Form** and cut apart. Distribute one answer form to each student. Remind students to fill in each answer circle completely and to erase completely if they wish to change an answer.

Directed Assessment

1 Instruct students to listen as you dictate the following Sample:
Sample

Trey and his <u>instructer</u> discussed Earth's <u>orbital</u> <u>velocity</u>. <u>All correct</u>
              A   B   C   D

Say, "Are any of the first three underlined words misspelled?" Pause for replies. Inform students that the letter *A* is below the underlined word that is misspelled. (**instructor**) Guide students to the answer form that was previously distributed. Lead students to find the Sample box and fill in the appropriate answer circle containing the same letter. Say, "You will continue in the same way. You will read each sentence, choose the word that you think is misspelled, and fill in the corresponding circle on the answer form. If all the words are spelled correctly, fill in the fourth circle, labeled *D*, for *All correct*."

2 Assist students as needed while they read the sentences and complete the Test on their own.

1. The astronomer lectured about the recent solar eclipse.
2. A bizarre interruption abruptly ended the movie.
3. The telescope showed the composition of a spiral galaxy.
4. Numerous star clusters are visible in the universe.
5. The girls intended to convince their parents to go on an escapade.
6. The moon's density and phases will be discussed at the centennial gala.
7. The defective satellite could not transmit images of the moon's craters.
8. The astronaut was expressive when asked to recount mission details.
9. The contemporary innovation transformed the space industry.
10. Dr. Lin received an award nomination for his manuscript on astronomy.
11. The energy of the hurricane and tornado was astounding.
12. Sylvia won a trophy for her essays on nuclear energy.
13. The moon's elliptical orbit has the tendency to affect Earth's tides.
14. In selenology, the term *mare* is a misnomer.
15. Visibility of the moon's albedo, or reflectivity, was very clear.
16. Ron recited an extemporaneous poem about an invincible mosquito.
17. A gaseous solar prominence can rupture the sun's atmosphere.
18. Pollution of Earth's ozone distorts the luminosity of constellations.
19. Carlyn constructed a model of Earth's mantle in the cafeteria.
20. The attorney was accountable for the supervision of the case.
21. Vick read about the sun's magnetic field, corona, and photosphere.
22. A palomino and burro walked across the vast plateau.
23. A bureau of the government arrested the traitor.
24. Brit will supervise the format of the bicentennial celebration.
25. We decided to renovate the structure by using adobe.

3 Refer to **BLM SP5-36G Lessons 31–35 Answer Key** when correcting the Test.

Word Bank

A *a*

_____   _____
_____   _____
_____   _____

_____

autumn

B *B*

_____   _____
_____   _____
_____   _____

C *C*

D *D*

coastline

E *E*

F *F*

_____ _____

_____ _____

_____ _____

_____ _____

_____ _____

_____ _____

G *G*

_____ _____

_____ _____

_____ _____

_____ _____

gorges

H *H*

_____ _____

_____ _____

_____ _____

_____ _____

I _I_

_____   _____   _____
_____   _____   _____
_____   _____   _____

J _J_

_____   _____   _____
_____   _____   _____
_____   _____   _____

K _K_

_____   _____   _____
_____   _____   _____
_____   _____   _____

kelp

L *L*

M *m*

marsupial

N *n*

O o

P p

phases of the moon

Q q

R $\mathcal{R}$

S $\mathcal{S}$

songbirds

T $\mathcal{T}$

U $\mathcal{U}$

V $\mathcal{V}$

W $\mathcal{W}$

woodlands

X *x*

Y *y*

Z *z*

Pronunciation Key

Letters written within slashes on this key represent common phonemes, the smallest units of distinct sound in English. Listed to the right are variant spellings for these sounds.

Consonants

/b/	**b**i**b**, **b**a**b**y, **b**u**bb**le
/ch/	**ch**ild, mu**ch**, pa**tch**, na**t**ure, ques**ti**on
/d/	**d**ay, sa**d**, la**dd**er
/f/	**f**ish, o**f**ten, o**ff**, **ph**one, cou**gh**
/g/	**g**o, bi**g**, wi**gg**le, **gh**ost, lea**gue**
/h/	**h**ot, **h**urry, **wh**o
/j/	**j**ump, **j**u**dge**, **g**ym, ran**ge**
/k/	**k**eep, **c**up, si**ck**, ti**ck**le, pi**c**nic, anti**que**, s**ch**ool
/l/	**l**ook, ta**ll**, **l**i**l**y, a**ll**ey, penci**l**
/m/	**m**y, co**m**e, **m**o**mm**y
/n/	**n**o, **n**i**n**e, wi**nn**er, **kn**ow
/ng/	ri**ng**, si**ng**ing
/p/	**p**ie, ho**p**e, a**pp**le
/kw/	**qu**een, **qu**iet, **ch**oir
/r/	**r**ed, **r**ose, nea**r**, a**rr**ow
/s/	**s**ee, le**ss**on, mi**ss**, **c**ity, dan**ce**
/sh/	**sh**e, wi**sh**, **s**ugar, ma**ch**ine, na**ti**on, spe**ci**al
/t/	**t**ie, ea**t**, **t**a**tt**le, walk**ed**
/th/	**th**ink, bo**th** (breath)
/<u>th</u>/	**th**is, ei**th**er (voice)
/v/	**v**ase, sa**v**e
/w/	**w**e, **w**ell
/hw/ or /w/	**wh**at, **wh**y, **wh**ether
/y/	**y**es, **y**ellow, on**i**on, mill**i**on
/z/	**z**oo, fu**zz**y, ma**z**e, ha**s**
/zh/	mea**s**ure, vi**s**ion

Vowels

/ā/	**a**ble, d**a**te, **ai**d, p**ay**, **eigh**t, gr**ea**t
/a/	p**a**t, **a**pple
/ä/	f**a**ther (same sound as /o/)
/är/	f**ar**m, **ar**m, sp**ar**kle, h**ear**t
/ē/	m**e**, b**ee**, m**ea**t, ch**ie**f, c**ei**ling, lad**y**, vall**ey**
/e/	b**e**t, **e**dge, m**e**ss, r**ea**dy, fr**ie**nd
/ī/	**I**, f**i**ne, n**igh**t, p**ie**, b**y**
/i/	h**i**s, **i**t, g**y**m
/ō/	b**o**ne, **o**pen, c**oa**t, sh**ow**, s**ou**l
/o/	t**o**p, **o**tter, b**o**ther (same sound as /ä/)
/ò/	s**o**ft, **o**ften, **a**lso, h**au**l, c**augh**t, dr**aw**, b**ough**t
/oi/	j**oy**, f**oi**l, r**oy**al
/oo/	b**oo**k, p**u**ll, sh**ou**ld
/o͞o/	p**oo**l, t**u**be, t**o**, st**ew**, fr**ui**t, gr**ou**p
/yo͞o/	**u**se, f**ue**l, p**ew**, **you**, bea**u**ty
/ou/	**ou**t, n**ow**, t**ow**el
/u/	h**u**t, l**o**ve, c**ou**ple, an**o**ther (used in stressed syllables)
/âr/	**air**, c**are**, b**ear**, January
/ôr/	f**or**, t**or**n, c**or**n, ch**ore**, w**ar**m
/îr/	**ear**, p**ier**ce, w**eir**d
/ûr/	t**ur**n, w**or**d, th**ir**d, t**ur**tle, f**er**tile, h**ear**d (used in stressed syllables) furth**er**, col**or** (used in unstressed syllables)
/ə/	schwa—the /u/ sound in unstressed syllables: **a**like sudd**e**n penc**i**l cott**o**n circ**u**s

Spelling Dictionary

The Guide Words are two words at the top of the page in a dictionary. These two words are the first and last words defined on a page.

broadest   **centennial**

broadest   centennial

An Entry Word is a word being defined. A dot is used to show syllable division. Multisyllable words are separated into syllables. Syllable division and pronunciation can differ.

bur·eau

bur·eau /ˈbyoor ō/ n. 1 a chest of drawers; a dresser. *The scientific book was placed on the bureau.* 2 an office or agency. *The news bureau reported the accident.*

bur·ro /ˈbur ō/ n. a small donkey. *The astronomer used a burro to carry his telescope to the desert.*

bu·si·ness·es /ˈbiz nə sɪz/ n. pl. plural of BUSINESS; companies. *Three businesses promised to support our school fund-raising drive.*

C

cac·tus /ˈkak təs/ n. a plant that has succulent stems and branches with spines instead of leaves and is found in desert areas. *The saguaro cactus can reach a height of over fifty-five feet.*

ca·fe·ter·i·a /ka fə ˈtir ē ə/ n. an eating area where guests take food to their own tables. *We discussed the spelling quiz while eating in the cafeteria.*

cal·ci·um /ˈkal sē əm/ n. a silvery metallic element. *Polyps produce calcium that helps to form the base of the*

...layer
...hat
...anopy

...throughout the canyon.

car·ni·vore /ˈkär nə vôr/ n. a meat-eating animal. *Each carnivore at the zoo...*

The Pronunciation shows how to say the word.

/ˈbyoor ō/

cau·tious /ˈkô shəs/ adj. being alert to watch for danger; careful. *Are you cautious*

The Part of Speech follows the pronunciation. An entry word may have more than one part of speech.

bur·eau /ˈbyoor ō/ *n.* 1 a chest of drawers; a dresser. *The scientific book was placed on the bureau.* 2 an office or agency. *The news bureau reported the accident.*

A Sample Sentence helps in understanding the definition.

bur·eau /ˈbyoor ō/ n. 1 a chest of drawers; a dresser. *The scientific book was placed on the bureau.* 2 an office or agency. *The news bureau reported the accident.*

A Definition is the meaning of the word. A word may have more than one definition.

bur·eau /ˈbyoor ō/ n. 1 **a chest of drawers; a dresser.** *The scientific book was placed on the bureau.* 2 **an office or agency.** *The news bureau reported the accident.*

A

ab·do·men /'ab də mən/ *n.* the third section of an insect's body. *The abdomen of a scorpion fly can curve over its back.*

a·brupt·ly /ə 'brupt lē/ *adv.* suddenly. *The speaker abruptly ended his discussion of the sun's activity.*

ab·sorp·tion /əb 'sôrp shən/ *n.* the process of being absorbed. *Absorption of water through the seed coat is necessary for growth.*

a·bun·dance /ə 'bun dənts/ *n.* a great supply. *Farmers enjoy having an abundance of crops to sell.*

ac·cel·er·ate /ak 'se lə rāt/ *v.* to move faster. *Rocket boosters accelerate the space shuttle from Earth into space.*

ac·ces·si·ble /ak 'se sə bəl/ *adj.* able to be easily reached. *The new ramp at Moonlight Shores makes the beach easily accessible.*

ac·count /ə 'kount/ *n.* a report or explanation of something that has happened or been observed. *Professor Ruthe gave an account of the diverse forest vegetation.*

ac·count·a·ble /ə 'koun tə bəl/ *adj.* responsible. *Jesus wants us to hold one another accountable in our actions.*

ac·cu·mu·late /ə 'kyōō myə lāt/ *v.* to make a heap or pile; to amass. *During a winter storm, snow can accumulate in massive piles.*

ac·cus·tomed /ə 'kus təmd/ *adj.* to have familiarized or become used to. *Have you become accustomed to cold temperatures?*

a·chieve /ə 'chēv/ *v.* to accomplish. *Tucker wants to achieve a high score on his science project.*

ac·tive·ly /'ak tiv lē/ *adv.* in an active manner. *The chipmunks were actively storing food for the winter.*

¹ad·dress /ə 'dres/ *v.* to speak about. *Our science teacher will address the subject of currents.*

²ad·dress /'a dres/ *n.* directions for delivery on an envelope. *The heavy rainfall smeared the address on the letter.*

ad·e·quate /'a di kwət/ *adj.* sufficient to meet a need. *Adequate water will help the seed grow.*

ad·jec·tive /'a jik tiv/ *n.* a word that describes a noun. *Loving is an adjective that perfectly describes Jae's personality.*

ad·mire /əd 'mī ûr/ *v.* to look or marvel at something or somebody. *We will admire the view of the canyon from a mountain summit.*

ad·mit·tance /ad 'mi tənts/ *n.* permission to enter. *After buying a ticket, Alexis received admittance into the zoo.*

ad·mit·ting /ad 'mi ting/ *v.* action of acknowledging; confessing. *Sandy was admitting that she forgot to turn the heater off.*

a·do·be /ə 'dō bē/ *n.* clay mixed with straw and baked in the sun used to make bricks. *Early Spanish settlers used adobe to construct houses.*

adobe

ad·vi·sa·ble /əd ˈvī zə bəl/ *adj.* prudent; wise. *It is advisable to wear sunscreen when playing outdoors.*

aer·o·naut·ics /âr ə ˈnȯ tiks/ *n. pl.* plural of AERONAUTICS; the science of flight. *Jamison wanted to study aeronautics at the Air Force Academy.*

af·fect /ə ˈfekt/ *v.* to have an influence on. *Does the moon greatly affect the earth's tides?*

af·fec·tion /ə ˈfek shən/ *n.* fondness; love. *God has great affection toward each of His children.*

af·ford /ə ˈfȯrd/ *v.* to be able to bear the cost. *The boys can afford to pay their entrance into the zoo.*

a·gent /ˈā jənt/ *n.* one who is authorized to act for a company. *Mr. Santos is an agent for the Volcanic Study Agency.*

ag·gra·vate /ˈa grə vāt/ *v.* to make worse, disturb, or annoy. *Scratching a mosquito bite will aggravate it.*

air·craft /ˈâr kraft/ *n. pl.* plural of AIRCRAFT; vehicles made for traveling through the air. *The aircraft were taking off from the airport.*

al·be·do /al ˈbē dō/ *n.* the fraction of light that is reflected by an object. *The moon's albedo* /al ˈbē dō/ *reflected a magnificent glow.*

al·ley /ˈa lē/ *n.* a narrow street. *The bus driver drove through the alley to get to the main street.*

al·low·ance /ə ˈlou ənts/ *n.* a budgeted amount of money. *Raymond was given a travel allowance for his vacation.*

al·pine /ˈal pīn/ *adj.* relating to the elevated slopes above the timberline of a mountain. *Alpine tundra contains no trees because of the high altitude.*

al·ter·nate /ˈȯl tûr nāt/ *v.* to take turns; rotate. *Shirley and Gerron alternate turns watering the flower garden.*

al·though /ȯl ˈthō/ *conj.* even though. *Although it was raining, Dave took a tour of the fertile valleys.*

a·nat·om·y /ə ˈna tə mē/ *n.* a branch of natural science that deals with the structure of organisms. *Anatomy is a basic area of study for doctors during medical school.*

an·chor /ˈang kûr/ *v.* to hold in place. *How does God anchor the earth in the solar system?*

a·ne·mo·ne /ə ˈne mə nē/ *n.* a sea animal that looks like a flower. *The anemone used its tentacles to attach itself to the rock.*

an·nu·al /ˈan yə wəl/ *adj.* occurring once a year; yearly. *Is Easter an annual celebration?*

a·non·y·mous /ə ˈno nə məs/ *adj.* not named or identified; unidentified. *An anonymous author wrote a poem about the desolate tundra.*

ant·arc·tic /ant ˈärk tik/ *adj.* relating to the region near or on the South Pole. *Antarctic tundra does not contain large animals.*

an·ten·na /an ˈte nə/ *n.* one of a pair of sensory organs on the head of an insect. *Did you know that an antenna also has three parts?*

a·pos·tro·phe /ə ˈpos trə fē/ *n.* a punctuation mark that is used to indicate the omission of letters or numbers, the possessive case, or the plural form. *The apostrophe in the word* wouldn't *replaces the letter* o *in* not.

ap·par·ent /ə ˈpâr ənt/ *adj.* visible; easily understood. *It is apparent that Isaiah has a bird since he brought it on Pet Day.*

ap·ply·ing /ə ˈpli ing/ v. putting into action. *Some farmers are busy applying pesticides to their crops.*

ap·point /ə ˈpoint/ v. to select a person for an official position or job. *The committee will appoint Lucas to the forest ranger department.*

a·qua·mar·ine /ä kwə mə ˈrēn/ adj. a pale, blue-green hue. *Shallow Caribbean waters may be aquamarine in color.*

a·qua·tic /ə ˈkwä tik/ adj. living or growing in water. *Algae are types of aquatic organisms.*

arc·tic /ˈärk tik/ adj. relating to the region near or on the North Pole. *Arctic tundra occurs on or around the North Pole.*

ar·id /ˈa rəd/ adj. extremely dry with very little rainfall. *Camels are able to live in an arid climate.*

ar·ti·cle /ˈär ti kəl/ n. a nonfiction story in a newspaper or magazine. *Enrique read an interesting article about owls in the newspaper.*

art·ist /ˈär tist/ n. a person who is skilled in creating art, especially paintings and sculptures. *John Audubon was an artist who enjoyed drawing birds.*

as·sem·bly /ə ˈsem blē/ n. a group of people gathered for legislation, worship, or entertainment. *The spelunker discussed how to explore a cave at an assembly.*

as·sign·ment /ə ˈsīn mənt/ n. that which is assigned; a task. *Our assignment was to transplant plants into larger containers.*

as·tro·naut /ˈas trə nȯt/ n. a person trained to perform tasks in space. *Brooke decided to study to become an astronaut.*

a·stro·no·mer /ə ˈstro nə mūr/ n. a person who makes observations of matter that is outside of the earth's atmosphere; space scientist. *An astronomer maps where stars are in the sky.*

a·stro·no·my /ə ˈstro nə mē/ n. the scientific study of the order of the universe, including the stars and planets. *Darrah's favorite area of study was astronomy.*

ath·lete /ˈath lēt/ n. a person trained in games, sports, or exercises that require skill. *Annie exercises six times a week and is a serious athlete.*

at·mo·sphere /ˈat mə sfir/ n. the mass of air surrounding the earth. *The atmosphere is categorized into five different layers.*

a·toll /ˈa tȯl/ n. a circular coral reef that surrounds an island and a lagoon. *The largest atoll in land area is Christmas Island.*

at·tempt /ə ˈtempt/ v. to make an effort to accomplish or do; try. *Porter will attempt to run a marathon next year.*

at·ten·tive /ə ˈten tiv/ adj. holding in thought; paying close attention to. *The students were attentive to the message in chapel.*

at·tor·ney /ə ˈtûr nē/ n. a lawyer. *The observatory committee hired an attorney to represent them.*

au·di·ence /ˈȯ dē ənts/ n. those who come to see and hear a program. *The audience clapped for the graduates.*

au·to·graphs /ˈȯ tə grafs/ n. pl. plural of AUTOGRAPH; written signatures. *Robin was able to get ten autographs on her space center brochure.*

au·tumn /ˈȯ təm/ n. the season between summer and winter; fall. *Autumn is the season for harvesting crops.*

a·vi·ar·y /'ā vē âr ē/ *n.* an enclosed place where birds are kept. *Mr. Cavender built an aviary for his ten birds.*

a·vi·a·tion /ā və 'ā shən/ *n.* the process of designing, manufacturing, and flying an airplane. *Leon checked out books about helicopters, jets, and aviation.*

a·vo·ca·do /ä və 'kä dō/ *n.* a pulpy green or brown fruit having yellow-green flesh. *The avocado was sliced and arranged on a plate.*

a·void /ə 'void/ *v.* to stay away from. *Amber will avoid hiking off the main forest trail.*

ax·is /'ak səs/ *n.* an imaginary straight line around which an object rotates. *God created the earth to rotate around an axis.*

B

bar·na·cles /'bär ni kəlz/ *n. pl.* plural of BARNACLE; small marine crustaceans that adhere themselves to rocks, ships, wharfs, or ocean animals. *How many barnacles did you count in the tidal pool?*

ba·ro·me·ter /bə 'ro mə tûr/ *n.* an instrument that measures changes in atmospheric pressure and is used for weather forecasting and determining altitude. *The meteorologist used a barometer to assist him in his forecast.*

bar·ri·er /'bâr ē ûr/ *n.* **1** a type of coral reef that lies parallel to a coastline with a lagoon between the reef and the shore. *A barrier reef is like a long wall that is parallel to a coastline.* **2** something that blocks or hinders movement. *The road crew placed a barrier on the street to prevent people from driving on the new asphalt.*

ba·sin /'bā sən/ *n.* a low area of ground surrounded by higher terrain. *The Continental Divide is a drainage basin in North America.*

beige /'bāzh/ *adj.* a pale tan hue. *Ash from Mount Saint Helens turned our car beige.*

be·lief /bə 'lēf/ *n.* something believed. *My belief in God is solid as a rock.*

bi·cen·ten·ni·al /bī sen 'te nē əl/ *adj.* a two-hundredth anniversary. *In 1976, the United States celebrated its bicentennial birthday.*

bi·lat·er·al /bī 'la tə rəl/ *adj.* relating to two sides. *A mayfly has bilateral wings on its body.*

bi·o·graph·ies /bī 'o grə fēz/ *n. pl.* plural of BIOGRAPHY; written accounts of someone's life that can be in the form of an article, a book, or produced into a movie. *Caleb read two biographies about Sir George Airy, an astronomer.*

bi·zarre /bə 'zär/ *adj.* odd. *An exploding star forms a bizarre shape.*

bliz·zard /'bli zûrd/ *n.* a heavy snowstorm with strong winds. *The powerful blizzard lasted for three days.*

bot·an·ist /'bo tə nist/ *n.* a scientist who studies plants. *A botanist discovered many uses for the peanut plant.*

avocado

broad·est /'bró dist/ *adj.* widest. *The Mississippi River Valley flows through one of the broadest river valleys.*

bruised /'broozd/ *v.* past tense of BRUISE; to have injured. *Sasha bruised her foot falling off her bicycle.*

bur·eau /'byoor ō/ *n.* **1** a chest of drawers; a dresser. *The scientific book was placed on the bureau.* **2** an office or agency. *The news bureau reported the accident.*

bur·ro /'bûr ō/ *n.* a small donkey. *The astronomer used a burro to carry his telescope to the desert.*

bu·si·ness·es /'biz nə səz/ *n. pl.* plural of BUSINESS; companies. *Three businesses promised to support our school fund-raising drive.*

C

cac·tus /'kak təs/ *n.* a plant that has succulent stems and branches with spines instead of leaves and is found in desert areas. *The saguaro cactus can reach a height of over fifty-five feet.*

ca·fe·ter·i·a /ka fə 'tîr ē ə/ *n.* an eating area where guests take food to their own tables. *We discussed the science quiz while eating in the cafeteria.*

cal·ci·um /'kal sē əm/ *n.* a silver-white metallic element. *Polyps produce calcium that helps to form the base of a reef.*

ca·len·dar /'ka lən dûr/ *n.* a table listing days and dates. *The calendar shows days on which the zoo is closed.*

ca·noe /kə 'noo/ *n.* a light, narrow boat powered by oars or paddles. *Donnie paddled out in his canoe to see the stars one night.*

can·o·py /'ka nə pē/ *n.* the uppermost layer of a forest, consisting of treetops that form a type of ceiling. *The forest canopy was very dense.*

can·yon /'kan yən/ *n.* a deep, narrow valley. *Wildflower seeds were scattered throughout the canyon.*

car·ni·vore /'kär nə vôr/ *n.* a meat-eating animal. *Each carnivore at the zoo receives a daily ration of meat.*

cart·il·age /'kär tə lij/ *n.* a strong elastic tissue. *Sharks have skeletons that are made of bendable cartilage.*

ca·tas·tro·phe /kə 'tas trə fē/ *n.* a sudden disaster. *After the catastrophe, many countries sent relief aid.*

cau·tious /'kò shəs/ *adj.* being alert to watch for danger; careful. *Are you cautious when you ride your bicycle?*

ca·vern /'ka vûrn/ *n.* a large cave. *My class enjoyed touring the beautiful cavern.*

cei·ling /'sē ling/ *n.* **1** the height of the lower part of a cloud covering. *The cloud ceiling at the beach was very low.* **2** the top part of a room or object. *A crystal chandelier hung from the ceiling.*

cen·ten·ni·al /sen 'te nē əl/ *adj.* a one-hundredth anniversary. *Many people attended the centennial celebration in Philadelphia.*

canoe

cen·ti·grade /ˈsen tə grād/ *adj.* a temperature scale based on one hundred degrees between the freezing and boiling points of water at sea level. *A centigrade scale is divided into 100 degrees.*

chalk·board /ˈchȯk bôrd/ *n.* a dark colored surface for writing and drawing with chalk. *Cindi drew a butterfly and a flower on her chalkboard.*

cham·ber /ˈchām bûr/ *n.* a room; a natural or artificial enclosed space. *A cave can have more than one chamber.*

cher·ish /ˈchâr ish/ *v.* to treasure. *Monique will cherish the necklace her grandmother gave to her.*

chil·ly /ˈchi lē/ *adj.* noticeably cold. *Rachel felt a chilly wind when she reached the mountaintop.*

chlor·o·phyll /ˈklôr ə fil/ *n.* the green pigment found in plants. *Do all green leaves contain chlorophyll?*

cho·co·late /ˈcho kə lət/ *n.* a food prepared from roasted cacao beans. *A bar of chocolate was named for the Milky Way galaxy.*

choos·ing /ˈchoo zing/ *v.* selecting. *Which desert plant are you choosing for your science project?*

chores /ˈchôrz/ *n. pl.* plural of CHORE; tasks. *One of Isabel's chores is to feed her dog.*

Chris·ti·an·i·ty /kris chē ˈa nə tē/ *n.* the faith of the followers of Christ. *Followers of Christianity believe that Jesus rose from the dead.*

cir·cu·la·tion /sûr kyə ˈlā shən/ *n.* the continuous movement of blood through the vessels of the body. *Circulation is a function of the cardiovascular system in a body.*

cir·cum·scribe /ˈsûr kəm skrib/ *v.* to draw a line around. *The divers will circumscribe an area on the map for today's dive.*

cit·i·zen /ˈsi tə zən/ *n.* a member of a community. *It is the duty of every eligible citizen to vote.*

clas·si·fi·ca·tion /kla sə fə ˈkā shən/ *n.* organization; a system of sorting according to type. *Do you know the classification for the Andromeda galaxy?*

cli·mate /ˈkli mət/ *n.* the average condition of the weather over a period of years. *Many woodland ecosystems have a semiarid climate.*

clus·ters /ˈklus tûrz/ *n. pl.* plural of CLUSTER; groupings. *Clusters of stars are found within galaxies.*

coast·line /ˈkōst lin/ *n.* the outline of a coast. *There are many tidal pools up and down the coastline.*

co·coa /ˈkō kō/ *n.* a brown powder used to make chocolate. *Cocoa is grown on plantations that are situated in river valleys.*

cof·fee /ˈkȯ fē/ *n.* a drink made by brewing the ground seeds of a coffee plant. *Jeannie enjoys drinking coffee with cream and sugar.*

cog·ni·tion /kog ˈni shən/ *n.* the state of knowing; awareness. *Her scientific cognition was astounding.*

col·umns /ˈko ləmz/ *n. pl.* plural of COLUMN; pillars. *Many columns are formed in caves by water seeping through the roof.*

com·fort·a·ble /ˈkumpf tûr bəl/ *adj.* enjoying contentment; cozy. *Scuba divers wear comfortable wet suits to keep their bodies warm.*

com·mer·cial /kə 'mûr shəl/ *adj.* business-related. *Commercial fishing boats often use sonar to detect schools of fish.*

com·mon /'ko mən/ *adj.* familiar. *Snow is a common sight on the top of tall mountain ranges.*

com·mo·tion /kə 'mō shən/ *n.* a state of confusion with much movement. *There was quite a commotion when our pet hamster escaped.*

com·pas·sion /kəm 'pa shən/ *n.* pity. *Jesus showed His compassion by dying on the cross for sinners.*

com·plaint /kəm 'plānt/ *n.* an expression of dissatisfaction; grievance. *Natalie never had a complaint about the hike up Mount Rainier.*

¹com·plex /'kom pleks/ *n.* a building or group of housing units. *Is your apartment complex near the shore?*

²com·plex /kom 'pleks/ *adj.* hard to analyze. *The prediction of rip currents is often a complex science.*

com·po·si·tion /kom pə 'zi shən/ *n.* the different parts of which something is made. *Scientists study the composition of a star's outer layers.*

com·pound /'kom pound/ *adj.* composed of two or more things together. *Roberto had a compound fracture in his arm after he fell.*

com·press /kəm 'pres/ *v.* to squeeze or press together. *To stop a wound from bleeding, you should compress the area.*

con·cave /kon 'kāv/ *adj.* curved or rounded inward; with a curved or inward shape. *A concave hideout in a rock or coral is beneficial to aquarium fish.*

con·clu·sion /kən 'kloo zhən/ *n.* thoroughly coming to a close or end; end. *Football is a sport that begins at the conclusion of summer.*

¹con·duct /'kon dəkt/ *n.* behavior. *Calista's conduct was a reflection of her love for the Lord.*

²con·duct /kən 'dukt/ *v.* to take part in the management of something. *We will conduct an experiment on tides and currents.*

con·duc·tion /kən 'duk shən/ *n.* the act of leading or carrying. *High winds provided conduction for ashes across the state.*

con·fig·ure /kən 'fi gyûr/ *v.* to arrange, design, or set up something for a specific purpose or in a particular way. *Kenji decided to configure his fish tank after the one at school.*

¹con·flict /'kon flikt/ *n.* opposing action. *The small sailboat was in conflict with the strong current.*

²con·flict /kən 'flikt/ *v.* to fail to be in agreement. *My ideas for the project conflict with the plans of the director.*

con·formed /kən 'fôrmd/ *v.* past tense of CONFORM; molded. *Jesus' will was perfectly conformed to His Father's will.*

con·form·ing /kən 'fôr ming/ *v.* agreeing; complying. *Conforming to the rules during an ocean expedition is important.*

con·grat·u·late /kən 'gra jə lāt/ *v.* to express rejoicing to someone for an achievement or special occasion. *Mr. Agustin will congratulate his students after their chapel skit.*

con·i·fer /'ko nə fûr/ *n.* a type of evergreen tree or shrub that produces cones and has thin, needlelike leaves. *The old conifer was one hundred feet tall.*

¹con·sole /ˈkon sōl/ *n.* an electronic device that connects to a television set. *We used our computer game console to play a DVD about the ocean.*

²con·sole /kən ˈsōl/ *v.* to comfort. *We prayed with Gina to console her after the loss of her puppy.*

con·stel·la·tions /kont stə ˈlā shənz/ *n. pl.* plural of CONSTELLATION; groups of stars. *Some constellations are visible only certain times of the year.*

con·struc·ted /kən ˈstruk təd/ *v.* past tense of CONSTRUCT; built. *The observatory was constructed in 1957.*

con·tact /ˈkon takt/ *n.* a touch. *Our class was told to not make contact with the cave walls.*

con·tem·por·ar·y /kən ˈtem pə rär ē/ *adj.* happening during the same period of time; modern; current. *The telescope was built with a contemporary design.*

con·tin·ued /kən ˈtin yōōd/ *v.* past tense of CONTINUE; to have maintained without an interruption. *Jamal continued working on his chores until he was finished.*

con·tin·u·ous /kən ˈtin yōō əs/ *adj.* uninterrupted in space, time, or order. *A rip current pulled a swimmer past the continuous line of waves.*

con·tor·tion /kən ˈtôr shən/ *n.* in a thoroughly twisted state out of its normal shape. *The contortion of a butterfly can be seen as it leaves its chrysalis.*

¹con·tract /ˈkon trakt/ *n.* a written agreement. *The contract for the purchase was signed by both buyer and seller.*

²con·tract /kən ˈtrakt/ *v.* to become less in size. *The pupils in our eyes contract in bright light.*

con·trac·tion /kən ˈtrak shən/ *n.* a drawing out or pulling together; reduction in size; tightening. *The human heart alternates between contraction and expansion.*

con·tra·dict /kon trə ˈdikt/ *v.* to speak in opposition; deny. *Many people contradict the theory of evolution on Earth.*

con·ven·ient /kən ˈvēn yənt/ *adj.* easy to get to; accessible. *A convenient way to learn about coral is to read a book.*

con·ver·sa·tion /kon vûr ˈsā shən/ *n.* talk between two or more people. *Two divers engaged in conversation before exploring the trench.*

con·versed /kən ˈvûrsd/ *v.* past tense of CONVERSE; to have spoken and exchanged thoughts in a conversation. *The two scientists conversed about the many different species of fish.*

con·vert /kən ˈvûrt/ *v.* to turn into something different. *We plan to convert our patio into a greenhouse.*

con·vert·i·ble /kən ˈvûr tə bəl/ *adj.* able to be turned. *Davit put the potted shrub into his convertible car.*

con·vince /kən ˈvints/ *v.* to thoroughly persuade another person to share one's opinion. *You do not have to convince me that God created galaxies.*

constructed

cor·nu·co·pi·a /kôr nə ˈkō pē ə/ *n.* a goat's horn filled with fruit, vegetables, and grains that is used for decoration and symbolizing abundance. *A cornucopia is a decoration often seen during fall months.*

co·ro·na /kə ˈrō nə/ *n.* the outermost layer of the sun's atmosphere. *When viewed through a telescope, the sun's corona looks like a crown.*

cor·rupt·ing /kə ˈrup ting/ *v.* continually breaking away from what is good; ruining; damaging. *Some divers are corrupting reefs by taking pieces of coral.*

coun·ter·act /koun tûr ˈakt/ *v.* to do the opposite of. *To counteract a low test grade, Margot turned in extra credit.*

coun·tries /ˈkun trēz/ *n. pl.* plural of COUNTRY; nations. *Countries in the northern hemisphere have spring weather in April.*

cour·a·geous /kə ˈrā jəs/ *adj.* having the quality of bravery; brave. *The hero acted in a courageous manner.*

court·room /ˈkôrt rōōm/ *n.* a room where court is convened. *The courtroom was quiet before the trial.*

cra·ters /ˈkrā tûrz/ *n. pl.* plural of CRATER; bowl-shaped depressions formed by the impact of an object. *The surface of the moon contains numerous craters.*

crowd·ed /ˈkrou dəd/ *adj.* packed; full. *The crowded campground contained numerous motor homes.*

crunch·i·er /ˈkrun chē ûr/ *adj.* more crunchy. *Are brown leaves crunchier than green leaves when you step on them?*

crys·tal /ˈkris təl/ *n.* a type of quartz that is almost transparent. *Lily had a necklace made of crystal.*

cu·mu·la·tive /ˈkyōō myə lə tiv/ *adj.* inclined to gradually heap up, build, or amass. *The winter storms had a cumulative effect on the road conditions.*

cur·few /ˈkûr fyōō/ *n.* a specific hour when one restricts his or her activity. *My brother's curfew is 11:00 P.M.*

cur·tain /ˈkûr tən/ *n.* cloth covering for a window; a drapery. *Nicole pushed aside the curtain to see the view from her window.*

D

de·act·i·vate /dē ˈak tə vāt/ *v.* to make something inactive or ineffective; to reverse activation or effectiveness. *Deena will deactivate the alarm to the laboratory in the morning.*

de·cel·er·ate /dē ˈse lə rāt/ *v.* to move slower. *A drag chute helps the space shuttle decelerate when it lands.*

de·cid·ed /di ˈsī dəd/ *v.* past tense of DECIDE; made a choice. *The geological team decided to survey the structure of the canyon.*

de·ci·du·ous /di ˈsi jə wəs/ *adj.* describes trees or shrubs that shed their leaves every fall. *The deciduous tree had leaves of yellow and red.*

deciduous

de·ci·sion /di 'si zhən/ *n.* conclusion. *The oceanographers reached a decision about where to dive.*

deep·est /'dē pəst/ *adj.* lowest. *Can you name the deepest valleys in the world?*

de·fec·tive /di 'fek tiv/ *adj.* faulty; flawed. *The globe was defective since it would not rotate.*

de·fin·ite·ly /'de fə nit lē/ *adv.* an adverb formed from *definite;* surely. *It is definitely warmer in the summer.*

de·lic·ate·ly /'de li kət lē/ *adv.* gingerly; carefully. *May delicately added a tower to her sand castle.*

de·li·cious /di 'li shəs/ *adj.* especially tasty. *The fresh tuna was delicious.*

de·liv·er·ance /di 'li və rənts/ *n.* a rescue. *We have deliverance through Jesus Christ from the evil one.*

dense /'dents/ *adj.* tightly compacted; pressed together. *It was difficult to hike through the dense clumps of bushes.*

den·si·ty /'dent sə tē/ *n.* the amount of mass in a certain volume of space. *The density of an object is determined by dividing mass by volume.*

de·po·sit /di 'po zət/ *n.* a placement of sediments. *A vast mineral deposit was found in the mountainous area.*

de·pres·sions /di 'pre shənz/ *n. pl.* plural of DEPRESSION; indentations in the surface; trenches. *Trenches are deep, narrow, underwater depressions.*

de·scribe /di 'skrib/ *v.* to give a thorough account. *Can you describe what you saw while exploring the trench?*

de·scrip·tion /di 'skrip shən/ *n.* thorough account. *The encyclopedia contains a description of how trenches are formed.*

de·serts /'de zûrts/ *n. pl.* plural of DESERT; very warm areas of land receiving less than ten inches of rainfall annually. *Most deserts have a small area of water called an oasis.*

de·sign /di 'zīn/ *n.* decorative pattern; plan. *Choose a design for your aquarium before you go to the store.*

de·stroy /di 'stroi/ *v.* to ruin. *Pollution can destroy the natural habitat of a forest.*

de·struc·tion /di 'struk shən/ *n.* ruin. *The collapse of the tripod caused destruction of the telescope's lens.*

de·tails /'dē tālz/ *n. pl.* plural of DETAIL; small elements that work together. *Adam put all the details that he could into his report on volcanoes.*

de·ter·mi·na·tion /di tûr mə 'nā shən/ *n.* the state of being thoroughly committed to achieving an end or a goal; willpower. *Galileo had the determination needed to face opposition.*

de·tour /'dē toor/ *n.* a variation from the direct route or normal course of action; delay. *There was a traffic detour near the marina.*

di·a·mond /'dī ə mənd/ *n.* a hard gem, made from crystals of carbon, that is formed under tremendous pressure and heat. *The diamond is the hardest of all known minerals.*

dic·tate /'dik tāt/ *v.* to command; to speak out loud or give orders. *She will kindly dictate each team member's responsibilities.*

dic·tion·ar·ies /'dik shə när ēz/ *n. pl.* plural of DICTIONARY; reference books. *The library contains dictionaries printed by different companies.*

dif·fer·ence /'di fə rənts/ *n.* a contrast between two people or things. *Do you know the difference between tree coral and brain coral?*

dis·count /'dis kount/ *adj.* reflecting a reduced price. *Keisha drove to the discount supply store for aquarium filters.*

dis·cov·er·y /dis 'ku və rē/ *n.* the process of learning or finding something; recognition. *The discovery of a new fish species excited the scientists.*

dis·rup·tion /dis 'rup shən/ *n.* the state of breaking something apart or interrupting; an interruption. *Pollution in the ocean causes a disruption in the reef's ecosystem.*

dis·sat·is·fied /dis 'sa təs fid/ *adj.* not satisfied or pleased; disappointed. *Ray was dissatisfied with his science test grade so he studied harder.*

dis·sect /di 'sekt/ *v.* to cut apart. *After learning about caves, we will dissect owl pellets.*

dis·tort /di 'stôrt/ *v.* to twist something out of its normal shape. *Will a dragonfly distort itself when it molts?*

dor·mant /'dôr mənt/ *adj.* inactive. *Some seeds can be dormant for a long time.*

doubt·ful /'dout fəl/ *adj.* unlikely. *It is doubtful that the tourists will take the entire forest tour.*

dunes /'dōōnz/ *n. pl.* plural of DUNE; a hill of sand formed by the wind. *Tony enjoys riding his all-terrain vehicle up and down sand dunes.*

dur·a·ble /'door ə bəl/ *adj.* able to last for a long time. *Plastic containers are durable.*

dur·a·tion /doo 'rā shən/ *n.* the period of time in which something lasts. *Sam slept the entire duration of the desert drive.*

du·ti·ful /'dōō ti fəl/ *adj.* motivated to accomplish work. *Dutiful students complete their class work on time.*

E

ea·si·ly /'ēz lē/ *adv.* the characteristic of being without difficulty. *Are you easily distracted when doing your work?*

ech·o /'e kō/ *n.* a sound that bounces back over and over as it hits surfaces. *Simone heard an echo after shouting into the valley.*

e·clipse /i 'klips/ *n.* a partial or total obscuring of one celestial body by another. *A lunar eclipse may be total or partial.*

e·co·sys·tem /'ē kō sis təm/ *n.* a group of living and nonliving things that interact with each other in an environment. *Algae are part of the ocean's ecosystem.*

ef·fect /i 'fect/ *n.* **1** a result. *Spring tides are an effect of the moon's gravitational pull.* *v.* **2** to bring about; to make a change happen. *Exhaust pollutants can effect a change in the quality of air.*

e·lec·tric·al /i 'lek tri kəl/ *adj.* related to electricity. *Denny used an electrical heater to provide warmth to the cabin.*

e·lite /i 'lēt/ *n.* the best of a group. *NASA employees represent the scientific elite.*

el·lip·ti·cal /i 'lip ti kəl/ *adj.* shaped like an ellipse; oval. *Many galaxies are elliptical in shape.*

em·bry·o /'em brē ō/ *n.* a young seed plant still contained within the seed. *If you open a bean seed, you can see the embryo.*

em·ploy·ment /im 'ploi mənt/ *n.* the paid work that somebody does. *Reagan found employment with the national park system.*

en·er·gy /'e nûr jē/ *n.* effort; power. *The energy from nuclear fusion causes a star to shine.*

en·joy·a·ble /in 'joi ə bəl/ *adj.* capable of taking pleasure or satisfaction in. *It was an enjoyable day to see God's creation in the forest.*

e·nough /i 'nuf/ *adj.* sufficient. *Did you include enough information in your report?*

en·sem·ble /än 'säm bəl/ *n.* a group of performers. *The choral ensemble held a concert outdoors.*

en·ter·tain /en tûr 'tān/ *v.* to keep or hold in the mind; to allow a thought. *Philippians 4:8 exhorts us to entertain thoughts that are pure.*

en·trance /'en trənts/ *n.* a way of getting in; a door; entry. *The entrance to the dive shop is on the west side of the building.*

en·ve·lope /'en və lōp/ *n.* an enclosing case or cover. *Dr. Schmidt placed the survey results into an envelope.*

en·vi·sion /in 'vi zhən/ *v.* to see in one's mind. *Linda can envision herself swimming in an ocean current.*

e·qua·tor /i 'kwā tûr/ *n.* an imaginary circle around the earth, equidistant from the poles, dividing the earth into the northern and southern hemispheres. *The equator is the line from which latitudes on Earth are measured.*

e·qui·dis·tant /ē kwə 'dis tənt/ *adj.* equally distant. *The north and south poles are equidistant from the earth's equator.*

e·qui·nox /'ē kwə noks/ *n.* either of the two days of the year when day and night are the same length. *An equinox occurs during spring and fall.*

e·ro·sion /i 'rō zhən/ *n.* a steady wearing away of soil by natural forces such as water, wind, or ice. *Through erosion, the surface of the earth is constantly changing.*

e·rup·tion /i 'rup shən/ *n.* an instance of erupting. *The eruption of Mount Vesuvius destroyed the town of Pompeii.*

es·ca·pade /'es kə pād/ *n.* an unusually adventurous action; adventure. *Late at night the boys went on an escapade to view a comet.*

es·says /'e sāz/ *n. pl.* plural of ESSAY; nonfiction writings about personal points of view. *Norman read many essays about the universe.*

es·ti·mate /'es tə māt/ *v.* to make a guess based on facts. *Experts estimate that the north tundra covers twenty percent of Earth.*

e·va·por·ates /i 'va pə rāts/ *v.* changing from solid or liquid to vapor or steam. *Dry air evaporates moisture from the ground.*

ev·er·green /'e vûr grēn/ *adj.* describes a type of tree or shrub that keeps its leaves throughout the year. *The evergreen forest was blanketed in snow.*

e·vil /'ē vəl/ *adj.* sinful; wicked. *God will protect us from every evil scheme of the enemy.*

eruption

ex·change /iks ˈchānj/ v. trade. *Ross and Wes decided to exchange the souvenirs they purchased.*

ex·claim /iks ˈklām/ v. to speak or call out loudly. *Max began to exclaim in order to get everyone's attention.*

ex·clu·sion /iks ˈkloo zhən/ n. the state of being left out; rejection. *There was an exclusion of certain players on the football team.*

¹ex·cuse /ik ˈskyooz/ v. to remove responsibility. *Mrs. Gonzales will excuse her class from an assignment.*

²ex·cuse /ik ˈskyoos/ n. a good reason. *There is no excuse for poor quality work.*

ex·o·skel·e·ton /ek sō ˈske lə tən/ n. the hard, outer covering of an animal. *All of an insect's soft body parts are protected by an exoskeleton.*

ex·ports /ek ˈspôrts/ v. sends things out from one country into another country. *The Philippines exports butterflies to museums in the United States.*

ex·pose /ik ˈspōz/ v. to put something into view and allow it to be seen; uncover. *The wind and rain will slowly expose the mountainside.*

ex·pres·sion /ik ˈspre shən/ n. a word, sign, or phrase that represents a feeling. *Ty's facial expression was comical when he saw the giant beetle.*

ex·pres·sive /ik ˈspre siv/ adj. full of feeling. *Buzz Aldrin was expressive while describing the moon's soil.*

ex·tem·por·a·ne·ous /ek stem pə ˈrā nē əs/ adj. something composed, performed, or said on the spur of the moment; impromptu. *A scientist made an extemporaneous comment about stars.*

ex·ter·mi·nate /ik ˈstûr mə nāt/ v. to end the existence of something. *Opponents of Galileo tried to exterminate his teachings.*

ex·trac·tion /ik ˈstrak shən/ n. the process of drawing something out of another thing; removal. *The extraction of starfish from tidal pools is illegal.*

F

Fah·ren·heit /ˈfâr ən hīt/ adj. a temperature scale where the boiling point of water is 212 degrees. *Water freezes at thirty-two degrees Fahrenheit.*

faith·ful /ˈfāth fəl/ adj. loyal. *The Lord preserves all those who are faithful to Him.*

fa·vor·a·ble /ˈfā və rə bəl/ adj. helpful; advantageous; good. *Warm soil and water are often favorable conditions for plant growth.*

feath·ers /ˈfe thûrz/ n. pl. plural of FEATHER; plumage; the external covering of a bird. *Most birds lose their feathers every year and grow new ones.*

fes·tiv·als /ˈfes tə vəlz/ n. pl. plural of FESTIVAL; celebrations usually centered around a theme. *Many festivals occur during the fall season.*

feathers

fish·er·ies /ˈfi shə rēz/ *n. pl.* plural of FISHERY; businesses that sell, harvest, or process fish. *Fisheries are a vital source of food for people who live on the coast.*

flat·tened /ˈfla tənd/ *adj.* in a compressed shape. *The Milky Way has a flattened shape, like a coin.*

flawed /ˈflȯd/ *adj.* imperfect. *The sale rack was filled with flawed items.*

fluc·tu·a·tion /flək chə ˈwā shən/ *n.* the state of changing back and forth continually, often from high to low levels or from one thing to another. *The fluctuation of tides is an integral part of life in a tidal pool.*

fo·li·age /ˈfō lē ij/ *n.* leaves, flowers, and branches. *The foliage in the flower garden is very colorful.*

for·eign /ˈfȯr ən/ *adj.* belonging to a country outside one's own country. *It is useful to study a foreign language in school.*

for·mal /ˈfȯr məl/ *adj.* following an established form, rule, or custom. *A wedding is a formal occasion.*

for·mat /ˈfȯr mat/ *n.* an arrangement. *Our teacher told us the format for our research paper.*

fos·ter /ˈfȯs tûr/ *v.* to nurse; to give or receive care. *A mother cat will foster her new kittens.*

frac·tion /ˈfrak shən/ *n.* a broken part or a piece of something; a fragment. *A fraction of the algae plant was floating atop the water.*

fra·gile /ˈfra jəl/ *adj.* easily broken or damaged; delicate. *Derrell decided not to climb onto the fragile mountain cliff.*

frag·ment /ˈfrag mənt/ *n.* a small, broken piece or section. *A fragment of rock broke off the cliff as the wind rushed by.*

fra·grance /ˈfrā grənts/ *n.* a pleasant smelling scent. *The lavender plant has a lovely fragrance and is used in perfume.*

freck·les /ˈfre kəlz/ *n. pl.* plural of FRECKLE; small brown spots on the skin. *Ling-mei has freckles on her cheeks and nose.*

freight /ˈfrāt/ *n.* goods to be shipped by rail. *Could seismic activity delay the arrival of the freight?*

fright·ened /ˈfri tənd/ *v.* past tense of FRIGHTEN; to have been made afraid. *Jasmine was frightened when she heard about the avalanche danger.*

fu·sion /ˈfyo͞o zhən/ *n.* a state of putting or melting together; combination. *The surgeon will examine the X-rays for fusion of the broken bones.*

G

gar·den·ing /ˈgär də ning/ *n.* planting and working in a garden. *Livia enjoys gardening in the spring.*

gar·nish·es /ˈgär ni shəz/ *n. pl.* plural of GARNISH; items that enhance the appearance or flavor of food. *Nina used sprigs of parsley as garnishes for her salad.*

gas·e·ous /ˈga sē əs/ *adj.* having the form of gas. *A nebula is a cloud of gaseous material from an exploding star.*

germ·i·nate /ˈjûr mə nāt/ *v.* to sprout. *Pumpkin seeds take about four days to germinate.*

gla·cier /ˈglā shûr/ *n.* a large body of ice that moves down a valley or slope; ice mass. *Risa learned that a glacier can carve the landscape.*

glob·u·lar /ˈglo byə lûr/ *adj.* having the shape of a globe or globule. *Stars in globular galaxies rotate around a bright nucleus.*

gor·ges /ˈgôr jəz/ *n. pl.* plural of GORGE; deep, narrow canyons or valleys that are formed through river erosion. *One of the most famous gorges in the world is the Grand Canyon.*

go·vern·ment /ˈgu vûrn mənt/ *n.* the act or process of having control; people who rule. *The government funds the research for astronomy.*

gra·nite /ˈgra nət/ *n.* a fiery rock composed of mica, feldspar, and quartz. *The granite on Mount Rushmore was blasted and sculpted.*

gra·vi·ta·tion·al /gra və ˈtā shə nəl/ *adj.* describes the force of gravity. *The moon exerts a gravitational pull on the tides.*

gro·cer·ies /ˈgrō sə rēz/ *n. pl.* plural of GROCERY; goods sold in a grocery store. *Les bought some groceries before his hike through the canyon.*

guar·di·an /ˈgär dē ən/ *n.* a person who is responsible for the care of someone. *Miguel and his guardian vacationed in the Canary Islands.*

guessed /ˈgest/ *v.* past tense of GUESS; made a judgment without enough knowledge to be certain. *Mario incorrectly guessed that green is the only color of algae.*

guest /ˈgest/ *n.* a visitor. *A guest from La Jolla Aquarium spoke at the assembly today.*

gym·na·si·um /jim ˈnā zē əm/ *n.* a large room used for indoor sports. *We played basketball in the gymnasium.*

H

ha·bi·tat /ˈha bə tat/ *n.* the environment in which an animal normally lives. *A reindeer's habitat is the tundra.*

hap·pen·ing /ˈhap ning/ *v.* to be occurring as a result of something. *Can you describe what is happening when water turns into snow?*

hap·pi·ness /ˈha pē nəs/ *n.* the quality of being joyful; gladness. *Jesus fills our lives with happiness.*

har·di·ness /ˈhär dē nəs/ *n.* the quality of withstanding harsh conditions. *The hardiness of the old tree was evident during the strong winds.*

har·mon·y /ˈhär mə nē/ *n.* a pleasing combination of musical notes. *The finches sang in harmony with each other.*

har·vest·ers /ˈhär və stûrz/ *n. pl.* plural of HARVESTER; people gathering a crop. *The crops are picked by harvesters.*

head·ache /ˈhed āk/ *n.* a pain in the head. *Trina had a headache from the change in altitude during her hike.*

heard /ˈhûrd/ *v.* past tense of HEAR; to have perceived a sound or been informed of something. *Have you heard about our field trip to the tidal pools?*

hea·vi·est /ˈhe vē əst/ *adj.* the most heavy. *The heaviest pumpkin weighed fifty pounds.*

he·mi·sphere /ˈhe mə sfîr/ *n.* a half of a sphere; a half of the earth. *Europe, Asia, Africa, and Australia are in the eastern hemisphere.*

her·bi·vore /ˈûr bə vôr/ *n.* a plant-eating animal. *An animal that primarily eats plants is an herbivore.*

herd /'hûrd/ *n.* **1** a large group, of animals or people, congregated in one area. *A herd of sheep grazed near the ocean cliff.* *v.* **2** to gather or assemble together. *Mrs. Wilson will herd the group of students onto the bus.*

hi·ber·nate /'hī bûr nāt/ *v.* to be or become inactive during the winter. *Bears are one example of animals that hibernate during the winter.*

hoarse /'hôrs/ *adj.* sounding harsh or rough, characterized by a husky voice. *Mr. Manning's voice was hoarse because he had a sore throat.*

horse /'hôrs/ *n.* a domesticated animal with four legs, mane, hooves, and a tail. *Algae can be a nutritional supplement for the hooves of a horse.*

hu·man /'hyōō mən/ *adj.* relating to persons. *Human beings need to be careful to protect the woodland ecosystem.*

hum·ble /'hum bəl/ *adj.* meek; respectful. *Jesus wants all of us to be humble and serve one another.*

hur·ri·cane /'hûr ə kān/ *n.* a tropical storm with winds exceeding 74 miles per hour. *The hurricane hit the Hawaiian Islands last month.*

I

i·ci·cle /'ī si kəl/ *n.* a hanging ice spike that is formed by the freezing of dripping water. *As the weather turned warmer, an icicle fell off a tree branch.*

i·de·al /ī 'dē əl/ *adj.* best; perfect. *The ideal agent in shaping and forming valleys is rivers.*

i·den·ti·fy /ī 'den tə fī/ *v.* to recognize and name. *Can you identify the flora and fauna of the tundra landscape?*

ig·ne·ous /'ig nē əs/ *adj.* fiery; relating to fire. *Igneous rock is formed when volcanic rock hardens.*

il·lum·in·ate /i 'lōō mə nāt/ *v.* to make, supply, or brighten with light; light up. *Schools of fish in coral reefs can illuminate the waters.*

i·ma·gi·nar·y /i 'ma jə när ē/ *adj.* related to something imagined; make-believe. *Tristan invented an imaginary land for a story.*

im·per·fec·tion /im pûr 'fek shən/ *n.* a defect, flaw, or blemish; not perfection. *The crack in the insect model was an imperfection.*

im·po·lite /im pə 'līt/ *adj.* rude; not polite. *Our teacher warned us not to be impolite while at the museum.*

im·por·tant /im 'pôr tənt/ *adj.* valuable in content or relationship; significant. *It is important to protect our environment.*

im·ports /im 'pôrts/ *v.* brings things into one country from another country. *The United States imports insects from other countries.*

im·po·si·tion /im pə 'zi shən/ *n.* a state of placing an unreasonable burden upon someone; excessive task or obligation. *Is it an imposition for you to meet five times in a week?*

hurricane

im·pres·sion /im 'pre shən/ *n.* **1** a mark or imprint made by pressing in. *The astronaut's boot left an impression on the lunar soil.* **2** belief; understanding. *What impression did you get from the chapel message?*

in·act·ive /i 'nak tiv/ *adj.* idle; sluggish; not active. *Moths are inactive during the day and active at night.*

in·au·di·ble /i 'nȯ də bəl/ *adj.* not able to be heard. *Without a microphone, the speaker's voice was inaudible.*

in·ca·pa·ble /in 'kā pə bəl/ *adj.* lacking ability; not able to do something. *Insects are incapable of living at the North and South Poles.*

in·clud·ed /in 'klo͞o dəd/ *v.* past tense of INCLUDE; made a part of. *Are you included in the family of God?*

in·com·plete /in kəm 'plēt/ *adj.* unfinished; not complete. *Metamorphosis for a butterfly is incomplete at the pupa stage.*

¹in·crease /in 'krēs/ *v.* to make greater. *Currents increase the nutrients in ocean water.*

²in·crease /'in krēs/ *n.* an addition. *Sabrina experienced an increase in her test scores when she studied.*

in·cre·di·ble /in 'kre də bəl/ *adj.* not able to believe; amazing or extraordinary. *An incredible amount of snow fell in the mountains.*

in·cre·du·lous /in 'kre jə ləs/ *adj.* having a quality of unbelieving. *Ashley gave an incredulous stare when she saw the snowflake crystal.*

in·de·struc·ti·ble /in di 'struk tə bəl/ *adj.* not able to be destroyed or ruined. *Coral is not indestructible since it can be damaged by storms.*

in·duct /in 'dukt/ *v.* to take into; install. *The college will induct Dr. Brown as the geology department head.*

in·er·tia /i 'nûr shə/ *n.* the resistance to a change of motion. *Inertia is the resistance to a change in motion.*

in·form /in 'fôrm/ *v.* to shape thoughts; communicate knowledge. *Mr. Smith will inform Mrs. Smith that he will be late for dinner.*

in·form·a·tive /in 'fôr mə tiv/ *adj.* full of news and facts. *The encyclopedia of insects contains informative details.*

in·frac·tion /in 'frak shən/ *n.* a break in a rule or law; a violation. *The game warden ticketed Ed for the infraction of littering the lake.*

in·no·cent /'i nə sənt/ *adj.* free from sin or guilt; uncorrupted. *Jesus was innocent, yet He chose to take our sins upon Himself.*

in·no·va·tion /i nə 'vā shən/ *n.* a new idea. *One scientist's innovation led to the development of space telescopes.*

in·scrip·tion /in 'skrip shən/ *n.* an engraving or writing within an area or object. *A plaque with an inscription was left on the moon during Apollo 11.*

in·spec·tion /in 'spek shən/ *n.* a state of looking into and examining something. *An inspection of Earth's divisions showed Abe four hemispheres.*

inspection

in·struc·tor /in 'struk tûr/ *n.* a person who builds knowledge; a teacher. *Mrs. Montgomery is a fine instructor.*

in·su·late /'int sə lāt/ *v.* to reduce the passage of heat, sound, or electricity from something by surrounding it with some material. *Goose down is used to insulate winter vests and jackets.*

in·tact /in 'takt/ *adj.* not touched or broken; unbroken. *The cave opening was intact after the earthquake.*

in·tel·li·gence /in 'te lə jənts/ *n.* ability to learn. *God gave each one of us the intelligence to learn about Him.*

in·ten·ded /in 'ten dəd/ *adj.* planned; envisioned. *The intended destination of the module was the Sea of Tranquility.*

in·ten·tion /in 'tent shən/ *n.* a purpose or plan held in mind. *Your heart's intention should be to share Jesus with others.*

in·ter·ac·tion /in tûr 'ak shən/ *n.* a state of communication or collaboration among two or more people; the combined action of two or more things. *There was interaction among twenty-five nations at the conference.*

in·ter·cept /in tûr 'sept/ *v.* to receive something by coming in between. *When I threw the ball to my friend, my dog tried to intercept it.*

in·ter·nal /in 'tûr nəl/ *adj.* inner; interior. *It is possible to see the internal organs of baby flying squirrels.*

in·ter·rup·tion /in tə 'rup shən/ *n.* a break in a conversation or activity. *The fire drill caused an interruption in our class schedule.*

in·ter·sect /in tûr 'sekt/ *v.* to divide by passing through. *Lines of latitude and longitude intersect.*

in·ter·sec·tion /in tûr 'sek shən/ *n.* the location where lines intersect. *Jessica used coordinates to find the intersection on the map.*

in·ter·ti·dal /in tûr 'ti dəl/ *adj.* relating to the region that is between the low-tide and high-tide zones. *The intertidal zone is an important part of the ocean's ecosystem.*

¹in·val·id /in 'va lǝd/ *adj.* not valid. *The expired coupon was invalid.*

²in·va·lid /'in və lǝd/ *n.* a sickly or disabled person. *Members of the church took meals to the invalid to help him recover.*

in·ver·te·brate /in 'vûr tə brāt/ *n.* an animal that does not have a backbone. *The insect is the only invertebrate that has wings.*

in·vin·ci·ble /in 'vint sə bəl/ *adj.* not able to be conquered. *Jesus' resurrection from the dead proved that He was invincible.*

in·vi·si·ble /in 'vi zə bəl/ *adj.* not able to be seen. *Rip currents are invisible, but dangerous to swimmers.*

ir·ri·ta·ble /'îr ə tə bəl/ *adj.* easily bothered; annoyed. *Most people are irritable when they are tired.*

J

jour·ney /'jûr nē/ *n.* a suggesting of travel from one place to another; a path or passage. *What kind of journey will God lead you on?*

ju·ve·nile /'jōō və ni əl/ *adj.* young; immature. *A juvenile rabbit is called a bunny.*

K

kelp /'kelp/ *n.* large, brown seaweed. *Flies like to swarm around kelp that washes up onto the beach.*

kind·ness·es /ˈkind nə səz/ *n. pl.* plural of KINDNESS; kindly acts. *The family received the kindnesses of others with joy.*

L

land·scape /ˈland skāp/ *n.* the landform of an area. *A desert landscape consists mostly of sand.*

la·ti·tude /ˈla tə tōōd/ *n.* **1** the distance north or south of the equator that is measured in degrees and time. *Latitude identifies locations north and south of the equator.* **2** an imaginary line joining points on the earth's surface that are equidistant north or south of the equator. *The parallels of latitude are horizontal lines.*

la·va /ˈlä və/ *n.* molten rock; magma that breaks the surface. *A great quantity of lava started to flow down the mountain.*

le·gend /ˈle jənd/ *n.* a folktale. *The legend of Big Foot is often told around the campfire.*

lib·er·ty /ˈli bûr tē/ *n.* the state of being free. *We have liberty in Jesus Christ our Lord.*

li·chen /ˈli kən/ *n.* a complex, plant organism consisting of both fungi and algae. *Lichen can be found growing on trees, rocks, and other surfaces.*

light·ning /ˈlīt ning/ *n.* a flash of light caused by the passing of electricity in a thunderstorm. *Lightning was seen during the thunderstorm in the canyon.*

light·weight /ˈlīt wāt/ *adj.* not heavy. *Is an ostrich a lightweight bird since it can weigh up to 345 pounds?*

lime·stone /ˈlīm stōn/ *n.* a sedimentary rock. *Many caves are formed from limestone.*

lin·en /ˈli nən/ *adj.* woven flax. *Did Rachael tear her linen shirt on a manzanita branch?*

lith·o·sphere /ˈli thə sfîr/ *n.* the part of the earth's mass consisting of the crust and the mantle. *Trenches extend into the lithosphere.*

lon·gi·tude /ˈlon jə tōōd/ *n.* **1** the distance east or west of the prime meridian that is measured in degrees and time, and is used to determine standard time. *Longitude represents a distance from the prime meridian.* **2** the arc of the earth's equator that is intersected between a meridian and the prime meridian. *The meridians of longitude divide the earth into twenty-four time zones.*

loos·en /ˈlōō sən/ *v.* to make less tight. *Since my shoe was too tight, I decided to loosen the laces.*

lum·ber·jack /ˈlum bûr jak/ *n.* a person who cuts trees for lumber. *The strong lumberjack used a chain saw to cut down a tree.*

lum·i·nos·i·ty /lōō mə ˈno sə tē/ *n.* the state of emitting or reflecting light. *The luminosity of stars is the only source of light in the universe.*

lum·i·nous /ˈlōō mə nəs/ *adj.* quality of emitting or reflecting light. *The luminous school of fish reflected vivid colors.*

M

ma·chi·ner·y /mə ˈshē nə rē/ *n.* a group of machines. *Royal Observatory machinery emits a prime meridian laser beam.*

ma·ga·zines /ˈma gə zēnz/ *n. pl.* plural of MAGAZINE; periodicals with articles. *Joan bought some magazines for her long flight to the Himalayas.*

mag·ma /ˈmag mə/ *n.* molten rock below the earth's surface. *Magma formed a bulge in the side of the mountain.*

mag·ne·tic /mag 'ne tik/ *adj.* having the quality of magnetism. *We will be studying magnetic fields in science today.*

ma·jor /'mā jûr/ *adj.* great in importance; serious. *Forest fires are a major problem after volcanic eruptions.*

man·age·ment /'ma nij mənt/ *n.* the handling or supervising of something. *Will was asked to lead the management of the tundra expedition.*

man·tle /'man təl/ *n.* the layer between the earth's crust and its core. *The thickest layer of the earth is the mantle.*

man·u·script /'man yə skript/ *n.* a piece of handwritten text that can be submitted to be published. *The mission team reviewed the launch manuscript very carefully.*

mar·e /'mär ā/ *n.* a dark, flat area on the moon's surface. *The word* mare /'mär ā/ *comes from the Latin word for* sea.

Mar·i·an·a /mâr ē 'a nə/ *adj.* the name of a trench located near the Mariana Islands in the Pacific Ocean. *The Mariana Trench is the deepest seafloor trench in the world.*

mar·ine /mə 'rēn/ *adj.* relating to the sea. *The marine biologist enjoyed his job immensely.*

mar·riage /'mâr ij/ *n.* the state of being husband and wife. *The marriage of my grandparents spanned fifty-seven years.*

mar·su·pi·al /mär 'sōō pē əl/ *n.* a mammal whose offspring partially develop in a pouch on the mother's abdomen. *A kangaroo is a marsupial.*

mar·vel /'mär vəl/ *v.* to be amazed. *I often marvel at the beauty of God's creation.*

mea·sur·ing /'me zhə ring/ *v.* finding the size of something. *Reid was measuring the distance on a Mercator projection map.*

mem·branes /'mem brānz/ *n. pl.* plural of MEMBRANE; layers of tissue that are soft and thin. *Did you know that gill membranes are designed to help fish breathe?*

mem·or·i·al /mə 'môr ē əl/ *n.* related to something that honors or remembers an event. *New trees were planted as a memorial to the brave firemen.*

mem·or·y /'me mə rē/ *n.* a state of remembering and retaining knowledge. *Since Abi had a good memory, she was asked to lead the forest tour.*

mer·i·di·ans /mə 'ri dē ənz/ *n. pl.* plural of MERIDIAN; the imaginary lines of longitude that arc between the north and south poles and cross the equator at right angles. *The meridians of longitude converge at the earth's poles.*

met·al /'me təl/ *n.* an element or compound that is solid at room temperature, is easily molded, and conducts electricity well. *The gold miners found precious metal in the woodland streams.*

mid·night /'mid nīt/ *n.* twelve o'clock at night. *The geologist's lecture on river erosion ended at midnight.*

mi·grate /'mī grāt/ *v.* to move from one place to another. *Geese migrate south every winter and return north every spring.*

marsupial

mis·nom·er /mis 'nō mûr/ *n.* a wrong name or term. *Astronomers used a misnomer when identifying the moon's dark areas.*

missed /'mist/ *v.* past tense of MISS; did not attend. *Laura missed the field trip to the aquarium because she was ill.*

mis·sion·ar·ies /'mi shə när ēz/ *n. pl.* plural of MISSIONARY; those who teach the gospel to others. *The missionaries planted several new churches in Asia.*

mist /'mist/ *n.* small water droplets falling in the atmosphere that is a form of rain. *We hurried home in the mist before the heavy rain began to fall.*

mois·ture /'mois chûr/ *n.* wetness; condensed liquid in a small quantity. *In the newness of the morning, many leaves were full of moisture.*

mo·le·cules /'mo li kyōōlz/ *n. pl.* plural of MOLECULE; the smallest particles of a substance. *Galaxies contain not only stars, but complex molecules of gas.*

mol·ten /'mōl tən/ *adj.* liquefied by intense heat. *Molten rock accumulates below the earth's surface.*

mon·ey /'mu nē/ *n.* coins and paper with value used for payment. *Anya bought souvenirs from the gift shop with her own money.*

mos·qui·to /mə 'skē tō/ *n.* a biting insect. *Quentin swatted a large mosquito.*

mo·tiv·ate /'mō tə vāt/ *v.* to make somebody interested in and commited to something. *What will motivate you to study the different effects of erosion?*

moun·tains /'moun tənz/ *n. pl.* plural of MOUNTAIN; large ridges of land that project out of the terrain, often with steep slopes and rocky areas. *Joseph wrote a report about the mountains in the European Alps.*

mul·ti·ply·ing /'mul tə pli ing/ *v.* the action of increasing. *Falling leaves are quickly multiplying as the gentle breeze blows.*

mus·cles /'mu səlz/ *n. pl.* plural of MUSCLE; groups of body tissues that can contract and expand to produce movement. *Trent stretched his leg muscles before the track-and-field meet.*

mu·sic·al /'myōō zi kəl/ *adj.* related to music. *Andrea studies musical theory in college.*

mys·ter·y /'mis tə rē/ *n.* something not easily or immediately understood. *It is a mystery to me how desert seeds grow with little water.*

N

naugh·ty /'nȯ tē/ *adj.* not behaving; disobedient. *The naughty child asked the Lord for forgiveness.*

ne·ces·sar·i·ly /ne sə 'sâr ə lē/ *adv.* the characteristic of being necessary; certainly. *Some crops are not necessarily ripe enough when they are harvested.*

neigh·bor·ly /'nā bûr lē/ *adj.* acting like a friendly neighbor. *People provided neighborly assistance after the volcanic explosion.*

neith·er /'nē thûr/ *conj.* not one or the other. *Neither Ramon nor Pedro attended the field trip to the cave.*

mountains

neph·ew /ˈne fyo͞o/ *n.* the son of a brother or sister. *My nephew rode a camel at the theme park.*

ner·vous /ˈnûr vəs/ *adj.* uneasy. *The young zoologist felt nervous when entering the lion's enclosure.*

nest·ling /ˈnest ling/ *n.* a baby bird that is not ready to leave the nest. *A crane nestling can fly when it is ten weeks old.*

nom·in·ate /ˈno mə nāt/ *v.* to name as a candidate. *The committee will nominate a candidate for the prize.*

nom·in·a·tion /no mə ˈnā shən/ *n.* a state of naming someone to a position or proposing something for an award. *The astronaut accepted the managerial nomination reluctantly.*

nom·in·ee /no mə ˈnē/ *n.* one who is named as a candidate. *Dr. Salazar will be the nominee for the award in astronomy.*

non·fic·tion /non ˈfik shən/ *adj.* something told or written that is factual; not false. *The most important nonfiction book is God's Word, the Bible.*

non·sense /ˈnon sents/ *adj.* words or actions that have no meaning or are silly and foolish; not sensible; silliness. *It is nonsense to believe that God's Word is untrue.*

nor·mal /ˈnôr məl/ *adj.* ordinary. *It is normal for baby mammals to stay near their mother.*

no·tice·a·ble /ˈnō tə sə bəl/ *adj.* likely to be noticed. *That sunburn on your shoulders is quite noticeable.*

nour·ished /ˈnûr ishd/ *v.* past tense of NOURISH; to feed. *Newborn opossums are nourished inside their mother's pouch.*

nu·cle·ar /ˈno͞o klē ûr/ *adj.* of or relating to atomic forces. *The sun produces energy by means of nuclear fusion reactions.*

nu·cle·us /ˈno͞o klē əs/ *n.* the control center of a cell. *Each cell in algae contains a nucleus.*

nu·tri·ents /ˈno͞o trē ənts/ *n. pl.* plural of NUTRIENT; nourishing substances. *Corals receive nutrients from the algae that live in them.*

O

o·be·di·ent /ō ˈbē dē ənt/ *adj.* willing to obey; compliant. *The Lord wants us to be obedient to His Word.*

o·beyed /ō ˈbād/ *v.* past tense of OBEY; followed a command; complied. *We obeyed the rangers and evacuated before Kilauea erupted.*

ob·struct /əb ˈstrukt/ *v.* to block; hinder. *Does that desk obstruct your view of the screen?*

oc·curred /ə ˈkûrd/ *v.* past tense of OCCUR; to have come to mind or happened. *When the avalanche occurred, many people volunteered to help.*

off·spring /ˈȯf spring/ *n. pl.* plural of OFFSPRING; babies. *Rabbits may have four or more offspring per litter.*

on·ions /ˈun yənz/ *n. pl.* plural of ONION; root vegetables. *Onions grow below the ground.*

op·po·si·tion /o pə ˈzi shən/ *n.* a state of placing or believing something opposite. *The community was in opposition to coastal land development.*

or·bi·tal /ˈôr bə təl/ *adj.* related to a path in which a heavenly body moves around another heavenly body. *The orbital path of the earth is an elliptical shape.*

or·chard /ˈôr chûrd/ *n.* an area of land where fruit trees are grown. *Oliver visited the orchard and picked a basket of peaches.*

or·di·nar·y /'ôr də när ē/ *adj.* common; usual. *A short growing season is an ordinary occurrence on the tundra.*

or·gan·isms /'ôr gə ni zəmz/ *n. pl.* plural of ORGANISM; living things. *Starfish and algae are examples of organisms found in tidal pools.*

or·gans /'ôr gənz/ *n. pl.* plural of ORGAN; independent structures made of tissues and cells that perform a specific function in an organism. *Shawn became a pathologist to study diseased organs.*

ought /'ȯt/ *v.* forced by duty. *One ought to put fresh cut flowers in water.*

out·doors /out 'dôrz/ *adv.* outside. *Seth and Logan ventured outdoors for an adventure.*

o·zone /'ō zōn/ *n.* a three-atom form of oxygen. *Ozone helps protect Earth from the sun's harmful radiation.*

P

Pa·ci·fic /pə 'si fik/ *adj.* the name of the largest ocean in the world. *The Pacific Ocean is home to many species of fish.*

pa·lo·mi·no /pa lə 'mē nō/ *n.* a cream-colored horse. *The palomino was running in the pasture.*

par·a·chute /'pâr ə sho͞ot/ *n.* a large, fabric canopy used to slow down the descent of a person or object. *Shantal's parachute opened when she pulled the cord.*

par·al·lel /'pâr ə lel/ *adj.* similar; resembling each other. *A parallel feature of tundra biomes is the hindrance of tree growth.*

par·don·ing /'pärd ning/ *v.* action of forgiving; absolving. *The judge is pardoning the criminal in the courtroom.*

par·rot /'pâr ət/ *n.* a brightly colored bird that can mimic a person's words. *The red parrot began to sing, "Row, row, row your boat."*

par·tial /'pär shəl/ *adj.* incomplete. *The oceanographer had a partial list of the fish he wished to study.*

par·ti·cu·lar /pûr 'ti kyə lûr/ *adj.* specific. *House cats often prefer a particular type of cat food.*

pa·tience /'pā shənts/ *n.* the ability to endure waiting, a problem, or a delay without becoming upset. *One must have patience while waiting for tides to recede.*

pa·tients /'pā shənts/ *n. pl.* plural of PATIENT; individuals who receive medical treatment. *Our class will write friendly notes to the nursing home patients.*

pat·tern /'pa tûrn/ *n.* a repetitive order. *Geologists study the pattern of movements in the earth's crust.*

peer /'pîr/ *v.* **1** to look closely or carefully. *What will you see when you peer into the tidal pool?* *n.* **2** a person of equal standing with someone else. *Brittney is Maria's peer because they are both in the same grade.*

per·form·ance /pûr 'fôr mənts/ *n.* something done before an audience; show. *While at the zoo, our class attended a performance featuring birds.*

per·formed /pûr 'fôrmd/ *v.* past tense of PERFORM; did something before an audience. *Four birds performed tricks they had learned.*

per·fume /'pûr fyo͞om/ *n.* a substance that gives a pleasant scent. *The salesclerk showed Grandma a lovely bottle of perfume.*

per·i·o·dic /pîr ē 'o dik/ *adj.* occurring at regular intervals. *The course of a current can undergo periodic changes.*

perm·a·frost /'pûr mə fròst/ *n.* a permanently frozen layer of ground. *A distinctive feature of most tundra soil is its permafrost.*

pha·ses /'fā zəz/ *n. pl.* plural of PHASE; particular appearances in a recurring change of cycles. *The moon goes through many phases as it orbits around Earth.*

pho·to·sphere /'fō tə sfîr/ *n.* the luminous surface layer of the sun. *A picture of the photosphere showed sunspots.*

pho·to·syn·the·sis /fō tō 'sint thə səs/ *n.* the process that allows green plants to make food from water, carbon dioxide, and sunlight. *Most algae make their own food through photosynthesis.*

phy·si·cal /'fi zi kəl/ *adj.* relating to the body. *Doctors should be familiar with the physical structure of the body.*

phy·si·cian /fə 'zi shən/ *n.* a medical doctor. *The physician checked the patient's pulse before allowing her to dive.*

phy·sics /'fi ziks/ *n.* a science that deals with matter and energy. *Alex took a class in physics last year.*

pier /'pîr/ *n.* a structure that is built out over a body of water for use as a walkway. *The students will walk on the pier after exploring the tidal pools.*

pig·ment /'pig mənt/ *n.* a natural coloring in plants and animals. *The pigment in maple leaves changes during the fall.*

pis·til /'pis təl/ *n.* the part of the flower where seeds are formed. *The bee landed on the pistil with its feet.*

plant·like /'plant lik/ *adj.* having the qualities of a plant. *Algae are plantlike organisms that lack a root system.*

plat·eau /pla 'tō/ *n.* a level area of land that is raised sharply above adjacent land on at least one side. *Tessa observed the stars from the plateau.*

plea·sant /'ple zənt/ *adj.* agreeable; enjoyable. *Diving and exploring a coral reef is a pleasant adventure.*

plu·mage /'plo͞o mij/ *n.* the feathers of a bird. *Tropical birds have brightly colored plumage.*

po·li·ti·cian /po lə 'ti shən/ *n.* one who practices politics. *Our governor has been a life-long politician.*

pol·lin·ate /'po lə nāt/ *v.* to transfer pollen to the pistil of a flower. *A hummingbird can pollinate a flower.*

po·lyp /'po ləp/ *n.* a young, single coral. *A polyp will float in the water and attach itself to a rock.*

pon·cho /'pon chō/ *n.* a blanket-like cape. *Esteban put on his waterproof poncho.*

post·script /'pōst skript/ *n.* lines written after the text has ended. *The author added a postscript that listed contributions to the book.*

prac·ticed /'prak təsd/ *v.* past tense of PRACTICE; to have repeated an action so as to master it. *Our team practiced softball all summer long.*

pier

pre·cious /ˈpre shəs/ *adj.* valuable. *Natural pearls are precious gems.*

pre·ci·pi·ta·tion /pri si pə ˈtā shən/ *n.* rainfall; snowfall. *April showers provided much needed precipitation.*

pre·dic·tion /pri ˈdik shən/ *n.* telling of a future event; outlook. *The team's prediction is that they will receive a good grade.*

preen·ing /ˈprē ning/ *v.* cleaning, smoothing, and rearranging the feathers on a bird. *Birds use their bill or beak and their feet when preening.*

pre·ferred /pri ˈfûrd/ *v.* past tense of PREFER; to have liked better. *Mason preferred the black coat over the blue one.*

pre·paid /prē ˈpād/ *v.* past tense of PREPAY; paid in advance. *Charles prepaid for the tickets to the natural history museum.*

pre·pare /pri ˈpâr/ *v.* to get ready. *Mom will prepare turkey and stuffing for dinner tonight.*

pre·scrip·tion /pri ˈskrip shən/ *n.* written instructions or directions. *Galileo's work became a prescription for later scientific thought.*

pre·sence /ˈpre zənts/ *n.* the condition of being present. *The presence of algae in the ocean is vital to marine life.*

pre·sents /ˈpre zənts/ *n. pl.* plural of PRESENT; gifts. *One of Trisha's presents was a book about marine plants and animals.*

pres·sure /ˈpre shûr/ *n.* the application of force. *Igneous materials move toward areas of lower pressure.*

pro·ceed /prō ˈsēd/ *v.* to go forward with something; to continue to do something. *Dr. Kern will proceed with his lecture on valleys.*

pro·cla·ma·tion /pro klə ˈmā shən/ *n.* the state of announcing something; announcement. *The teacher's proclamation about the field trip excited the class.*

¹pro·duce /prə ˈdo͞os/ *v.* to make available to be seen. *Our teacher will produce a map of the Gulf Stream.*

²pro·duce /ˈprō do͞os/ *n.* fresh fruits and vegetables. *The local grocer carries wonderful produce.*

pro·fit /ˈpro fət/ *n.* **1** money received from a sale after costs are subtracted. *Fishermen make a profit selling fish and algae.* *v.* **2** benefit. *It will profit Coy to practice his math facts each night.*

pro·gress /ˈpro grəs/ *n.* a step forward; an advancement. *Much progress has been made in understanding how seeds grow.*

pro·mi·nence /ˈpro mə nənts/ *n.* a cloud-like mass of gas that arises from the chromosphere of the sun. *An astronomer will explain the prominence shown in the video.*

pro·mo·tion /prə ˈmō shən/ *n.* a forward advancement in a job, grade, or position. *The ceremony of promotion was held at the beginning of the summer.*

pro·phet /ˈpro fət/ *n.* a person who speaks for God. *Do you think the prophet Jonah saw algae inside the great fish?*

precipitation

pro·verb /'pro vûrb/ *n.* a short saying or principle. *The fifth graders will be discussing each proverb in the Bible.*

prox·im·i·ty /prok 'si mə tē/ *n.* the closeness of one thing to another. *The swimmer was in close proximity to the shore.*

pup·pet·ry /'pu pə trē/ *n.* the art of producing or operating puppets. *Sarah learned about puppetry at summer camp on Mount Whitney.*

pur·chased /'pûr chəsd/ *v.* past tense of PURCHASE; to have bought. *Jesus purchased our salvation through His death on the cross.*

pur·i·fy /'pyoor ə fī/ *v.* to make pure. *If we confess our sins, Jesus will purify our hearts.*

pur·pose /'pûr pəs/ *n.* intention. *Steve's purpose in going to the zoo was to study mammals.*

pur·suit /pûr 'soot/ *n.* a chase. *The pursuit to catch the thief running in the sand was difficult.*

Q

quiche /'kēsh/ *n.* a pie with an egg-and-cream mixture and meat and vegetable ingredients. *Patsy baked a quiche for the space center's party.*

R

rai·sin /'rā zən/ *n.* a sweet, sun-dried grape. *One raisin dropped from the bag of trail mix.*

rea·son·a·ble /'rēz nə bəl/ *adj.* not extreme or unusual; logical. *Divers must be reasonable and not spend long periods underwater.*

re·called /ri 'kȯld/ *v.* past tense of RECALL; to have brought back to mind; remembered. *Deborah recalled that she needed to bring flowers to the party.*

re·cap·ture /rē 'kap chûr/ *v.* to take back again. *Danae tried to recapture her hamster.*

re·cede /rē 'sēd/ *v.* to go back from a certain point or level. *The canyon community hopes that the river waters will soon recede.*

re·ceived /ri 'sēvd/ *v.* past tense of RECEIVE; to have acquired. *Have you received Jesus as your Savior?*

re·cent /'rē sənt/ *adj.* current; new. *We took a recent field trip to learn about woodland animals.*

re·cog·nize /'re kig nīz/ *v.* the act of knowing someone or something again. *Do you recognize the leaves from an oak tree?*

¹re·cord /ri 'kȯrd/ *v.* to copy for future use. *We will record the science program to view later.*

²re·cord /'re kûrd/ *n.* an official document. *The witness' testimony was entered into the record of the trial.*

re·count /ri 'kount/ *v.* to report; to tell in detail. *Each astronaut will be asked to recount mission details.*

re·cy·cle /rē 'sī kəl/ *v.* to process so as to regain usefulness. *Recycle your newspapers instead of discarding them.*

re·flec·ti·vi·ty /rē flek 'ti və tē/ *n.* the brightness or luminosity of an object. *The reflectivity of the moon comes from the sun.*

re·flex·es /'rē flek səz/ *n. pl.* plural of REFLEX; automatic responses. *Baseball players need sharp reflexes to make plays quickly.*

re·fu·sal /ri ˈfyoo zəl/ *n.* a related form of *refuse*; to take a stand against something. *Melanie's refusal to give in to temptation was a sign of her faith.*

re·fuse /ri ˈfyooz/ *v.* to deny, give back, or disprove. *Did Lea refuse to believe the results of the tundra study?*

re·fus·ing /ri ˈfyoo zing/ *v.* the act of denying, giving back, or disproving. *Brody is refusing to study for his test on the tundra terrain.*

re·gres·sion /ri ˈgre shən/ *n.* a backward trend; a decline. *A major forest fire caused a regression in the growth of the forest.*

reign /ˈrān/ *v.* to exercise power; to rule. *Jesus will reign for all eternity.*

rein·deer /ˈrān dîr/ *n. pl.* plural of REINDEER; large deer, with antlers on both the male and female species, that are found in the Northern Hemisphere. *A herd of reindeer was seen grazing on the tundra.*

re·ju·ve·nate /ri ˈjoo və nāt/ *v.* to make youthful again. *The spring thaw seemed to rejuvenate the mountain meadow.*

re·lieve /ri ˈlēv/ *v.* to stop something unpleasant. *Kirk took some medicine to relieve his headache.*

re·mit·tance /ri ˈmi tənts/ *n.* payment sent for goods or services. *The zoo receipt showed the amount of the remittance.*

ren·o·vate /ˈre nə vāt/ *v.* to make new again; to restore. *Astronauts began to renovate the Hubble Space Telescope in 1993.*

re·port·ing /ri ˈpôr ting/ *v.* telling information again. *I will be reporting on science news for our school paper.*

res·cue /ˈres kyoo/ *v.* to save from danger. *Jesus died on the cross to rescue us from the evil one.*

re·sig·na·tion /re zig ˈnā shən/ *n.* a state of accepting something reluctantly against your desired position. *Nala displayed no signs of resignation when asked to combine teams.*

re·signed /ri ˈzīnd/ *v.* past tense of RESIGN; to have shown signs of accepting something reluctantly; accepted. *Bret eventually resigned that the weather was not going to clear up.*

re·sur·rec·tion /re zə ˈrek shən/ *n.* the rising again to life. *Easter is the celebration of Jesus' resurrection.*

re·tro·spect /ˈre trə spekt/ *n.* a look back to think about or review. *"In retrospect, I should have done more research," Cora said.*

re·verse /ri ˈvûrs/ *v.* to turn back to the original thought, belief, or position. *Did the lecture on the tundra biome reverse your ideas for your project?*

re·vise /ri ˈvīz/ *v.* to correct and improve text by looking over it again. *Kelly will revise her report about trees in the forest.*

re·vi·sion /ri ˈvi zhən/ *n.* a state of correcting and improving text. *The environmental report went through a revision last month.*

re·vi·val /ri ˈvi vəl/ *n.* a renewal of life. *Our school experienced a revival during Spiritual Emphasis Week.*

re·vive /ri ˈvīv/ *v.* to bring back to life. *The doctors were able to revive the victims of the accident.*

re·vo·lu·tion /re və ˈloo shən/ *n.* the action of a heavenly body going around in orbit; orbit. *Earth's revolution around the sun takes 365.25 days.*

rhym·ing /ˈrī ming/ *v.* putting into rhyme. *Were you rhyming the words to make a poem?*

ring /'riŋ/ n. **1** a circular band used to hold, hang, or connect things. *Randy's key ring fell into the tidal pool while he was exploring.* v. **2** to give a clear tone by moving. *Mr. Tomo will ring a bell when it is time to leave the beach.*

ro·ta·tion /rō 'tā shən/ n. the action of rotating. *A current's direction is caused by the rotation of the earth.*

rough·ly /'ru flē/ adv. approximately. *Mr. Mordue needed roughly two hours for his hemispheres lecture.*

roy·al /'roi əl/ adj. magnificent; majestic. *Have you seen the royal sequoias in California?*

rup·ture /'rupt shûr/ v. to cause a break in something. *Overinflating a tire may cause it to rupture.*

S

sal·a·ry /'sa lə rē/ n. wages earned on a regular basis; money earned. *Mrs. McIntire earns a salary as a tour guide.*

sa·lin·i·ty /sə 'li nə tē/ n. relating to salt; salt content. *As you move inland, an estuary's water salinity decreases.*

sal·mon /'sa mən/ n. pl. plural of SALMON; fish with pink flesh. *Salmon swim upstream to lay their eggs.*

sand·wich·es /'sand wi chəz/ n. pl. plural of SANDWICH; slices of bread with a filling between them. *Tia made several egg salad sandwiches.*

sa·tel·lite /'sa tə lit/ n. an object that orbits a larger object. *The moon is the only natural satellite of Earth.*

sa·tis·fac·tor·y /sa təs 'fak tə rē/ adj. adequate; acceptable. *Jonathan did a satisfactory job in preparing for the tundra tour.*

sau·cer /'sȯ sûr/ n. a small, shallow dish in which a cup can be placed. *Grandma Butler let me use her floral cup and saucer.*

scald /'skȯld/ v. to burn with hot liquid or steam. *The recipe directions said to scald the milk, then let it cool.*

scales /'skālz/ n. pl. plural of SCALE; flat, round, and rigid covering plates. *God designed fish with protective scales.*

sci·en·tist /'sī ən tist/ n. a person who specializes in observing, studying, and experimenting. *The scientist conducted a survey about the tundra's flora and fauna.*

scis·sors /'si zûrz/ n. a cutting instrument with two blades. *Colby used scissors to cut out pictures for a project on hemispheres.*

scratch·i·ness /'skra chē nəs/ n. the quality of being irritating. *The scratchiness of my throat disappeared after drinking water.*

sculp·ture /'skulp chûr/ n. a three-dimensional work of art; model. *The cardiologist studied a medical sculpture of a human heart.*

sea·floor /'sē flôr/ n. the floor of a sea or an ocean. *The deep-sea anglerfish lives near the dark seafloor.*

rotation

seal·ing /ˈsē ling/ v. **1** closing something firmly or securely so as to make it watertight or airtight. *The barnacle was sealing itself as the tide lowered.* **2** fastening something with a seal. *Lynn was sealing the envelope as the postman walked into the office.*

search·ing /ˈsûr ching/ v. seeking. *The lion was searching the grasslands for prey.*

sea·son·al /ˈsēz nəl/ adj. related to a season or time of year. *A seasonal storm is a common occurrence during winter.*

sea·weed /ˈsē wēd/ n. a plant that grows in the sea; alga; kelp. *Some seaweed can grow to be three hundred feet tall.*

se·cede /si ˈsēd/ v. to formally withdraw from an organization. *Because of disagreements, ten members of the club decided to secede.*

sec·tion /ˈsek shən/ n. a piece separated from a whole. *A section of the cave was off-limits to visitors.*

sed·i·ment /ˈse də mənt/ n. a material deposited by water, wind, or ice; a residue. *The small stream carried sediment from the mountain to the lake.*

seed·ling /ˈsēd ling/ n. a young plant grown from a seed. *Ken grew a sunflower seedling in potting soil.*

seg·men·ted /ˈseg men təd/ adj. divided into sections or parts. *An insect has three segmented body parts.*

sel·e·nol·o·gy /se lə ˈno lə jē/ n. the study of the moon. *Did you know that the study of the moon is called selenology?*

sem·i·ar·id /se mē ˈa rəd/ adj. very dry with little rainfall. *Semiarid regions have an annual rainfall of ten-to-twenty inches.*

sen·ses /ˈsen səz/ n. pl. plural of SENSE; specialized functions by which a person or animal receives information about the physical world. *Senses enable people to experience the world around them.*

sen·si·ble /ˈsent sə bəl/ adj. showing good judgment; wise. *Sensible scuba divers always dive with a buddy.*

se·pals /ˈsē pəlz/ n. pl. plural of SEPAL; unique leaves that enclose the petals of a flower. *As the flower bud opened, the sepals unfurled.*

se·par·ate /ˈse pə rāt/ v. to divide. *Does the mountain separate the two valleys?*

shelv·ing /ˈshel ving/ n. a sloping area or surface. *The shelving on the mountainside was very steep and dangerous.*

shield /ˈshēld/ n. a protective cover. *Sunglasses are a shield that protects our eyes from ultraviolet rays.*

shoul·der /ˈshōl dûr/ n. the place where the arm attaches to the trunk of a body. *The arm at the shoulder is a freely movable joint.*

shrubs /ˈshrubz/ n. pl. plural of SHRUB; low plants with woody stems. *Woodland shrubs can provide food for animals.*

shrubs

sig·nals /ˈsig nəlz/ *n. pl.* plural of SIGNAL; marks that give notice. *Hot, dry weather and high winds are signals of fire danger.*

sin·cere /sin ˈsîr/ *adj.* truthful; without hypocrisy. *Ivan was sincere when he asked the Lord into his heart.*

sink·hole /ˈsingk hōl/ *n.* a hollow place. *The stream disappeared into the sinkhole.*

skel·e·tal /ˈske lə təl/ *adj.* resembling a skeleton. *A skeletal base provides protection for polyps from predators.*

skel·e·ton /ˈske lə tən/ *n.* the supportive framework of bones and cartilage of humans and vertebrate animals. *The bones in a human skeleton are connected by ligaments.*

snow·capped /ˈsnō kapt/ *adj.* to have a covering of snow. *The snowcapped top of Pikes Peak is often photographed.*

so·cial /ˈsō shəl/ *adj.* relating to society. *Mr. and Mrs. Garcia met at a social function.*

so·lar /ˈsō lûr/ *adj.* relating to the sun. *Planets in our solar system revolve around the sun.*

sol·stice /ˈsōl stəs/ *n.* either of the two days of the year when day or night are at their longest length. *The summer solstice occurs on or about June 22.*

song·birds /ˈsông bûrdz/ *n. pl.* plural of SONGBIRD; birds that sing musical tones. *Most songbirds are perching birds.*

sought /ˈsòt/ *v.* past tense of SEEK; to have looked and asked for. *Jason sought his neighbor's help to find his lost puppy.*

source /ˈsôrs/ *n.* a point of origin or procurement. *Jesus' atonement on the cross is the source of our faith.*

sparse /ˈspärs/ *adj.* thin and widely spread; infrequent. *Extremely tall trees are sparse in the woodland areas.*

spe·cies /ˈspē shēz/ *n. pl.* plural of SPECIES; a category or kind of animal. *There are over twelve thousand species of ants.*

spi·ral /ˈspī rəl/ *adj.* winding around a center and gradually receding from it. *The Milky Way is a spiral galaxy.*

spring·time /ˈspring tīm/ *n.* the season of spring. *Daffodils and crocuses bloom in springtime.*

squir·rel /ˈskwûr əl/ *n.* a small or medium-sized rodent. *The squirrel climbed high into the tree.*

sta·lac·tites /stə ˈlak tīts/ *n. pl.* plural of STALACTITE; formations resembling an icicle that hang from the ceiling or sides of a limestone cave. *Stalactites grow downward from the ceiling of caves.*

sta·lag·mites /stə ˈlag mīts/ *n. pl.* plural of STALAGMITE; formations rising from the floor of a limestone cave. *Stalagmites grow upward from the floor of caves.*

sta·men /ˈstā mən/ *n.* the part of the flower that produces pollen. *A rose has more than one stamen.*

straight·en·ing /ˈstrāt ning/ *v.* action of making something tidy. *Reina was straightening up the skis in her closet.*

stream·lined /ˈstrēm līnd/ *adj.* contoured. *Fish bodies are streamlined for swimming efficiency.*

strength /ˈstrengkth/ *n.* the quality of being strong. *We were surprised by the strength of the current.*

struc·ture /ˈstruk chûr/ *n.* a building. *The main structure in the observatory houses the telescope.*

stur·di·er /ˈstûr dē ûr/ *adj.* more solid; more sturdy. *Grandpa's new ladder is sturdier than his old one.*

sub·duc·tion /səb 'duk shən/ *n.* the process by which one crustal plate is forced under an adjacent plate. *Trenches are formed by the subduction of tectonic plates.*

sub·mar·ine /'sub mə rēn/ *n.* undersea vessel. *The submarine explored the deep trench.*

sub·mit·ting /səb 'mi ting/ *v.* to present or propose for a review. *Raji was submitting his video essay on seasons and climate.*

sub·stan·tial /səb 'stant shəl/ *adj.* ample. *The crew received substantial information about the ocean floor.*

sub·zer·o /səb 'zē rō/ *adj.* below zero. *Many subzero temperatures were reported throughout the region.*

su·gar·y /'shoo gə rē/ *adj.* sweet; containing sugar. *Dr. Micah ate a sugary treat at the navigational conference.*

suite /'swēt/ *n.* a group of rooms. *The Barker family stayed in a suite at the hotel for their vacation.*

sum·mer·time /'su mûr tīm/ *n.* the summer season. *Outdoor activities are often done during the summertime.*

sum·mit /'su mət/ *n.* highest point; top. *Many people have tried to climb to the summit of Mount Everest.*

su·per·vise /'soo pûr vīz/ *v.* oversee; manage. *Bryn will supervise the science project for her team.*

su·per·vi·sion /soo pûr 'vi zhən/ *n.* the action of supervising; management. *Careful supervision of the team made the project run smoothly.*

sup·ply·ing /sə 'plī ing/ *v.* the action of providing. *Farms are supplying consumers with vegetables.*

sur·face /'sûr fəs/ *n.* the uppermost part. *A red sailboat bobbed up and down on the water's surface.*

sur·vey /'sûr vā/ *n.* a determination of the measurement of a large land area. *Scientists made a geodetic survey when volcanic activity ceased.*

sur·vi·val /sûr 'vi vəl/ *n.* the continuation of life. *Animals' survival in the winter often depends on summer foraging.*

sweet /'swēt/ *adj.* **1** tasting like sugar. *Sweet foods such as syrup and ice cream contain algae.* **2** kind. *Olivia is a very sweet and polite young lady.*

symp·tom /'simp təm/ *n.* an indication of an illness. *A fever can be a symptom of the flu.*

sys·tems /'sis təmz/ *n. pl.* plural of SYSTEM; a group of parts that work together to perform a task. *Reproductive systems in some plants produce seeds.*

T

tel·e·scope /'te lə skōp/ *n.* a device used for viewing objects at a distance. *In 1990, an orbiting telescope was released into space.*

tel·e·vise /'te lə vīz/ *v.* to broadcast a far distance to be seen. *They will televise the tundra documentary tomorrow evening.*

tem·per·ate /'tem pə rət/ *adj.* describes a moderate climate that lacks extremes in temperature. *Temperate forests are not too hot and not too cold.*

tem·per·a·ture /'tem pûr choor/ *n.* the measure of heat. *The temperature during the summer months is usually warm.*

ten·den·cy /'ten dənt sē/ *n.* an inclination in which somebody reacts or something behaves. *The moon has the tendency to orbit Earth in an elliptical path.*

teph·ra /ˈte frə/ *n.* pyroclastic material made of rock fragments and ash formed by an explosion of magma. *Geologists found tephra hundreds of miles from the explosion site.*

ter·ra·ces /ˈtâr ə səz/ *n. pl.* plural of TERRACE; flat sections of old floodplains, usually left attached to the side of a valley, that have been formed by erosion. *Terraces can be cut by the powerful forces of a rushing river.*

ter·rain /tə ˈrān/ *n.* landscape; ground. *The terrain of most tundra contains grasses, shrubs, and moss.*

ter·ri·tor·y /ˈtâr ə tôr ē/ *n.* an area of land. *Many caves were found when people explored the territory.*

ther·mo·me·ter /thûr ˈmo mə tûr/ *n.* an instrument that is used to determine temperature. *The thermometer broke and did not show an accurate reading.*

thick·et /ˈthi kət/ *n.* thick growth of shrubs. *A deer was caught by its antlers in a thicket.*

thor·ax /ˈthôr aks/ *n.* the middle section of an insect's body. *An insect's wings and legs are attached to the thorax.*

thor·ough·ly /ˈthûr ō lē/ *adv.* completely. *Becka thoroughly understood the lecture on formation of valleys.*

tide /ˈtīd/ *n.* the systematic rise and fall of ocean water, generally occurring every six hours. *Clams migrate with the tide to evade preying birds.*

tied /ˈtīd/ *v.* past tense of TIE; to have fastened or attached by knotting. *The fisherman securely tied his boat to the dock.*

tim·ber·line /ˈtim bûr līn/ *n.* the upper limit of tree growth in mountains. *Since we hiked past the timberline, there were no trees.*

to·bog·gan /tə ˈbo gən/ *n.* a flat-bottomed sled. *Miranda bought a new toboggan for her winter vacation.*

tol·er·ate /ˈto lə rāt/ *v.* to bear. *Arctic animals are able to tolerate cold temperatures.*

to·po·graph·ic /to pə ˈgra fik/ *adj.* relating to topography; describes a type of map that shows elevations of landforms. *Daron consulted a topographic map of the ocean floor before diving.*

tor·na·do /tôr ˈnā dō/ *n.* a destructive thunderstorm, accompanied by a funnel-shaped cloud. *The tornado did no damage to the town.*

trai·tor /ˈtrā tûr/ *n.* a person who betrays another's trust. *The traitor ran away under the darkness of the night sky.*

trans·formed /trants ˈfôrmd/ *v.* past tense of TRANSFORM; changed. *Copernicus' ideas transformed the way scholars saw the solar system.*

trans·fu·sion /trants ˈfyo͞o zhən/ *n.* a state or process of transferring fluid into a vein or artery. *Reiko received a fluid transfusion during her hospital stay.*

trans·port /ˈtrants pôrt/ *v.* to carry from one place to another. *Birds transport seeds from one place to another.*

tied

trans·port·a·ble /trants 'pôr tə bəl/ *adj.* able to be carried from one place to another. *Cargo is transportable by ship.*

trans·port·ing /trants 'pôr ting/ *v.* carrying across a distance. *Mrs. Milano is transporting the students' science fair projects.*

trea·sur·y /'tre zhə rē/ *n.* a collection of valuable items. *The observatory museum holds a treasury of astronomical tools.*

tri·pod /'trī pod/ *n.* a stand that has three legs for support at its base. *Neil Armstrong mounted a camera on a tripod to take pictures.*

tro·phy /'trō fē/ *n.* an award given in acknowledgment of a victory. *Brent won a trophy for his stellar painting.*

trop·i·cal /'tro pi kəl/ *adj.* relating to a region that is very warm, frost-free, and has sufficient moisture. *Coral reefs are only located in warm, tropical waters.*

typ·ist /'tī pist/ *n.* one who types. *The typist used the computer keyboard to enter the notes.*

U

un·der·sea /ən dûr 'sē/ *adj.* underwater. *Undersea exploration is advancing our knowledge of trenches.*

u·ni·for·mi·ty /yoo nə 'fôr mə tē/ *n.* the quality of having always the same form. *The uniformity of the scientists' observations supported a theory.*

u·ni·fy /'yoo nə fī/ *v.* to make into one. *The coach's pep talk will unify the team.*

u·ni·lat·er·al /yoo ni 'la tə rəl/ *adj.* relating to one side. *Wings are not unilateral since they are on both sides of the body.*

u·ni·verse /'yoo nə vûrs/ *n.* all the matter and energy in existence; cosmos. *The Lord God created the entire universe.*

up·set·ting /əp 'se ting/ *adj.* disturbing; distressing. *When Jorge heard the upsetting news, he went to the Lord in prayer.*

V

va·ca·tion /vā 'kā shən/ *n.* a time off from normal activities. *Have you decided what to do during your vacation?*

val·ley /'va lē/ *n.* a low area of ground, surrounded by higher terrain, with a large extent in one direction. *A valley can be completely surrounded by higher ground.*

val·u·a·ble /'val yə bəl/ *adj.* capable of having value. *That gold ring looks valuable.*

val·ue /'val yoo/ *n.* worth or importance of something. *The value of the mountain-climbing lesson was tremendous.*

ve·ge·ta·tion /ve jə 'tā shən/ *n.* plant life in an area. *The vegetation in the area included many old olive trees.*

ve·lo·ci·ty /və 'lo sə tē/ *n.* a measure of an object's speed and direction; speed. *The velocity of the moving ball was slowed by friction.*

undersea

verb·al /ˈvûr bəl/ *adj.* relating to or consisting of words. *Amy gave a verbal description of the valley's terrain.*

ver·dict /ˈvûr dikt/ *n.* a decision; the outcome from the information presented during a trial. *The jury returned a not-guilty verdict to the judge.*

ver·nal /ˈvûr nəl/ *adj.* relating to the season of spring. *The vernal equinox occurs during the spring.*

ver·sion /ˈvûr zhən/ *n.* an account that is turned to reflect a particular viewpoint. *Rhiana told her version of the story to her parents.*

ver·te·brates /ˈvûr tə brāts/ *n. pl.* plural of VERTEBRATE; animals with backbones. *Are all mammals, including bats, vertebrates?*

vi·si·bil·i·ty /vi zə ˈbi lə tē/ *n.* the farthest distance at which something can be seen. *Visibility during a blizzard is very limited.*

vi·si·ble /ˈvi zə bəl/ *adj.* able to be seen; noticeable. *The moon is visible from Earth.*

vi·tal /ˈvi təl/ *adj.* necessary to maintain life. *Water is vital for plants and animals.*

vi·tal·i·ty /vi ˈta lə tē/ *n.* the capacity to live and grow. *Vitamins help our body to have vitality.*

vi·va·cious /vi ˈvā shəs/ *adj.* having the quality of liveliness; perky; lively. *A vivacious little robin perched on a branch.*

vi·vid /ˈvi vəd/ *adj.* bright; lifelike. *The tulips bloomed in vivid shades of red and pink.*

vol·ca·no /vol ˈkā nō/ *n.* a mountain or hill formed by the accumulation of materials in the earth's surface. *Mount Shasta is a dormant volcano.*

vol·ley·ball /ˈvo lē bȯl/ *n.* a game played by hitting a ball over a net using one's hands. *Cara and her sisters enjoy playing volleyball.*

vol·umes /ˈvol yo͞omz/ *n. pl.* plural of VOLUME; written pages often combined into book form. *Xavier read through the volumes of mountain-climbing information.*

W

wear·ing /ˈwâr ing/ *v.* having on the body. *A secretary bird looks like it is wearing a shirt and pants.*

wear·y /ˈwîr ē/ *adj.* tired. *I did not want to leave the zoo even though I was weary.*

whis·per /ˈhwis pûr/ *n.* a very low voice or sound; a murmur. *Cary spoke in a whisper so he would not disturb the quiet camp.*

wood·lands /ˈwood ləndz/ *n. pl.* plural of WOODLAND; areas covered by trees and shrubs. *Erin enjoyed the field trip to the woodlands.*

¹wound /ˈwo͞ond/ *n.* an injury. *The sailor's foot received a wound from a sharp splinter.*

²wound /ˈwound/ *v.* past tense of WIND; to turn completely around. *I wound the alarm clock before setting the time.*

wring /ˈring/ *v.* to squeeze or twist something to extract moisture. *Kristen will wring out the wet bathing suits after the beach outing.*

Y

youth·ful·ness /ˈyo͞oth fəl nəs/ *n.* the characteristic of being young. *An animal's youthfulness can be seen by looking at its teeth.*

Index

Note: Page numbers refer to the student page inserts in the Teacher Edition. Lesson numbers preceded by TE refer to Teacher Edition content.

Note: Page numbers refer to the student page inserts in the Teacher Edition. Lesson numbers preceded by TE refer to Teacher Edition content.

Note: Page numbers refer to the student page inserts in the Teacher Edition. Lesson numbers preceded by TE refer to Teacher Edition content.

© *Spelling Grade 5*

Note: Page numbers refer to the student page inserts in the Teacher Edition. Lesson numbers preceded by TE refer to Teacher Edition content.